Relevance Theory

Over the past twenty years, relevance theory has become a key area of study within semantics and pragmatics. In this comprehensive new textbook, Billy Clark introduces the key elements of the theory and how they interconnect. The book is divided into two parts, first providing an overview of the essential machinery of the theory, and second exploring how the original theory has been extended, applied and critically discussed. Clark offers a systematic framework for understanding the theory from the basics up, building a complete picture, and providing the basis for advanced research across a range of topics. With this book, students will understand the fundamentals of relevance theory, its origins in the work of Grice, the relationship it has to other approaches, and its place within recent developments and debates.

BILLY CLARK is a senior lecturer in English Language in the School of Media and Performing Arts at Middlesex University. He has considerable experience teaching relevance theory at undergraduate and postgraduate level and was editor of the 'Foundations of Linguistics' section for the *Encyclopedia of Language and Linguistics* edited by Keith Brown.

CAMBRIDGE TEXTBOOKS IN LINGUISTICS

General editors: P. AUSTIN, J. BRESNAN, B. COMRIE, S. CRAIN, W. DRESSLER, C. EWEN, R. LASS, D. LIGHTFOOT, K. RICE, I. ROBERTS, S. ROMAINE, N.V. SMITH.

Relevance Theory

Relevance Theory

BILLY CLARK

Middlesex University

CAMBRIDGE
UNIVERSITY PRESS

CAMBRIDGE UNIVERSITY PRESS

Cambridge, New York, Melbourne, Madrid, Cape Town,
Singapore, São Paulo, Delhi, Mexico City

Cambridge University Press
The Edinburgh Building, Cambridge CB2 8RU, UK

Published in the United States of America by Cambridge University Press, New York

www.cambridge.org
Information on this title: www.cambridge.org/9780521702416

First published 2013

Printed and bound in the United Kingdom by Bell and Bain Ltd

A catalogue record for this publication is available from the British Library

Library of Congress Cataloguing in Publication data

Clark, Billy.
  Relevance theory / Billy Clark.
    p. cm. – (Cambridge textbooks in linguistics Relevance Theory)
  Includes bibliographical references and index.
  ISBN 978-0-521-87820-3 (Hardback)
1. Relevance. 2. Semiotics. 3. Language and languages. I. Title.
  P99.4.R44C57 2013
  401'.43–dc23
                                                    2012036512

ISBN 978-0-521-87820-3 Hardback
ISBN 978-0-521-70241-6 Paperback

for Bessie and Bill

Contents

Figures and tables

Tables

Preface

Aims

The main aim of this book is to provide an introduction to relevance theory. Relevance theory aims to describe and explain how humans understand the world and how we understand each other. In other words, it is a theory of both cognition and communication. In neither case, however, does the theory attempt to say all that there is to say about the phenomenon it aims to explain. On cognition, the theory makes a claim about how we allocate our cognitive resources in general but does not make specific claims about the majority of cognitive systems and processes. On communication, the theory makes a claim about how we use cognitive resources when we recognise that someone has openly produced an act of intentional communication, verbal or nonverbal, but it has less to say about covert or accidental forms of information transmission. In other words, relevance theory aims to tell part of the story of how we think and understand the world (cognition) and how we convey thoughts and understand each other (communication).

Relevance theory has been influential in a number of areas but it has arguably been most influential in the area of linguistic pragmatics, which aims to explain how we understand each other when we communicate in language. The book focuses mainly on linguistic communication but it also considers some cases of nonverbal communication, what the theory has to say about cognition more generally and the relationship between the accounts of cognition and of communication. While the explanation of communication presupposes assumptions about cognition, neither account fully depends on the other (one could be shown to be false while the other is broadly true, and vice versa). The book aims to explain the technical notion of 'relevance' assumed by the theory, the meaning of the claim that human cognition is 'geared' towards the maximisation of 'relevance', and the ways in which considerations of relevance guide the processes of human communication (for communicators and audiences).

Key features

I have written this book with more than one audience in mind. It should be useful for readers with no prior knowledge of linguistic pragmatics or relevance theory, for readers who have done some work on these previously, and for more advanced researchers who are looking to develop their understanding of this theory in particular. In later chapters, fairly recent ideas are explained and critically discussed with a view to developing the debate in some areas.

I have tried to write in an accessible style and to keep things as simple as possible. Of course, the extent to which things can be kept simple depends partly on the nature of the topics being discussed and the book covers some fairly tricky topics. While the level of difficulty varies from chapter to chapter, the chapters build on each other to some extent. You should find that you can follow the argument overall if you work through the book in order and do not try to move on before you are fairly confident at each stage about your understanding of the discussion so far. Some parts of the book may be usable as stand-alone readings. The first section of the book (Chapters 1 to 4) could be used to introduce the main assumptions of relevance theory, its origins in previous work and its relationship to other approaches.

Organisation

The book is divided into two main Parts. Part I, consisting of the first four chapters, provides a relatively uncritical overview of the main parts of the theory, explaining what it aims to achieve and how it attempts to do this. As with any theory, all of the important assumptions of the theory are open to debate. At this stage, the focus is mainly on presenting the theory clearly. More critical discussion is reserved until Part II. Chapter 1 contains a brief summary of the main ideas behind the theory so that you can begin to develop a sense of what it is trying to achieve and how. Chapters 2, 3 and 4 flesh this out in distinct ways. Chapter 2 considers the origins of the theory, mainly in the work of Paul Grice, and its relationship to other post-Gricean work. Chapter 3 looks more closely at the definition of relevance and the two Principles of Relevance which constitute the main general claims made by the theory. Chapter 4 considers how they are used in explaining cognition and communication. By the end of Chapter 4, you will have been introduced to the essential machinery of the theory and you should be able to propose and test your own relevance-theoretic explanations of particular utterances and other communicative phenomena. You should also be ready to interrogate the ideas more closely and to look in more detail at specific components of the theory. Part II of the book helps you to do this in two ways. First, it explores particular theory-internal notions in more detail. Second, it considers ways in which the original theory has been extended, applied and critically discussed. Chapters in Part II of the book will help you to extend your understanding of the details of the theory and also to consider various kinds of critical discussion and responses to that criticism. Taken as a whole, the book presents a comprehensive overview of the main features of the theory so that readers should understand the fundamentals, the relationship to other approaches, and a number of relevant developments and debates.

Each chapter discusses and illustrates the relevant ideas and contains a number of exercises which can be used to test your understanding. There are further exercises on the book's website at: www.cambridge.org/billyclark. The exercises are designed to be suitable for classroom work and also for working through on your own. The website also contains suggested answers so that you can check whether you are on the right track. Of course, in many cases there is no one definitively correct answer so these often indicate the direction in which you might develop an answer rather than just stating what the answer should be. While the exercises can be saved until the end of the chapter, some of them are designed to be tackled at the point in the chapter where they appear. My own view is that all of the exercises will be most effective if you pause to work on them when they are introduced and then read on. You might, of course, prefer to read through a chapter first if you are in a hurry or if you believe that you already have a reasonable understanding of the topics being discussed.

Key notions in the theory are briefly explained in an Appendix at the end of the book. This can be used to check your understanding of these notions and it can also be read as a quick reminder of the key components of the theory. Technical terms are presented **in bold** at critical points in the text. There are a number of other typographical conventions adopted in the text, explained more fully on page xix. For ease of understanding, in examples with an unnamed speaker or communicator, the communicator will be referred to with a female pronoun and the addressee with a male pronoun. For consistency, when communicators are named, the communicator will usually be thought of as female and the addressee as male.

At the end of each chapter, there are brief suggestions for initial further reading on topics just covered. The resources section at the end of the book lists some key reading on relevance theory, including useful websites, and concludes with a fuller bibliography containing all of the sources mentioned in the book.

Acknowledgements

I am obviously in debt to Dan Sperber, Deirdre Wilson and all of the researchers in relevance theory and in pragmatics who have contributed to developing accounts of how we understand each other and the world. By far my greatest debt is to Deirdre Wilson, who has offered limitless advice, encouragement and intellectual inspiration throughout the time I have known her. I am also grateful to a large number of people who have discussed relevance theory with me over the years. I have had interesting formal and informal discussion in bars, cafés, classrooms, conferences, corridors, kitchens, libraries and street corners with a huge number of people (not all of them working in relevance theory). I would particularly like to thank Nick Allott, Diane Blakemore, Regina Blass, Richard Breheny, Noel Burton-Roberts, Robyn Carston, Annabel Cormack, Alan Durant, Nigel Fabb, Charles Forceville, Thorstein Fretheim, Anne Furlong, Lorna Gibb, Marjolein Groefsema, Liliane Haegeman, Jonathan Hope, Jill House, Elly Ifantidou, Reiko Itani, Corinne Iten, Mark Jary, Katarzyna Jaszczolt, Napoleon Katsos, David Keeble, Ruth Kempson, Patricia Kolaiti, Geoff Lindsey, Barbara MacMahon, Tomoko Matsui, Jacques Moeschler, Steve Nicolle, Eun-Ju Noh, Ira Noveck, Nicky Owtram, Anna Papafragou, Adrian Pilkington, Alyson Pitts, George Powell, Anne Reboul, Xose Rosales Sequeiros, Villy Rouchota, Kate Scott, Sylvia Shaw, Neil Smith, Hanna Stöver, Naoko Togame, Christoph Unger, Rosa Vega Moreno, Begoña Vicente, Tim Wharton, Beata Zacharska, Mai Zaki and Vlad Zegarac. I am, of course, grateful to students in many institutions who have helped me to understand the topics discussed here and how to explain them to others, and I am particularly grateful to students who studied meaning with me from 2010 to 2012 and who used and commented on early versions of some of the chapters here. Helen Barton, Liz Davey, Jill Lake and colleagues at Cambridge University Press have been patient, positive and a pleasure to work with throughout the time it took to produce the book. I would also like to acknowledge the financial support of the Department of English, Languages and Philosophy at Middlesex University, which granted me a period of leave in which to work on the book, and the British Library (and the people in it) for providing a friendly environment to work in. Finally, I'd like to thank Ohna, Apoa and Kiloh for all kinds of support and for putting up with the dysfunctional communicator who shared their living space while he worked on a book about how communication works (and sometimes doesn't).

Typographical conventions

There are a number of typographical conventions used during the book, some of which are standard conventions and some of which I have adopted just for this book. Here are the ones I think you may not already be aware of.

bold text	technical terms
italics	linguistic expressions / wordforms
{CURLY BRACKETS AND SMALL CAPITAL LETTERS}	concepts
SMALL CAPITAL LETTERS	concepts (i.e. brackets are sometimes omitted for simplicity)
{CURLY BRACKETS AND SMALL CAPITAL LETTERS}*	'adjusted', or 'ad hoc', concepts (see Chapter 8) (asterisk indicates adjustment)
{CURLY BRACKETS AND SMALL CAPITAL LETTERS}**	distinct 'adjusted', or 'ad hoc', concepts (an extra asterisk is added for each adjustment)
SMALL CAPITAL LETTERS*	'adjusted', or 'ad hoc', concepts with brackets omitted for simplicity
'inverted commas'	interpretations
[_____] blank slots in square brackets with text beneath	representations of inferences to be made (with linguistically encoded guidance as to how to fill the slot shown beneath it)
[text in square brackets]	material which has been inferred in fleshing out semantic representations to derive explicatures

To sum up and partly illustrate this, linguistic forms are represented *in italics*, concepts in {CURLY BRACKETS AND SMALL CAPITAL LETTERS}, interpretations in 'single quotation marks'. For example, we might say that the linguistic form (or word) *music* names the concept {MUSIC} and that someone who utters it in a specific context might mean to communicate that 'listening to music is one of my hobbies'.

PART I

Overview

1   A first outline

Topics: expectations and meanings; sentences, utterances and propositions; communication and cognition

1.1   Overview

The ideas introduced in this chapter are presented more fully in the remaining chapters of Part I before the more critical and exploratory discussion in Part II. The chapter begins with a very brief summary of the central ideas behind relevance theory. It then considers some issues about terminology before presenting a fuller introduction to the theory, looking at some of the key ideas involved in explaining communication from a relevance-theoretic point of view.

One of the key ideas assumed by relevance theory, and shared by most other approaches, is that we can make a fundamental distinction between coded and inferred communication. This distinction can then be exploited in making a distinction between linguistic semantics and pragmatics. This chapter considers some of the kinds of things which can be linguistically encoded (and which therefore fall within the scope of linguistic semantics) and some of the kinds of things which can be pragmatically inferred (and which therefore fall within the scope of pragmatics). We then take our first look at the theoretical ideas proposed by relevance theory to explain how we work out communicated meanings, in particular at the two Principles of Relevance, the presumption of optimal relevance and the relevance-guided comprehension heuristic which follows from these. Finally, we consider the nature of explanations of communication proposed within relevance theory.

The aim at this stage is to present the key ideas behind the theory quickly so that you have a general idea of how the theory works before moving on to develop a fuller understanding of the details in the rest of Part I and to explore the trickier issues discussed in Part II. To keep this initial overview brief, I have made a number of simplifying assumptions and ignored a number of issues which we will discuss more fully later. If you have questions about the details, or notice any possible inconsistencies here, make a note of them as you go. Two of the exercises in this chapter (Exercise 1.2 and Exercise 1.9) invite you to think a bit more fully about questions which have occurred to you while reading this chapter. Each subsequent chapter contains an exercise which invites you to go back to this list and consider whether any of your initial questions have been answered at that stage.

Part I of the book is relatively uncritical. You should bear in mind, though, that many if not all of the assumptions made by relevance theorists have been questioned to varying degrees. In Part II, some of these debates will be explored more fully. For now, the focus is on explaining the various components of the theory and how they are used. The key notion in relevance theory is, of course, the notion of 'relevance' itself, which has a technical definition distinct from any of its everyday uses. This technical definition will be introduced and explained in Chapter 3. At this stage, the definition will not be explained fully as the aim is to begin with an understanding of the broad outline of the approach rather than to spell out the technical details.

1.2   Expectations and meanings: a short summary

This section presents a very brief summary of the essential idea behind relevance theory: that intentional communication gives rise to expectations which help us to decide what the communicator intends to convey. This is not the only thing which relevance theory claims, but it is a central part of the theory and I hope that beginning with this short introduction will make it easier to develop a fuller picture as you work through the rest of the book. The section begins by considering the idea that intentional communication creates expectations, briefly considers the kinds of meanings which these expectations help to explain, and then says a little about how the expectations help to give rise to the meanings.

1.2.1   Creating expectations

Pay no attention to this sentence. It is not relevant to you. Did you ignore either of the two sentences you have just read? I'm assuming that you didn't. I can't realistically expect readers of this book to follow an instruction not to pay attention to a sentence in this book. The existence of the book and the sentences within it provide evidence that I intended someone to read them. By typing these words onto my computer (as I am doing now) and agreeing to them being printed in a book which can be bought and read (as you are doing now), I have suggested that I think the words are relevant to the book's potential readers (including you). Similarly, whenever someone speaks to you in a language you know (or that they assume you know), they communicate this assumption. In a talk on relevance theory which I attended, Dan Sperber, one of the founders of relevance theory, began by saying something very similar to his audience:

(1)   Pay no attention to this utterance. It has no relevance to you.

His aim then was the same as my aim here: to show that it is not reasonable to expect someone you are addressing in a language they know (and which they assume that you know that they know) to take seriously the idea that you do not think the utterance you are producing is relevant to them. The act of communicating makes clear to the addressee that the communicator must think that what they are communicating is relevant to the addressee. The same point applies to nonverbal communication. If I approach you in the street, wave both hands at you and then point across the street, my behaviour makes clear to you that I think you will spot something worth noticing if you look across the street. Relevance theory can be understood as an elaboration of, and an attempt to account for, this intuition.

Whether language is involved or not, actions which make clear that someone intends to communicate something always create particular kinds of expectations in addressees. The general expectation can be roughly characterised as the assumption that there is an interpretation of the communicator's behaviour which the addressee will find it worthwhile to recover. This generalisation is the central insight behind the relevance-theoretic account of intentional communication. Understanding the way that acts of communication create this expectation is seen as the key to understanding how we interpret each other's utterances and also why we sometimes misunderstand each other. Notice, by the way, that I have not yet defined either the technical term 'relevance' or the kind of communication which gives rise to the expectation (we will see below that this is termed 'ostensive-inferential communication'). I am hoping that the initial discussion will be fairly clear without providing full definitions at this stage, If not, or if you are unsure about the details at any stage, make a note and add it to the list of questions you are invited to make in responding to Exercise 1.2 below. Later exercises will ask you to check whether your understanding of specific points becomes clearer as you work through the book.

1.2.2   How do we know what we mean?

How do we know what other people mean when they communicate with us? Explaining this is one of the central aims of relevance theory. There are a number of different kinds of question to ask about how we understand each other, including how we account for cases where we fail to understand each other. We'll begin to explore these in more detail, and to consider a fuller range of examples, in Section 1.4. Here, we'll consider just three kinds of question which relevance theory aims to answer:

a.   How do we manage to understand meanings which are not directly communicated?
b.   How do we work out which propositions communicators are directly communicating?
c.   Why do we sometimes misunderstand each other?

Here is a brief explanation of each question.

a.   How do we manage to understand meanings which are indirectly communicated?

It is easy to find examples of indirect communication. Here is an example from an exchange which happened when I was in my local corner shop recently and about to pay for two pots of cream cheese. The assistant at the till said to me:

(2)   They're three for two just now.

I had no problem in understanding that she meant I was entitled to a third pot of cream cheese at no additional cost. This is something she communicated indirectly. I was able to understand what she had said, realise that she meant me to derive an indirect meaning, and to derive that indirect meaning. One thing relevance theory aims to do is to provide an explanation of what is involved in deriving such indirect meanings.

b.   How do we work out which propositions communicators are directly communicating?

We'll look more closely at how to define the distinction between 'direct' and 'indirect' communication below. For now, the key thing to notice is that in order to work out that I was entitled to a third pot of cheese, I first had to work out what proposition the shop assistant was directly communicating. This might seem obvious, but there are a number of things I needed to work out in order to see what this proposition might be. I needed to work out, for example, that *they* referred to pots of cream cheese of the brand and size I was about to buy which were on sale in the shop I was in at the time when I was buying them, and that saying that *they're three for two* meant that the cost of three of them would be the same as the cost of two of them. I also needed to realise that *just now* meant during a period of time which included all of the time in which I was in the shop buying the cream cheese. A rough characterisation of what she was directly communicating, with components which were not explicitly stated in square brackets, might be (3):

(3)   [Pots of cream cheese of the type which you are about to buy] are [on sale in this shop under a special offer which means that if you buy] two [pots of that cream cheese which you are about to buy] [we will give you a third pot without charging you any more] [at the present time and for as long as the offer lasts]

This representation makes clear that I had to make a significant number of assumptions which go beyond what the shop assistant actually said in order to understand this everyday utterance.

c.   Why do we sometimes misunderstand each other?

The interpretation I've just outlined seems a fairly natural and obvious one and I am sure most people would have understood the utterance in the same way. However, it is possible to imagine a situation where someone might have misunderstood it. There are a number of ways in which communication might have gone wrong. Sometimes addressees don't notice that they're being addressed. If my attention was not focused fully on the shop assistant, I might not have heard her or I might have thought that she was talking to someone else. Perhaps less plausibly, I could have heard her and realised she was talking to me but still have misunderstood the utterance. This could happen because I don't know what *three for two* means or, even less plausibly, because I think she is telling me this for a different reason, e.g. to comment on the nature of special offers in some way. I might understand the main point she is trying to convey but misunderstand some parts of what she intended. I might, for example, think that she is making a negative comment about me because she thinks I'm silly not to have brought three pots of cheese to the counter, even if this is not what she intended.

There are a significant number of different ways in which things might go wrong when we communicate with each other. An adequate account will need to do as well at explaining misunderstandings as it does at explaining how we manage to understand each other when communication goes well. We will also expect an adequate theory to account for possibilities ranging from those where we are confident that communication has been successful to those where we are sure it has not and all of the grey areas in between.

1.2.3 Guiding interpretations

So how does the expectation raised by intentional communication help one person to understand what another person intended by their act of communication? The key idea within relevance theory is that addressees begin by assuming that the communicator has an interpretation in mind which justifies the expenditure of effort involved in arriving at it, i.e. which provides enough cognitive rewards for it to be worth expending the mental effort involved in reaching it. (As we'll see below, relevance theory explains this in terms of a technical definition of the term 'relevance'.) This could be understood as resting on assumptions about what it is rational for communicators to do and for addressees to expect. We might point out, for example, that it would seem less than rational for me to attract your attention and invite you to pay attention to something if I did not think it would be worth your while to do so. We will see below that a suitably developed understanding of this leads to fairly precise predictions about the particular interpretations addressees will arrive at. Before returning to my corner shop cream cheese, let's broaden the scope of our discussion by considering a fairly simple example of nonverbal communication.

Suppose you are standing in a chemist's shop and you begin to cough in a way that is hard for you to control. A stranger looks at you, makes eye contact, and then taps a box on the counter. What will you do? My guess is that you will look at the box to see what it contains. Suppose the box says that it contains a cough medicine. You will no doubt assume that the stranger is recommending that you try this medicine and that it might relieve your cough. Why did you decide this? Because it would make sense of the stranger's actions if this was what she intended to communicate. Notice that it is your expectation about her behaviour which led you to notice the medicine. Where did this expectation come from? Let's assume we always make hypotheses about the behaviour of other people that we notice. It is hard to see how you could explain the stranger's behaviour as anything other than an attempt to communicate with you. This in turn gave rise to the expectation that there would be an interpretation of her behaviour which would justify the effort you would have to expend in order to understand it. Because you expected this, you put the required amount of effort into looking at the box and looking for a relevant interpretation. Notice that there is no necessary connection between tapping a box and communicating that it contains medicine that might fix a cough. You will have arrived at this interpretation because you put the effort in and assumed there would be a relevant interpretation. We have said nothing yet about how you arrive at this specific interpretation, but we will see below that this account shares with all relevance-theoretic explanations the assumption that interpretations are guided by the presumption that the communicator must have had an interpretation in mind which would justify the effort involved in paying attention to her behaviour.

Now, let's go back to the cream cheese example. How does this account for example (2) above? First, we assume that I recognise that the shop assistant is talking to me. By uttering (2) she makes me think that there is an interpretation of (2) which it will be worth my while to derive. For this to be the case, it must be an interpretation which she will have thought of as more worthwhile than alternative utterances which she might have produced, such as (4):

(4)   Three pounds fifty-eight, please.

My job then is to work out what that interpretation might be. In this situation, it is not hard for me to come up with a reasonable interpretation. If I can buy three pots for the price of two, then a number of significant things follow from this, including:

(5) a.   I can have a third pot of cheese without paying any more for it.
    b.   The shop assistant thinks I don't know about the special offer.
    c.   The shop assistant is checking whether I want a third pot.
    d.   If I do want a third pot, I can get it now.
    e.   If I pick it up now before paying, I won't risk being suspected of shoplifting.

I can also see why the shop assistant will see this as more relevant than just asking me for payment for two pots of cheese, since it also suggests that she is being considerate which has positive implications for our social relationship.

This is the starting point for relevance-theoretic explanations of the interpretation of particular utterances. We will look at the rest of the story more closely below. Now what about our other two questions? The first was about how we work out such things as that *they* refers to pots of cheese for sale at the time of the utterance in the shop where the exchange is taking place. The answer to this question is very similar to the answer to the previous question. In fact, recognising the intended referent of *they* is required in order to arrive at the interpretation sketched above, so we might simply say that these are sub-tasks within the overall task of working out the intended interpretation of the utterance as a whole. This is indeed what relevance theory suggests. We will develop our understanding of how this goes in the rest of the book, looking at how the sub-tasks in comprehension take place and interact with each other in constructing interpretations.

Finally, what about the possibility of misunderstanding? Within relevance theory, this is explained in terms of a mismatch between the speaker's estimate of the set of assumptions the hearer can and will access when hearing the utterance and what the hearer does in fact access, i.e. between the kinds of **contextual assumptions** which the speaker thinks the hearer will access and those the hearer actually does access. We will consider the nature of the process of accessing contextual assumptions more fully in Chapter 7. Assumptions which are probably required in order for me to understand the utterance include:

(6) a.   The shop assistant is talking to me.
    b.   *They* refers to pots of cheese.
    c.   The shop assistant is trying to be helpful.

If I miss (6a), I am not likely to think much about what proposition the shop assistant is expressing or to make the right assumptions about such things as the intended referent of *they*. If I miss (6b), I might not realise that this is relevant to my cream cheese purchase. If I miss (6c), I might go for a more critical interpretation than the shop assistant intended. And so on. We will develop a more detailed account of misunderstandings below. For now, one thing to notice is that an addressee who misunderstands an intended meaning and a successful interpreter will share the expectation that the communicator is aiming for an interpretation that justifies the effort involved in processing it.

Exercise 1.1 encourages you to think about the kinds of expectations created by communicators and how we understand each other.

Exercise 1.1

- The chapter discussed the impossibility of being taken seriously if you ask someone not to pay attention to something you express in a language they know. This follows because producing the utterance automatically creates the assumption that you have in mind to communicate something which you believe the addressee will be interested in. The example with the cough medicine showed that these expectations can arise in the same way for verbal and nonverbal communication. Imagine you walk into a public space, say a coffee bar, where several people are sitting around. Consider:

(a) other things you might do to make clear to one or more people in the room that you are attempting to communicate something to them

(b) how you might behave in order to avoid the possibility that someone will think you are trying to communicate with them

Exercise 1.2 asks you to note questions you have at this stage about relevance theory in particular or about language and meaning in general.

Exercise 1.2

• The main aim of this book is to help you to understand relevance theory more fully. This means discussing a wide range of topics, many of which are quite complicated. I hope that you will be aware of your understanding developing as you read the book and that you will become more confident to discuss some of the general and specific arguments and issues as you work through the book. To help you to think about this, and to be aware of how you are developing your understanding, make a list now of questions you have about how relevance theory works or about linguistic meaning in general. Later exercises will ask you to return to this list, adding to it where new questions emerge and noting the extent to which existing questions have been answered as you work through the book. Make a list now in any format which you think is useful and keep it in an accessible place so you can refer to it, add to it and edit it as you work through the book. Don't wait to be prompted by exercises, though. Have a look at your list whenever you think it would be useful, or when you come across something in the book or elsewhere which you think is relevant to any of these questions. I don't expect to have answered all of your questions by the end of the book, but I do hope to have answered some, partially answered others, and suggested the lines along which answers could be developed to yet others. I would be very happy to receive feedback from readers, asking questions, commenting on the extent to which you think I have answered questions, or raising any other issues. There is a discussion section on the website (www.cambridge.org/ billyclark) where questions can be posted and answered, and a link to send questions directly to me.

1.3   Sentences, utterances and propositions

As with any subject, there are a number of technical terms used in linguistic semantics and pragmatics that it is important to understand before looking at work in this area. This is particularly problematic for terms which have a slightly different meaning, or a variety of meanings, in everyday usage. An obvious example is the term **ambiguous**. In everyday language, this is used to refer to a range of cases where an expression has more than one meaning. In current linguistics, the term refers only to linguistic expressions which have more than one encoded sense (such as the word *ball*, which can refer to a spherical object or a gathering where people dance, among other things). This section considers three other terms which it is important to distinguish in work on linguistic meaning: **sentence**, **utterance** and **proposition**.

Utterances are physical entities which we perceive aurally (if spoken) or visually (if written or signed) whereas **sentences** (and the words they are made up of) are linguistic entities. An utterance is written or spoken by a particular person at a particular time and in a particular space. This morning, I have produced several utterances. One of them was to say (7) to my wife and another was to send the text message in (8) to a friend:

(7)   What time do you have to leave this morning?

(8)   I could be there by around 5.30.

A sentence is a more abstract entity which does not take account of properties such as speaker, time and place of utterance. Because of this, we can think of my utterances of (7) and (8) as utterances of the sentences *What time do you have to leave this morning?* and *I could be there by 5.30*. Those sentences existed before I produced the utterances and might well have been uttered by other people in other situations before. They might well, of course, be uttered again. At the same time, not all of the sentences of English have ever been uttered. In fact, it's quite easy to think of a sentence which is likely never to have been realised in an utterance. I'm guessing that (9) is not something anyone has uttered before this moment as I type it:

(9)   A lecturer will use any hoojamaflip they can to avoid being discombobulated by the glare of a mongoose.

To say that 'the same sentence' has been uttered by different speakers on different occasions must mean that different utterances (sounds or images) are taken to be realisations of the same sentence of English. The same point applies to words (we can produce different realisations of the same word on different occasions).

The notion of a **proposition** is another kind of abstraction, this time focusing on logical properties. The sentence *I could be there by around 5.30* does not express any proposition but my utterance in (8) did. I expected my friend Dónal to work out that I meant that I, Billy, could be in the square where we had planned to meet by approximately 5.30 p.m. on the 17th of March 2012. Propositions can be expressed by the specific concrete realisations of sentences which we refer to with the term 'utterance'. Thoughts also have propositional content so we might say that part of my intention in uttering (8) was to lead to Dónal entertaining a thought with the same propositional content.

Exercise 1.3 is designed to help you develop your understanding of the differences between the three terms 'sentence', 'utterance', 'proposition'.

Exercise 1.3

- We saw in the chapter that we use words such as sentence, utterance and proposition loosely in everyday speech. We use some of these more often than others, of course. The difference between everyday and technical uses of *sentence* is perhaps easier to illustrate than the others. To begin with, see if you can explain why I must be speaking loosely if I underline part of a student essay and write the following in the margin: *'This is not a sentence'*.
- Now propose a technical definition for each of the terms:

  sentence: _____

  _____

  utterance: _____

  _____

  proposition: _____

  _____

1.4   Communication and cognition: a fuller overview

Now that we have a general idea of how relevance theory aims to explain communication, and have become more sensitive to issues about how to use terminology, we are ready to look in slightly more detail at the relevance-theoretic picture of linguistic and non-linguistic communication. In this section, we begin by looking at an example designed to indicate the broad question which linguistic, philosophical and pragmatic theories may help to answer: what is involved in linguistic and non-linguistic communication? We consider the difference between coded and inferred communication which forms the basis for the distinction between semantics and pragmatics. We consider some of the kinds of meanings which can be linguistically encoded, and therefore fall within the scope of linguistic semantics, and some of the things which can be pragmatically inferred, and so fall within the scope of pragmatics. We move on to look at the two Principles of Relevance which represent the central theoretical apparatus of the theory, at the presumption of optimal relevance which follows from these, and at the relevance-guided comprehension heuristic which relevance theory claims we follow when working out interpretations. Finally, we consider how all of these ideas are brought together in relevance-theoretic explanations.

1.4.1   Linguistic and non-linguistic communication

Consider this scenario. A woman is sitting in a dimly lit room with an open book in front of her. A man comes in and a noise comes out of the woman's mouth. The man presses a switch on the wall and a light comes on. This is an ordinary, everyday sequence of events made slightly strange by the unusual way in which I have described it. Phrasing it in this way helps us to see that it illustrates a question which philosophers and linguists have been trying to answer for millennia: what is the connection between the noise made by the woman and the behaviour of the man? To some extent, answering this question involves answering the question 'what is language?' which is a central question explored within linguistics. Going beyond that, it involves answering the question 'what is linguistic communication?' which presupposes an answer to the question 'what is language?' Chomsky (for example, 1986: 1–14) has suggested that linguistics should be concerned with three questions: What is language? How is language acquired? How is language put to use? He suggests that the first question is logically prior to the other two since we cannot explain how language is acquired or how it is put to use unless we have some understanding of what it is. This book, like pragmatic theories in general, and relevance theory in particular, will presuppose an answer to the first question (broadly Chomskyan in the case of relevance theory) and attempt to develop a partial answer to the third question.

We begin to explain what is going on in the dimly lit room by saying that the noise represented an expression in a language the two individuals share. Let us move towards a more typical description by supposing that the woman was speaking English and that her utterance was:

(10)   Could you put the light on please?

We've now taken a step towards explaining things, but of course we need to answer many other questions before we can claim to have given a full explanation, including (all but not only) these:

- how did the man recognise this as an utterance in English?
- how did he recognise each word?
- how did he recognise the larger structures (morphological and syntactic) which the words are combined into? (how did he 'parse' it?)
- how did he know what each word meant or referred to?
- how did he know what the speaker meant by the utterance as a whole?

One way of thinking about the study of language or linguistics is as an attempt to explain how some human noises (spoken utterances), movements (signed utterances) or visual products (written utterances) come to have effects on other humans. As Chomsky suggests, a full explanation of what happened in the dimly lit room would involve explaining what human language is, how it is acquired and how it is used. The part of the question which this book addresses is the part about how language is used. The answers will take for granted that someone else will work on answering questions about what language is and how it is acquired, about how phonemes and words are recognised, and so on. In some places, we will assume particular answers to some of the other questions. What relevance theory addresses directly is how we work out the meanings and referents of words and what individuals mean by producing them at a particular time and place. Assuming that someone else will be working on the explanations of the other things, relevance theory aims to explain how we work out for what purpose a particular person at a particular time produced an utterance realising a particular sequence of words. In the case of (10), we hope to explain how the man entering the room knew that the woman was asking him, relatively politely, to put the light on.

Moving on a little, there are a number of other kinds of things which relevance theory aims to explain. These are questions addressed by all theories of linguistic pragmatics. First, consider some other things which the woman in example (10) could have said to the man. These might include:

(11)   Put the light on.

(12)   It's really dark in here.

(13)   It's terrible getting old. I can hardly focus on this print.

She could also, of course, have chosen to communicate without using words at all. She might, for example, have held up her glasses and the book and hoped that it was clear what she intended by this.

Any theory of pragmatics should be able to explain intuitions we have about the differences between these options. (11), for example, is less polite than (10), while (12) and (13) are less direct than (10) or (11). The nonverbal method is more risky than the spoken utterances in that it is more likely that she will be misunderstood. These differences are related to further differences. I might feel better about putting the light on for you if you ask politely than if you are very direct. What follows from the request is less clear and less easy to pin down when you are less direct. And so on. A pragmatic theory should explain the different effects of different ways of formulating a request or another kind of utterance and also the differences and similarities between linguistic and non-linguistic communication. One key part of an explanation of this involves drawing a distinction between coded meaning and inferred meaning. This is discussed in the next sub-section.

1.4.2   Codes and inference

Although relevance theory aims to explain both verbal and non-verbal communication, we will begin here by focusing mainly on cases of linguistic meaning. To understand what is involved in accounting for linguistic meaning, we need to make a clear distinction between linguistic semantics and pragmatics. On the relevance-theoretic approach, the first step towards this is to make a distinction between **coded meaning** and **inferred meaning**. Let's begin by considering what's involved in coded communication. A code is a system where a particular signal always communicates the same message. Another way to say this is to say that in coded communication the same 'input' always leads to the same 'output'. Classic examples include traffic lights, where a red light always means 'stop' and a green light always means 'go', or Morse code, where three dots always mean 'S', three dashes always mean 'O', and so on. We could also consider codes which are used by machines and are not normally visible to human communicators, such as the binary machine code used by computers, or the source code underlying web pages which 'tells browsers how to display pages' (note that we usually describe this metaphorically). What are the definitional characteristics of a code? The most important one is surely that the same signal is always linked unambiguously to the same message. Every single time a sequence of three dots appears as a unit in Morse code, this represents 'S'. Every single time web browser software reads the source code marker '' it represents characters following the symbol as bold until the end of the scope of the command is indicated with the symbol ''. And so on.

If we ask ourselves whether human language functions in the same way as a code, it is easy to see that it does not. Take any example of human language, say the utterance in (14):

(14)   It's here.

Does this utterance always communicate the same thing to everyone who hears or sees it? Clearly not. It could be used to communicate many different propositions. A few of the possibilities are represented in (15):

(15) a.   The book Billy has been looking for is on the kitchen table.
     b.   The 2014 World Science Fiction Convention will be taking place in London.
     c.   The 2014 World Science Fiction Convention is currently taking place in London.
     d.   The 2014 World Science Fiction Convention will be taking place in England.
     e.   Rodin's sculpture 'The Thinker' is in room 3 of the Musée Rodin.
     f.   Rodin's sculpture 'The Thinker' is in France.
     g.   Rodin's sculpture 'The Thinker' is in the book on my coffee table.
     h.   Billy Clark has found directions to the Musée Rodin on the website he is currently looking at.

These possibilities reflect some of the ways in which this utterance can give rise to different interpretations. The pronoun *it* could refer to a book, a conference, a work of art, a pictorial representation of a work of art, and many other things. The present tense form *is* could refer to something currently happening, due to happen in the future, happening habitually, and so on. The word *here* could refer to many different, more or less precise locations. Of course, there are many more possibilities than these. How does the hearer know which sense to go for? The answer has to be that they make inferences, i.e. they use knowledge from sources other than the linguistic meanings of the words to work out what they think the speaker must have meant. We'll consider the nature of these inferences in more detail later, but for now the important thing to notice is that no code establishes a mapping between *it's here* and any of the propositions it can be used to express. If my daughter says (14) (*It's here*) after her mother has asked her:

(16)   Do you know where dad's book is?

then it's rational to decide that (16) must mean that the book I am looking for is somewhere close to my daughter. This is clearly not part of the linguistically encoded meaning of the linguistic expression. It is inferred based on non-linguistic assumptions (including that the speaker has just been asked where her dad's book is).

Another way to talk about the distinction between coded and inferred linguistic communication is to say that there is always a gap between the linguistic meanings of expressions and what speakers actually communicate, and that this gap is filled by inference. Relevance theory assumes a fairly well developed account of this gap as the basis for its distinction between linguistic semantics and pragmatics. In the next section we run through a number of things which can be linguistically encoded before moving on to consider some of the kinds of inference we need to make in order to understand each other.

Before moving on, it is worth drawing attention to possible sources of confusion based on different possible uses of the terms 'code' and 'infer'. First, there are a number of ways in which the word *code* can be used in everyday language. It can refer to a system of conventions or behaviours, e.g. the 'Highway Code' is a set of instructions for how to behave when driving and the 'Country Code' is a set of ways of behaving when in the countryside. More loosely, we might say that there are codes of behaviour for particular social situations (e.g. formal dinner parties, university seminars) and activities (e.g. playing sports, responding to fire in a public building, use of mobile phones). In this book, we will be using the term to refer only to a fully explicit system which always links the same input with the same output. In the next section, we will look at some of the kinds of input and some of the kinds of output which can be part of a linguistic system.

A different and more specific possible source of confusion arises with the term 'infer'. In everyday language, the term is used in two senses, one of which is synonymous with 'imply'. We will be using it with only one of these senses. Within pragmatics, to **infer** something is to derive it as a conclusion on the basis of a number of premises. This is related to its sense in logic where inference rules are used to check the validity of arguments. To take one example, the logical rule of *and-introduction* tells us that we can conclude a conjunction of two propositions when we know that each one is true:

(17)   and-introduction
         Premise: P
         Premise: Q
         Conclusion: P & Q

This states that, given any proposition (represented by the 'propositional variable' *P*) and any other proposition (represented by the 'propositional variable' *Q*), we can conclude the conjunction of the two premises. To take an example of an inference you might make in a real-life context, suppose you have heard of a writing competition open to Scottish people under the age of 25 and you know that your friend Ella is Scottish but you're not sure of her exact age. To know that Ella can enter the competition you need to know that she is Scottish and under 25 (*P & Q*) but you only know that she is Scottish (*P*). If you notice a form on the table indicating that she is 23, you can infer that she is under 25 (*Q*) and so form the conjunction of the two propositions (*P & Q*, or 'Ella is Scottish and under 25').

To take a conversational example, suppose I ask you whether you have seen the new TV version of *Pride and Prejudice* and you reply:

(18)   I never watch period dramas.

I can infer from this that you have not seen the series and also why you have avoided it. I do this by combining the contextual assumption that *Pride and Prejudice* is a period drama with the proposition that you have expressed about never watching period dramas.

Within pragmatics, we would say that I have inferred these conclusions and that you have implied, or more technically, **implicated** them. However, in everyday conversation some speakers use the word *infer* to mean 'communicate indirectly', i.e. as a synonym of *imply*, rather than 'work out indirectly'. This can be illustrated by the exchange in (19):

(19)   KEN: Do you want me to work out the bill for you?
          BEV: What are you inferring by that? That I can't count?

Bev here is asking whether Ken is trying to imply that Bev can't count. It's easy to see how this usage has developed since there are contexts where both the 'communicate' and the 'work out' sense could be reasonable. Imagine, for example, if Bev had responded to Ken's question with (20) or if I responded to your question about *Pride and Prejudice* by saying (21):

(20)   Are you inferring I can't count?

(21)   Are you inferring that *Pride and Prejudice* is a period drama?

In these contexts, the utterances are consistent with the use of *infer* to mean both 'come to the conclusion that' and 'communicate indirectly that'. Most word meanings are acquired after hearing other people use the words rather than through explicit instruction. Anyone trying to work out what *infer* means from utterances such as (20) and (21) has evidence consistent with either sense of *infer* and so the door is open for semantic change. The important thing for us is not whether a particular usage is correct, but just to note that, within pragmatics in general and within this book in particular, inference is a cognitive process. Communicators communicate or imply but their utterances do not infer.

Exercise 1.4 encourages you to think about the differences between codes and inference.

Exercise 1.4

- Consider Bev's utterance in the following exchange:
    KEN: Will you be in tomorrow evening? I'm expecting a package.
    BEV: It's my swimming evening.
  How much of what Bev communicates can we think of as 'encoded'? How much do you think is 'inferred'?

1.4.3   Linguistic semantics: what we encode

In this section we look briefly at a number of ways in which meanings can be linguistically encoded and so develop our understanding of what kinds of things are part of linguistic semantics. We will look both at the kinds of linguistic forms which can encode meanings and the kinds of meanings which can be encoded.

What kinds of things can have a linguistic meaning? Most likely to spring to mind for most people is that *words* have linguistic meanings. Words are certainly capable of encoding linguistic meaning. Some gestures clearly do not encode anything, e.g. tapping on an object does not encode any particular thing about the object or anything else. Gestures which do seem to encode something, e.g. nodding your head to mean 'yes', are cultural but not part of a particular language. Intonation (pitch movement) and punctuation are more tricky cases. Intonation is discussed briefly in Chapters 10 and 11. Since punctuation is not present in speech and the conventions governing it are difficult to pin down (despite how often it is explicitly discussed), we will not consider it more fully in this book.

Let's start from the assumption that linguistically encoded meanings are associated with words and ways of putting them together. So we might say that the difference between (22) and (23) is that one of them contains the word *chocolate* and the other the word *cheese*:

(22)   He does like chocolate.

(23)   He does like cheese.

And that the difference between (23) and (24) is that one of them has declarative syntax while the other has interrogative syntax (remember that we're ignoring the possible effects of different intonation patterns for now):

(24)   Does he like cheese?

This is a reasonable starting point, but I'll complicate it just a little bit by pointing out that, strictly speaking, it is morphemes rather than words which encode meanings. The difference between (25) and (26) is that one of them has the present tense morpheme (here -*es* pronounced /ɪz/) where the other has the past tense morpheme (here -*ed* pronounced /t/):

(25)   John practises every day.

(26)   John practised every day.

Carrying on now with the assumption that meanings are encoded by morphemes and ways of putting them together, we will conclude this section with a quick survey of some of the kinds of things which can be encoded. In each case, this is a brief and over-simplified account but it should be enough to serve our purposes for now.

Some words encode concepts

It seems that some words encode concepts. The word *chocolate* encodes the concept {CHOCOLATE}. The word *cheese* encodes the concept {CHEESE} and so on.

(27)   I like chocolate.

(28)   I like cheese.

Some words 'point' to concepts

Some words do not encode concepts but seem to point us in the direction of particular things we can work out from the context. Words like *he, here* and *now* do not encode any specific concept but when we hear them we make assumptions about particular concepts the speaker has in mind.

(29)   He's here now.

In the linguistics literature, expressions such as these are usually referred to as examples of 'deixis' (traditionally pronounced roughly as 'dyke-sis' but now often pronounced 'day-ixis'). A technical definition might say that deictic expressions are those where we need to have contextual information in order to know what the expression refers to.

Some words are vague

Some words do not seem to encode clearly defined concepts, at least at first. If you ask me whether my daughter is *tall*, how tall does she need to be for her to count as tall? If a dentist asks you whether touching one of your teeth with a dental instrument is *painful*, how do you know how much discomfort you have to feel before it counts?

(30)   Is your daughter tall?

(31)   Is your toothache painful?

Some of these examples are easier to clarify than others. You might tell me what height you have in mind which counts as tall. Your dentist might blow cold air on individual teeth so that you can compare the painful tooth with others. The nature of these two examples is different. While both TALL and PAINFUL are matters of degree, it seems that there must be an inherently vague borderline between what counts as TALL and what does not. With the concept PAINFUL, there might be pragmatic or social reasons to hesitate about using the word *painful* even if the concept is clearly defined and a particular sensation falls under that description to a minimal degree. Other cases are more difficult. What does it mean, for example, to say that a particular country is a *democracy*?

(32)   I'm glad we live in a democracy.

Different speakers will have different ideas about what counts as a democracy and even individual speakers might not be able to say exactly what they have in mind.

Word order affects meaning

There are systematic differences between utterances based on the way words are ordered. There has been a large amount of work on how to account for this and there are a number of different approaches. For now, we'll simply acknowledge that there's a sense in which (33)–(35) are all about the same thing (about John being polite) but that the speaker is saying something different about the possibility of John's politeness in each case.

(33)   John is polite.

(34)   Is John polite?

(35)   Be polite, John.

Roughly (we'll see some of the ways in which this is only roughly accurate in Chapter 11), the speaker in (33) seems to be saying that John is polite while in (34) she is asking whether John is polite and in (35) she is telling John to be polite.

This very quick survey falls far short of an account of linguistic semantics. I hope, though, that this brief discussion gives a sense of the ways in which meanings can be linguistically encoded. The next step is to see whether we can identify what is encoded by a range of particular utterances. Imagine I ask you whether John is coming to tomorrow night's party and you reply as in (36):

(36)   He is.

It is clear in this context that you are telling me that John is coming to the party tomorrow night. But this can't be a linguistically encoded meaning, since an utterance of the same linguistic expression in a different context would have a different meaning. If you say it to me after I have said it's a shame that Robbie isn't very good at football, then it will mean that you think that Robbie is good at football. And so on. So how much of the meaning of an utterance is linguistically encoded? The best way to investigate this is to look at specific example utterances and identify what parts of their meanings we need to work out in context. In other words, to look at what is involved in pragmatic interpretation at the same time as considering what is linguistically encoded. The next section considers what kinds of things we pragmatically infer.

1.4.4   Linguistic pragmatics: what we infer

There is always a significant gap between what is linguistically encoded and what speakers actually intend by their utterances. Recognition of this gap has been termed the 'underdeterminacy thesis' (e.g. by Carston 2002a: 19–30) to reflect the idea that linguistically encoded meanings always significantly underdetermine intended meanings. The gap between what is encoded and the meanings we eventually arrive at is filled by pragmatic inference. What kinds of things can be inferred?.

Exercise 1.5 encourages you to think about what kinds of inferences we need to make in order to understand utterances.

Exercise 1.5

- There are a number of different kinds of inference involved in working out what a speaker intends on a particular occasion. In each of these examples, consider some of the inferences the hearer will need to make in understanding the utterance (in cases with two utterances, focus on what B has said and how A will understand it):
  (i)   This vacuum cleaner really sucks.
  (ii)   Robbie thinks the underground is closed and there's a night bus stop round the corner.
  (iii)   My teacher says we can.
  (iv)   Looks like it's too late.
  (v)   Sarah thinks we're all going to die.
  (vi)   A: Do you think Bob will like cheese?
        B: He's Welsh.
  (vii)   I think everyone's here now.
  (viii) My new flat is near the shops.
  (ix)   You're not having dinner.
  (x)   That's probably not the brightest star in the galaxy.
  (xi)   A: What did Frieda say?
        B: You look sad.
  (xii)   A: Ozzy Ozbourne's coming to dinner.
        B: I'll bring a bat.
  Now see if you can organise the inferences into types, e.g. there might be some inferences about the sense of an ambiguous word, others about the overall aim of the speaker, and so on.

The activities in Exercise 1.5 should have suggested a range of kinds of inferences we make in understanding each other. Here are some of the different things you might have suggested and which pragmaticists have focused on in recent work.

Indirect communication

Let's return to example (2) above, reprinted here as (37):

(37)   *(shop assistant to customer about to pay for two pots of cream cheese)*
They're three for two just now.

One thing I inferred from this utterance was that the shop assistant was letting me know that I was entitled to another pot of cream cheese without having to pay extra. We'll see below that the technical term for the inference that I am entitled to a third pot is an 'implicature'. For now, we can think of implicatures as 'indirect communication'. What makes this indirect is that it is derived by combining the main proposition 'directly' communicated (that pots of cream cheese are currently for sale under an offer where three pots cost the same as two pots) together with other contextual assumptions (including that I am about to pay for two pots). The fact that I can have one more pot without paying extra does not follow from either the proposition alone or the contextual assumptions alone.

'Direct' communication

We'll see below that there is some dispute about how exactly to characterise what I am calling 'direct communication' here, but I hope that what I have in mind will be clear enough for now. Before working out what the assistant in my corner shop was indirectly communicating, I had to work out what she was directly communicating, which we might roughly characterise as (38) (a simplified version of (3) above):

(38)   Pots of cream cheese in this shop are on sale in a 'three-for-two' offer (where if you pay for two, we give you three) at this moment in time.

One thing to notice (bearing in mind the discussion in 1.3 above) is that in order to represent a proposition we have to use an utterance in English. To understand what proposition is expressed by (38), we'd need to know the referents of *this shop* and *this moment in time*, among other things. What's important for now, though, is to notice that understanding the shop assistant involved making a number of decisions, including that *they* referred to pots of cream cheese on sale in the shop, that *three for two* meant that three pots were available for the same price as two pots, and that *now* meant 'at this moment in time'. Understanding what she intended by *they* involved making a decision about the referent of the pronoun. Most linguists would also think of *now* as a referring expression.

There are a number of other questions we might need to answer in working out what someone directly communicated, including how to disambiguate ambiguous expressions, how to work out what has been 'missed out' in elliptical utterances and how to decide exactly what is intended by vague expressions. All three of these are illustrated in example (39):

(39)   Yes, unless the crown is painful.

To understand (39), you need to know which sense of the ambiguous word *crown* is intended (e.g. a cover put over a tooth to repair it or an item of royal headgear), to work out what proposition *yes* indicates agreement with, to work out the ellipsed (or 'left out') material between *yes* and *unless* (to work out what will be happening so long as the crown isn't painful), and also to decide how much pain would count as painful in this situation. As we saw above, {PAIN} is a vague concept and what counts as painful for one person or in one situation might not count as painful to someone else or in another situation. Example (39) was uttered by me after my wife asked me whether the outcome of my visit to the dentist meant that I did not need to go back until my next routine check-up. Her exact utterance was (40):

(40)   So is that you for six months then?

These examples show that we have some work to do before we understand what has been 'directly' as well as indirectly communicated, and we expect our pragmatic theory to explain this.

Whose thoughts are being communicated?

In some cases, we need to decide whether the thoughts being represented are those of the speaker or of someone else. Suppose, for example, that I see you are looking at horoscopes in the paper, ask you what it says about me, and you reply:

(41)   You've got something on your nose.

I will have to decide whether you are telling me that my horoscope says that I have got something on my nose (obviously not a very likely interpretation) or whether you are telling me that I have something on my nose because that seems more important right now than telling me about my horoscope. One way to think about this is to think of propositions as being 'embedded' under descriptions indicating who they are being attributed to. The two interpretations of (41) could be represented as (42a) for the attribution to the horoscope and (42b) for your statement of your own belief:

(42) a.   (Your horoscope says that) you have something on your nose.
     b.   (I am informing you that) you have something on your nose.

There are, of course, more complicated possibilities. Suppose I see you eating a chocolate cake and seeming to enjoy it and I say:

(43)   You don't like chocolate.

It is unlikely in this situation that I am informing you that you do not like chocolate. A more natural interpretation is one where I am reminding you that you have said in the past that you did not like chocolate and drawing attention to the contrast between what you said in the past and your behaviour now. We might represent this as (44) or (45):

(44)   [You said in the past that] you do not like chocolate.

(45)   [Until now I was under the impression that] you do not like chocolate.

Is the utterance ironic?

Within relevance theory, ironical interpretations are seen as closely related to interpretations where the proposition expressed is attributed to someone other than the speaker. Here are three examples. First, consider (46) uttered in response to the suggestion of inviting a particular person to a party:

(46)   That's a really good idea. There'll be so much less to clear up if no-one comes.

Here, the speaker is attributing to the person who made the suggestion the thought that inviting the person they have in mind is a good idea. To recognise the utterance as ironic, we need to recognise that the speaker is attributing the thought to the hearer and dissociating herself from it. Clearly, she thinks it's a bad idea, that inviting this person will mean that no-one else (or at least significantly fewer people) will come to the party, that it would be ridiculous to focus on not having much to clear up as the sign of a successful party, and so on.

Now, consider (47), uttered in London on a particularly unpleasant, windy and rainy day in August:

(47)   Ah, the great British summer!

Here again it is clear that the speaker is not thinking that British summers are particularly great. In fact, she thinks they're not. So who is she attributing this positive thought to? This time, it is less clear that she has one person in mind. More likely, she is representing a general hope that the summer will be good or just holding up the idea to ridicule without really focusing on one individual or group as the source of the idea.

In some cases, it is less clear exactly what attitude the speaker is expressing or who they might be attributing the thought to, and arguably more problematic to explain the utterance in this way. I heard a teenager say (48) when watching a rather eccentric performer on a TV programme:

(48)   I love this guy.

One thing to notice here is that we need to decide what exactly *love* means in this context, i.e. exactly what kind of attitude would be intended if she meant to be understood non-ironically as expressing a straightforwardly positive attitude? While it was clear that she did not mean to be taken literally, it was not clear to me exactly how strongly she meant to dissociate herself from the idea that she loved the performer. Was she 'ironically' enjoying the performance so that she did in fact have a positive attitude, or loving the fact that she thought it was terrible? Or something more complicated? And who was she attributing the thought that she might have 'loved' him to? We will look at ironical interpretation, including complex cases such as this, in more detail in Chapter 10.

How literal is the utterance?

Literalness is not a straightforward notion. In an everyday intuitive sense, we would usually think that someone is speaking literally if they aim to communicate that they believe a fairly straightforward interpretation of the proposition they seem to have directly expressed. Ironical utterances would be taken as non-literal because the speaker does not intend to be taken as believing what they have said. There is another dimension on which we can consider whether or not an utterance is literal, which has to do with how we understand the proposition itself. Suppose I mention to someone that I am working on this book and they reply:

(49)   You've been working on that book for a billion years.

Clearly, they do not think that either one thousand million or one million million (depending on your definition of *billion*) years have elapsed since I started working on the book. To understand them, I need to recognise that they mean to be understood as less than fully literal. They do mean to communicate some things which are connected with what they have said, e.g. that I have been working on the book for a very long time, that anyone would find it surprising that I have been working on it for so long, and so on, but not that a billion years have elapsed since I started work. This is an example of an overstatement, or 'hyperbole'. We also speak loosely in other ways. I might, for example, tell you that:

(50)   There were a hundred people at my birthday party.

even if I haven't counted them, or that:

(51)   Brighton is sixty miles away.

even when I know the distance is not exactly sixty miles. Deciding how literally a speaker intends her utterance to be taken is another thing that hearers need to infer. Questions about both of these dimensions of literalness are discussed in more detail in Chapters 8 and 9.

Is the utterance metaphorical?

Just as ironical utterances are related to cases where the speaker is attributing a thought to someone else, metaphorical utterances are related to non-literal utterances. Consider (52), for example:

(52)   My father was a rock.

The speaker here does not mean that their father was not a human being or that he was a mass of stone. This is different from loose talk and hyperbole because we can't explain it by saying that I have overstated or approximated the truth. It is similar to loose talk and hyperbole in that there are similarities between what has been said and what the speaker intends. In this case, the rock-like similarities have to do with qualities such as being strong, durable, resistant to forces of change, and so on. Metaphor has traditionally been thought of as a case where the speaker expresses a relationship of similarity by speaking as if the similarity were absolute. Some approaches suggest that metaphors are understood to express more or less the same as a related simile. Utterance (52) would then be taken to express more or less the same as (53):

(53)   My father was like a rock.

The question this raises is how to explain the difference between metaphors and similes, particularly given our intuition that (52) and (53) do not give rise to exactly the same effects. Most speakers feel that a metaphorical utterance is more creative and harder to paraphrase than a related simile. One thing to note is that a simile such as (53) is literally true whereas a metaphor such as (52) is not. Questions about how to account for metaphor are also discussed in more detail in Chapter 9.

Is the utterance vague?

Vagueness is another tricky notion. There is a sense in which all utterances are vague, since all utterances leave some things to be worked out in context. An ambiguous expression can be seen as vague in that an utterance containing it will have more than one possible interpretation. Utterance (54), for example, is vague between a reading where the speaker would like a piece of sports equipment to be brought to the picnic or a reading where she would like a small flying mammal to be brought to the picnic:

(54)   When you come to the picnic, can you bring a bat?

If we assume that picnicking people often like to play communal games, we can see why the 'sports equipment' interpretation is more likely here. In most cases, this vagueness is temporary and hearers quickly work out the intended sense.

Similarly, referring expressions are vague in that understanding them depends on assigning referents to them. So (55) has as many possible interpretations as there are possible referents for *she*:

(55)   She doesn't really enjoy opera.

There are also cases where utterances are vague in a more serious and ultimately irreconcilable way, i.e. where it is not possible to decide exactly what the speaker intended even with access to all the necessary contextual assumptions. Some of these arise because of vague terms such as *democracy*:

(56)   We will not be satisfied until there is democracy in this country.

Some arise because the concepts being communicated are open to several interpretations and the speaker does not want to be committed to any particular one of them. This might be illustrated by religious statements such as (57):

(57)   God is within me.

There are also cases where the speaker is unable to convey anything precise because their own understanding is vague, e.g. when they are talking about complex emotions. In such cases, the speaker might make it clear that they cannot be precise, verbally as in (58) or nonverbally as in (59):

(58)   I can't explain it. I feel kind of good and bad at the same time?

(59)   I just feel kind of *[raises and drops shoulders with a heavy sigh]*

In fact, there is a word in current English usage which encodes a vague response:

(60)   A: What did you think of the concert?
        B: It was kind of meh

The word *meh* suggests a lack of engagement and indecision about whether to respond positively or negatively (for a journalistic comment on the spread of this word, see Hann 2007).

In understanding utterances, then, we also need to think about how precise or detailed our characterisation of the intended interpretation should be.

Is the utterance literary?

Related to vagueness in some ways, and itself a fairly controversial issue, is the question of whether an utterance is literary. Consider (61)–(63):

(61)   O, how I faint when I of you do write

(62)   Remember office keys

(63)   *This is just to say*
        I have eaten
        the plums
        that were in
        the icebox
        and which
        you were probably
        saving
        for breakfast
        Forgive me
        they were delicious
        so sweet
        and so cold   (William Carlos Williams, 'This Is Just To Say'. Tomlinson 2000: 72)

(61) is the opening line from Shakespeare's 80th sonnet. (62) is the text of a note I left on the kitchen table to remind myself to bring my office keys to work on

my first day back after a trip. (63) is a poem by William Carlos Williams. Shakespeare's sonnet has consistently been interpreted as a work of literature. As far as I know, my note has only been interpreted (by me) as a relatively trivial note reminding me to do something. William Carlos Williams's poem has been much discussed since it highlights questions about what makes something count as literary. If you believe texts are either literary or not, then (61) would presumably count as literary, (62) would not, and your decision on (63) will depend on what you think determines literariness. If you believe literariness is a property of interpretations, then presumably all three might be interpreted as literary. On this view, contextual assumptions will explain why (61) is more likely to be interpreted as literary than (62) and why the literariness of (63) is less clear. There is, of course, nothing to stop someone from treating an everyday utterance such as (62) as if it were a literary work.

Misunderstandings

While we often understand each other relatively well, we also often misunderstand or only partially understand each other.

(64)   Can you read what you've just written?

A long time ago, when teaching (for me) involved writing on an overhead projector, a student said (64) to me while I was lecturing. Oversensitive to the fact that my handwriting was very bad, I defended myself by pointing out that I was saying it all aloud at the same time. The student explained that he appreciated that and was simply asking me to read aloud the specific passage I had just written, so that he could be sure his notes were accurate.

(65)   I'd like one.

Recently, I was offering chocolate ice cream bars to a group of children when a grownup said (65) to me. I gave her one of the bars and she said thank you. It was only later that I realised she was slightly offended that I hadn't offered her one in the first place and that she'd had to ask. Unlike with (64), in this case I understood most of what was intended but missed part of her intention. Had I realised what she intended, I would have apologised for missing her out first time around.

As well as explaining cases where understanding each other is fairly straightforward, we also expect our pragmatic theory to explain cases such as (64) where the interpretation is not the intended one and cases such as (65) where the interpretation is only partially successful.

Disputed meanings

Related to misunderstandings are cases where a dispute arises about what a particular utterance was intended to communicate. A number of cases have been much discussed. Jenny Thomas (1995: 16–17) discusses (66), an utterance which was alleged to have been made in 1952 by Derek Bentley, who was being restrained by a police officer at the time. His friend Christopher Craig then shot and killed another police officer.

(66)   Let him have it.

There is no dispute that Craig shot and killed the policeman. However, Bentley was jointly prosecuted with Craig and eventually executed. Part of the prosecution case depended on the interpretation of (66). The prosecution argued that Bentley intended to encourage Craig to shoot the police officer. However, an alternative interpretation would be that Bentley was asking Craig to hand over the gun to the police officer.[1] In fact, there has since been some dispute about whether Bentley even uttered (66) at all. Both Craig and Bentley denied that either of them had said it. Bentley was eventually pardoned posthumously in 1998. (For fuller discussion of examples such as these, see Durant 2010; for discussion of this example, see Thomas 1995: 17.)

I hope you now have a sense of the range of things which we infer when understanding each other and which we would therefore expect a pragmatic theory to explain. Relevance theory aims to explain this range of phenomena in terms of two generalisations about human behaviour: the Cognitive (or First) Principle of Relevance and the Communicative (or Second) Principle of Relevance. The next section discusses these two principles and the technical definition of relevance which they presuppose.

Exercise 1.6 asks you to look more closely at a number of examples and to consider what is involved in understanding them.

Exercise 1.6

- For each of the following examples, identify TWO inferences which the hearer needs to make in order to understand them (again, focus on B's utterance where there are two speakers):
  (i)   I think you are being economical with the truth there.
  (ii) Reading your essay is like talking to someone on the phone in a neighbourhood with patchy coverage.
  (iii) *(while playing cards to indicate that the dealer should deal the speaker another card)* Hit me.
  (iv) A: Did Robbie tell you what he thought of the song I wrote?
        B: It's rubbish.
  (v)   A: Would you like a piece of this cake?
        B: Are there nuts in it?

1.4.5   Two Principles of Relevance

The two Principles of Relevance constitute generalisations about cognition and communication. The more general **Cognitive Principle of Relevance** is a claim about human cognition in general:

(67)   First, or Cognitive, Principle of Relevance
        Human cognition tends to be geared to the maximisation of relevance.

What does this mean? To understand it, we need to know what 'relevance' is and what 'maximisation' means. Relevance theory is based on a technical notion of 'relevance' as a property of sights, sounds, thoughts, utterances, memories, conclusions of inferences (and, more generally, inputs to cognitive processes) defined in terms of a balance between **cognitive effects** and **processing effort**. This can be understood informally and more technically. Informally, we can compare two stimuli in terms of the number of effects they have and see that the stimulus with more effects will seem better to justify the effort involved in processing it. Imagine I look out of the window and see that:

(68)   There is a robin in the garden.

This is significant to me to some extent. I now know more things about the world than I did before I looked out of the window. Now consider I look out and see:

(69)   There is a robin and a fox in the garden.

This is more significant since I know more than I would have known from the first stimulus. Now consider a third possibility. I look out of the window and I see:

(70)   There is a robin and a tiger in the garden.

This is even more significant than either (68) or (69). Why? Informally, we can say that this is because it 'tells me more', or perhaps 'something more significant', than either of the other possibilities. More technically, we can make a list of what follows from each possibility and see a significant difference between them. From (68) we might list the following new assumptions:

(71) a.   There is a robin in the garden.
     b.   Anyone who is interested in robins might want to look in the garden.

and not much else. From (69) I can come up with the following list:

(72) a.   There is a robin in the garden.
     b.   There is a fox in the garden.
     c.   Anyone who is interested in robins might want to have a look in the garden.
     d.   Anyone who is interested in foxes might want to have a look in the garden.

and not much more (unless there are other contextual assumptions which suggest more). This is more significant than the assumptions in (71) but not much more. In different contexts, the details might change. I might, for example, know someone who is terrified of foxes, in which case it follows that I should tell them not to go into my garden. If I have chickens or small vulnerable animals in the garden, then it follows that I need to do something to protect them. The important thing for now is to notice that seeing two new creatures in the garden is more significant ('relevant') than noticing one.

What about utterance (70)? We can come up with a longer list of things which follow from this. With the change from a fox to a tiger, of course, we can access the same assumptions about a tiger as we did about a fox:

(73) a. There is a robin in the garden.
    b. There is a tiger in the garden.
    c. Anyone who is interested in robins might want to have a look in the garden.
    d. Anyone who is interested in tigers might want to have a look in the garden.

But foxes, while less common than robins in many parts of England, are not too unusual in gardens where I live in London (and getting more and more common). By contrast, a tiger in my garden would be a big surprise. Seeing a tiger would contradict existing assumptions I have about the likelihood of seeing tigers when I look in my garden and it will have alarming new implications about how dangerous it would be to go out into my garden. It will also make me wonder how the tiger got there and whether other dangerous animals might be on the prowl. A far from exhaustive list of assumptions I might conclude from seeing a robin and a tiger might be:

(74) a. There is a robin in the garden.
    b. There is a tiger in the garden.
    c. Anyone who is interested in robins might want to have a look in the garden.
    d. Anyone who is interested in tigers might want to have a look in the garden.
    e. My garden is very dangerous.
    f. Anywhere near my garden is very dangerous.
    g. It is possible to see tigers on the loose in London.
    h. Other wild creatures might be on the loose in London.
    i. I should warn everyone I know to stay indoors.
    j. I should phone the police to report it.

So seeing a tiger would be far more 'relevant' to me than seeing a robin or a fox. Notice that the assumptions which follow from the presence of a tiger are so significant and unexpected that the presence of a robin is likely to seem much less relevant than it would otherwise have been. In fact, it would be odd in most contexts to utter (70) after having noticed a tiger.

To form a definition of **relevance** based on these insights, we need to have a definition of what counts as an 'effect'. Relevance theory defines **cognitive effects** for an individual as adjustments to the way an individual represents the world. Seeing a robin in my garden means that I now know that there is a robin in my garden so I have changed the way in which I am representing the world. Relevance theory claims that the more cognitive effects a stimulus has, the more relevant it is. Seeing a tiger in the garden gives rise to more cognitive effects than seeing a robin so this is a more relevant stimulus.

The more cognitive effects a stimulus has, the more relevant it is. But we can assess relevance not only in terms of the amount of effects derivable from a stimulus. **Processing effort** also plays a role. Sperber and Wilson claim that the more mental effort involved in processing a stimulus the less relevant it is. Compare (75) and (76):

(75)   I can see a tiger in the garden.

(76)   When I look outside, I can see a tiger in the garden.

Assuming that the tiger is the most significant thing to notice in the garden and that nothing significant follows from the suggestion that I need to look to see the tiger, then (75) is a more relevant stimulus than (76). This follows because it will enable us to derive a similar range of effects but with less effort needed to process the words.

Now consider two other possible utterances, (77) and (78):

(77)   There's a tiger in the garden.

(78)   There's a tiger in the garden and the square root of 729 is 27.

Assuming that nothing significant follows from the mathematical information about the square root of 729, then (77) is a better way of informing someone about a tiger than (78). This is because the range of effects derivable in each case are similar but (78) requires the hearer to exert more effort in processing it. Examples such as this explain why the definition of relevance is based on assumptions about effort as well as effects.

Now we have an informal definition of relevance, we need to know what is involved in **maximising relevance**. Here is a definition:

(79)   Maximising relevance
         To maximise relevance is to produce the greatest amount of cognitive effects for the
         least amount of processing effort.

The claim expressed in the **Cognitive Principle of Relevance**, then, is that the goal of human cognition is to derive as many cognitive effects as possible for as little effort as possible. As we look at, listen to, and otherwise perceive the world, we are looking for relevance: that is, we are aiming to derive as many cognitive effects as possible for as little effort as possible. And our minds are organised in such a way as to help us achieve that. We will look at the implications of this more closely in Chapter 3.

The claim about our expectations when we are understanding acts of communication is that we are also looking for relevance, but we are not entitled to assume that every utterance will be maximally relevant to us. Instead, we are entitled to assume that it will be optimally relevant:

(80)   Second, or Communicative, Principle of Relevance
         Every utterance conveys a presumption of its own optimal relevance.

To understand this, we need to know what it means to presume that an input is optimally relevant:

(81)   Presumption of optimal relevance

a.   The ostensive stimulus is relevant enough for it to be worth the addressee's effort to process it.

b.   The ostensive stimulus is the most relevant one compatible with the communicator's abilities and preferences.

The idea here is that recognising that someone is speaking to us creates an expectation that their utterance will be worth the effort required to understand it, and moreover that it is the most relevant one they were both willing and able to make. We do not presume that the utterance is the most relevant conceivable one (providing as many effects as possible for as little effort as possible) but that it is at least relevant enough to be worth processing, and the most relevant one that the speaker was both able to think of and willing to use at the time. If you require my attention, then you imply that you think it will be worth my while to interpret your behaviour. If you do not convey anything worth communicating, or put me to unnecessary effort, then it will not be worth my while to process your stimulus. So I look for an interpretation which will confirm the assumptions that:

a.   you have in mind an interpretation that it is worth my while to derive

b.   your stimulus can be interpreted in such a way as to provide enough effects to justify the effort involved in processing it

c.   you are putting me to no more effort than is required, given your abilities and preferences

Since any act which is clearly intended to communicate something gives rise to these assumptions, it does not make sense to attempt to communicate something which contradicts them. This is why it is not possible to take seriously an utterance such as the one near the beginning of this chapter, repeated here as (82):

(82)   Pay no attention to this utterance. It has no relevance to you.

In the next sub-section, we will take our first look at how the presumption of optimal relevance can be used to explain particular interpretations of acts of verbal and nonverbal communication.

Exercise 1.7 encourages you to explore your understanding of the notion of relevance and the two principles of relevance.

Exercise 1.7

*   In each of the following examples, consider which of the two options would be most relevant in the given context and why (note that the answer might not be totally clear in every case):
    (i)   A: What did you do at school this afternoon?
          B: a. We did some maths and then the teacher read us a story.
               b. First, we sat on the carpet at the front and the teacher spoke to us all about what we'd be doing for the rest of the day. Then she got us to sit at our tables and we got our maths books out...
    (ii) *(to a bus conductor as the speaker gets on to a bus)*
          a. One to the town centre please.
          b. Can I have a ticket to the town centre please? My friend Robbie is visiting today so I'm meeting him at the station and taking him to the shops before we go out for the evening.
    (iii) A: Do you fancy a coffee?

B: a. I don't drink coffee.
    b. Beyoncé's playing a gig in London next week.

1.4.6 Relevance-theoretic explanations: a comprehension heuristic

So it is part of the nature of human cognition that we are always looking for as many effects as possible for as little effort as possible. At the same time, any utterance or act of intentional communication conveys a presumption of optimal relevance. How can this help us to explain cognition in general and how we understand acts of intentional communication in particular?

For cognition in general, there is relatively little to say here. Faced with a range of stimuli, our minds are so organised that we automatically tend to pick out the one that is likely to yield the most cognitive effects for the least processing effort. For instance, our perceptual systems seem to have developed in ways which make it more likely that we notice relevant stimuli. We might, for example, be particularly skilled at reading human expressions. As I walk down a crowded city street, I will be looking to notice what is relevant. I will pay particular attention to other humans, noticing anyone familiar, looking at signs, posters and other places where relevant information might be displayed. I will also be good at noticing acts of intentional communication and at assessing the likelihood that they are relevant to me. A poster on a bus shelter is an act of intentional communication and so I can expect a certain amount of relevance from this. If someone talks to me at the bus stop, this also creates expectations. I am able to see that the relevance of an utterance from a real person talking directly to me is likely to be higher than the relevance of a poster, partly because this person has designed their communicative act with me in mind while the poster is designed to communicate with a large number of people not individually known to the creators of the poster. Given this, I will pay attention to the person talking to me rather than ignoring her and reading the poster instead. It is worth mentioning here that relevance theory assumes that we focus our attention in this way automatically, as a result of the way our cognitive system is organised. As Carston (2002a: 5–10) points out, while we tend to talk about 'the speaker' and 'the hearer' producing and understanding utterances, relevance theory sees these processes as being carried out by domain-specific cognitive systems and sub-systems which function in this way automatically and not under conscious control. In Dennett's (1969) terms, these are 'subpersonal' rather than 'personal' processes.

We might also speculate here about ways in which attempts to maximise relevance vary from individual to individual, from situation to situation, or from cultural group to cultural group. Walking through a city, I will pay more attention to other human beings than other things such as pigeons, trees or lamp-posts. I will pay enough attention to try to avoid walking into any of them but I will also look a little more closely at humans, perhaps because I think they are more likely to talk to me or because they are more likely to be irritated if I get in their way as they try to negotiate the streets. On my bicycle, I will pay more attention to pigeons than when I'm walking and maybe more attention to them than I would have done if I hadn't once hit a pigeon while cycling (neither of us came to any harm) and noticed the dangers if they don't get out of my path quickly enough. My daughter, who is nervous of pigeons, might pay them more attention than someone else would. And so on.

When it comes to intentional communication, the claim is that the presumption of optimal relevance will guide my attempt to work out what is being communicated. How does this work exactly? The **presumption of optimal relevance** leads to predictions about what addressees will do when they recognise that someone is acting in a way that is manifestly intended to communicate something (in relevance-theoretic terms, when they recognise an act of **ostensive-inferential communication**). The first part of the presumption of optimal relevance says that the communicator has in mind an interpretation which will justify the expenditure of processing effort in accessing it. This means that the addressee is looking for an interpretation with enough effects to provide this justification and that he will not settle for an interpretation which does not meet this criterion. Suppose, for example, you say to me:

(83)   I'm a human being.

I cannot assume that you are letting me know which biological species you belong to. This would simply be informing me of something I already know and so would not justify the effort involved in processing your utterance. Therefore I will go further and consider other possibilities. Perhaps you are reminding me that you have human qualities and that it would not be appropriate to expect you to behave in ways that go beyond or fall below what humans are capable of. This would be appropriate, for instance, if I have just asked you whether you feel sorry for someone who you have had to treat harshly in some way. The fact that the interpretation has to be 'relevant enough' explains why we keep looking beyond initial, fairly trivial, possibilities which would not justify the processing effort involved.

Suppose you have said (83) to me and I have considered this as a possible interpretation. Should I now go further and wonder whether there might be something even more significant which you intended to communicate? The presumption of optimal relevance predicts that I should not. If you could see that I would come up with this interpretation and that it would meet my expectations of relevance, it would be putting me to unnecessary effort to expect me nevertheless to go further, consider another possible interpretation and then weigh it up against the first one I considered. Sperber and Wilson (1986: 168–9) illustrate this by considering the following example:

(84)   George has a big cat.

They point out that the word *cat* is ambiguous, including a frequently used sense in which it refers to a domesticated cat of the kind many people keep as pets and a less familiar sense in which it refers to a member of the larger cat family which includes lions, tigers, leopards, and so on. So (84) could indicate either that George has a pet cat which is larger than most pet cats or that he has a tiger or lion or similar animal. Relevance theory predicts that a hearer in an everyday situation in England will choose the common-sense interpretation of *cat*, which is more accessible and therefore easier to process, unless something particular in the context suggests otherwise. This is because the second clause of the presumption of optimal relevance says that the speaker will have produced the 'most relevant' utterance consistent with her abilities and preferences. If the speaker has two possible ways of communicating something, then they should choose the one that is more accessible and easier for the hearer to process. If George has a tiger or a leopard or similar, the speaker could have said something like (85), (86) or (87):

(85)   George has a tiger.

(86)   George has a leopard.

(87)   George has a tiger or a leopard.

Communicating this by uttering (84) would require the hearer to access a perfectly acceptable interpretation (i.e. one that justifies the effort involved in accessing it) and then to move on to consider other possibilities which might be more relevant and choosing one of them. This would involve unnecessary effort given the availability of less effortful alternative formulations such as (85)–(87). If the hearer accesses the 'domestic cat' interpretation of (84) and thinks the speaker could have intended the utterance to be relevant on that interpretation, then there is no need to look further for an alternative interpretation. One way of summarising this is to say that there is at most one interpretation of an utterance which will satisfy the hearer's expectations of relevance. As Sperber and Wilson put it, 'either the first interpretation consistent with the [communicative] principle of relevance is communicated ... or nothing is communicated at all' (Sperber and Wilson 1986: 169).

The relevance-guided comprehension heuristic follows from these assumptions. Given that addressees should not stop looking for an interpretation until they find one which provides enough effects to justify the effort involved in interpreting the utterance, and given that the first such interpretation found is the only one which could be intended, then addressees should begin by considering interpretations in order of accessibility (i.e. in the order in which they become accessible) and stop when they find one which meets this expectation. While earlier discussions presented this same account of the procedure of utterance interpretation, it is only in more recent discussions (see, for example, Wilson and Sperber 2004; Sperber and Wilson 2005) that it has been presented explicitly as a **relevance-guided comprehension heuristic**:

(88)   Relevance-guided comprehension heuristic
   a.   Follow a path of least effort in deriving cognitive effects: test interpretations (e.g. disambiguations, reference resolutions, implicatures, etc.) in order of accessibility.
   b.   Stop when your expectations of relevance are satisfied.

We will look in Chapters 3 and 4 at how this heuristic constrains interpretation in more detail; for now, the important thing to note is that relevance theory does not predict that interpreters explicitly weigh up interpretations or assess their relevance in detail. Rather, the prediction is that they follow a relatively simple heuristic which involves looking for an interpretation and stopping as soon as they find one which satisfies their expectations of relevance.

Before moving on, we should consider what role is played by the reference to 'abilities and preferences' in the presumption of optimal relevance, particularly since this was not explicitly mentioned in earlier formulations of the presumption.[2] Sperber and Wilson introduced this idea in the 1995 second edition of the book *Relevance* to take account of the fact that communicators might not always be able or willing to produce the most relevant utterance possible. Suppose, for example, that I am allergic to nuts but you do not know this. If you tell me that you have made a hazelnut tart, you cannot be trying to warn me not to eat it. It is relevant to me to know that the cake contains nuts and I will be able to act on this knowledge, but I cannot assume that this was part of what you intended to communicate. This is a case where a relevant interpretation is ruled out because it is not consistent with what I assume about your abilities.

Now suppose that I ask you what you thought of my cake and you tell me it was very nice. I might nevertheless conclude that you didn't enjoy it. Why would you say you liked it when you didn't? Because you prefer not to hurt my feelings by letting me know what you really thought. We make assessments such as this all the time and, of course, this is one reason why positive comments are often extended and repeated ('I really enjoyed the cake. It was fantastic. Really! …' and so on).

So the presumption of optimal relevance says that addressees are entitled to assume that communicators have provided at least enough effects to justify the effort involved in deriving them and have made their utterance even more relevant to the extent that this is consistent with their abilities and preferences. We look for an interpretation which would give rise to enough effects and we stop looking when we find one which satisfies our expectations of relevance. We will look at this heuristic and how it constrains interpretations in more detail in Chapter 4. This chapter concludes by considering the lines along which this approach aims to explain three specific examples, starting with (89):

(89)   *(spoken by a stranger in the street outside a pub, holding a cigarette)* Excuse me, have you got a light?

We will focus for now on just two aspects of the interpretation of this utterance: which sense of the ambiguous word *light* is intended and how the hearer knows whether the speaker is just asking for information or something more.

How does the hearer know which sense of *light* is intended? The fact that the speaker is holding a cigarette suggests that she might be asking for a 'light' in the sense of something to light her cigarette with. The idea of someone asking for something to light their cigarette with is a fairly common everyday scenario. So there is a very accessible interpretation on which the speaker is asking the hearer whether they have a match or a lighter, and asking either to use the match or lighter or to have the hearer help them light their cigarette. This will suggest something like the following range of inferred conclusions:

(90) a.   The speaker is asking whether I have a match or a lighter to light their cigarette with.
     b.   The speaker wants me to let them use my match or lighter or to help them light their cigarette with it.
     c.   If I help them, I will have been sociable and friendly.
     d.   If I help them, they will be grateful.

This range of effects is clearly enough to justify the effort involved in processing the utterance and there is no obvious, more plausible or more accessible interpretation. When the hearer accesses this interpretation and sees that it is one which the speaker could have chosen to communicate, he can decide that this is the intended interpretation. Any other interpretation would not satisfy the hearer's expectations of relevance.

What if the hearer accesses a different interpretation? Suppose, for example, it just pops into the hearer's head that the speaker might be asking about something like a torch or that the speaker is just curious about whether the hearer possesses any kind of light? Neither of these interpretations would satisfy the hearer's expectations of relevance. If the speaker intended either of these, then they were expecting the hearer to go beyond the most accessible likely interpretation, perhaps first accessing and rejecting it (compare the earlier utterance about George's cat). This would mean putting the hearer to extra effort beyond what is required for the more likely interpretation. Further, the speaker could have produced a different utterance which would have made it clear what they meant, for example:

(91)   Do you have a torch or something to light up the pavement with?

This would have made it clear that a different sense of *light* was intended. Given that the speaker did not use an utterance like this, the evidence suggests that they did intend to ask for a match or a lighter. As ever, the first interpretation that the addressee accesses and which the communicator could have intended to be consistent with the presumption of optimal relevance is the one the addressee should choose as the intended interpretation. Alternatives are rejected if the speaker could not have thought of them or if they would involve moving beyond an otherwise relevant and more accessible alternative.

Accounts of how we do such things as assigning reference or recovering ellipsis follow a similar pattern:

(92)   KEN: Is Kirstin coming for a drink after the show tonight?
              BEV: She said she would.

Clearly, 'Kirstin' is a very accessible referent for the word *she* here and the
most likely candidate for the ellipsed material is that she said she would 'come
for a drink after the show tonight'. The hearer can make these assumptions
quickly and use them to derive enough effects to justify the effort involved
in interpreting the utterance. The speaker clearly could have envisaged these
choices and any other interpretation would involve extra processing effort
which would not be rewarded with extra cognitive effects. Given this, the
speaker must have intended to communicate that Bev is saying that Kirstin said
she would come for a drink after the show tonight.

Here is an example to illustrate a relevance-theoretic account of the recovery
of implicated (indirect) assumptions. At first, it seems to be a fairly straightforward example.

(93)   KEN: Have you heard the new My Chemical Romance album?
              BEV: I've kind of gone off emo, actually.

If Ken knows that My Chemical Romance are considered an 'emo' band, then he
can infer that Bev has not heard the album because she has stopped listening to
music by emo bands. This means he can conclude not only an answer to his
question but also some more information about why Bev hasn't heard the album,
about Bev's current listening habits, and so on. This is clearly enough to justify
the effort involved in processing the utterance and it did not involve any unnecessary processing effort. Any other interpretation would involve more effort so Ken
will conclude that this must be what Bev intended to communicate.

Notice that this interpretation would be arrived at even if Ken didn't know what
emo was or that My Chemical Romance were considered an emo band. The
members of My Chemical Romance have frequently denied that they are or ever
were an emo band and Ken might well agree with this assessment. Even if
Ken thinks like this, though, he will decide that Bev is communicating that she
has not listened to the album because she doesn't listen to emo and considers
My Chemical Romance an emo band. This follows partly from knowing that My
Chemical Romance are generally considered an emo band and partly because
producing this utterance makes an interpretation like this accessible. If Bev
intends anything other than this, she will fail to communicate it because Ken
cannot be expected to access an alternative interpretation and because any alternative Ken does come up with will involve extra, and not clearly justified,
processing effort. Of course, the situation might be different if it is clear to Ken
and Bev that they share different contextual assumptions, e.g. if Ken and Bev have
agreed that they think My Chemical Romance are not an emo band and that they
do not listen to them because they have a strong allegiance to 'proper' emo music.
In this situation, the implicature might be that Bev is listening to My Chemical
Romance again now that she has lost some of her interest in other kinds of music.

The account of this example so far is fairly straightforward. We could, however, move on to consider whether Bev's utterance provides evidence for any further assumptions. Let's assume our first interpretation where Ken has decided that Bev does not listen to My Chemical Romance because Bev has gone off emo music. What else might follow from knowing that Bev doesn't listen to emo? Perhaps Ken will wonder whether Bev thinks less than she used to of people who like emo. Ken's question provides evidence that Ken is interested in My Chemical Romance so Bev has provided evidence that she thinks of Ken as being interested in an emo band. Perhaps this suggests that Bev is holding negative assumptions about Ken.

This illustrates the notion that implicatures can vary with regard to how determinate they are and how strongly they are communicated. Let's assume that Ken concludes the following range of assumptions based on Bev's utterance:

(94) a.   Bev thinks My Chemical Romance are an emo band.
      b.   Bev has not heard the new My Chemical Romance album.
      c.   Bev does not like emo music.
      d.   Bev has not heard recent albums by other bands she considers emo.
      e.   Bev does not think much of people who like emo.
      f.   Bev thinks Ken likes emo.
      g.   Bev thinks negatively about Ken's taste.

(94a–c) are strongly communicated assumptions. It is hard to see how Ken could fail to conclude these or how Bev could deny having communicated them. (94d–g) are less strongly evidenced and more deniable by Bev. This begins to give an idea of how relevance theory tackles indeterminacy in communication and how it addresses some of the social aspects of communication. These questions will be explored in more detail in Chapters 7 and 11.

So far we have only taken a quick look at how relevance theory explains interpretations. The next exercise gives you the opportunity to work on further explanations along relevance-theoretic lines. The details of the relevance-theoretic approach will be developed more fully in the rest of the book.

Exercise 1.8 asks you to explain the interpretation of a few examples in relevance-theoretic terms, based on the presumption of optimal relevance.

Exercise 1.8

- Suggest a relevance-theoretic explanation of the interpretation of the following utterances (where there is more than one utterance, focus on the final one in the exchange). Make reference to the presumption of optimal relevance and to the relevance-guided comprehension heuristic in your answers.
    (i)   A: Got any plans for tonight?
           B: Andy's in town for the evening.
    (ii)   A: Ken and Bev asked me if those biscuits are sweet or savoury.
           B: They're crackers.
    (iii) That's the worst meal I've ever had.
    (iv)   (on a sign on a motorway)
           Delays possible.

1.5 Summary

In this chapter we have looked briefly at the domain of relevance theory with the aim of giving an initial sense of what it tries to account for and how. We have begun by focusing mainly on linguistic communication, while recognising that relevance theory has something to say about non-linguistic as well as linguistic communication and about cognition as well as communication. We identified the key question as 'how do we work out what other people are trying to achieve by communicating with us?' We identified a few areas where we need to be careful with terminology, referring in particular here to the terms 'sentence', 'utterance', 'proposition', 'code', 'infer', 'imply'. We made a distinction between encoded and inferred communication and linked this to the way relevance theory distinguishes between linguistic semantics and pragmatics. We looked at a range of linguistic forms which can encode meanings and at a range of things which can be encoded. We looked at a range of kinds of things which need to be inferred. We looked at the two Principles of Relevance: the Cognitive Principle of Relevance and the Communicative Principle of Relevance. Finally, we had our first look at the kinds of explanations proposed within relevance theory and the relevance-guided comprehension heuristic which is at the centre of these explanations. Everything we have looked at in this introductory chapter will be looked at again later in the book and fuller accounts will be developed. In the next chapter we begin this process by looking at how relevance theory developed from earlier work in pragmatics, in particular from the dramatic breakthrough made in the 1960s by the philosopher Paul Grice.

Exercise 1.9 asks you to look at the list of questions you have come up with so far and to think about the kinds of things which might count as answers to each one.

Exercise 1.9

- Exercise 1.2 asked you to make a list of questions you had about relevance theory in particular and about linguistic meaning in general. Have a look at the list now and consider whether you think you are in a better position to answer any of them now than you were before. Make a note of any ways in which your understanding has developed. If you feel that you are a little closer to an answer without actually having an answer, make a note of that too (e.g. you might feel that you know more about where to look for particular answers without actually knowing what the answers are).

1.6 Further reading

I have indicated further reading during the chapter. Here, as at the end of each chapter, I indicate just a few starting points to follow up the main ideas from the chapter. A fuller range of sources is indicated on the book's website at www.cambridge.org/billyclark. As with most chapters, the main sources for ideas discussed here are by Sperber and Wilson. The book *Relevance* (Sperber and Wilson 1986) is the classic source. Wilson and Sperber 2004 and Sperber and Wilson 2005 are shorter summaries. Other introductory articles are: Blakemore 1995; Carston and Powell 2006; Clark 2011; Yus 2006, 2010. Blakemore 1992 is an introduction aimed at readers who are less familiar with ideas about linguistic semantics and pragmatics than my target audience for this book. Wilson and Sperber's more recent book (Wilson and Sperber 2012) gathers important work on a number of topics and will be most useful to develop your understanding of ideas discussed in Part II.

2   Origins and alternatives

Grice, relevance theory and modern pragmatics

Topics: Grice and meaning; Grice's 'theory of conversation'; critiques of Grice; the development of relevance theory; other approaches

2.1   Overview

Now that we've had a first look at relevance theory as a whole, this chapter fleshes out the picture by considering how it developed from the ground-breaking work of Paul Grice. Grice made arguably the most significant breakthrough so far in our understanding of how we infer contextual meanings and laid the foundations for most if not all recent work in pragmatics. His work inspired a number of others to develop their own approaches. Most significantly for this book, it was in exploring and critiquing Grice's work that Sperber and Wilson came up with the insights that led to the development of relevance theory. The chapter begins with an outline of Grice's work on natural and non-natural meaning before discussing Grice's 'Theory of Conversation' (the scare quotes reflect the fact that, as we will see, what Grice proposed was misnamed in at least two ways: first, it was not a fully-fledged theory; second, it was not only about conversation). In general, responses to Grice's ideas were very positive. At the same time a number of problems were identified. Particular issues include the vagueness (acknowledged by Grice when he first presented his ideas) about what exactly 'relevant' might mean and the sense that some of the ideas he suggested might be redundant (more than one of the components of his theory seem to be designed to do the same job). We consider how exploring these issues led Sperber and Wilson to define 'relevance' in a radically different way and to propose replacing Grice's account with something new. It is worth noting right away that some subsequent discussion has made the mistake of seeing relevance theory as an essentially Gricean approach in which the number of maxims has been reduced to one. This is incorrect. Relevance theory is broadly Gricean in assuming that general pragmatic principles guide interpretations and that the principles involved are broadly rational. However, the Principles of Relevance are not maxims which communicators aim to follow but generalisations about what communicators actually do. The chapter ends with an indication of some other possible ways of building on or replacing Grice's approach. We look in particular at the ideas proposed by two 'neo-Griceans': Larry Horn and Stephen Levinson.

2.2   Grice and meaning

Paul Grice worked on a wide range of topics in linguistics and philosophy (for a clear and thorough overview, and an intellectual biography of Grice, see Chapman 2005). He is best known, though, for work in two areas: his work on 'logic and conversation', which has influenced most if not all subsequent work in pragmatics, and his influential work on meaning. Relevance theory builds on Grice's work in both of these areas. Grice's work on meaning predates his work on pragmatics and it can also be thought of as coming first logically, since the work on meaning aims to distinguish different kinds of meaning, one of which defines the domain of his pragmatic principles. Given this, it makes sense to consider Grice's work on meaning before considering his work on pragmatics. We will see below how relevance theory builds on Grice's approach both with regard to understanding the nature of different kinds of meaning, including intentional communication, and in developing an account of the pragmatic principles which guide interpretation.

It is very common for courses on linguistic meaning (semantics or pragmatics) to begin by considering what we mean when we talk about 'meaning'. Discussion often begins by considering a paper eventually published in 1957 (Grice 1957) in which Grice presented ideas he had been working on and publicly discussing since at least 1948.[1] Grice considered a number of different ways in which we use the words *mean* and *meaning* and established a distinction between kinds of meaning which he called 'natural' and kinds which he called 'non-natural'. He pointed out differences between utterances such as (1) and (2):

(1)   Those spots mean she's got measles.

(2)   Those three rings on the bell (of the bus) mean that the bus is full.

One difference is that we cannot say things like (3) without sounding odd, whereas (4) is perfectly natural:

(3)   Those spots meant measles, but he didn't have measles.

(4)   Those three rings meant the bus was full, but it wasn't actually full.

Grice suggested that examples such as (1) were cases of 'natural meaning' while examples such as (2) were cases of 'non-natural meaning' or '**meaning$_{NN}$**'.

Grice's 'natural meaning' is the kind of meaning involved when we are able to infer from something in the world that something else must be the case, often because of a perceived causal relationship. The classic example of this is the assumption that *smoke means fire* which is true to the extent that all smoke is caused by fire. Similarly, in (1), the presence of the spots is taken to be evidence of measles. Given this, it would be odd to say that we can conclude that the patient has measles because of the spots and then to say that the patient did not have measles after all.

'Non-natural meaning' involves the existence of a particular kind of intention. The three rings 'mean' that the bus is full in that the conductor intends us to infer this from his behaviour. It would not be unreasonable to say that the conductor intended to communicate that the bus was full while not knowing all of the facts and so not realising that there were, in fact, still some seats available.

Grice discussed several examples to establish the particular kind of intention involved in non-natural meaning. His conclusion was that it was not enough for someone to intend for someone else to conclude something, as in (5) where:

(5)   *I ... leave B's handkerchief near the scene of a murder in order to induce*
            the detective to believe that B was the murderer.   (Grice 1957: 381–2)

If the detective in this situation decides that B was the murderer because of the handkerchief, Grice suggests, this is not because he recognises an intention to communicate this, but just because the presence of the handkerchief suggests this.

Nor is it enough to say that the intention includes an intention for the interpreter to recognise the intention, as in (6) where:

(6)   *Feeling faint, a child lets its mother see how pale it is (hoping that she may*
            draw her own conclusions and help)   (Grice 1957: 382)

Here the mother might decide that the child is ill and that the child intends for her to decide this, but the conclusion is based on the way the child looks and not on the recognition of the child's intention.

Grice argued that for something to count as an example of meaning$_{NN}$ we need more than the intention to make an audience think something and recognition of the intention to inform. We also need the very recognition of the intention itself to be involved in giving rise to the conclusion reached by the audience. Here is a summary of Grice's account of meaning$_{NN}$:

(7)   'A meant$_{NN}$ something by x' is (roughly) equivalent to 'A intended the utterance
            of x to produce some effect in an audience by means of the recognition of this
            intention'   (Grice 1957: 385)

Grice illustrated this by considering an example where one person is leading another to conclude that his wife has been unfaithful either by showing a photograph of the wife with another man or by drawing a picture of this. For Grice, only the drawing would count as meaning$_{NN}$. It is true that showing the photograph will lead to the conclusion and that the intention to communicate this will be recognised, but the conclusion would follow from the photograph alone and this rules it out as a possible example of non-natural meaning. With the drawing, the conclusion follows from recognition of the intention to communicate this by drawing the picture.

Wharton (2009: 18–37) reports (and this is confirmed by my own experience) that students are often confused by Grice's discussion of the contrast between showing a photo and drawing a picture. They point out, quite correctly in my opinion, that the husband who is shown the photo may well conclude that his wife has been unfaithful and that his friend intends to communicate this by showing the photograph. For Grice, though, the important point is that the photograph alone provides enough evidence. One way in which I have tried to make Grice's proposal clearer to my students is to suggest that the man shown the photograph can conclude both (8) and (9) without considering (10):

(8)   My friend is showing me a photograph of my wife being unfaithful.

(9)   My wife has been unfaithful (because of the photograph).

(10)   My friend is telling me that my wife has been unfaithful (by showing me the photograph).

Notice that in this case (9) follows from the photograph alone. In the case of the drawing, the man concludes:

(11)   My friend is drawing a picture of my wife being unfaithful.

(12)   My wife has been unfaithful (because my friend is attempting to communicate this to me by drawing the picture).

In this case, (12) follows from recognising the intention behind the drawing and would not follow from the drawing on its own. This is a crucial difference for Grice. Classroom discussion of the photograph and the drawing often involves questions about truthfulness. However, the focus for Grice here was not on truthfulness but on the way in which conclusions are communicated. Questions about truthfulness are discussed more fully below.

Grice also discusses cases where what is intended is not to inform the hearer but to get them to act in a certain way. He refers to these as 'imperatives or quasi-imperatives'. Here is how he explains these examples:

> I have a very avaricious man in my room, and I want him to go; so I throw a pound note out of the window. Is there here any utterance with a meaning$_{NN}$? No, because in behaving as I did, I did not intend his recognition of my purpose to be in any way effective in getting him to go. This is parallel to the photograph case. If on the other hand I had pointed to the door or given him a little push, then my behaviour might well be held to constitute a meaningful$_{NN}$ utterance, just because the recognition of my intention would be intended by me to be effective in speeding his departure. Another pair of cases would be (1) a policeman who stops a car by standing in its way and (2) a policeman who stops a car by waving.   (Grice 1957: 384)

These examples seem to make things a bit clearer. Notice that Grice says that his pointing or pushing the avaricious man 'might well' be taken to be a case of meaning$_{NN}$ because recognition of his intention 'would be' intended to encourage him to leave. It seems, then, that there is room for some uncertainty here. If I intend to have my intention to communicate recognised, then my behaviour 'might well' be taken as meaning$_{NN}$. Returning to the photograph case, then, it seems that the way is open for us to say that whether or not this is taken as a case of meaning$_{NN}$ depends on a number of other factors, including the precise intentions of the photograph-showing man and how the betrayed husband interprets the photograph.[2]

Grice's discussion of meaning was important and influential. The main reason it is important for us here is that the scope of Grice's pragmatics is determined by the definition of meaning$_{NN}$. In Grice's terms, it is cases of meaning$_{NN}$ which pragmatic theories aim to explain. In Chapter 3, we'll look at what relevance theory assumes about the kinds of communication which pragmatic theories should aim to explain. We will see that one way in which relevance theory differs from Grice is that the scope of pragmatics is not seen as covering cases of meaning$_{NN}$ but the wider category of 'ostensive communication' (Wharton 2009 also discusses reasons for this shift).

Exercise 2.1 encourages you to think about the distinction between natural and non-natural meaning.

Exercise 2.1

- Consider whether each of the following examples should count as an example of Gricean 'natural' or 'non-natural' meaning. Give reasons for each answer. In some cases, you might think that there are elements of natural and non-natural meaning in the same act of communication. Indicate where you think this is so and, again, explain why:
    (i)   Your flatmate's shoes by the front door indicating to you that she has come home from work.
    (ii) Whistling loudly to your friends on a crowded beach so that they can find you.
    (iii) A cyclist screaming as a car almost drives into her.
    (iv) A letter to your local library asking for you not to be fined for returning a book after its due date.
    (v)   Holding up a book and waving it at someone who lost it earlier and has been frantically searching for it.

2.3   Grice and pragmatics: a 'theory of conversation'

Grice's work on meaning was important and influential. His work on pragmatics was also hugely important. Why were Grice's ideas seen as such a significant breakthrough? The answer is that, to a large extent, Grice's work can be seen as the first really significant progress in trying to answer the questions mentioned in Chapter 1 about how we try to understand each other and why communication sometimes fails. In Grice's terms, his proposal suggests an explanation of how we manage to 'mean more than we say'. Questions like this have been discussed for a very long time. Chapman (2005: 87), for example, points out that Aristotle discussed questions of meaning such as how *two* entails *one* but not vice versa, and Horn (2004: 3) suggests that 'the contrast between the said and the meant ... dates back to the fourth-century rhetoricians Servius and Donatus'. Despite this long-standing interest, no previous discussion had suggested anything approaching an explanation of how exactly we manage to work out the specific, intended meanings of utterances or other communicative acts based on their underspecified initial meanings. The next subsection presents a brief summary of what Grice suggested.

2.3.1   A brief summary

The most well-known source for Grice's ideas on inference in conversation is the series of William James lectures he gave at Harvard in 1967 (Grice 1967). For several years, these circulated as photocopies so that the ideas were well-known and much discussed before they were officially published, initially as separate papers, and finally together in one place, alongside other significant work, in the 1989 collection *Studies in the Way of Words* (Grice 1989). They inspired arguably all subsequent work on linguistic pragmatics because they suggested an explanation for how we make inferences about what speakers are indirectly communicating. The key was a distinction between 'what is said' by an utterance and what Grice termed its 'implicatures', i.e. propositions which it communicates indirectly. Grice coined the terms 'implicate' and 'implicature' to avoid confusions which might arise if he used existing words which might be understood in more than one way.

While Grice discussed a number of different types of implicature, the focus of early discussions of his ideas was mainly on the particular types of implicature illustrated by (13)–(15):

(13)   A: I need some paper tissues.
          B: There's a newsagent on the next corner.
          Implicature: The newsagent is likely to be open and to be able to sell you some
                        paper tissues.

(14)   A: How do you think my lecture went?
          B: Some of the students enjoyed it.
          Implicature: Not all of the students enjoyed your lecture.

(15)   A: How's your essay going?
          B: Isn't the weather strange these days? I think it might rain tonight. What do
             you think?
          Implicature: I don't want to talk about my essay as it's not going very well at all.

Note that I've indicated just one implicature for each example here (although these are complex propositions for 13 and 15). In each case, there are likely to be further implicatures. (14), for example, is likely to be understood as implicating that B didn't expect the lecture to go well and perhaps that she didn't expect any of the students to enjoy the lecture. We'll explore the 'open-endedness' of interpretations, and how implicatures can lead in turn to further implicatures, later in the book, particularly in Chapter 7. The key thing for now is Grice's suggestion that in each of these cases what is meant by B's utterance is 'more than what was said'.

Grice's account depends on the assumption that we follow rational principles in communicating. He formulated these as 'maxims of conversation'. We'll look at the specific maxims more closely in Section 2.3.3. We'll begin here by sketching the general idea behind them.

Grice assumed that conversation is a cooperative activity and that it is therefore rational to assume that speakers will be cooperative. For Grice, to be cooperative meant to produce utterances which are informative, truthful, relevant and formulated in an appropriate manner. Here is a very brief indication of how these assumptions might be involved in explaining the interpretations outlined in (13)–(15). We'll refer here to the notions of 'informativeness', 'truthfulness' and 'relevance' but we won't mention the 'manner' of the utterance. As we'll see below, the notion of manner is significantly different from the notions referred to in Grice's other maxims.

Let's start with example (13). Is B's utterance (*There's a newsagent on the next corner*) informative enough? Yes, if we think that B thinks the newsagent's shop is likely to be open and able to sell A some tissues. If, on the other hand, B knew that the newsagent had closed down or did not stock paper tissues, then this utterance would not be informative enough and would mislead A into thinking he could go and find some tissues there. Is B's utterance truthful? Again, if it is not, then A will be misled by the utterance. Is B's utterance relevant? Yes, if B thinks the newsagent's shop is open and able to sell A some tissues. If B is just mentioning a closed-down or tissueless shop to A, then we cannot see how this utterance is intended to be relevant. Grice's proposal, then, is that A reaches the above interpretation by starting from the assumption that B intends her utterance to be seen as informative, truthful and relevant. B's utterance is assumed to be true and its informativeness and relevance depend on the assumption that the shop might be able to sell A some tissues. So the assumption that B is following the maxims leads A to assume that B is communicating more than just that there exists a newsagent's shop on the next corner.

(14) is a more complicated example. Most adult speakers of English tend to assume that an utterance of the form *some X are Y* suggests that not all X are Y. Unless there is something special in the context to suggest otherwise, then, *some of the students enjoyed it* will suggest here that not all of the students enjoyed the lecture. Why should this be? Grice's approach would suggest that this is because it would not be informative enough to say only that some of the students enjoyed the lecture if you knew that all of them did. On similar lines, we could argue that it would be relevant to know that all of the students enjoyed it if they did and so not relevant enough in this case to say only that some of the students enjoyed it. As before, there is little to say about truthfulness here beyond that A will assume that B is saying something true and something that she has enough evidence for.

What about example (15)? This is perhaps the most discussed kind of example in Grice's approach. The key thing to notice here is that B's utterance seems on the face of it not to be cooperative. In particular, it seems to be blatantly avoiding an attempt to say something relevant. In this context, anything other than a statement about how B's essay is going will not seem relevant. So how does A understand the utterance? Grice suggests that we start from the presupposition that utterances will be relevant 'at some level'. If B's utterance is not relevant at the level of what seems to be directly communicated (which Grice termed the level of 'what is said'), then B must be indirectly communicating (or 'implicating') something that is relevant. Given this, we look for an indirectly communicated proposition (an 'implicature') that would be relevant. What we come up with is the assumption that B is deliberately avoiding discussion of the essay because it is not going well. Once again, we could also propose an explanation which refers to the notion of informativeness. Here we would say that an utterance which does not tell us anything about the essay is not informative enough and so we assume that the speaker must be implicating something else that is informative enough. We then come up with the assumption that B is avoiding the subject because the essay is not going well. Notice two things here. First, there is a difference between blatantly avoiding the subject, as here, in such a way as to make it clear that you are avoiding the subject, and more covert attempts to 'change the subject' and avoid a tricky conversation. Second, notice that once again the notion of truthfulness does not seem particularly important, except inasmuch as we assume that B is telling the truth when commenting on the weather.

This brief sketch leaves many important aspects of, and questions about, Grice's approach unexplored. We will discuss these in more detail below. First, we consider one of the motivations for Grice's approach.

Exercise 2.2 asks you to consider how a range of examples might be taken to support Grice's suggestion that notions such as informativeness, truthfulness and relevance play a role in how we understand utterances.

Exercise 2.2

- B's utterances in each of the following examples could be seen as faulty with regard to how closely they follow Gricean assumptions about informativeness, truthfulness or relevance, i.e. they seem to fail to be appropriately informative, truthful or relevant:

  (i)   A: Have you had breakfast?
         B: I got up at 6 o'clock like I do every morning and had my usual meal. I started with a glass of orange juice and then had a cup of strong coffee and a bowl of cereal. Then I had an apple before I finished getting ready for work.

  (ii)   A: What did you do last night after you got home from work?
         B: Stuff.

  (iii) A: Do you enjoy working with Robbie?
         B: He's a dinosaur.

  (iv)   A: Why do you think this director's films are always so gloomy?
         B: When she was young, she was always the last to be picked for sports. And when they played star wars, they always made her be Jar Jar Binks.

  (v)   A: Any chance you could help me dig the garden this weekend?
         B: I think salted caramels are my favourite sweets.

For each example:

(a) describe the ways in which the utterance seems to depart from the expectation that it will be informative, truthful and relevant

(b) suggest possible 'implicatures' which the hearer might derive in order to preserve the assumption that these maxims are being observed.

2.3.2   Motivation: logical and natural languages

Grice's most famous paper outlining this approach was 'Logic and conversation' based on his 1967 lecture of the same name (Grice 1967, published as Grice 1975 and reprinted in Grice 1989: 22–40). Here, he introduced his account by exploring what might seem at first like a completely different question about language and communication (we will see below how it is related to the question of how we often say more than we mean). This was the notion that natural languages are vastly ambiguous, in contrast to logical languages. To understand this fully requires a certain amount of familiarity with logical languages. For now, I'm planning just to tell you about one logical language (the 'propositional calculus'), one logical symbol, namely '&', and some of the ways in which natural language expressions, such as English *and*, seem to diverge from it. First, here are a few words about what logical languages are and what they aim to do.

Originally, logical languages were devised as a way of assessing the validity of arguments. The idea is that a skilled speaker or writer might convince us of something not because it logically follows from what they have said but because they have managed to confuse us by the way in which they have presented the argument. The general idea might be illustrated by this extract from a comedy routine (which I remember being performed on television by the British comedians Eric Morecambe and Ernie Wise):

(16)   ERIC: Lend us a tenner.
           ERNIE: OK.
           (Ernie takes a five pound note out of his pocket along with some change)
           ERIC: Five'll do.
           (Eric takes the five pound note).
           ERIC: Now you owe me five.   (Morecambe and Wise show)

If Ernie is fooled by this, it is because he has been taken in by Eric's assertion that Ernie owes him five pounds which is based on the initial plan to lend him ten pounds. Pointing out the error might involve reminding Eric of what has just happened and that the correct conclusion would be that 'now Eric only owes Ernie five pounds rather than ten'.

Here is a more traditional example. Imagine we know that (17) is true:

(17)   All humans breathe oxygen.

Suppose we now learn that:

(18)   Billy is a human.

Logically, we can now infer that:

(19)   Billy breathes oxygen.

The inverse inference would not be valid. That is, if we know that all humans breathe oxygen (17) and then discover that Billy breathes oxygen (19), it does not follow that Billy is human (18), since of course it is possible that some things which are not human beings (other mammals, for example) also breathe oxygen. Logical languages were created so that we could represent the difference between a valid inference which could be represented in a simplified form such as (20) and an invalid inference which could be represented as (21):

(20)   Valid inference
            Premises: All X are Y
                          Billy is X
            Conclusion: Billy is Y

(21)   Invalid inference
            Premises: All X are Y
                          Billy is Y
            Conclusion: Billy is X

Let's now look at how one logical symbol, the operator '&', would be handled within one logical language, the 'propositional calculus'. Expressions in propositional calculus consist of a combination of 'propositional variables' represented here by capital letters (P, Q, R, etc.) which are to be understood as representing any possible proposition, and logical operators which represent specific connections between propositions. These are represented with symbols such as &, ¬, v, each of which stands for an operation similar to, but arguably different from, that expressed by natural language expressions such as *and*, *not*, *or*, etc. Each of the propositional variables P, Q, R, etc. are to be understood as standing for any proposition, i.e. any statement capable of being true or false. The precise value is not relevant since we're looking at the relationships between propositions. Given this, an expression such as (22) represents the conjunction of two propositional variables:

(22)   P & Q

(22) represents the truth of a proposition P and the simultaneous truth of a proposition Q. The meaning of '&' is represented in a truth table, the idea being that to know what '&' means is to know when a conjunction of two propositions would be true:

(23)   *Truth table for '&'*

P	&	Q
T	T	T
T	F	F
F	F	T
F	F	F

The first line here says that & (i.e. the conjunction of *P* and *Q*) is true when both *P* and *Q* are true. The other three lines tell us that the conjunction is false whenever at least one of the conjuncts (either *P* or *Q*) is false. One thing to notice, which is not represented explicitly in the table, is that the order of the conjuncts will have no effect on the truth of the proposition overall, i.e. *Q & P* is equivalent to *P & Q* (whenever one is true, the other is true, since both depend only on the simultaneous truth of the two propositions). While it is not represented here, the equivalence of the two conjuncts is something that can be proved using the tools of propositional calculus.

I hope this seems fairly straightforward. When we look at logical languages more closely, things become more tricky. Some of the difficulties arise because of the divergences between logical and natural languages which motivated Grice to develop his theory of conversation. Here is how Grice referred to them at the very beginning of 'Logic and conversation':

> It is a commonplace of philosophical logic that there are, or appear to be, divergences in meaning between, on the one hand, at least some of what I shall call the formal devices... and, on the other, what are taken to be their analogues or counterparts in natural language... Some logicians may at some time have wanted to claim that there are in fact no such divergences; but such claims, if made at all, have been somewhat rashly made, and those suspected of making them have been subjected to some pretty rough handling.   (Grice 1989: 22)

In his paper, Grice argues that we can defend a view on which the divergences do not exist and that different interpretations arise because of a distinction between the conventional meaning of linguistic expressions and meanings we infer in particular contexts.

> I wish... to maintain that the common assumption of the contestants that the divergences do in fact exist is (broadly speaking) a common mistake, and that the mistake arises from inadequate attention to the nature and importance of the conditions governing conversation.   (Grice 1989: 24)

To see how Grice's account addresses the issue, and supports the view that the divergences may not be as big as has been supposed, we'll consider how we interpret the meaning of the English word *and* in specific contexts and compare this with the meaning of the logical connective &.

According to the truth table for '$\&$' in (23) an expression of the form $P \& Q$ will be true when P is true and Q is also true, and otherwise false. The meaning of $\&$ is that it conveys the truth of both of its conjuncts. Now consider these natural language examples:

(24)   Aberdeen is in Scotland and Paris is in France.

(25)   Jess said goodnight and went to bed.

(26)   My train was cancelled and I missed the start of the lecture.

If the word *and* corresponds closely to the logical connective $\&$, then each of (24)–(26) will simply express the truth of both of their conjuncts. (24) will communicate that Aberdeen is in Scotland and that Paris is in France. (25) will communicate both that Jess said goodnight and that she went to bed. (26) will communicate that my train was cancelled and that I missed the start of the lecture. If this is all they communicate, then we should be able to change the order of the conjuncts with no change in meaning since, as we mentioned above, $P \& Q$ is logically equivalent to $Q \& P$. This seems to work for (24) (provided we do not assume any specific contextual assumptions which would affect the interpretation) so that (27) seems to have more or less the same meaning as (24):

(27)   Paris is in France and Aberdeen is in Scotland.

But (28) does not seem to mean the same thing as (25):

(28)   Jess went to bed and said goodnight.

and (29) does not seem to mean the same thing as (26):

(29)   I missed the start of the lecture and my train was cancelled.

It seems that (25) communicates something about a temporal relationship which changes when the conjuncts are reversed. When we hear (25), we assume that Jess first said goodnight and then went to bed. When we hear (28), we assume that Jess first went to bed and then said goodnight. Examples like this have led to the suggestion that there is a 'temporal *and*' in English as well as a 'logical *and*' which corresponds to the logical connective '$\&$'. (26) seems to communicate something about a causal relationship which changes when we reverse the conjuncts. When we hear (26) we assume that I missed my train and as a result of that I missed the start of the lecture. In other words, there seems to be a 'causal *and*' as well as a 'logical' and a 'temporal' one. This causal relationship seems to disappear when we hear (29). We might think here that the two events are linked because they are two separate things which have frustrated or upset me. We might even assume that the cancelled train happened on the way home from the lecture rather than the other way round. (As ever, the particular contextual assumptions available will affect the interpretation. The important point is that reversing the conjuncts seems to change the interpretation.)

Examples like this have led to the suggestion that there is a 'causal *and*' in English alongside the other senses.

So far, then, we have suggested that the word *and* in English is at least three ways ambiguous:

(30)   Senses of the English word *and*
          logical *and*:   '&'
          temporal *and*:   'and then'
          causal *and*:   'and as a result'

This seems problematic for anyone hoping to develop a systematic account of the meanings of expressions in English and other languages. Looking more closely, the situation is even more complicated. First, many other expressions in English seem to have more than one meaning. Consider the following, for example:

(31)   Everyone doesn't like chocolate.

(32)   Would you like cake or a biscuit?

(33)   If you wash my car, I'll give you five pounds.

Does (31) mean that there is no-one who likes chocolate (it's true of everyone that they don't like chocolate) or just that there are some people who don't (it's not the case that everyone likes chocolate)? Does it refer to everyone in the universe or everyone in some smaller group? Does (32) allow the possibility of the hearer having both cake and a biscuit? Does (33) rule out the possibility that the speaker gives the hearer five pounds even if they don't wash the car? In a logical language, we would represent these different possibilities with different symbols. In English, and in other natural languages, expressions such as these seem to be consistent with more than one meaning.

These are a few of the wide range of examples suggesting that natural languages are less precise than logical languages. Similar examples exist in all languages. Possibly even more worrying is that the range of possibilities for particular words seems similar across languages. This is odd given standard assumptions about the arbitrariness of word meanings. Why should different languages select the same range of meanings for their equivalents to the English word *and*? (If you speak another language, try translating (24)–(26) to see whether the same range of interpretations is possible.) We do not normally expect ambiguous words in one language to be ambiguous in similar ways in different languages. The English word *chap*, for example, is a fairly informal way of referring to a male person and can also refer to something cowboys wear on their trousers, a painful eruption which might appear on lips and a knock on a door or hard object. I do not know of any other language where there is a word which shares all of these meanings. Even if there were a word with these meanings in any other language, it would still be surprising that language after language has the same range of meanings for a word corresponding to English *and*.

Finally, it is possible that there are even more senses of *and*. Consider this example:

(34)   Mark went to the kitchen and made a cup of tea.

Here we do not only assume that Mark made the tea after having gone to the kitchen. We also assume that he made the tea while he was in the kitchen. So we might suggest the existence of a 'locative *and*' (with a reading such as 'and in that place') to cover cases such as this.

How does Grice propose to account for this range of interpretations while maintaining the claim that natural languages do not diverge much from logical languages? The key is his distinction between saying and implicating as illustrated in examples (13)–(15), repeated here as (35)–(37):

(35)   A: I need some paper tissues.
        B: There's a newsagent on the next corner.
        Implicature: The newsagent is likely to be open and to be able to sell you some
                paper tissues.

(36)   A: How do you think my lecture went?
        B: Some of the students enjoyed it.
        Implicature: Not all of the students enjoyed your lecture.

(37)   A: How's your essay going?
        B: Isn't the weather strange these days? I think it might rain tonight. What do
           you think?
        Implicature: I don't want to talk about my essay as it's not going well at all.

In (35), the speaker *says* that there is a newsagent but *implicates* that it is likely to be open. In (36) the speaker *says* that some of the students have enjoyed the lecture. This is consistent with all of the students having enjoyed it (if all of them enjoyed it then some of them did) but the speaker is taken to *implicate* that not all of the students enjoyed it. In (37), the speaker makes some comments about the weather, rather than directly answering the question, and so is taken to be *implicating* that she doesn't want to talk about how her essay is going. Grice suggests that the different ways of understanding the utterances containing *and* can be explained by assuming that the utterances give rise to implicatures about temporal ordering, causal relations, and so on.

How did Grice propose to explain the derivation of implicatures? He suggested that intentional communication is a cooperative task and that it is governed by rational principles. In particular, he suggested that communication was governed by a cooperative principle which could be explained more fully in terms of a number of maxims and sub-maxims. The maxims exploit more formally expressed versions of the notions of 'informativeness', 'truthfulness', 'relevance' and 'manner' which we mentioned informally above. The next section outlines these 'tools' and how they help to explain utterance interpretation.

2.3.3   Explanations: the maxims of conversation

As mentioned above, Grice proposed to explain utterance interpretation by assuming that we expect each other to be cooperative when engaging in conversation. More specifically, he proposed that we assume that we all follow certain norms, or 'maxims', of conversation. Here is a statement of the Cooperative Principle and the maxims of conversation:

(38)   Grice's Cooperative Principle and maxims of conversation
        Cooperative Principle
        Make your conversational contribution such as is required, at the stage at which it occurs, by the accepted purpose or direction of the talk exchange in which you are engaged.
        Maxim of Quality
        Try to make your contribution one that is true:
(i)   do not say what you believe to be false
(ii)   do not say that for which you lack adequate evidence.
        Maxim of Quantity
(i)   make your contribution as informative as is required
(ii)   do not make your contribution more informative than is required.
        Maxim of Relation
        Be relevant.
        Maxim of Manner
        Be perspicuous, specifically:
(i)   avoid obscurity of expression
(ii)   avoid ambiguity
(iii)   be brief (avoid unnecessary prolixity)
(iv)   be orderly.

In brief, the claim is that we expect people who are contributing to a conversation to be informative but not too informative, to be truthful, to base their statement on adequate evidence, to be relevant and to speak in an appropriate manner. Grice suggested that related maxims applied to all cooperative behaviour. If I ask you to put two tablespoons of sugar into my cake mix I expect you to put two tablespoons in, not one or three. If I ask you to pass me a hammer, I don't expect you to pass me a spanner. And so on. The Cooperative Principle and maxims represent similar principles applied to conversation. Here is a brief comment on each one to indicate the kind of thing Grice had in mind and to help you to consider how plausible they each seem at first glance.

The maxim of quantity says that we should provide enough information but not too much. If you ask me how to get to the post office from here, you will expect me to say something like (39) rather than (40) or (41):

(39)   It's on the second corner after the traffic lights, next door to the town hall.

(40)   First, lift up your left foot, move it to the front and place it on the ground. Then, raise your right foot…

(41)   Walk.

Intuitively, (40) seems to be too informative, since we assume that you already know how to walk. (41), on the other hand, would not be informative enough, since we assume that you already know walking is involved but expect to be told a bit more.

At this point, you might be thinking that (40) and (41) are not necessarily faulty utterances and that their over-informativeness and under-informativeness could be intended to communicate something. If so, that observation is absolutely right and key to Grice's account, as we'll see below. Part of Grice's idea is that deliberately 'deviant' utterances, e.g. ones which are overinformative or underinformative, give rise to interpretations which go beyond what has been directly communicated. For now, though, it's enough to notice that there's a sense in which these utterances are 'faulty'.

The maxim of quality usually seems reasonable at first glance, although we will see that there are reasons to doubt that it has a role to play in explaining communication. The claim here is simply that we expect each other only to say things that are true or well evidenced. We are not expected to, and we do not expect others to, make false contributions or to say things which we have little evidence for. If I ask you whether you are hungry, I expect you to say yes only if you are. If I ask you how to get to the post office and you don't know where it is, I don't expect you to give me directions which are only based on guesswork. If you continually tell me obvious lies, I will find this infuriating and perhaps even conclude that you are effectively not communicating with me. In Grice's terms, this would be uncooperative behaviour.

Grice acknowledged that the maxim of relation was problematic in that he did not know how to define 'relevant'. Wilson and Sperber's attempts to address this problem led eventually to the development of relevance theory. Grice said:

> Though the maxim itself is terse, its formulation conceals a number of problems that exercise me a good deal: questions about what different kinds and focuses of relevance there may be, how these shift in the course of a talk exchange, how to allow for the fact that subjects of conversation are legitimately changed, and so on. I find the treatment of such questions exceedingly difficult, and I hope to revert to them in later work.   (Grice 1989: 27)

Grice never did manage to formulate a clear definition of what it would mean to be relevant. But it is possible to use something like the everyday notion of 'relevance' in developing Gricean explanations. Roughly, this notion is of 'having to do with the topic we're discussing'. Of course, this formulation is not clear enough to count as a definition but it is clear enough to play a role in explaining the interpretation of some utterances. It is fairly uncontroversial, for example, to suggest that B's utterance in (42) is not relevant to A's question:

(42)   A: I saw an amazing programme on BBC3 last night.
          B: I've got a really weird itchy feeling behind my ear.

The maxims of manner are about how utterances are formulated rather than what they 'say'. The idea here is that it would be odd in most contexts to say something like:

(43)   Inclement liquid precipitation is predicted for this evening.

rather than:

(44)   They say it's going to rain tonight.

This is partly because the phrase *inclement liquid precipitation* is an unnecessarily obscure way of describing rain.

The second sub-maxim does not, of course, mean that we should never use any ambiguous expressions, but instead that we should not use expressions which the hearer will not be able to disambiguate. It's fine to use a word like *flat* if we can tell that it's intended to refer, say, to a tyre with a puncture rather than a small place to live, or to some other sense. Grice seems to have in mind cases where the addressee cannot tell which of two or more possible meanings a communicator intends in a particular situation.

'Be brief' and 'be orderly' are generally assumed to be fairly clear. It would be odd if I asked whether you were tired and you produced a very long answer such as (45) where a simple 'yes' would answer my question.

(45)   I am uttering my belief and reporting my own sensation when I tell you in answer to
         your question that tiredness is something which I am currently experiencing.

Similarly, it would be odd to tell me about a meal you recently ate with the various parts of the meal arranged in the following way:

(46)   Between the starter and the main course we had a delicious sorbet. I had a nice chat
         with Robbie before we left home. Dessert was a chocolate fondant. The main course
         came with green beans and courgettes on the side. I had a coffee afterwards. I started with
         baby artichokes. Then I had sea bream. They gave us little amuse-bouches when
         we arrived.

While Grice did not claim that everything we say conforms to the maxims, he did claim that we always assume communicators are following the maxims overall. This idea is grounded in Grice's view that verbal communication is a rational and cooperative activity. The maxims represent what it is rational to expect of each other in communication. They play a key role in the derivation of particular kinds of implicature, the notion which Grice uses to explain cases of indirect communication. What generates implicatures is the assumption that the maxims are being followed. Grice discussed a number of ways in which the maxims could be involved in generating implicatures (and so leading us to understand 'more than has been said' from an utterance).

First, some implicatures follow just from the assumption that the maxims are being observed (if the speaker did not intend to communicate the implicature then the maxims would be violated). Grice's first example of this was:

(47)   A: I am out of petrol.
            B: There's a garage round the corner.

Most people, including students who I have shown this example to in class, do not think at first about the assumption that B must think the garage is likely to be open and selling petrol. This becomes clear when we think about how A would react if the garage turned out to be closed down and B said that he had known this at the time. In glossing this, Grice said:

> B would be infringing the maxim 'Be relevant' unless he thinks, or thinks it possible, that the garage is, or at least may be, open, etc.
>
> (Grice 1989: 32)

So it is rational in this context to conclude that the speaker thinks the garage might be open. Notice, by the way, that Grice is using the undefined notion of 'relation' in his explanation here. Notice also that we could equally have used the maxim of quantity, pointing out that a speaker who knew the garage had closed down or had no petrol would not be being informative enough if he only said the garage was there but did not say anything about the unavailability of petrol. Notice also that this account is based on assuming that the speaker is being rational.

The second way in which the maxims generate implicatures is where there is a perceived 'clash' between more than one maxim. Grice's first example of this is (48):

(48)   A: Where does C live?
            B: Somewhere in the South of France.

B's utterance here infringes the first maxim of quantity as it does not provide as much information as is required, i.e. it is not precise enough about where C lives. Grice suggests that A will assume that this arises because giving enough information would involve infringing the second maxim of quality by saying something which B does not have adequate evidence for. In other words, A assumes that B fails to tell A enough about where C lives because B does not know exactly where C lives. Following one of these maxims would mean not following the other so B compromises by sticking to the second maxim of quality but not to the first maxim of quantity. This suggests a sense in which the maxim of quality is seen as more important than the maxim of quantity.

The third way in which Grice saw the maxims as being involved in explaining interpretations is one which people have tended to see as the most interesting and which has been very much discussed in work since Grice. This is where the maxims are exploited by 'ostentatiously flouting' them. In Grice's words, this is:

> a procedure by which a maxim is flouted for the purpose of getting in a
> conversational implicature by means of something of the nature of a figure
> of speech   (Grice 1989: 33)

Note, though, that cases like this cover a wide range of utterances, many of them
not counting as what most people would describe as a 'figure of speech'. Grice
goes on to explain them by saying:

> In these examples, though some maxim is violated at the level of what is said, the
> hearer is entitled to assume that that maxim, or at least the overall Cooperative
> Principle, is observed at the level of what is implicated.   (Grice 1989: 33)

Grice's first example of this kind of implicature is (49), which is to be read as
the text of a reference letter written by a lecturer for a former pupil who has
applied for a philosophy job:

(49)   Dear Sir, Mr. X's command of English is excellent, and his attendance at tutorials has
          been regular. Yours, etc.

Grice points out that it is very clear in the context of a letter of reference that we
expect to be informed of more than the applicant's attendance and ability with
English. So the letter violates the first maxim of quantity at the level of what is
said. The letter reader knows, though, that the writer must be being cooperative
overall and so there must be an implicature which is informative enough. What
is implicated here is that Mr X is not very good at philosophy and that the letter
writer does not want to write this down explicitly. This pattern is now very well
known within pragmatics and provides the basis of at least a partial (not always
fully explicit) explanation of a wide range of kinds of implicature. Perhaps the
key thing to notice here, given its importance in the development of relevance
theory, is that Grice is assuming that working out what is being communicated
involves making rational inferences about the communicator's intentions.

Grice does not claim that all utterances always follow the maxims. He points
out that we sometimes explicitly 'opt out', e.g. we might say that we refuse to
say everything we know about something, and sometimes surreptitiously opt
out, e.g. by lying or pretending not to know as much as we do. The most
important cases, though, are ones where the maxims are involved in explanations of indirect communication based on rational inference.

Grice does not claim that all implicatures are based on context and inference.
He envisages a category of 'conventional implicatures' which are conventional
in the sense that they are encoded by linguistic expressions:

(50)   He is an Englishman; he is, therefore, brave.

Grice claims that the causal connection between being English and being brave
is encoded by the word *therefore* rather than depending on inference in a
specific context. We will look at problems with this notion in Chapter 11 and
compare how these kinds of phenomena are handled within relevance theory.

Conversational implicatures are implicatures which depend on the context.
For Grice, they come in two varieties: 'generalised conversational implicatures'

do not need specific contextual motivation while 'particularised conversational implicatures' arise only in specific contexts. (51) is one of Grice's examples to illustrate the notion of generalised conversational implicature:

(51)   I broke a finger yesterday.

We would usually assume that the finger that was broken belongs to the speaker and is biologically attached to her hand. This implicature could be cancelled either contextually, say if we know that the speaker makes porcelain fingers for a living, or linguistically, if the speaker carries on to say that the finger is someone else's.

A particularised conversational implicature, by contrast, arises only when there are specific contextual reasons for deriving it. What does (52) implicate?

(52)   Andy is a film producer.

I am assuming not much follows for you from this. Imagine, though, that the speaker of (52) knows that you have written a film script, that you are looking for advice on how to get it made, and that you are wondering who to invite to a party tomorrow night. Given these contextual assumptions, it is clear, among other things, that the speaker is implicating that you should invite Andy to the party. This is not a generalised conversational implicature since it arises only given these specific contextual assumptions. There has been considerable discussion of the notion of generalised conversational implicatures, with some theorists (e.g. Hawkins 1991; Horn 1989; Huang 1991, 2007; Levinson 2000) developing the idea and others (including relevance theorists) questioning the validity of the distinction between generalised and particularised conversational implicatures.

To sum up, Grice's key insight (for us) is the idea that understanding utterances is a rational activity in which we make inferences about the communicator's intentions. He makes a number of important distinctions, between saying and implicating, between conventional and conversational implicatures, between generalised and particularised conversational implicatures. These distinctions are summarised in Figure 2.1.

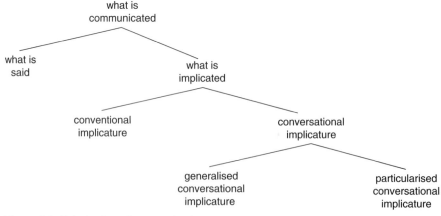

Figure 2.1 *Grice's view of communication*

We will look more closely at some of the implications of this in the next section. One thing to notice right away is that the pragmatic principles proposed by Grice, in the form of his maxims of conversation, apply only to the context-dependent aspects of communication, i.e. to the derivation of conversational implicatures.

Exercise 2.3 encourages you to explore Grice's ideas in more detail.

Exercise 2.3

- Attempt an explanation of how A might understand B's utterance in each of the following exchanges:
  - (i)   A: The train I take to work has just been cancelled.
        B: My car's still out of action.
  - (ii)   A: I bought you a ticket for that concert on Saturday.
        B: But I hate classical music!
  - (iii)   A: Do you think the new Zadie Smith book's any good?
        B: John's been reading it.
  - (iv)   A: How did you manage to break the toaster?
        B: I just pressed the 'cancel' switch and it cut out.
  - (v)   A: Do you think you could look after my dogs for me while I'm away?
        B: I will, although I can't say I'll enjoy it.

In each case, your account should say 'what is said', 'what is implicated' and how the hearer works out what is implicated.

Make a note of any problems you have in applying Grice's ideas and of any problems you think these examples raise for Grice's approach.

2.4 Problems and possibilities: critiques of Grice

As mentioned above, Grice's approach has been very influential and all work in pragmatics since can be understood as either a development of, or an alternative to, Grice's approach. Relevance theory counts as both, developing the notion of pragmatic principles with some grounding in rationality and replacing the notion of maxims of conversation which are followed by communicators with the proposal of general principles which describe what communicators do when interacting. This section considers some of the critical discussions of Grice's work, focusing particularly on Wilson and Sperber's (1981) discussion which led ultimately to the development of relevance theory.

Grice's work was a breakthrough because it suggested a way of explaining how we understand things which are communicated indirectly or, more generally, how we make inferences about the intentions of communicators. His ideas were applied by a range of theorists and in a number of areas beyond pragmatics, including in developing accounts of linguistic semantics, philosophy of language, philosophy of mind, psychology, second language acquisition and stylistics. A number of theorists focused on critiquing and developing the insights and, in so doing, developed pragmatic theories of their own.[3] The work of some of these theorists will also be mentioned briefly when discussing particular topics throughout the book.

Wilson and Sperber's first critique (Wilson and Sperber 1981) acknowledged the significance of Grice's insights while also pointing out areas where there seemed to be room for improvement. They said:

> Although specific proposals have been made for extending, supplementing or modifying Grice's machinery, it seems no exaggeration to say that most recent theories of utterance-interpretation are a direct result of Grice's William James Lectures.
>
> The value of Grice's work derives not so much from the detail of his analyses as from the general claim that underlies them. Grice has shown that given an adequate set of pragmatic principles – to which his conversational maxims are a first approximation – a wide range of what at first sight seem to be arbitrary semantic facts can be seen as consequences of quite general pragmatic constraints. The broad outline of this position is extremely convincing, and we have relied on it in our own recent research. However, it seems to us that its detail needs considerable modification if any further progress is to be made.   (Wilson and Sperber 1981: 155)

The aim of Wilson and Sperber's paper is to begin this process of modification. The three main suggestions for improvement, which can be understood as early steps in the development of relevance theory, are:

(a)   the maxims seem to be involved in recovering what is said as well as what is implicated
(b)   there is more to what is said than recovery of linguistic meaning, disambiguation and reference assignment
(c)   the maxims do not all seem to be equally important, and some may not even be needed, in explaining interpretations.

The first two of these are presented under one heading in the paper, but I think it is easier to follow the argument if we separate them here. (This paper also pointed out problems with Grice's account of figurative language, which will be discussed in Chapters 9 and 10.)

Points (a) and (b) are about Grice's notion of 'what is said' and are important in deciding how exactly to make the division between semantics and pragmatics. This issue has been one of the most discussed topics in the study of linguistic meaning since Grice's work. Figure 2.2 is a simplified diagram showing how Grice's approach drew the distinction.

Later, we will see that several other issues have been identified with Grice's notion of 'what is said'. We'll leave these aside for now, though, and begin by considering the kinds of meanings which Grice sees as semantic and the kinds which he sees as pragmatic. Grice's approach is fairly uncontroversial in assuming that linguistic semantics is involved in recovering 'what is said'. What this means is that some aspects of what is said are linguistically encoded.

Figure 2.2 *The semantics–pragmatics distinction according to Grice (1975)*

What we know about the linguistically encoded meanings of words tells us something about what the speaker has said. For example, if I use the word *muffin*, then you know that this word refers to a particular kind of bread or cake (depending on your precise understanding of what a muffin is). Grice also claimed that some *implicatures* can be linguistically encoded. These are what he termed 'conventional implicatures'. We will look at critical discussion of this notion in Chapter 11 below. First, we will consider each of the three areas discussed by Wilson and Sperber which we have just mentioned.

(a)   The maxims are involved in recovering 'what is said'
        Grice sees the scope of his maxims, i.e. of his envisaged pragmatic principles, as governing the recovery of (generalised or particularised) conversational implicatures.

Wilson and Sperber point out that Grice says very little about how hearers come to recognise those aspects of 'what is said' which are not linguistically encoded. For Grice, there are two such phenomena: recognising the intended sense of an ambiguous expression and recognising the referents of referring expressions. Wilson and Sperber (1981: 156–8) point out that these seem also to be inferred and so should fall under the scope of pragmatic principles. They discuss this example:

(53)   Refuse to admit them.

This utterance contains an ambiguous word, *admit* (including at least a sense we might describe as 'confess to' and a sense we might describe as 'allow to enter') and a referring expression, *them*. With no contextual information to help us decide which sense is intended for *admit* or which entities are the intended referents for *them*, then more than one sense is plausible and *them* could refer to any group of people or things. If, however, we imagine (53) said in response to the question in (54):

(54)   What should I do when I make mistakes?

then we will disambiguate *admit* in favour of the 'confess to' sense and we will assume that *them* refers to the original speaker's mistakes. Wilson and Sperber point out that this decision can be explained in terms of the maxims and particularly the maxim of relevance. If the speaker does not intend to refer to the mistakes asked about and to suggest that they should be confessed to,

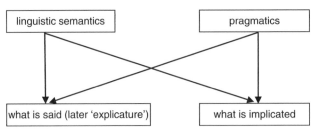

Figure 2.3 *The semantics–pragmatics distinction according to Wilson and Sperber (1981)*

then the utterance will not be seen as answering the question and so will not be understood as relevant.

Now imagine (53) is a response to the different question in (55):

(55)   What should I do with the people whose tickets have expired?

Here we will assume that *admit* means 'allow to enter' and that *them* refers to the people with expired tickets. Again, this can be explained in terms of the maxim of relation. If the speaker did not intend this sense and this referent, then the utterance would not be answering the question and so would not be relevant.

Wilson and Sperber conclude, therefore, that the maxims are involved in working out 'what is said' as well as in working out implicatures. As they put it, 'the semantics–pragmatics distinction cross-cuts the distinction between saying and implicating' (Wilson and Sperber 1981: 157). Figure 2.3 shows in simplified form how Wilson and Sperber proposed to revise Grice's semantics–pragmatics distinction.

(b)   There is more to recovering 'what is said' than disambiguation and reference assignment

A second point Wilson and Sperber made in this paper was that there is more to recovering 'what is said' than just disambiguation and reference assignment. To show this, they present an example where a hearer who only disambiguates ambiguous expressions and assigns referents to referring expressions will not have done enough to be able to identify what the speaker has said. The example is (56):

(56)   John plays well.

Suppose, they suggest, that this is said to a companion by someone who is watching John Smith play the violin. In this situation, the hearer will surely decide that the referent of *John* is John Smith and that the intended sense of *play* is one which relates to musical instruments rather than, say, games or acting. If this were all they did, then their representation of what is said would be as in (57):

(57)   John Smith plays a/some musical instrument well.

But the hearer of (56) in this context will decide something stronger, namely (58):

(58)   John Smith plays the violin well.

Again, it seems possible to explain this in terms of the maxims. Wilson and Sperber suggest that the maxim of quantity might be the key to a Gricean account here. (58) is clearly more informative than (57) and it is (57)'s lack of informativeness which suggests it is not a likely candidate for what the speaker is 'saying'. Wilson and Sperber point out that this inference has the property, which Grice saw as definitional for implicature, of being cancellable, since it can be explicitly denied without giving rise to contradiction or pragmatic oddity, in utterances such as (59):

(59)   John plays well – he just doesn't play the VIOLIN well.

As mentioned in Chapter 1, and as discussed in more detail throughout the book, a wide range of inferences is involved in working out 'what is said' by an utterance. The key suggestions to notice here are that pragmatics is involved in accounting for the recovery of what is said and that there is more to recovering what is said than just disambiguation and reference assignment. Redrawing the semantics–pragmatics distinction in ways that recognise these points is an important aspect of Wilson and Sperber's development of relevance theory in later work.

(c)   Not all of the maxims seem to be necessary

When they wrote this critique of Grice's work in 1981, Wilson and Sperber had not yet fully developed their definition of relevance or the two Principles of Relevance. At this stage, they had in mind a way of defining relevance and one principle of relevance rather than two. Since both of these early formulations have been replaced by different notions, this book will not consider them in any detail; but the ideas were well enough developed for Wilson and Sperber to suggest that all of Grice's maxims could be replaced by one properly defined principle of relevance. They considered each of the maxims in turn and concluded that:

(a)   in a theory based on a well-defined principle of relevance, the maxims of quantity are redundant

(b)   there are problems with the maxims of quality: in some cases, they are subsumed by a principle of relevance while in others they make different, and incorrect, predictions

(c)   the maxim of relation is, of course, subsumed by a well-defined principle of relevance

(d)   two of the maxims of manner ('avoid obscurity of expression' and 'be orderly') are subsumed by a well-defined principle of relevance and the other two are unnecessary.

Rather than asking you to move back in time to consider the early formulations of the 1981 paper, we will base our discussion here on the more recent relevance-theoretic view of how the Communicative Principle of Relevance governs interpretations. Exercise 2.4 asks you to consider how this principle might justify conclusions (a)–(d). We will then move on to consider these points in more detail, and the more general idea that a theory based on a properly defined Communicative Principle of Relevance can provide a superior account of the phenomena Grice's maxims aim to explain.

Exercise 2.4 encourages you to explore some of Wilson and Sperber's proposals about how Grice's approach should be modified.

Exercise 2.4

- B's utterance in each of the following exchanges illustrates at least one problem for Grice's theory of conversation:
  - (i)   A: I reckon John should represent us at the union meeting on Saturday.
          B: Well, he's definitely got the guts for it.
  - (ii)   A: Does that new student talk in class?
          B: Too much, if you ask me.
  - (iii) A: You really do far too much for everyone, and now they want you to take on even more work.
          B: Life!
  - (iv)   A: Did you see how John lost it when they told him he'd lost his job? He screamed the place down.
          B: You could say he's unhappy.

See if you can identify the nature of the problem and how Wilson and Sperber might propose to solve it.

Now that you have attempted to explore these ideas yourself, we will quickly remind you of how the more recent formulation of the **Communicative Principle of Relevance** aims to account for the interpretation of a range of utterances and then consider each of (a)–(d) in turn.

As explained in Chapter 1, the **presumption of optimal relevance** underpins a comprehension procedure on which interpreters:

(a)   follow a path of least effort in deriving effects

(b)   stop when expectations of relevance are satisfied.

As we saw, this makes very specific predictions about a wide range of utterances. How does it relate to conclusions (a)–(d) above? Let's consider each in turn.

(a)   the Communicative Principle of Relevance makes the maxims of quantity redundant

It is fairly easy to see how this follows. Recall Grice's example:

(60)   A: I'm out of petrol.
        B: There's a garage round the corner.

Grice's explanation of A's reasoning in understanding B's utterance is as follows:

(a)   B has said that there's a garage round the corner.
(b)   B must be following the maxims, including the maxims of quantity.
(c)   If B thought the garage round the corner was closed or out of petrol, then it would not be informative enough to say that the garage is there without indicating this.
(d)   Therefore, B must think that the garage is or is likely to be both open and able to sell petrol.

The Communicative Principle of Relevance says that B's utterance communicates a presumption of its own optimal relevance. We could explain the interpretation by pointing out that the utterance would not be optimally relevant if the speaker knew that the garage was closed or suspected it might be closed. An alternative explanation might focus on the relevance-guided comprehension heuristic and simply point out what relevance theory predicts a hearer will do, which is, of course, to:

(a)   follow a path of least effort in looking for an interpretation
(b)   stop as soon as a plausible candidate is found (where a 'plausible' interpretation is one which satisfies the hearer's expectations of relevance).

Following a path of least effort will lead the hearer very quickly to the hypothesis that B is suggesting a way to remedy the problematic lack of petrol. The prediction is that as soon as A thinks of this possibility and decides that this is something B could have intended, A will stop searching for an interpretation and assume that this is what B intended. Given A's stated problem with petrol, it is of course very likely that A will already be anticipating an answer relevant to this problem. If so, then of course an interpretation which assumes that the garage round the corner will solve the problem will be accessed straight away. At this point, the hearer need go no further and will assume that B is telling him about a garage that is likely to be able to sell him some petrol. Since relevance theory claims to be able to account for all utterances with reference to the Communicative Principle of Relevance, of course it is no surprise that it claims to account for examples such as these.

(b)   problems with the maxim of quality

Wilson and Sperber have consistently argued against the view that there exists any kind of convention that speakers should aim to be strictly and literally truthful when communicating (see, for example, Wilson and Sperber 2002). There are a number of problems with this view. One is that speakers often produce utterances which are not strictly true but which are relevant and do not seem problematic in any way. Typical examples are loose uses or rough approximations such as (61) and (62):

(61)   A hundred people showed up to my party.

(62)   Aberdeen is five hundred miles from London.

(61) is a perfectly appropriate utterance even if the number of people who came to the party is not exactly one hundred. (62) is fine even if the distance between the two cities is not exactly five hundred miles. In fact, there are cases where we seem to prefer an inaccurate answer to an accurate one, e.g. someone who lives in Issy-les-Moulineaux just outside the city limits of Paris might well answer as in (63) when asked where they live by someone they have just met, rather than with a strictly true answer such as (64) or (65):

(63)   In Paris.

(64)   Just outside Paris.

(65)   In Issy-les-Moulineaux.

Sperber and Wilson (1990) suggest that this follows because we are looking for relevant rather than strictly true interpretations. If we think that someone lives in Paris, a number of relevant assumptions follow from this, such as (66)–(69):

(66)   The speaker lives in an urban environment.

(67)   The speaker knows their way around Paris very well.

(68)   It is easy to get to the centre of Paris from the speaker's house.

(69)   It might be nice to stay at the speaker's house when I visit Paris.

A strictly true answer might not lead to these conclusions. If I think you live outside Paris, I might think your home is not convenient for Paris, that it is fairly rural, and so on. So there are good reasons to prioritise relevance rather than truth when choosing how to formulate utterances.

Wilson and Sperber have also pointed out problems with the role of the maxim of quality in explaining figurative utterances, including ironic and metaphorical utterances. We will consider these in Chapters 9 and 10.

(c)   the maxim of relation

Of course, the maxim of relation will seem to be redundant if we now have a technical definition of relevance. Even within Grice's own account, the maxims of quantity and relation often seem to perform the same role, suggesting that a Gricean definition of 'relevance' might simply amount to equating it with quantity. The new technical definition of relevance does have something in common with the Gricean notion of quantity, since the relevance of a phenomenon partly depends on how many assumptions follow from it. Both the Gricean notion of quantity and the presumption of optimal relevance use the term 'enough'. In the Gricean account, utterances need to provide 'enough' information and no more. In the relevance-theoretic account, utterances are presumed to provide enough cognitive effects to justify the effort involved in processing them.

(d)   problems with the maxims of manner

The first thing to notice about the maxims of manner is that they are seldom used in Gricean explanations, with the work mainly being done by the maxims of quantity and relation. Given this, we might expect to find that they are made redundant in a similar way by the principles proposed within relevance theory. This seems to be the case for at least the first three maxims of manner, which are about avoiding obscurity, avoiding ambiguity and being brief. The fourth manner maxim, 'be orderly', seems to be slightly different from the others. We'll begin here by considering the first three manner maxims, all three of which seem to be based on the possibility of the formulation of utterances having more or less of a particular quality. In all three cases, it seems that the maxim is made redundant by the presumption of optimal relevance.

The first maxim of manner says 'avoid obscurity'. Wilson and Sperber (1981: 172) suggest that the idea of avoiding obscurity 'obviously follows' from their assumptions at the time about relevance. On Grice's account, a tutor commenting on a student's writing should say (70) rather than (71):

(70)   You use a lot of long words.

(71)   Your writing is sesquipedalian.

If a speaker produces (71) rather than (70), then their utterance will violate the first maxim of manner at the level of 'what is said'. The hearer, assuming that the maxims must be being obeyed at some level, will derive an implicature which is not obscure. Likely implicatures here might be that the speaker is being humorous or rude. Notice that it is not clear on Grice's account how exactly the hearer decides exactly which implicature to derive. Grice stressed that implicatures must be 'calculable', i.e. that it should be possible to spell out all of the steps involved in deriving particular implicatures. One weakness in Grice's account is that one of the stages in deriving implicatures is to look for a related proposition which could be being implicated. This seems to fall short of the calculability criterion and this shortcoming is particularly clear when we consider cases such as this where there are several possible implicatures. At the same time, on many occasions hearers may not be sure exactly what a speaker intended and our account should reflect and explain that possibility.

On a relevance-theoretic account, the key difference between (70) and (71) is that (71) will put the addressee to more effort than would have been required to process (70). Of course, one possibility is that the addressee will not understand the utterance. This will in turn have implications and possibly lead to implicatures, e.g. that the speaker is suggesting that the hearer is uneducated or intellectually inferior. Suppose you say (71) to me and I do know what *sesquipedalian* means. On a Gricean account, this will generate an implicature since violating a maxim at the level of 'what is said' leads to an implicature which does observe the maxims. On a relevance-theoretic account, the extra effort involved in processing the obscure term must lead to some increase in effects. One possibility is that the speaker is being humorous. Another might be that they are being deliberately rude. The interpretation will depend on the manifestness of particular contextual assumptions, including assumptions about the speaker's 'preferences and abilities'. If I know that you do not think of yourself as intellectually superior to me, or even that you think we are equally 'overeducated', then I am likely to see this as a humorous formulation. If I think that you look down on me for not being as well educated as you and you often make snide remarks about this, then I am likely to decide that you are deliberately being rude. Of course, misunderstandings can arise when the speaker makes a false assumption about what is manifest to the hearer, e.g. I might be ashamed of being less well educated than you while you think of us as intellectual peers. Grice himself may have intended to be humorous when formulating his maxims by using the word *perspicuous* rather than a word such as *clear* and including the unnecessary parenthetical ('avoid unnecessary prolixity') after the maxim 'be brief'.

The second manner maxim says to avoid ambiguity. This can be understood in more than one way. In current linguistic theory, the term **ambiguity** usually refers to linguistic expressions which encode more than one meaning, e.g. the noun *seal* can refer, among other things, to a sea creature or something which holds an opening closed, e.g. on an envelope. Grice cannot have intended the maxim to mean that we should never utter ambiguous expressions, so this means that he must have been using the term to refer either to unresolvable ambiguity or more generally to utterances which are open to more than one interpretation. Of course, every utterance is open to more than one interpretation and pragmatic theories aim to explain how we arrive at one. So Grice must have intended this maxim to mean that we should avoid utterances which can not be resolved to one interpretation. What happens when speakers produce utterances where more than one interpretation is possible? Again, one possibility is misunderstanding. When my wife and I told people the name we had chosen for our first child, several of our friends responded by saying:

(72)   What kind of name is that?

We took them to be asking for information about the cultural or geographical origin of the name but of course there is another interpretation on which this is a rhetorical question implicating that they find the name ridiculous (note that these alternative interpretations do not follow from a linguistic ambiguity). On Grice's account, this is a case of inadvertently violating the second maxim of manner and of course we knew what people really meant and sometimes joked about the double meaning.

What about cases where the speaker deliberately leaves her utterance open to more than one interpretation. In a discussion of the book *Relevance* (Sperber and Wilson 1986), Morgan and Green (1987: 727) discuss this utterance produced by Mozart in the film *Amadeus* after the performance of a new opera by the composer Salieri:

(73)   I never knew that music like that was possible.

Mozart's utterance here is consistent with a positive or a negative interpretation, depending on whether the music Mozart couldn't previously conceive of is surprisingly good or surprisingly bad. Given contextual assumptions made available by the rest of the film, we come to see that the point of the utterance is that it frustrates Salieri because it is not clear exactly how it should be interpreted. We strongly suspect, though, that Mozart's attitude is quite negative and this is confirmed when the conversation continues and Mozart's next utterance, uttered in a fairly stylised way, is just as equivocal:

(74)   SALIERI: You flatter me.
            MOZART: Oh no! One hears such sounds and what can one say, but – Salieri!

Salieri here is trying to establish whether or not Mozart is indeed flattering him and Mozart produces another utterance just as equivocal as the previous one. Morgan and Green raise this example to show that interpretations can be successful even when there is no one clear intended interpretation. Sperber and Wilson suggest that this is to be explained in terms of 'layering'. As they put it:

> ... deliberate ambiguity at one level can be used as a nonambiguous ostensive stimulus at another level. By putting Salieri in a situation in which he cannot tell whether he is being complimented or insulted, Mozart makes it manifest that there is much less mutual understanding between them than Salieri might wish. Moreover, Mozart does so in a manifestly intentional way: the failure of the first-level communication successfully communicates Mozart's sense of distance from Salieri on a second level.   (Sperber and Wilson 1987b: 751)

There is an interesting difference between the Gricean account and the relevance-theoretic account of cases such as these. On Grice's account, a hearer will notice that there is an unresolvable 'ambiguity' here and then work out why the speaker has produced an utterance like this. On the relevance-theoretic account, the hearer simply begins to look for an interpretation, following the relevance-theoretic comprehension heuristic, and stops when he finds an interpretation that satisfies his expectations of relevance. In some cases, the 'ambiguity' is easily resolvable. If I tell you that I enjoyed watching the seals when I went to the sea life centre, you will know that I am referring to a kind of sea creature rather than something which holds items together. This follows because you can easily access the interpretation on which I am telling you about sea creatures and assume that I am expecting you to do so. When my friends responded as in (72) to information about my baby's name, two interpretations were fairly accessible. One was the fairly polite question about the name's origin. The other was the less polite one implying that the speaker found the name bizarre or objectionable. In most cases, I was able to judge quite quickly that my friends would not be rude enough to communicate such a negative response to something which I might well be quite sensitive about. The less polite interpretation could be used as the basis for more humorous discussion partly because it was accessible and, of course, a bit risky since it might have offended me. With Mozart's utterance in (73), the interpretation is straightforward if we have access to contextual assumptions about what Mozart thinks of Salieri's music. Salieri does not have access to these assumptions and so his attempt at interpretation is frustrated. For Grice, Mozart's utterance gives rise to implicatures because Salieri notices a violation of the maxim which says 'avoid ambiguity'. For relevance theory, the implicatures follow because of the salience of incompatible interpretations and the absence of contextual assumptions which can guide the interpretation in one direction or the other.

The third maxim of manner says to 'be brief'. Brevity is of course a gradable notion and utterances can be more or less brief. For Grice's account to work, hearers will need to notice the existence of a briefer alternative which the speaker could have used instead. This kind of example will follow similar lines to cases involving the previous two manner maxims. In some cases, brevity and informativeness will overlap:

(75)   I went out into the open air and placed one foot in front of another for a period of time.

(76)   I went for a walk.

(75) is less brief than (76) and also more informative. Grice could explain this by referring to either maxim. As ever, the account will involve noticing violation of maxims at the level of 'what is said' and deriving an implicature which does follow the maxims. Grice's own example is arguably less likely to be explained in terms of informativeness. He compares the suitably brief (77) with the 'overly prolix' (78):

(77)   Miss X sang 'Home Sweet Home'.

(78)   Miss X produced a series of notes that corresponded closely with the score of 'Home Sweet Home'.

Grice imagines an interpreter's reasoning process in glossing these examples as follows:

> Why has he selected that rigmarole in place of the concise and nearly synonymous *sang*? Presumably, to indicate some striking difference between Miss X's performance and those to which the word *singing* is usually applied. The most obvious supposition is that Miss X's performance suffered from some hideous defect. The reviewer knows that this supposition is what is likely to spring to mind, so that is what he is implicating.   (Grice 1989: 37)

A relevance-theoretic explanation will again be very similar but couched in relevance-theoretic terms. (78) is more effortful than (77) and so must lead to more cognitive effects. A report that someone *sang* 'Home Sweet Home' will lead to a representation of a performance of the song. A report that they *produced a series of notes that corresponded closely* with its score suggests some but not all of the properties of an act of singing. So the inference will be that this performance fell short of what we would refer to as singing.

Wilson and Sperber (1981: 173) suggest that the maxim of brevity is 'at the very least … misstated', pointing out that there is vagueness about how to measure brevity and that there are cases where a longer utterance may be more relevant than a shorter one. The examples they give are:

(79) a.   Peter is married to Madeleine.
     b.   It is Peter who is married to Madeleine.

(80) a.   Mary ate a peanut.
     b.   Mary put a peanut into her mouth, chewed and swallowed it.

They point out that there are cases where the second, longer ('by any measure') examples in (79) and (80) would be more appropriate than the first, shorter, one. As they put it:

> … the (a) and (b) members differ not in their logical implications, but in the relative importance assigned to them. By changing the linguistic form [of their utterance] … the speaker can draw attention to certain of its logical implications. If these are the implications on which the relevance of the utterance depends, the speaker will have done [her] best to indicate to the hearer how its relevance is to be established.   (Wilson and Sperber 1981: 173)

The maxim which says 'be orderly' seems to be different from the others in that it is hard to imagine an utterance which would be perceived as a deliberate violation intended to generate an implicature. Consider, for example, the difference between (81) and (82), the kinds of examples for which Grice seems to have designed this maxim:

(81)   He read a chapter of his book and went for a walk.

(82)   He went for a walk and read a chapter of his book.

(81) will lead us to think that he first read the book and then went for a walk. (82) will lead us to think that he first went for a walk and then read a chapter of his book. While we could argue that the difference follows because we assume that the speaker has told us first about what he did and then about what he did next, we could not suggest that there is something 'deviant' about the formulation of (82). It could not be described as 'disorderly' in any way. It seems, then, that this maxim operates in a slightly different way from the others.

We simply assume that speakers are orderly and therefore that events reported in a conjoined sentence are reported in the order in which they occurred. A more typical example discussed in the literature is the contrast between (83) and (84):

(83)   He dived into the pool and swam a length.

(84)   He swam a length and dived into the pool.

We would usually interpret (83) as suggesting that the diving preceded the swimming and (84) as being a case where the swimming preceded the diving. Gricean accounts treat this as a case of generalised conversational implicature. Part of the explanation depends on general assumptions we make about the world, such as that diving into water usually precedes swimming. This alone does not explain the order of events we would usually infer when hearing (84). We might suggest that we notice the marked ordering and so infer an implicature. However, the ordering is not marked if we assume that the swimming preceded the diving. In fact, this is the expected order given the maxim. So there is something unusual about this maxim in that it is not clear how we will notice it has been violated and if we do notice we then conclude that it has not been violated at all.

Wilson and Sperber (1981: 174) suggest that we do not need to assume a maxim of orderliness to explain the contrast between (83) and (84). In a number of works, most extensively in her 2002 book (Carston 2002a), Robyn Carston has developed a relevance-theoretic account of these examples. This account depends on the assumption that we always need to make an inference about when or under what circumstances a reported event is taking, did take or will take place. When we hear that *he dived* we need to make an inference about when he dived. When we hear *he swam a length*, we need to make an inference about when he swam. The straightforward assumptions for (83) follow from their accessibility and the fact that they lead to enough effects to justify processing the utterance. The oddity of (84) follows from the fact that we will have already made an estimate of time for the swimming and now need to integrate an assumption about diving with an accessible assumption that diving usually precedes swimming. The key thing to notice here is that the assumptions about 'order' are not derived as implicatures but simply follow from separate assumptions about the time reference of separate reported events. We will come back to examples like this in Chapter 5.

At the conclusion of their discussion of the maxims, Wilson and Sperber (1981: 174) suggest that most of the maxims are unnecessary and that the rest can be 'reduced' to 'a principle of relevance'. In later works, of course, they no longer referred to the replacement of the maxims as involving 'reduction' and of course they also changed significantly the way they thought about the 'principle' (now two principles) of relevance.

2.5   The development of relevance theory

Building on insights arising from their critique of Grice, Sperber and Wilson developed their suggestion that considerations of relevance guide the processes of utterance interpretation. The view that emerged follows Grice in seeing utterance interpretation as being about recognising the intentions of communicators but differs from his approach in several ways, some of which are considered in this section. The aim is to give you a sense of how relevance theory is simultaneously a development from Grice's insights and something quite different from Grice's approach. This list of differences is not exhaustive but should be enough for an initial overall impression.

(a)   the pragmatics of 'what is said'

As we just saw, relevance theory sees a role for pragmatics in guiding inferences about 'what is said'. Within relevance theory, a term which replaces 'what is said' (to some extent – we will discuss the details more fully below) is the **proposition expressed**. This is the proposition represented by the communicator's chosen linguistic expression. If I utter (85), the proposition I am expressing could be any of a vast number of propositions, including (86) and (87):

(85)   She read it on the tube.

(86)   Julia read an article about relevance theory while travelling on the London Underground transport system.

(87)   Joni saw that the toothpaste she was using contained fluoride by reading this on the container the toothpaste was in.

Deciding which proposition has been expressed is a pragmatic process. Linguistic expressions encode information which helps to identify the proposition expressed and pragmatic inference is involved in working out the rest. By contrast, Grice's approach assumed that pragmatic principles (for Grice, the maxims) were involved only in the recovery of conversational implicatures.

(b)   the underdeterminacy of 'what is said'

As we have seen, what is linguistically encoded vastly underdetermines what is communicated by an utterance. This is not just because we infer implicatures but also because what is encoded falls far short of telling us 'what is said', or the proposition expressed by an utterance. By contrast, Grice's approach assumed that the only things beyond recovering linguistically encoded content which were involved were disambiguation and reference assignment.

(c)   the definition of relevance

The definition of **relevance** was a focus of Wilson and Sperber's first work together. The notion is now defined in terms of **positive cognitive effects** and processing effort. A cognitive effect is an adjustment in an individual's representation of the world. A 'positive' cognitive effect is a cognitive effect that is worth having (we will discuss the role of the qualifier 'positive' in Chapter 3). Other things being equal, the more positive cognitive effects a stimulus gives rise to, the more relevant it is. Other things being equal, the more processing effort involved in deriving cognitive effects from a stimulus, the less relevant it is. Of course, Grice himself did not propose a full, formal definition of the term 'relevance'.

(d)   Principles of Relevance

As mentioned in Chapter 1, and as will be discussed more fully in Chapter 3, relevance theory proposes two principles: the Cognitive Principle of Relevance and the Communicative Principle of Relevance. The existence of two principles was recognised in the 'postface' to the second edition of the book *Relevance* in 1995. Until then, the Cognitive Principle had not been termed as such but just discussed as a generalisation about cognition. This led to some confusion and so this generalisation was recast as a principle of the theory. The Cognitive Principle says that human cognition is geared towards the **maximisation of relevance**. The Communicative Principle says every ostensive stimulus conveys a presumption of its own **optimal relevance**.

The two Principles of Relevance are law-like generalisations about human cognition and communication. By contrast, the exact status and nature of Grice's maxims was never fully clear. Are they social conventions which need to be learned or somehow acquired? Are they psychological generalisations? Are they culture-dependent? Questions such as these were not explicitly answered in Grice's proposal and have been discussed to varying degrees in more recent work on pragmatics. Relevance theory makes more explicit claims about the nature of the Principles of Relevance.

(e)   explicatures and implicatures

Following on from the new understanding of the semantics–pragmatics distinction and the notion of 'what is said', Sperber and Wilson coined the term 'explicature' to refer to communicated propositions which are constructed by developing the linguistically encoded logical form of an utterance. Explicatures are partly encoded and partly inferred. The technical term 'explicature' replaces, and is quite different from, Grice's notion of 'what is said'.

Within relevance theory, 'implicatures' are communicated propositions which are not explicatures. There is no notion of 'conventional implicature' and the phenomena Grice handled in this way are treated differently, as linguistically encoded 'prompts' to guide the inferential stage of utterance interpretation. These come under the heading of 'procedural meaning', discussed in more detail in Chapter 11. The distinction between 'generalised' and 'particularised' conversational implicatures is dissolved. What Grice would have termed 'generalised conversational implicatures' are simply implicatures, i.e. pragmatically inferred propositions which are not explicatures.

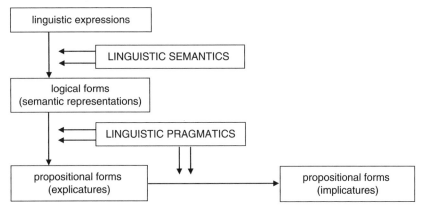

Figure 2.4 *Simplified summary of the semantics–pragmatics distinction for relevance theory*

(f)   literal and figurative uses of language

As we will see in Chapter 9, the relevance-theoretic account of the distinction between literal and non-literal language is quite different from the one proposed by Grice. Grice assumed that utterances had literal meanings which were always accessed and then, in some cases, rejected and replaced with non-literal, sometimes figurative interpretations. Relevance theory does not assume that literal interpretations are always accessed, nor that they have any special status.

(g)   the semantics–pragmatics distinction

Within relevance theory, the distinction between semantics and pragmatics is a distinction between linguistically encoded meanings and contextually inferred meanings. **Linguistic semantics** is the bridge between linguistic expressions and their semantic representations. These semantic representations, termed **logical forms**, are representations with logical properties which vastly underdetermine interpretations. Pragmatics explains how these are enriched so that we can understand the propositions expressed and communicated. Communicated propositions which are developments of logical forms are termed **explicatures** and other communicated propositions are **implicatures**. Figure 2.4 is a simplified representation of the division of labour between linguistic semantics and pragmatics.

(h)   no maxims

Now that we have a sense of the relevance-theoretic view, we can go back again to look at each of Grice's maxims and see how they are subsumed or rejected by relevance theory.

i.   maxims of quantity

Wilson and Sperber (1981) point out, as several others have done (e.g. Horn 1989, 1992; Levinson 1983, 1987a, 2000), that it is not clear how we are to measure degrees of information in such a way as to know what will count as 'informative enough' or 'more information than is required'. Within the new formulation of relevance theory, interpreters are looking for an interpretation that provides enough effects to justify the effort involved in processing the utterance. This might sound vague at first, but it turns out to make more precise predictions than follow from the maxims of quantity and it seems that any utterance which would count as underinformative or overinformative in Grice's terms will either fail to provide enough effects to justify the effort involved in interpretation or put the hearer to unjustifiable effort. Consider (88)–(90) as responses to a question about how to get to the Post Office:

(88)   Walk.

(89)   First, lift up your left foot, move it to the front and place it on the ground. Then, raise your right foot...

(90)   It's on the second corner after the traffic lights, next door to the town hall.

In Grice's terms, (88) would count as not informative enough and (89) as over-informative. In each case, this apparent violation at the level of what is said would generate a conversational implicature and so these would be cases of 'flouting', i.e. ostentatiously violating one or more maxims in order to generate implicatures. The likely candidates in each case involve the speaker being rude, in (88) by implicating unwillingness to cooperate and not valuing the hearer's needs, and in (89) by acting as if the hearer is so stupid that he needs to be reminded of how to carry out the action of walking somewhere. In (90), the amount of information is 'enough' because it enables the hearer to know what to do in order to get to the Post Office. In relevance-theoretic terms, there is no notion of violating or flouting a maxim. Rather, these generalisations explain how we interpret utterances as we do. Hearers look for a set of propositions which the speaker intends to communicate, which would justify the effort involved in deriving them and which do not put the hearer to unjustifiable effort. A salient feature of (88) is that it does not enable the hearer to know how to get to the Post Office. The hearer already intends to walk and is clearly asking for information about which direction to walk in, how long it will take, and so on. So, among the propositions derivable from (88) are that the speaker has not provided enough information to enable the hearer to find his way to the Post Office, that the speaker is not cooperating, and so on. The answer also implicates that the speaker thinks it will be relevant to explain to the hearer that getting to the Post Office will involve walking, which in turn implicates that the hearer might not have been aware of this obvious assumption. Some of these same propositions follow from (89), namely those which have to do with the speaker choosing not to provide the information which the speaker is looking for. On top of this, (89) implicates that the hearer does not know what's involved in walking and needs to be told how to move his legs and feet in order to walk somewhere. In (90), the hearer can straightforwardly access the information needed to know how to get to the Post

Office. In cases like this, then, the Communicative Principle of Relevance is able to explain effects which the maxims of quantity were designed to explain.

ii.   maxims of quality

Wilson and Sperber point out problems with the maxims of quality. An example they discuss in the 1981 paper (Wilson and Sperber 1981: 172) is (91) when uttered by a patient to a doctor:

(91)   I'm ill.

As they point out, the doctor is in a better position than the patient to know whether the utterance is true or adequately evidenced. But no-one would suggest that the patient is unjustified in uttering (91) or claim that any special implicatures follow from this usage. There are many cases where we make utterances which are strictly false without giving rise to implicatures because of it. These include loose uses such as (92)–(95):

(92)   A hundred people came to my lecture.

(93)   Nobody understood a word I said.

(94)   Aberdeen is five hundred miles north of London.

(95)   Andy lives in Paris.

If we discover that the exact number of people who came to the lecture is not exactly 100, say 98 or 101, we will not judge the speaker of (92) as a liar because of this. If we find one person who understood a word or two at my lecture, again this does not make my utterance in (93) misleading. Aberdeen is not exactly five hundred miles from London and not exactly due or magnetic north from there, but (94) is a perfectly acceptable utterance. If the speaker of (95) lives in Issy-les-Moulineaux, technically just outside the boundary of the city of Paris, we will not normally say that she has lied. The key thing, as relevance theory predicts, is that in each case the hearer can access enough positive cognitive effects to justify processing the utterance. In the case of (92), the important implications follow equally from any number of lecture-goers which is around a hundred (e.g. that there were more people than expected, that we ran out of handouts, etc.). Nothing that is communicated depends on the number being exact. Therefore it's acceptable to use the round number which is easier to process. Similarly, (93) is an acceptable way of making clear that most of my audience could not understand most of what I said, or the main points; (94) is an acceptable way of indicating the rough location of Aberdeen relative to London; (95) is an acceptable utterance as long as nothing depends on knowing exactly which administrative domain the speaker lives in. In fact, relevance theory predicts in each case that the strictly false utterance is more relevant than an exact statement which would involve more effort and therefore suggest effects which depend on the exactness. The question of whether truthfulness is important in utterance interpretation will be further discussed in Chapter 9.

iii.   maxim of relation

In the 1981 paper, Wilson and Sperber (1981: 172) simply state that it is clear that the maxim of relation is subsumed by their notion of relevance, a claim which has been explored in detail in work carried out since then. The key thing predicted by relevance theory is that we should be able to derive enough effects to justify the effort of interpreting the utterance. If the utterance seems to have no connection with any easily accessible contextual assumptions, then it is hard to see how this will be possible.

iv.   maxims of manner

The first maxim of manner says to avoid obscurity of expression. An obscure expression might make it impossible for the hearer to understand the utterance and so to derive effects from it. At the same time, the use of an obscure expression might help the hearer to access particular effects. Given this, there is no need within relevance theory for a separate statement about obscurity.

The second maxim of manner says to avoid ambiguity. As Wilson and Sperber point out, virtually every utterance contains an ambiguous expression in the technical sense of an expression which encodes more than one meaning. On this reading, this maxim would preclude almost every utterance. If it is understood in a broader sense, e.g. as 'avoid unresolvable ambiguity' or 'avoid utterances which do not lead to one clear interpretation', it will again be subsumed under the Communicative Principle of Relevance, since unresolvable ambiguity will either mean that effects can not be derived, or give rise to an interpretation on which the ambiguity is intended to give rise to effects. The most obvious cases would be jokes which play on words or creative texts which aim to give rise to richer effects through their ambiguity. A BBC radio programme which describes itself as 'a weekly discussion on topical issues within our academic institutions and research bodies' is called 'Thinking Allowed'. In print, we know that the second word is *allowed* but on the radio we cannot tell whether speakers are saying *allowed* or *aloud*. Both words fit the context. The participants are 'thinking aloud' and this is a place where 'thinking' is 'allowed'. In fact, the idea that thinking is 'permitted' in this context is intended in a slightly humorous way. It is typical of humorous plays on words like this that the sense which is slightly unusual is reflected in the way it is written. This is probably in order to make it more likely that we understand the pun and do not think the title is straightforwardly describing what the participants are doing in the discussion sessions.

The third maxim of manner says to be brief. As Wilson and Sperber point out, brevity can be measured in more than one way (number of words, number of syllables, amount of time spent producing the utterance, and so on). Even so, as we saw above, there are cases where a longer utterance might be more appropriate than a shorter one. Of course, there is a relationship between brevity and processing effort. While this relationship is not wholly straightforward, there will be many cases where a briefer formulation will be one which requires less effort to process.

Finally, the maxim which states 'be orderly' seems to be designed to deal with cases such as the use of *and* to convey 'and then'. As mentioned above, this seems different from other maxims since it will only ever be assumed that the maxim is observed at the level of 'what is said'.

As we have seen, then, relevance theory emerged from critical discussion of Grice's approach. Sperber and Wilson built on Grice's initial insight, namely the idea that interpretation is guided by rational principles. They proposed a technical definition of relevance and suggested principles which are different in kind from the maxims in that they are generalisations about human cognition and communication. Following Exercise 2.5, we will end this chapter by considering some alternative suggestions about how to develop fuller pragmatic theories from Grice's initial ideas.

Exercise 2.5 asks you to look at a new range of examples and compare a relevance-theoretic approach with a Gricean one.

Exercise 2.5

- Consider how A is likely to interpret B's utterance in each of the following examples:
    (i)   A: I thought you might fancy going for a run along the beach while you're here.
            B: I haven't run for over a year.
    (ii)   A: John says you're fed up with having to work such a long shift today?
            B: Give me a break.
    (iii)   A: Do you think I was wrong to ask John to help at the party?
            B: Well, it's not the best idea you've ever had.
    (iv)   A: Do you think I was wrong to ask John to help at the party?
            B: Not at all! That's the best idea you've ever had!
    (v)   A: They're saying John didn't show up for work today.
            B: How could they tell?
For each one, propose both a Gricean and a relevance-theoretic account. Compare the two approaches and consider how we might compare them and decide which offers the best explanation.

2.6   Other directions: 'post-Griceans' and 'neo-Griceans'

Relevance theory is not the only approach to pragmatics influenced by or developed since the work of Grice. While other approaches are not the main focus of this book, knowing something about other approaches should help you to understand the nature of the relevance-theoretic approach. Of course, there are differing views about a number of individual ideas proposed within relevance theory and we will also look at some of these later in the book. At this stage, though, we will only consider approaches which can be seen as aiming to develop ideas initially proposed by Grice. In this section, we will mainly look at two approaches which have been described as 'neo-Gricean' in that they retain some of the key ideas proposed by Grice while developing accounts which differ in their details (as opposed to relevance theory, which is usually described as only 'post-Gricean', since it moves further away from Gricean assumptions).

Despite not being formally published, Grice's approach was quickly recognised as an exciting development by many researchers. Given the tentative and programmatic nature of Grice's presentation, it was clear that there was work to do in developing a more complete and detailed account. At the same time, some theorists challenged specific claims made by Grice or proposed important changes. Keenan (1976), for example, questioned the universality of Gricean maxims, suggesting that Malagasy-speakers in Madagascar did not follow the first maxim of quantity in the same way as speakers in Western cultures. She suggested that Malagasy-speakers 'regularly provide less information than is required by their conversational partner, even though they have access to the necessary information' (Keenan 1976: 70). She gives the following example:

(96)   A: Where is your mother?
        B: She is either in the house or in the market.

Keenan suggests that an utterance such as B's here 'is not usually taken to imply that B is unable to provide more specific information needed by the hearer'. She says that: 'The implicature is not made, because the expectation that speakers will satisfy informational needs is not a basic norm' (Keenan 1976: 70). Keenan suggests that this divergence from what seems to be predicted by Grice's approach arises because information is treated differently by Malagasy-speakers (as a 'rare commodity' and a source of prestige). However, Brown and Levinson (1978: 298–9) point out that this variation in behaviour does not directly argue against Grice's proposal. Rather, this suggests that other factors can adjust what counts as 'informative enough' or possibly even over-ride particular maxims in some situations. Brown and Levinson go even further, suggesting that in fact we need to assume something like the maxims in order to explain what is going on here. This seems reasonable since it is hard otherwise to see why hearers of B's utterance in (96) would conclude that B knows where her mother is but is choosing not to say.

2.6.1   Horn's neo-Gricean approach

The two best-known neo-Gricean approaches are those proposed by Horn (1984, 1988, 1989, 2004) and Levinson (1987a, 1987b, 2000). In both cases, Grice's maxims are replaced by a smaller number of principles so that there is a sense in which they can be seen as 'reducing' a greater number of principles (or 'maxims') to a smaller number. Since the underlying idea is to assume principles understood along similar lines to the Gricean maxims, these approaches tend to be described as 'neo-Gricean'.

Horn proposes two principles. One is a 'Q' or 'Quantity' Principle which says that speakers should provide 'sufficient' information. The other is an 'R' or 'Relation' Principle which says that speakers should not say more than is necessary. Here are the two principles:

(97)   Q Principle:
                 Make your contribution sufficient;
                 Say as much as you can (given R)

(98)   R Principle:
                 Make your contribution necessary;
                 Say no more than you must (given Q)

At first glance, these might look like no more than restatements of Grice's maxims of quantity since they seem to amount to saying that speakers should provide as much information as is necessary and no more than is necessary. Horn does intend this, but he also argues that the Q Principle subsumes two of the maxims of manner ('avoid obscurity' and 'avoid ambiguity') and that the R Principle subsumes the maxim of relation and one of the maxims of manner ('be brief'). These relationships are presented in table form in Table 2.1.

Horn's approach, then, greatly reduces the number of maxims, suggesting, in effect, that a large part of what they are designed to explain can be accounted for in terms of a tension between a requirement to give enough information and a requirement not to give too much information.

One phenomenon which motivated Horn's approach and which this approach aims to explain is the existence of a range of cases where implicatures follow a particular pattern. These have been termed 'scalar implicatures' and are understood to arise because of the existence of 'scalar relationships' between stronger and weaker items. The scales which these items represent are now often referred to as 'Horn scales' reflecting the work Horn did in identifying and exploring them. Here are some examples:

(99)   Horn scales

            some   *all*
            one   *two*   *three*
            possibly   *probably*   *definitely*

In each of these cases, the use of an item on a particular scale is consistent with the use of items on its right. If I ate some of your chocolates, it is possible that I ate all of them. If I ate one, I may have eaten two. If something is possibly going to happen, it may be probable that it will happen. And so on. At the same time, the use of an item on a scale entails an item to its left. If I ate all of your chocolates, it is true that I ate some. If I ate two chocolates, I ate one. If something is probable, then it is possible. And so on. We can demonstrate these points by considering exchanges such as (100):

(100)   A: If you've got a teaching qualification, you can take part in the workshop.
            B: I've got three.

B's utterance implicates that B can take part in the workshop because having three teaching qualifications entails having one (and two).

Table 2.1 *Horn's principles and Grice's maxims*

Principle suggested by Horn	Replaces these Gricean maxims
Q Principle: 'Make your contribution sufficient; say as much as you can (given R)'	First maxim of quantity: 'make your contribution as informative as is required' Maxim of manner: 'avoid obscurity' Maxim of manner: 'avoid ambiguity'
R Principle: 'Make your contribution necessary; say no more than you must (given Q)'	Second maxim of quantity: 'do not make your contribution more informative than is required' Maxim of relation: 'be relevant' Maxim of manner: 'be brief'

An important observation made by Horn is that an utterance containing an item on one of these scales will tend to implicate the negation of items to its right on the scale. Consider the following examples:

(101)   I ate some of your chocolates.

(102)   I ate two of your chocolates.

(103)   I'll probably finish that essay tonight.

If I say (101), you will think that I did not eat all of your chocolates. If I say (102), you will think that I ate exactly two and not three or more. If I say (103), you will think it is not definite that I will finish the essay tonight. Horn suggests that these inferences follow from the Q Principle. If a speaker is aiming to 'say as much as you can', then choosing a particular point on a scale implicates that they cannot say anything higher on the scale. Without the Q Principle (101) might be produced by someone who ate all of the chocolates. The Q Principle says that someone who ate them all should say so.

The R Principle aims to explain inferences which move in the opposite direction, leading us to conclude that the speaker intends to communicate something stronger than what they have said. In these cases, the assumption is that we won't spell out something we're confident you can work out for yourself. Consider an utterance such as (104) said to my daughter as she is about to leave the house in the morning:

(104)   It's supposed to rain later.

When I say this, my daughter will infer that I am implicating that she should bring an umbrella or waterproof clothes with her when she goes out. The fact that I did not say so explicitly does not lead her to doubt whether I actually intended that. I have followed the R Principle and not spelled out something which I know she will be able to work out for herself, i.e. I have followed the instruction to say 'no more than you must'.

The pattern here then is one where two forces pull in opposite directions. How do we know which direction our inference should go in? This depends on what we know about the context. We know that news of rain often implicates that we should bring waterproof clothes or an umbrella, so saying (104) will implicate this unless something else in the context suggests otherwise. This, of course, is what Grice termed a 'generalised conversational implicature'. By contrast, we do not have a general assumption along the lines that anyone who ate some chocolates will have eaten all of them. So in the case of (101)–(103) the inference is based on the Q Principle, assuming that the speaker would have used the stronger term if she had been able to.

2.6.2   Levinson's neo-Gricean approach

Some of the thinking behind Horn's approach is shared by Levinson, who has developed his own approach in a series of publications over the years (including Atlas and Levinson 1981; Levinson 1987a, 1987b, 1995, 2000). In one of the key papers developing this approach (Levinson 1987a), he begins by pointing out what he calls an 'anomaly' in Grice's programme. As he points out, it seems that in some cases Gricean principles are used to explain enrichment from something weaker to something stronger while in other cases they are used to explain the assumed negation of something stronger. Levinson (1987a: 62–3) illustrated this conflict with reference to the following examples and the suggested implicatures indicated here:

(105)   Some of the miners voted for Thatcher.
          Implicates: Not all of the miners voted for Thatcher.

(106)   Bill turned the key and the engine started.
          Implicates: Bill turned the key and then, as a direct result, the engine started.

We can argue that the implicature in (105) follows from the speaker's decision not to say that all of the miners voted for Thatcher. If the speaker knew this, we would expect her to give enough information by telling us so. The fact that she has not said this means that she must either think that not all of the miners voted for Thatcher or not be sure whether they all did. The same reasoning applied to (106) might suggest that this utterance should implicate the opposite of what we do in fact assume. We could say that it would have been relevant to know that turning the key caused the engine to start and that failure to say so implicates that this was not the case. Instead, though, we enrich the interpretation and assume that the key turning caused the engine to start. In (105), then, Gricean principles lead to the implicature of the negation of something stronger. In (106), by contrast, they lead to the assumption of something stronger.

Levinson's approach is similar to Horn's in identifying principles which account for inferences in different directions. Horn's two principles are echoed in Levinson's work, with Levinson's I Principle doing the work of Horn's R Principle. Ultimately, Levinson develops an account based on three principles

Table 2.2 *Levinson's heuristics and Grice's maxims (based on Levinson 2000: 35–8)*

Heuristic suggested by Levinson	Replaces these Gricean maxims
Q Heuristic: 'What isn't said isn't'	First maxim of quantity: 'make your contribution as informative as is required'
I Heuristic: 'What is expressed simply is stereotypically exemplified, i.e. minimal specifications get maximally informative or stereotypical interpretations'	Second maxim of quantity: 'do not make your contribution more informative than is required'
M Heuristic: 'What's said in an abnormal way isn't normal'	Maxim of manner: 'be brief' Maxim of manner: 'avoid obscurity' Maxim of manner: 'avoid ambiguity'

and associated heuristics: a Q Principle, an I Principle and an M Principle. The Q Principle and the I Principle are similar to Horn's Q and R Principles. The M Principle is about how an utterance is formulated. Table 2.2 features Levinson's heuristics (which are briefer than the principles) with a summary of which Gricean maxims each heuristic is derived from and proposes to replace.

As we can see, Levinson shares with Horn the general idea of replacing Grice's maxims with a smaller number of principles. Horn and Levinson differ in exactly what set of principles, and how many of them, they propose. We'll finish our look at these approaches by considering three examples and how Levinson would explain them (one example for each of Levinson's heuristics):

(107)   John is over 5 feet tall.

(108)   I broke a finger yesterday.

(109)   He invited me in and gave me a warm liquid created from the ground beans of a coffee plant.

If we assume that (107) has given as much information as the speaker can give and therefore that 'what isn't said isn't', we will assume that John is over 5 feet tall but not over 6 feet tall. Being over 6 feet tall is consistent with being over 5 feet tall but we'd expect the speaker to let us know if he was even more than 6 feet tall. (108) is a classic Gricean generalised conversational implicature. We have access to standard assumptions about individuals having accidents which break fingers biologically attached to their hands. Since the speaker has said nothing to indicate otherwise, we assume it is one of these fingers which she has broken. In (109), the speaker has produced an unusual formulation where we know she could easily have said something much simpler, e.g. (110):

(110)   He invited me in and gave me a coffee.

Given the availability of a simpler formulation and the speaker's decision not to use it, we assume that there was something unusual about the drink she was given, e.g. that it was not well-made, it was unpleasant, etc.

2.7   Summary

In this chapter, we have seen how relevance theory has its origins in Grice's theory of conversation. Grice's approach was clearly a major breakthrough in understanding how we understand each other. Sperber and Wilson acknowledged this breakthrough and attempted to build on his insights. They critiqued the approach and, in attempting to remedy weaknesses, came up with a new approach of their own. Other theorists developed the ideas in different ways and, of course, debates have carried on among people working within the different approaches.

Exercise 2.6

As in every chapter, this final exercise asks you to adjust the list of questions you have come up with so far by compiling new questions which have occurred to you while reading this chapter and to think about the kinds of things which might count as answers to any questions you have come up with so far. First, add new questions to your ongoing list. Second, consider all of your questions and think about possible ways of answering them.

2.8   Further reading

Of course, the papers 'Meaning' (Grice 1957) and 'Logic and conversation' (Grice 1975) are the main sources for Grice's ideas on meaning and pragmatics respectively. I would recommend you look at these papers for a sense of Grice's style as well as his ideas, even though students are usually advised to start with a more accessible introduction. See the later collection of papers (Grice 1989) to follow up Grice's other ideas. On Grice and meaning, there are useful discussions in the book *Relevance* (Sperber and Wilson 1986: 21–4) and in Tim Wharton's book on nonverbal communication (Wharton 2009: 18–37). There are useful discussions of Grice's ideas about pragmatics in most introductory pragmatics textbooks. Levinson's 1983 discussion is a very clear and still very useful introduction (Levinson 1983: 97–166).

3   Principles of Relevance

Topics: relevance, cognition and communication; relevance and effects; relevance and effort; the Cognitive Principle of Relevance; the Communicative Principle of Relevance; ostensive-inferential communication; relevance-guided comprehension heuristic

3.1   Overview

Having summarised relevance theory in Chapter 1 and looked at how it developed from the work of Grice in Chapter 2, this chapter presents more detail on the key notions proposed and used by relevance theory. We look at the general claims relevance theory makes about human cognition and communication and at the two Principles of Relevance: the First, or Cognitive, Principle of Relevance and the Second, or Communicative, Principle of Relevance. We look at how relevance is defined in terms of cognitive effects and processing effort, and then at how relevance theory defines the kind of communication which the Communicative Principle of Relevance applies to. This is termed 'ostensive-inferential communication' to reflect the fact that communicators communicate ostensively (openly showing an intention to communicate) and that audiences make inferences about the intentions of communicators. We then look at the 'relevance-guided comprehension heuristic' which addressees follow when interpreting utterances and other ostensively communicative acts. This is a 'fast and frugal heuristic' (a term used by Gigerenzer *et al.* 1999) which is motivated by the Communicative Principle of Relevance and the presumption of optimal relevance. Understanding the ideas in this chapter is essential in order to understand exactly how relevance theory aims to account for how we understand each other, which is the topic of Chapter 4. When you have finished the current chapter, you will have developed your understanding of the key components of relevance theory and be in a position to understand how they are applied in particular explanations and analyses. We will move on to look more closely at how relevance theory explains specific interpretations in Chapter 4.

3.2   Relevance, cognition and communication

As pointed out above, relevance theory is based on law-like generalisations about cognition and about communication. The cognitive generalisation is about how human minds are so organised that they look for and notice
important aspects of our environment. The communicative generalisation is
about the expectations created by communicative acts. More fully and more
technically, the claim about cognition is that our minds are organised so that
they tend to 'maximise' relevance, i.e. to derive as many cognitive effects as
possible for as little effort as possible, and the claim about communication
is that acts of ostensive-inferential communication create expectations of
'optimal' relevance, i.e. that they will be at least relevant enough to justify
the effort involved in processing them and the most relevant ones consistent
with the communicator's abilities and preferences. This chapter provides a
fuller account of these generalisations. To understand the claims fully, we need
to know exactly how relevance is defined, what is involved in maximising and
optimising relevance, and how we recognise the acts of communication which
give rise to the presumption of optimal relevance and trigger the relevance-
guided comprehension heuristic. Before developing each of these in more detail,
this section gives a brief, informal sketch of the important differences between
cognition and communication, particularly with regard to how we look for
relevance in each case. We will begin by considering how our cognitive system
in general looks for relevance in the world around us. The first step in doing this
is to understand what we mean when we talk about cognition.

3.2.1   Cognition and relevance

So what is cognition? As ever, there are a number of different
answers. What the different answers share is the assumption that cognition
has to do with 'thinking'. Processes such as remembering, planning, evaluating
and so on are seen as 'cognitive' processes. Within contemporary cognitive
science, a common metaphor (although one whose accuracy is often questioned)
is to see the mind as a device for processing information. On this view,
cognition is the process of acquiring, storing and manipulating information.
A standard view, largely based on the work of the philosopher Jerry Fodor, is
that cognition involves representations and computations. Fodor's 1975 book,
The Language of Thought, (among other works) spells out the related idea that
human thinking is language-like. Relevance theory is located within this tradition and explicitly follows many aspects of Fodor's thinking, not only about the
'language of thought' but also about the idea that the mind is modular (Fodor
1983), i.e. that it contains a number of specialised modules, or 'input systems',
whose main role is to help us construct representations of the world based
on input originating in sensory data. Perhaps Fodor's most significant
and controversial claim is that one of these modules is specialised for dealing

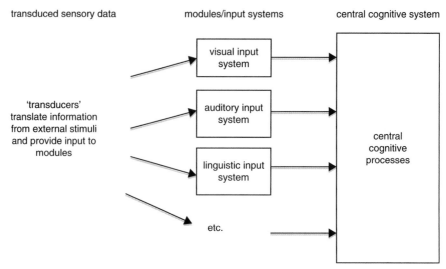

Figure 3.1 *A simplified representation of modular mental architecture (based on Fodor 1983)*

with linguistic input. These modular input systems take as input 'transduced' data from whichever source they specialise in, transform and enrich it, and provide representational input to a central system. This central system is the part of the mind where we 'think' by performing computations over our conceptual representations. This picture is represented in simplified form in Figure 3.1. Note that this diagram makes no claims or assumptions about the brain. The question of how generalisations at the more abstract level of 'mind' relate to the physical nature of the brain is of course one which is still being explored. Fodor's proposals are about the mind and make no direct claims about the brain.

There are several ways of explaining how and why Fodor developed his **modularity** thesis. One way to think about it is to say that Fodor is addressing the question of how information from different sources is related and integrated as we understand the world around us. I can come to know that it's raining because I see rain outside the window, because I hear rain, or because you tell me it's raining. One thing my mind has to do is to understand information coming from different sources and assess it, including in cases where information is contradictory – for example, if you tell me it isn't raining but I see rain outside the window. In this case, I will be likely to give greater weight to the evidence of my eyes than what you say and so decide that you are either mistaken or misinforming me.

Fodor's work is quite speculative and the evidence for his view of the mind as modular is controversial, but he points out that there is some evidence which supports it. One kind of evidence comes from the existence of phenomena such as optical illusions where the evidence of our eyes (i.e. from our vision module)

Figure 3.2 *The Müller-Lyer illusion (Müller-Lyer 1889)*

contradicts but is not over-ridden by more strongly evidenced information from other sources. A classic example is the 'Müller-Lyer' illusion (Figure 3.2) where two lines of the same length appear to have different lengths.

The two horizontal lines in Figure 3.2 are exactly the same length but the lower line looks longer than the higher one. The slanted lines at each end give rise to this illusion. What is important for Fodor's position is that we cannot choose to 'see' the lines as the same length even after we have measured them and established that they are the same length. This is because the visual input system, or 'module', is a self-contained unit and information from other sources cannot affect it. Fodor describes this property of modules by saying that modules are 'informationally encapsulated'. This property is often seen as the most important property of a module, but Fodor does mention a number of other properties of modular processes, including that they are fast, mandatory and domain-specific. Clearly, visual processing happens very quickly. As soon as we open our eyes, we are aware of what we can see. It is domain-specific in that it only deals with visual input. It is mandatory in that we cannot choose not to see something in our field of vision. Fodor suggests that there are good evolutionary reasons for modular processes to have these properties. For example, if something unexpected happens, it is important that we nevertheless recognise that it is happening. If a tiger appears on a London street one afternoon, it is in my interest to see it and recognise what it is rather than to miss it because I 'know' from experience that there will not be any tigers there.

The most controversial of Fodor's claims for modularity is the one associated with language. What evidence is there that linguistic input is handled by a domain-specific linguistic input system? As Fodor acknowledges, evidence in this area is hard to gather and assess. We can ask, though, whether linguistic processing seems to share the properties Fodor claims for modules in general. It is easy to see that linguistic processing is fast. Fodor (1983: 61) cites evidence from speech 'shadowing' where subjects listen to linguistic input through headphones and repeat what they have heard as quickly as they can. Fodor points out that the shadowing speech of many subjects lags only around a quarter of a second behind the input. Linguistic processing also seems to be mandatory. I always notice someone saying my name even when I am in a crowded environment, and it is not possible to listen to words in a language we know without recognising which words have been produced. Evidence for domain specificity is arguably less clear since we would need to find a way to create different predictions based on whether two kinds of processing shared a domain or not. We said above that informational encapsulation is perhaps the most important property of modules. What evidence is there for the informational encapsulation of linguistic processing? Again, the evidence is not fully clear but proponents of the modularity thesis might point to cases where we misunderstand despite clear contextual bias. Perhaps the clearest experimental support comes from work on lexical disambiguation. In a series of experiments which have been confirmed in repeated trials, Swinney (1979) showed that lexical access is not affected by contextual cues. Consider the ambiguous word *bug* as used in one of Swinney's examples:

(1)   He found several kinds of bug in the corner of the room.

The word *bug* has several different encoded meanings, including 'listening device' or 'small insect-like creature'. Swinney's experiments were based on a technique known as 'cross-modal priming'.[1] In this technique, subjects listen to utterances through headphones and respond to stimuli on a computer screen, i.e. they are exposed to stimuli from two different 'modes': auditory and visual. The task of subjects is to judge whether sequences of letters presented on screen are words of English or not. If they see a sequence such as '*sew*' they should press the 'YES' key since *sew* is a word of English. If they see a sequence such as '*wse*' they should press the 'NO' key since there is no English word *wse*. Swinney's technique is based on the fact that seeing a particular stimulus in one mode can 'prime' responses in another, making subjects respond to them more quickly. If subjects see the word *sew* on screen immediately after they have heard it through headphones, they respond to it more quickly than if they have not heard it recently. Importantly, the priming effect also applies to semantically related words. Subjects who have heard the word *sew* will also respond more quickly to the word *knit*, for example.

In the relevant part of his experiments, what Swinney did was to present subjects with words immediately after they had heard ambiguous words with semantically related senses. He presented the words in contexts which were biased towards relevant (semantically related) senses. So, for example, he presented the word *ant* immediately after subjects had heard the word *bug* in a context which favoured the 'insect-like creature' sense, such as:

(2)   He found spiders, cockroaches and several other kinds of bug in the corner of the room.

The word *ant* was shown as a prompt immediately after subjects had heard the word *bug*. Unsurprisingly, subjects responded more quickly to a word like *ant* than to an unrelated word such as *sew*. The really significant result, though, was that subjects also responded more quickly to the word *spy*, which is semantically related to a sense which the context is pointing away from. Repeated experiments show priming effects for words related to all senses of ambiguous words, regardless of how the context is biased.[2] This suggests that lexical access is a modular process unaffected by knowledge from contextual and other sources. The effect lasts only for a few hundredths of a second so that when a prompt is revealed as listeners hear the last word of (2) the priming effect only applies to the contextually relevant sense. Evidence such as this has been taken to support the view that our minds contain a Fodorian module specialised for dealing with linguistic input. This is some of the strongest evidence for the modularity thesis. The thesis and evidence have been much discussed and there is a body of work which has been taken to disconfirm it as well as to confirm it.[3] While a number of linguistic theorists make broadly Fodorian assumptions, there are also a number who reject this view. Cognitive linguists and functional linguists, for example, reject the separation of linguistic knowledge or processes from other areas of cognition. Chomsky assumes that there is an area of linguistic competence, or a 'language faculty', but he does not endorse the Fodorian position, partly because he is unsure about the relationship between 'input' and 'output' (for discussion, see Smith 2004: 15–24). Despite this difference, relevance theory is based on a broadly Chomskyan approach to language and on Fodorian assumptions about modularity. These ideas are constantly being explored and debated.

For Fodor, the function of modules is to deliver conceptual representations, i.e. thoughts, to the central cognitive system. The central system can then use these representations to perform computations of various kinds. If I have the thought that I should bring an umbrella with me whenever it's raining outside and I see that it's raining as I prepare to go out, I can conclude that I should bring an umbrella with me. Fodor's picture aims to explain how we 'think' by performing computations on conceptual representations (i.e. sentences in the 'language of thought'). The modules deliver some of the representations. Computations on representations deliver others. It is not clear exactly how far we can explain cognition in terms of the representational-computational model. One way of thinking about relevance theory is as an attempt to see how much we can explain in terms of such a model. The kinds of phenomena which pose challenges for this approach include what philosophers term '*qualia*' (pronounceable either as 'quail–ia' or as 'kwahl–ia'), i.e. the subjective sensation of our conscious experiences, and more general impressions. You might ask, for example, whether we can realistically hope to describe the 'feeling' of touching or tasting something, or the emotional sensations we have when responding to an artwork or literary work, in terms of systems of representations and computations over them.[4]

Thinking of the mind in this Fodorian way, what is it that the mind is trying to do? One of the main functions of the mind is to maintain a system of beliefs and to try to keep this system as accurate as possible in terms of how it represents the world. If something dangerous appears in my environment, it is important that I should notice it in order to avoid it. If something desirable appears, it is important that I notice it in order to try to take advantage of it. And so on. If this is on the right lines, then it makes sense that our minds are organised in such a way as to pick up on important new information. This may explain a number of facts about how we process data from the world, including: the fact that new-born babies attend to human language in their immediate environment and are particularly attuned to the voices of people they have 'heard' (with considerable loss of detail in the sounds, of course) while in the womb; the fact that we tend to perceive human faces quickly and even to perceive characteristics of human faces in other visual stimuli; our inability to 'switch off' utterances in languages we know and perceive them as pure noise; and so on. One way to think of these facts is that they are evidence of our goal of 'maximising relevance', deriving as many cognitive effects as possible from the environment for as little effort as possible.

There is one important way in which relevance theory departs from, or challenges, Fodor's approach. Fodor believes that we are not in a position to come up with testable hypotheses about central cognitive processes, including pragmatic inference. When considering central processes, Fodor often refers to scientific theorising as an example. As he points out, there are no boundaries on what might count as relevant evidence when constructing scientific theories. Absolutely anything might be relevant. Given this, Fodor argues, we cannot reasonably expect to come up with an adequate theory of central cognitive processes. He says:

> The reason that there is no serious psychology of central processes is the same as the reason there is no serious philosophy of scientific confirmation. Both exemplify the significance of global factors in the fixation of belief, and nobody begins to understand how such factors have their effects.   (Fodor 1983: 129)

Relevance theory can be seen as an attempt to challenge Fodor's pessimism by coming up with an account of one variety of central cognitive processes, i.e. those involved in pragmatic inference. It argues that we can come up with testable hypotheses about pragmatic inference because these processes are constrained by expectations of relevance. As we will see, there is an important difference between general expectations of relevance in cognition and expectations of relevance created by ostensive-inferential communication. In cognition in general, we are on the lookout for relevant information, i.e. information from which significant effects follow. We can assume that our cognitive system has developed in ways which will help us to notice what is relevant to us. But there is no reason to assume that there are any strong constraints carried by the stimuli provided in the world in general which guide or constrain the search for relevance. In communication, by contrast, we assume that communicators attempt to shape their communicative acts in ways which make it easier for us to see how they intend their behaviour to be relevant. Before moving on to consider the specific claims made by relevance theory about how we look for relevance when interpreting acts of communication, we need to make clear what we mean when we talk about 'communication'.

Exercise 3.1 encourages you to consider evidence relevant to Fodor's view that the mind is modular and that one module is specialised for linguistic processing.

Exercise 3.1

- Fodor suggests a range of properties characteristic of modules understood as input systems. These include: speed (processes are very fast), mandatoriness (we cannot choose not to perform modular processes or not to process modular input), domain specificity (they apply to a delimited range of input types), informational encapsulation (modular processes cannot be affected by input from other sources).
  a. Consider the Müller-Lyer illusion and make sure you understand why the processes involved in viewing seem to have the above properties and so to demonstrate modular input.
  b. See how many other varieties of modular processing you can think of (you might begin by thinking about senses – are there modular processes associated with each of these?).
  c. Consider what evidence you can find that linguistic processing is modular.

3.2.2 Communication and relevance

So what is **communication**? Again, there are several possible answers. The range of phenomena that could count as examples of communication is quite wide. We could say that computers are communicating with each other when software from one computer sends electrical energy in a particular form to another and causes software in the other computer to perform operations. We could say that a thermostat is communicating with a central heating system when a temperature sensor sends electricity to a pump or boiler causing it to switch off or on. While a wide range of phenomena have been described loosely as 'communication', many of these involve information transmission but not communication. Sperber and Wilson assume that there are only two possible theories of communication: a **code theory** and an **inferential theory**. What is needed, then, is a way of identifying the kinds of communication which the Communicative Principle of Relevance applies to. Once again, Sperber and Wilson took their cue from Grice, this time with reference to his notion of 'non-natural meaning', or 'meaning$_{NN}$' as discussed in Chapter 2. Once again, relevance theory has replaced the notion of meaning$_{NN}$ with another notion which defines the scope of pragmatics.

The kind of communication which relevance theory sees as giving rise to expectations of optimal relevance is **ostensive-inferential communication**. The double-barrelled name is designed to represent what is involved from the point of view of both the communicator and the audience. From the communicator's point of view, this involves producing an ostensive act, i.e. one which shows that the communicator is intending to communicate something. From the audience's point of view, this involves making inferences about the intentions of the communicator. An ostensive act is one which attracts the audience's attention and shows them something. Here is a nonverbal example:

(3)   *Ken and Bev arrive home. As Bev is locking the front door, Ken goes ahead to the kitchen. He comes back and stands in the hall holding up an empty milk bottle.*

This is ostensive behaviour. Bev cannot help noticing what Ken is doing and making inferences about it. With no other obvious explanation, she will decide that Ken is ostensively communicating with her. Now her task is to make inferences about what he is communicating. With no access to Bev's contextual assumptions, we can make some guesses about what this might be. We might think that he is suggesting that they leave a note out for the milkman asking for more milk tomorrow. Or maybe he's suggesting that one of them should pop out now for more milk. The more access we have to appropriate contextual assumptions, the more detailed our inferences can be and the more confident we can be that they're right. Suppose, for example, that Ken and Bev had this conversation on the bus on the way home:

(4)   KEN: I think we might be out of milk.
         BEV: I checked before I came out. There was over a pint left.
         KEN: Are you sure? We could get off a stop early and pop by the shop for a pint on the way home.
         BEV: I'm sure. It's fine.

We can see now that Bev will be inferring a rebuke, that she was wrong, that they should have picked up some milk on the way home, and so on. So Ken's action of holding up the empty bottle was ostensive and Bev made inferences about what he must mean by it.

   Verbal communication is an even clearer example. In almost all cases where someone writes or speaks to someone in a language the addressee knows, the only plausible explanation is that they are ostensively communicating and so the addressee makes inferences about what they intend to communicate. Here are three utterances Ken might have used in place of (or alongside) holding up the bottle:

(5)   I was right. The milk's finished.

(6)   There's no milk. Just this empty bottle.

(7)   So you checked before you came out, did you?

(8)   Hooray! LOADS of milk left!

There is an important difference between acts of ostensive-inferential communication and other stimuli in the world. Acts of ostensive-inferential communication create fairly strong expectations in their audiences about their relevance, i.e. about what kinds of effects we can expect to derive from them and about the amount of effort we might need to expend to achieve these effects. We will look at this in more detail below but we can give a brief illustration by considering differences in how you might respond to an ostensively communicative act of nonverbal communication and to other kinds of behaviour. Consider the difference between someone bending down to tie their shoelaces and someone who waves at you and then bends down to tie their shoelaces in a stylised manner. In the first case, you are likely to think little more than that they are tying their shoelaces. In the second case, you will recognise that the other person is intending to communicate something, wonder what it is, and get to work on interpreting their behaviour. Relevance theory claims that the expectation generated by the ostensiveness of this act is that the communicator has an interpretation of her behaviour in mind which she thinks you will find significant and that you will not be put to undue effort in arriving at it. We will spell out this claim more fully and more technically later in this chapter. The next two sections begin this process by discussing the definition of relevance which is used in the relevance-theoretic account of ostensive-inferential communication.

Exercise 3.2 encourages you to consider a range of scenarios which might involve ostensive-inferential communication.

Exercise 3.2

- Consider to what extent and how the behaviour described in the following examples involve ostensive-inferential communication:
    (i)   After you ask me whether my knee is better after I hurt it playing football, I stand up, squat down and stand up again.
    (ii)   Walking down a busy street, I stop, pick up a sweet wrapper and drop it into a nearby bin.
    (iii) After you have dropped a sweet wrapper in the street, I tap you on the shoulder and then pick up the sweet wrapper and put it in the bin.
    (iv)   While you and I are having a conversation, I slap my neck trying to hit a fly which has landed there.
    (v)   While you and I are having a conversation, I cover my mouth and cough.
    (vi)   After you ask me how I am feeling, I cover my mouth and cough.

3.3   Defining relevance: effects

Intuitively, and even before we have a definition of what counts as an 'effect', it seems reasonable to say that the more effects a stimulus has the more relevant it is. If I see a pigeon crossing the road in front of me as I cycle down the road on a normal day, this is more relevant than if I see a fallen leaf.

Both a leaf and a pigeon might make me have thoughts about leaves or pigeons. The pigeon is more relevant, though, since it has implications for my cycling. I need to slow down, keep an eye on it and make sure I don't cycle into it or have it fly into me. Moving to a more far-fetched scenario, seeing a tiger on the London streets would be more relevant still since it would not only have quite drastic implications about my safety and my cycling behaviour, but also over-turn some of my existing assumptions about the likelihood of tigers strolling around London, the safety of London streets in general, and so on. (Of course, we can imagine situations which would make leaves more important or tigers less important, but I have in mind for now only what is for me an everyday scenario.)

In order to define relevance more fully, we need to know what kinds of things can have a degree of relevance and to say what kinds of effects are the ones that make those things relevant. The kinds of things that can be relevant are, of course, the kinds of things that can have effects. The list includes utterances, thoughts, memories and interpretations. For now, we will consider the relevance of a stimulus (an utterance, of course, is one kind of stimulus).

So what kinds of effects can make a stimulus relevant? In the book *Relevance*, Sperber and Wilson start by discussing **contextual effects**. Since the second edition of the book appeared in 1995, they have replaced this with the term **cognitive effects**. The difference is that contextual effects are defined formally without reference to the kind of system which might give rise to them, while cognitive effects are effects which arise within a cognitive system, i.e. cognitive effects are contextual effects within a cognitive system. We can illustrate the notion of a contextual effect by looking at expressions in the logical language 'propositional calculus' which we mentioned in the previous chapter.

(9)   P

(10) $P \rightarrow Q$

(11)   Q

The arrow represents the 'material conditional'. While it is often informally described as corresponding to 'if ... then ...', so that (10) would be equivalent to *if P then Q*, there is of course an ongoing debate about the extent to which logical symbols do correspond to natural language expressions.[5] In the propositional calculus, the material conditional is understood as being false whenever the antecedent (in this case P) is true and the consequent (in this case Q) is false. In all other cases (i.e. when P is false or when P and Q are both true), the material conditional is true.

In a context consisting of the proposition P, it follows from $P \rightarrow Q$ that Q. Similarly, in a context consisting of the proposition $P \rightarrow Q$, it follows from P that Q. So (11) is a contextual effect of (10) in the context of (9) and also a contextual effect of (9) in the context of (10). We can say that P is relevant in a context containing $P \rightarrow Q$ since it implies the conclusion Q in that context and that $P \rightarrow Q$ is relevant in a context containing P since it implies the conclusion Q in that context. Looking ahead slightly, and moving away from purely logical thinking, if we know some proposition P then it is likely to be relevant to know that $P \rightarrow Q$ and vice versa. We can also say that the more contextual effects a proposition has in a given context, the more relevant it is. Suppose we assume a context containing the propositions (12) and (13):

(12) $P \rightarrow Q$

(13) $R \rightarrow S$

Which of (14) and (15) would be the most relevant?

(14)   P

(15) $P \& \neg S$

In this context, (15) would be more relevant because it allows us to derive the conclusions in (17) while (14) only allows us to derive the conclusion in (16):

(16)   Q

(17) a.   Q
     b. $\neg R$[6]

So we can say that a new proposition is relevant in a given context if it gives rise to contextual effects and that the more contextual effects it gives rise to the more relevant it is. As this is a purely technical, logical definition, we do not need to consider whether any individual has entertained or will entertain any of these propositions. The relationships between these propositions can be understood in purely logical terms.

As we said, a 'cognitive effect' is a contextual effect within a cognitive system. When an individual person derives conclusions on the basis of new or existing assumptions, these are cognitive effects. In the same way, we can say that a new assumption is relevant to an individual to the extent that it gives rise to cognitive effects and that the more cognitive effects it gives rise to, the more relevant it is for that individual at that time. Suppose, for example, that I am entertaining the assumptions (18) and (19):

(18)   If it's raining, Andy will take the bus home from work today.

(19)   If Andy remembers to buy the cheese, I'll make carbonara.

Given these assumptions, we can say that the assumption in (20) would be relevant:

(20)   It's raining.

We can also say that (21) would be more relevant than (20):

(21)   It's raining and Andy has remembered to buy the cheese.

On the basis of (20) we can conclude (22):

(22)   Andy will take the bus home.

On the basis of (21) we can conclude both (22) and (23):

(23)   I'll make carbonara.

Cognitive effects are not only about new conclusions following from a logical connection between existing and new assumptions. They also include cases where new information strengthens an existing assumption by providing stronger evidence in support of it and cases where new information contradicts and leads to the elimination of one or more existing assumptions. In a fairly early paper (Wilson and Sperber 1986) Wilson and Sperber illustrate ways in which new information can be relevant by discussing an example where an individual thinks they can hear rain outside. First, they consider a situation where the individual, suspecting it is raining, looks out of the window and sees that:

(24)   It IS raining.

This new information confirms and strengthens the individual's existing assumption. Next, they consider a situation where the same individual with the same assumption looks out of the window and sees:

(25)   It's not raining but there are branches from a tree making a noise like rain on the roof.

This new information is relevant because it contradicts and leads to the elimination of the existing assumption. Finally, the individual might have an assumption which can interact with new information to lead to new conclusions. For this purpose, we can imagine that the individual is entertaining assumption (18) about Andy taking the bus if it's raining. In this context, seeing the rain will lead to conclusion (20) that Andy will take the bus home. Wilson and Sperber suggest, then, that there are three kinds of contextual, and hence cognitive, effects which a new proposition can have:

a.   **strengthening** an existing assumption
b.   **contradicting** and leading to the elimination of an existing assumption
c.   **contextual implication**, where new information follows from the combination of new and existing assumptions but would not follow from either alone.

It is not obvious that giving rise to these three kinds of effects should be the only possible ways in which a stimulus can be relevant.

The conclusion at this stage, then, is that we can say that a stimulus or other input to cognitive processes is relevant to an individual to the extent that it gives rise to cognitive effects and that the more cognitive effects it has, the more relevant it is (to that individual at that time).

In more recent work (notably the 1995 postface to the second edition of *Relevance*), Sperber and Wilson refer to 'positive cognitive effects'. This is because it is possible for a stimulus to produce changes in an individual's beliefs which are intuitively not relevant, e.g. if they lead to false conclusions. Note that the question is not whether the initial assumption is false but whether it leads overall to a better (i.e. more accurate) or worse (i.e. less accurate) representation of the world. Sperber and Wilson (1995: 264) discuss the following pair of scenarios:

(26)   Peter is a jealous husband. He overhears Mary say on the phone to someone, 'See you tomorrow at the usual place.' Peter guesses rightly that she is speaking to a man, and infers, quite wrongly, that she has a lover and does not love him any more.

(27)   Peter is a jealous husband. He overhears Mary say on the phone to someone, 'See you tomorrow at the usual place.' Peter guesses wrongly that she is speaking to a man, and infers, rightly as it happens, that she has a lover and does not love him any more. (Mary's lover is a woman.)

In the first case, Peter's initial assumption (that Mary is talking to a man) is true but it leads to conclusions which are false. In the second case, Peter's initial assumption is false but it leads to true conclusions (as well as some false ones). Sperber and Wilson suggest that Peter's initial assumption in (26) was not relevant, even though it seemed to be at first, and that his initial assumption in (27) is relevant although false.

As well as noting that truth and relevance don't always go together in cases like these, Sperber and Wilson point out other cases, such as literary fiction, where we clearly derive relevant effects from strictly false utterances. They suggest that the conclusions we reach based on fiction are relevant even though the work of fiction is not itself true.

For reasons such as these, relevance theory now defines relevance in terms of **positive cognitive effects**, where 'positive cognitive effects' include true conclusions, warranted strengthenings or revisions of existing assumptions, and more generally, any effect 'which contributes positively to the fulfillment of cognitive functions or goals'. With this definition of a 'positive cognitive effect', relevance theory claims that a stimulus or other phenomenon is relevant if it leads to positive cognitive effects and that the more positive cognitive effects it has, the more relevant it is.

Exercise 3.3 explores the connection between relevance and positive cognitive effects.

Exercise 3.3

- In each of the following examples, consider which of the two possible responses by B would give rise to more positive cognitive effects (and make a note of any difficulties you have in judging this):
  (i)   A: What do you do for a living?
          B: a. I teach in a university.
             b. I teach pragmatics at university.

(ii)   A: Do you fancy a muffin?
         B: a. I missed breakfast, actually.
            b. The traffic's terrible today.
(iii)   A: Where do you live?
         B: a. In Finsbury Park.
            b. In Stroud Green, just north of Finsbury Park.
- Consider which response in each case is likely to be the more relevant of the two (and make a note of any difficulties you have in judging this).

Now that we have an initial definition of a 'cognitive effect', the next step is to consider the other factor used in the definition of relevance: effort.

3.4   Defining relevance: effort

As we have just seen, one part of understanding the definition of relevance involves reference to cognitive effects. These come in three main varieties: strengthening existing assumptions, contradicting and leading to the elimination of existing assumptions, and contextual implication (deriving new effects from the interaction of new and existing assumptions). Other things being equal, the more such effects a stimulus has, the more relevant it is. But relevance is not defined only in terms of cognitive effects. Sperber and Wilson point out that, other things being equal, the more mental effort involved in processing a stimulus or phenomenon (which involves accessing contextual assumptions and deriving positive cognitive effects), the less relevant that stimulus or phenomenon is. A number of factors are now known to affect **processing effort**. These include recency of use, frequency of use, perceptual salience, ease of retrieval from memory, linguistic or logical complexity and size of the context.[7]

Returning to our purely logical examples from the previous section, imagine again a logical context containing just the following assumptions:

(28) $P \rightarrow Q$

(29) $R \rightarrow S$

We have already concluded that (31) is more relevant than (30) in this context since more conclusions follow from it:

(30)   P

(31) $P \,\&\, \neg S$

Now compare (31) with (32):

(32) $P \,\&\, \neg S \,\&\, (P \lor \neg P)$

If you are new to logical symbols, this might look complicated. When you work through it, you should see that nothing follows from (32) in this context which does not follow from (31) (since the only difference between them is that (32) also expresses the necessary truth that *P* is or is not true). But (32) will require more processing effort than (31) and so the same effects come at a greater cost in terms of cognitive resources. Given this, Sperber and Wilson argue, (32) is less relevant than (31).

We can see that this reflects intuitions about relevance by considering again the example where an individual hears a noise outside and suspects that it's raining. In the example above, we imagined this individual looking out of the window and seeing that:

(33)   It IS raining.

Now imagine that the same person looks out of the window and sees:

(34)   It IS raining and there are three blackbirds on the roof.

Provided nothing follows from having seen the three blackbirds, then (34) is less relevant in this context than (33) since it requires more effort to process it but the extra effort does not lead to any extra effects.

Finally, we can illustrate this with reference to a spoken utterance. Suppose I ask you whether it is raining and you reply:

(35)   Yes, it is.

This response is relevant since it confirms my initial assumption, which counts as a positive cognitive effect. Now imagine you replied instead:

(36)   Yes it is raining and it rained in Aberdeen on the second of July 1864.

If nothing follows from knowing whether it rained in Aberdeen on 2nd of July 1864, then (36) is less relevant than (35). This follows because (36) requires more processing effort but does not lead to any extra cognitive effects.

With this balance between effects and effort in mind, Sperber and Wilson (1995: 266–67) propose the following classificatory and comparative definitions of relevance (a *classificatory* definition makes it possible to judge whether or not something counts as an example of what is defined, here whether an assumption or other phenomenon is relevant; a *comparative* definition allows us to compare different phenomena, here to compare how relevant assumptions or other phenomena are):

(37)   Relevance to an individual (classificatory definition)
            An assumption is relevant to an individual at a given time if and only if it has some
            positive cognitive effect in one or more of the contexts accessible to him at that time.

(38)   Relevance to an individual (comparative definition)
            Extent condition 1
            An assumption is relevant to an individual to the extent that the positive cognitive effects
            achieved when it is optimally processed are large.[8]

Extent condition 2
An assumption is relevant to an individual to the extent that the effort required to achieve these positive cognitive effects is small.

The comparative definition can also be expressed in this way:

(39)   Relevance of an input to an individual
    a.   Other things being equal, the greater the positive cognitive effects achieved by processing an input, the greater the relevance of the input to the individual at that time.
    b.   Other things being equal, the greater the processing effort expended, the lower the relevance of the input to the individual at that time.

What this amounts to is that the more positive cognitive effects a phenomenon has the more relevant it is and the more effort involved in achieving those effects the less relevant it is. In the next section, we consider what it means to 'maximise' relevance as envisaged in the Cognitive Principle of Relevance. After that, we will consider what it means to 'optimise' relevance as envisaged in the Communicative Principle.

Exercise 3.4 encourages you to explore the relationship between relevance and cognitive effort.

Exercise 3.4

- In each of the following examples, consider which of the two possible responses by B would require more processing effort (and make a note of any difficulties you have in judging this):
    (i)   A: What do you do for a living?
            B: a. I teach in a university.
               b. I'm employed in a teaching role in a university.
    (ii)   A: Do you fancy a muffin?
            B: a. I missed breakfast, actually.
               b. I missed breakfast and the traffic's terrible today.
    (iii)   A: Where do you live?
            B: a. In Finsbury Park.
               b. I live in Finsbury Park.
    (iv)   A: Where do you live?
            B: a. I live in Finsbury Park.
               b. I'm saying I live in Finsbury Park.
- Consider which response in each case is likely to be the more relevant of the two (and make a note of any difficulties you have in judging this).

3.5   Maximising relevance: the Cognitive Principle of Relevance

We have seen that relevance is defined in terms of positive cognitive effects and processing effort. The more effects a stimulus has the more relevant it is. The more processing effort involved in deriving those effects, the less relevant it is. The next step is to see how these ideas are used in the Cognitive Principle of Relevance, which deals with cognition in general, and the Communicative Principle of Relevance, which deals with ostensive-inferential communication in particular. We begin here with cognition in general.

The First, or Cognitive, Principle of Relevance seems fairly simple:

(40)   First, or Cognitive, Principle of Relevance
          Human cognition tends to be geared to the maximisation of relevance.

It simply states that our minds tend to allocate our attention and processing resources in such a way as to yield the greatest possible positive cognitive effects for the smallest possible processing effort. There is an assumption about evolutionary processes underlying this, which is that systems tend to evolve in ways which make them more efficient at carrying out their main goals or functions. If the function of a mind is to represent the world as accurately as possible, then we would expect it to evolve in ways which tend to make this happen fairly efficiently. This might not seem very exciting on its own, and relevance-theoretic research has focused far more on the Communicative than the Cognitive Principle of Relevance, but the Communicative Principle of Relevance, which is the one that explains how we make inferences about communicative intentions, is closely connected to this assumption; to use Sperber and Wilson's terms (1995: 263), the Communicative Principle is 'grounded' in the Cognitive Principle.

The idea is that our perceptual systems are constantly monitoring the environment for stimuli which are relevant to us, that our memories are organised so that they will retrieve relevant background information, and that our inferential systems are set up so as to maximise the cognitive effects we can derive. Processing in this way is seen as something that happens automatically, in ways that are generally outside our control. These 'subpersonal' processes are carried out by heuristics with a certain degree of rigidity, which may occasionally lead us astray.[9] A key thing to notice is that processes happen in this way just because of the way the mind is organised. These are not processes which we carry out intentionally. We pay attention to some things more than others, other humans perhaps being the most obvious object of our perception. If I am walking down the street, my perceptual systems will be on the lookout for stimuli which might be relevant. A sudden loud noise or the sound of a car will attract my attention. If I see other humans on the street, I will pay attention to them and make inferences about what they are doing. If I am with a friend, I will pay attention to her behaviour. If she bends down and starts to do something to her shoelaces, I will assume that she is tying her laces. If she makes eye contact with me, flashes her gaze over her shoulder and then bends down without touching her shoelaces or anything else, I am likely to think that she is trying to communicate with me. In this case, where I recognise an intention to communicate (and to make that intention itself clear) then the Second,

Communicative, Principle of Relevance will apply and my expectations of relevance will be significantly raised. The next section says something more about this.

3.6   Optimising relevance: the Communicative Principle of Relevance

The Second Principle of Relevance says:

(41)   Second, or Communicative, Principle of Relevance
          Every ostensive stimulus conveys a presumption of its own optimal relevance.

And the **presumption of optimal relevance** says:

(42)   Presumption of optimal relevance:
   (a)   The ostensive stimulus is relevant enough for it to be worth the addressee's effort to process it.
   (b)   The ostensive stimulus is the most relevant one compatible with the communicator's abilities and preferences.

As mentioned in Chapter 1, the idea behind the presumption of optimal relevance is that when an individual overtly claims the attention of another individual, she makes clear that she intends to communicate something to that other individual. This means that she expects that individual to use his cognitive resources to infer the intention behind her utterance or act of nonverbal communication. It follows from this that she must think that it will be worth the other individual's while to expend his effort in working out what it is that she intends to communicate. The communicator must think that what she is intending to communicate is worth the effort involved in processing it and that it will be relevant enough to justify paying attention to this stimulus rather than anything else the addressee could be paying attention to at the time. Cognitive resources are precious and we do not want to waste them in paying attention to phenomena which will not reward us with enough cognitive effects. This can be understood intuitively by thinking of situations where one person is clearly paying attention to something and someone else addresses them. If I am watching a TV programme and you speak to me, you must think that what you have to tell me is more worthy of my attention than the TV programme.

The presumption of optimal relevance has been formulated in different ways over the years. The formulation in (42) is the one presented in the 1995 postface to the second edition of *Relevance*. (42a) stipulates the minimal degree of relevance required: it says that there will be at least enough positive cognitive effects to justify the effort involved in interpreting the ostensive stimulus. (42b) says that the communicator is expected to go beyond this minimal degree of relevance – increasing the effects achieved and reducing the effort required – to the extent that this is consistent with her abilities and preferences. (42a) is easier to grasp at first than (42b). We will explore the thinking behind (42b) below. First, here are two more examples which suggest that this is on the right track.

(43)   He's a human being.

If I ask you what your new flatmate is like and you reply as in (43), I will not assume that you are simply communicating that your flatmate is a member of the human race. Why not? Because this is something I would already be assuming and no cognitive effects would follow from it. So I will decide that you must intend to do more than just let me know that you have a human being for a flatmate (rather than an entity of some other kind) and look for another interpretation. A likely candidate is that you are telling me that your flatmate has desirable human qualities, e.g. that they are able to empathise with you and other flatmates, to understand differences of opinion, compromise, and so on. Perhaps your previous flatmate was less forgiving, and so the key thing is a contrast with the previous one. Something along these lines will justify the effort involved in interpreting the utterance where a purely literal interpretation would not. This is an interesting example since we could argue that it is metaphorical even though its literal interpretation is true. This means it would not fit the classical, or the Gricean, account of metaphor which both assume that the speaker says something which is literally false and that this leads to the addressee treating the utterance as metaphorical. This is discussed in more detail in Chapter 9.

The contrast between the two utterances in (44) also illustrates how the presumption of optimal relevance works:

(44) a.   Hi Robbie, how are you?
     b.   Hi Robbie, how are you these days?

What is the difference between (44a) and (44b)? Linguistically, the difference is the presence of the two words *these days*. What effect do these extra words have on the interpretation? In most contexts, the hearer of (44a) would infer that the speaker wants to know how the addressee is around the present time. (44b) makes explicit that the speaker is interested in the hearer's well-being around now. However, the difference between them is not simply that a small part of the interpretation is linguistically encoded in one case and entirely inferred in the other. Rather, most English speakers report an intuition that the speaker of (44b) seems to be more genuinely interested in the hearer's welfare than the speaker of (44a). (44a) is a typical 'phatic' utterance, i.e. one designed more to be sociable than genuinely to request or pass on information.[10] Even someone who is quite ill might reply 'fine thanks' to (44a). Relevance theory predicts that (44b) will not receive the same interpretation because the speaker has put the hearer to more effort than would have been required to process (44a). If this extra effort does not lead to extra effects, then it is not justified and the speaker has put the hearer to unnecessary effort. Therefore, the utterance will not be optimally relevant. Given this, the hearer must look for something beyond the straightforward phatic interpretation which he thinks the speaker is intending to communicate. The most likely interpretation is that the speaker is genuinely interested in the hearer's well-being and even in contrasting how the hearer is 'these days' with how they have been at other times. Of course, the phatic element (the intention to create positive social assumptions) is still present in (44b), but it cannot be the whole story. The reply in (45) would be a much more likely response to (44b) than to (44a):

(45)   Better.

The first part of the presumption of optimal relevance says that the stimulus will be relevant enough for it to be worth the addressee's while to process it, i.e. that it will provide enough effects, at a low enough cost, to justify the effort required to understand it. The second part says that it will be as relevant as the communicator can make it given their abilities and preferences. We can consider what this means in terms of effort separately from what it means in terms of effects.

Taking effects first, this means that having achieved the minimal degree of relevance required by clause (42a), the communicator is expected to convey as many more effects as is compatible with her abilities and preferences. Suppose that more than one formulation of your utterance comes to mind, each of which would comply with the first part of the presumption by giving rise to enough effects to justify the effort involved in processing it. Let's imagine that you tell me you are going to go home and settle down to a bit of reading and I ask you what you are going to read. You might reply with any of the utterances in (46):

(46) a.   An academic article.
     b.   An article about language.
     c.   An article about pragmatics.
     d.   An article about relevance theory.
     e.   An article on explicatures and implicatures.

The most likely reason for choosing one of these over the others has to do with your ability to make an accurate guess about the assumptions I have about language, pragmatics, etc. (46e) would have the most cognitive effects for me, but many people might not know what 'explicatures' or 'implicatures' are.

The second part of the presumption of optimal relevance predicts that someone reading a book on explicatures and implicatures should utter (46e) if talking to me (since I do know what explicatures and implicatures are) unless either their abilities or preferences prevent them. Their abilities might prevent them if they do not know that I know about explicatures and implicatures. Their preferences might prevent them if they don't want me to know exactly what they're reading. A friend once told me about a conversation he had with a car salesperson who asked what he did for a living. The conversation went something like this:

(47)   A: So you're an academic. What's your subject?
         B: Linguistics.

A: Really. What kind of linguistics?

B: To do with meaning.

A: Semantics?

B: Yes, and also about how we understand each other in different contexts.

A: Oh, pragmatics? What kind? Would that be relevance theory? Or Levinson?

The salesperson was a linguistics graduate who had enjoyed working on pragmatics during his course. My friend could not have known that and so could not have known that more detail would have been relevant for this addressee.

The reference to abilities also covers cases where the communicator might not be able to think of a more relevant answer at the time, and this applies to effort as well as to effects. Sometimes, the easiest formulation to process doesn't come to mind at the time of speaking or the speaker just doesn't know about it. The reference to preferences covers any case where a speaker might choose not to say something, which could be for any of a number of reasons, including embarrassment, an intention to deceive, or an unwillingness to share particular information. Here are some relevant examples.

(48)   BEV: A neighbour of mine has said she'll look after the garden for me while I'm away.
        KEN: Is that Cathy?

(49)   BEV: I've got some reading to do for uni.
        KEN: For your Grice essay?

(50)   KEN: Did you enjoy the meal?
        BEV: Yes, thanks. I was really starving.
        KEN: You didn't really like it, did you?
        BEV: No, it was nice. I'm not mad about spicy food, though.

In (48), Bev refers to *a neighbour of mine* rather than giving the person's name because she has forgotten that Ken knows her neighbour Cathy. Saying 'Cathy said she'd look after the garden while I'm away' would be easier to process given that Ken knows her and would give rise to greater effects if Ken knows relevant things about Cathy. Bev has produced a less relevant formulation because she didn't manage to remember that Ken knew Cathy. (49) is similar. Here, Bev has forgotten that Ken knows about the Grice essay and will therefore be able to access assumptions about the essay if Bev mentions it directly. (50) is a case where Bev does not want to produce the most relevant utterance for social reasons. It would be relevant for Ken to know that Bev was not very keen on the meal and that this was because it is spicy. Bev prefers not to say this explicitly, though, because she does not want to offend Ken.

Here is one final comment on the presumption of optimal relevance. The discussion so far has suggested that relevance theory follows Grice in assuming a rational basis for pragmatic principles and processes. While this is a general assumption, at the same time it is not true that relevance theory assumes that we explicitly reason out every step in interpreting other people's utterances or communicative acts. This is not just because we tend to develop 'shortcuts' for specific processes but also because recent work (e.g. Sperber and Wilson 2002) suggests that we might have developed particular cognitive procedures which are specialised for interpreting communicative acts. Part of the evidence for this comes from the abilities of young children to understand other people while their cognitive and reasoning abilities are relatively underdeveloped. We will consider this issue again in Chapter 12. For now, though, note that there is no claim about exactly how we work through the steps in understanding each other and no claim that the underlying rational basis of the presumption of optimal relevance is reflected in actual reasoning in real time.

Exercise 3.5 encourages you to explore the presumption of optimal relevance in more detail.

Exercise 3.5

- Consider how A will interpret B's utterance in the following exchanges. How will A go about finding an interpretation? What makes the interpretation they have arrived at consistent with the presumption of optimal relevance:
  - (i)   A: How were things at work today?
          B: Busy enough.
  - (ii)   A: I've boiled the kettle.
          B: Great! Do you fancy a cup?
  - (iii)   A: Have you seen the paper?
          B: John was reading it earlier.
  - (iv)   A: Do you want me to nip out for more milk?
          B: The shops are a distance from here.

3.7   Ostensive-inferential communication

We have now defined relevance, seen what generalisation about cognition is expressed in the Cognitive Principle of Relevance, seen what generalisation about communication is expressed in the Communicative Principle of Relevance, and looked at the presumption of optimal relevance generated by acts of ostensive-inferential communication. The next step is to consider what kinds of things give rise to the presumption of optimal relevance. This means defining what we mean by **ostensive-inferential communication**, the phenomenon which gives rise to the presumption. The origin of this notion also lies in the work of Grice.

As we saw in Chapter 2, Grice's theory of conversation grew out of a long-term interest in language and meaning, and was preceded by his very influential work on meaning, discussed in his paper on 'Meaning', eventually published in 1957. As we saw, Grice argued that it is crucial for meaning$_{NN}$ not only that the communicator intends to produce an effect but also both that the audience should recognise that intention and that the recognition of the intention plays a role in achieving the effect. For Grice:

'A meant$_{NN}$ something by x' is (roughly) equivalent to 'A intended the utterance of x to produce some effects in an audience by means of the recognition of this intention.'   (Grice 1989: 220)

Strawson (1964) reformulated Grice's analysis to separate out the three sub-intentions Grice envisaged:

(51)   To mean something by *x*, *S* must intend:
    (a)   *S*'s utterance of *x* to produce a certain response *r* in a certain audience *A*
    (b)   *A* to recognise *S*'s intention (a)
    (c)   *A*'s recognition of *S*'s intention (a) to function as at least part of *A*'s reason
           for *A*'s response *r*   (based on Strawson 1964 [1971])

Sperber and Wilson share the view of other theorists that there is a significant insight here. They review a number of issues which have been discussed with this and come up with their own proposal (Sperber and Wilson 1986: 21–4).

There are several ways in which Sperber and Wilson's approach differs from Grice's. First, the phenomenon they aim to characterise as covered by the Communicative Principle of Relevance is 'ostensive-inferential communication' rather than 'meaning$_{NN}$'. The change from 'meaning' to 'communication' is not trivial. Grice's discussion of 'meaning$_{NN}$', of course, was designed to address issues raised by the fact that 'meaning' has more than one meaning. The focus, then, is on ways in which meanings can be conveyed. One action can simultaneously convey natural and non-natural meanings. Sperber and Wilson's focus is on acts of communication. These can, of course, also convey both what Grice called 'natural meaning' and 'meaning$_{NN}$'. The key thing for relevance theory, though, is a particular way of interpreting behaviour. What kicks off this kind of interpretation, for Sperber and Wilson, is the recognition that another piece of behaviour is ostensively communicative, i.e. that it make clear an intention to communicate.

Sperber and Wilson's notion of 'ostensive-inferential communication' refers to two kinds of behaviour: ostension by the communicator and inference by the addressee. Once the addressee has recognised that a particular act is an ostensive one, then the presumption of optimal relevance guides the addressee in interpreting that act. Second, they define it in terms of two intentions: an 'informative intention' (to make manifest a set of assumptions) and a 'communicative intention' to make the informative intention manifest. Third, they define a notion of manifestness, which is then used in defining three further notions: mutual manifestness, cognitive environment and mutual cognitive environment. This section explains all of these terms. There is rather a lot of terminology here. First, here is a relatively informal statement of what is involved in *ostensive-inferential communication*:

(52)   Ostensive-inferential communication
    (a)   The informative intention
           The intention to inform an audience of something.

(b)   The communicative intention
       The intention to inform the audience of one's informative intention.

Perhaps the first thing to strike you will be that this is similar to Grice's notion of 'meaning$_{NN}$' in that it involves two intentions, one of which is to inform the audience about the other. Here are fuller statements of each of the **informative and communicative intentions**:

(53)   Informative intention
        An intention to make manifest or more manifest to the audience a set of assumptions I.

(54)   Communicative intention
        An intention to make it mutually manifest to audience and communicator that the communicator has this informative intention.

And here is a fuller statement of the definition of ostensive-inferential communicaton:

(55)   Ostensive-inferential communication
        The communicator produces a stimulus which makes it mutually manifest to communicator and audience that the communicator intends, by means of this stimulus, to make manifest or more manifest to the audience a set of assumptions I.

This is quite tricky for anyone who has not come across discussion of this before. The account shares some properties of Grice's approach, including the notion that it is about intentions and the notion that the stimulus makes clear that it is by means of this stimulus itself that the communicator intends to achieve these effects. To understand the definitions, we need to understand each of the notions they involve. We'll begin with the notion of 'manifestness'.

The notion of **manifestness** is weaker than the notion of 'knowledge'. It is notoriously difficult to decide exactly what is involved in 'knowing' something. It is also not clear that we need the notion of knowledge in order to explain communication. If I tell you that there will be a strike on the London Underground system tomorrow, do you now 'know' that there will be one? Technically no, because it is always possible that the strike will not take place. It seems more reasonable to say that you have evidence to support the suggestion that there will be a strike (fairly good evidence if you decide that you can trust me). Many of the assumptions we hold are held tentatively to varying degrees. Here are some things I believe:

(56)   My mother and my father were both born in Scotland.

(57)   I have lived in London since 1985.

(58)   I am not afraid of spiders.

(59)   I enjoy good company.

(60)   I don't like period dramas.

Do you believe them? Probably you take (56) and (57) on trust. You might wonder whether I am really not afraid of spiders, whether I might be saying this to appear brave, or even whether there might be some self-deception here. (59) requires you to decide what '*good company*' means and again you might question the accuracy of my statement. (60) depends partly on exactly what I mean by '*period dramas*'. What is clear, though, is that if I say these utterances then I might succeed in communicating the propositions they express and you might end up accepting them. The notion of manifestness helps us to capture this since an assumption can be manifest to someone without actually being entertained or believed. Here is the definition Sperber and Wilson propose:

(61)   Manifestness
        An assumption is manifest to an individual at a given time if and only if he
        is capable at that time of representing it mentally and accepting its
        representation as true or probably true.[11]   (Sperber and Wilson 1986: 39)

Something is manifest if it is possible for an individual to perceive it or infer it. Sperber and Wilson make an analogy with the notion of visibility. What is visible to you at a given time includes things you are not actually aware of but which are in the visual environment so that you will see them if you look for them. On the analogy with the notion of a visual environment, Sperber and Wilson also define a **cognitive environment** as follows (again I've changed 'facts' to 'assumptions'):

(62)   Cognitive environment
        The cognitive environment of an individual is a set of assumptions that are
        manifest to him.

As manifestness is a weaker notion than knowledge, more things can be manifest than are 'known' (just as more things are visible than are actually seen). An assumption can be manifest to an individual without actually being entertained. Also, notice that 'manifestness' is a matter of degree. We can think of assumptions as more or less manifest. If you think it's probably raining because of the sounds you are hearing, then this assumption is manifest to you. If you see the rain, it is more manifest (because better evidenced). And so on.

   Your cognitive environment at any moment consists of all the assumptions which are manifest to you, whether you are actually entertaining them or not. Here are three assumptions which I believe are manifest to you at the moment:

(63)   You are reading a book.

(64)   Billy has lived in London for over twenty years.

(65)   Queen Victoria never saw a living mammoth.

Were you entertaining any of them before you read them here? If not, then they are definitely more manifest to you now. Other things in your cognitive environment which you might not be mentally representing include things that are visible or audible but which you might not be paying attention to (I can't make guesses about those). Notice that, since the assumptions which are manifest to you include ones which you have never entertained, the contents of your cognitive environment are not all actually mentally represented at the time at which they are manifest.

We can understand communication as being about adjusting the manifestness of each other's assumptions. By talking to you or nonverbally communicating with you, I make assumptions manifest or more manifest to you. To put it another way, I adjust your cognitive environment.

The notion of manifestness also plays a role in the relevance-theoretic account of context. The set of assumptions which are typically used as context-ual assumptions are the ones which are manifest or can become manifest to you at the time of utterance. Even if you don't know that I am Scottish I can make this manifest to you, and expect you to use this as a contextual assumption, by answering a question like (66) as in (67):

(66)   Do you like country and western music?

(67)   Most Scottish people do.

Here, my utterance makes manifest (or more manifest) that I am Scottish and I can expect you to use this assumption in understanding my utterance even if you did not know it before.

The definition of ostensive-inferential communication refers to the notion of **mutual manifestness**. At first, you might assume that something which is manifest to each of us is mutually manifest. However, this is not enough. What is required is not just that each of us is capable of entertaining some-thing and accepting it as true, or probably true. This would include cases where two people are aware of something but neither knows that the other is aware of it, e.g. we might both know that our friend Jess is afraid of spiders but each think that we are the only one Jess has told about this. It is not even enough for it to be manifest to each of us that it is manifest to the other. This would include cases where you and I both know something and each knows that the other knows it, but we do not know that we share more knowledge than this about each other's beliefs. Without going through all of the logical possibilities, the key thing to stress is that the overtness, or transparency, of ostensive-inferential communication depends on the intention to inform being genuinely mutually manifest, which involves a kind of 'infinite regress' such that:

(68)   It is manifest to A that it is manifest to B that X
         It is manifest to B that it is manifest to A that X
         It is manifest to B that it is manifest to A that it is manifest to B that X
         It is manifest to A that it is manifest to B that it is manifest to A that X
         and so on...

Before discussing examples which fall short of this, it is worth emphasising that the notion of mutual manifestness includes a notion of infinite regress but that this avoids well-known problems posed by this for approaches which assume mutual knowledge. For mutual *knowledge*, it is necessary to go through infinitely regressing stages in order to establish mutual knowledge (mutual knowledge requires A to know that B knows that A knows … and so on). For mutual *manifestness*, this is not necessary. If something is mutually manifest, it would be possible to go through stages of checking whether it is manifest to A that it is manifest to B that … etc. But this is not required. It is manifest to A that it is manifest to B (…and so on) even if no-one actually checks through the various stages. One way in which something can be instantly mutually manifest to two people is if some information becomes manifest to them at the same time and they can see each other becoming aware of it. Suppose, for example, that we are watching television together. Anything said or shown by the television programme is mutually manifest. Another way to make something mutually manifest would be for one of us manifestly to inform the other of it.

So what role does the notion of mutual manifestness play in explaining ostensive-inferential communication? First, it plays a role in the definition of a **mutually cognitive environment**, which is the set of assumptions which are mutually manifest to two or more individuals. We can describe the effects of communication between two or more individuals as adjustments to their mutually cognitive environments. Second, it plays a key role in the definition of ostensive-inferential communication, which involves two intentions: an informative intention to make manifest or more manifest a set of assumptions and a communicative intention to make the informative intention mutually manifest.

Taking the communicative intention first, how can a communicator make an intention to inform mutually manifest? The best way is to do something which has no other explanation than that the communicator is ostensively communicating. By far the most effective way of doing this is to produce a written or spoken utterance in a language the addressee knows. If I turn to a stranger near a busy pub counter and say:

(69)   It's impossible to get served in here, isn't it?

it is automatically mutually manifest that I am intending to communicate with him. Why else would I go to the trouble of producing a well-formed sequence of English sounds? The other person can now get to work on making inferences about the content of my informative intention, working out what exactly I am trying to communicate (in this case, there will be a significant social element, expressing shared frustration, implying togetherness in adversity, and so on).

Similarly, any piece of writing makes mutually manifest that the communicator has an intention to inform. A sign written in chalk on a board outside a pub following a serious fire in Camden Town, London, in February 2008 said:

(70)   We're not on fire! Come and have a pint.

On a board on the other side of the door, another sign read:

(71)   Free beer for police and fire brigade.

The person who wrote these intended to inform passers-by in a mildly humorous way that the pub was open as usual and to express gratitude to the police and fire services by announcing free beer (which they might or might not be able to accept). It is clear that anyone seeing these signs will (be able to) entertain the assumption that they were written in order to inform passers-by of these things.

Nonverbal communication can also make clear that it is intended to inform. As the barperson ignores me and the person next to me for the umpteenth time, I might turn towards him, make eye contact, raise my eyebrows, shrug my shoulders, shake my head and smile wryly. Again, it is hard to see what else the other person can think besides that I intend to communicate something. In this case, I assume he will think that I am again expressing togetherness, friendliness and resigned acceptance of the fact that there is very little we can do about the situation. In most cases of nonverbal communication, what is communicated is less precise than what can be communicated verbally. One of the special things about human language is that it allows us to formulate utterances which communicate very precise assumptions. It is also more likely for nonverbal communication to be relatively vague, in some cases misunderstood, and even for the intention to communicate not to be noticed. For some reason, I have a good reputation for attracting the attention of bar staff and being served, even in very busy pubs. For some equally unclear reason, I am much less skilful at attracting the attention of staff in restaurants. In many cases, my communicative intention is manifest to me and others at the table but not to the staff whose attention I am trying to attract.

When the communicator succeeds in making her intention to inform the audience of something mutually manifest, the presumption of optimal relevance is also made mutually manifest and the addressee will work on recovering the intended interpretation. In cases where the intentions of the communicator are not clear, the addressee will put in a little more effort in the belief that there must be an interpretation which would justify it. If you are looking behind a bar to see whether they stock a particular brand of whisky, you might give up looking after you've tried and failed to spot it for a few seconds. If you've just asked me whether the bar stocks it and I point behind the bar, you will give up less quickly because my behaviour suggests that it is there (of course, you might also just decide that the whisky is there, even if you still can't actually see a bottle of the whisky for yourself).

What happens when full ostensive-inferential communication is not achieved? There are a number of possibilities. One is that no communication takes place at all. If I pass a stranger on the street and we avoid eye contact, any inferences I make about them (e.g. 'he's in a hurry', 'I like his shoes', etc.) are not communicated. I have inferred them based only on the Cognitive Principle of Relevance, deriving as many positive cognitive effects as I can for as little effort as possible.

In some cases, there is intentional information transmission but not ostensive-inferential communication. There are several good examples in the book *Relevance* (Sperber and Wilson 1986: 38–64) but here is one of my own. Imagine I am very pleased with myself because I have managed to complete a particularly fiendish cryptic crossword in record time. I might decide to leave the page with the completed crossword on the kitchen table in the hope that my wife will notice I've done it and be impressed. If I succeed, then I have intentionally conveyed some information to her (I have caused her to think that I completed the crossword quickly), but this is not ostensive communication since she has not recognised my intention to inform her of this. We might call this covert information transmission. There is an informative intention but no communicative intention. One reason I might do this is because I want her to think positively and maybe even explicitly praise me, but I don't want to imply that I was proud or looking for the praise.

Suppose I do the same thing but that this time she decides that I have left the crossword out deliberately in the hope that she notices it. In other words, she has recognised my informative intention. However, I still did not intend her to recognise it, or to make it mutually manifest to both of us that I had this intention. It is only when it becomes mutually manifest to both of us that ostensive-inferential communication has occurred. If I walk into the kitchen holding the paper open at the page with the completed crossword, then I will be ostensively communicating, i.e. making mutually manifest my intention to inform her of something.[12]

There are important, and quite subtle, social implications which follow from all of this. When an informative intention becomes mutually manifest, it in turn makes mutually manifest a range of implicatures which would not exist without the act of ostensive communication. 'Communicating' covertly can be a way of avoiding the creation of social obligations and relationships which we want to avoid. These examples are very interesting and relevance theory has interesting things to say about them, but they do not count as examples of ostensive-inferential communication and so do not give rise to the presumption of optimal relevance or trigger the relevance-guided comprehension heuristic. In the next chapter, we will consider how the presumption of optimal relevance and the relevance-guided comprehension heuristic can help explain the interpretation of utterances and nonverbal communicative acts.

3.8   A comprehension heuristic

As we saw in Chapter 1, the **relevance-guided comprehension heuristic** looks like this:

(72)   Relevance-guided comprehension heuristic
   (a)   Follow a path of least effort in deriving cognitive effects: test interpretations (e.g. disambiguations, reference resolutions, implicatures, etc.) in order of accessibility.
   (b)   Stop when your expectations of relevance are satisfied.

This is not really a new piece of machinery within the relevance-theoretic framework. Rather, it is a formal statement of what was already implicit in the theory, namely that interpreters proceed by looking for the intended interpretation in the least effortful way and stop when they arrive at an interpretation which gives rise to enough effects to justify the effort involved in arriving at it. As mentioned above, following the heuristic is a sub-personal process which happens automatically rather than a conscious, explicit process. Wilson and Sperber (2004: 613–14) point out that this procedure follows from the presumption of optimal relevance:

> Given clause (b) [of the presumption of optimal relevance], it is reasonable for the hearer to follow a path of least effort because the speaker is expected (within the limits of her abilities and preferences) to make her utterance as easy as possible to understand. Since relevance varies inversely with effort, the very fact that an interpretation is easily accessible gives it an initial degree of plausibility (an advantage specific to ostensive communication). It is also reasonable for the hearer to stop at the first interpretation that satisfies his expectations of relevance, because there should never be more than one. A speaker who wants her utterance to be as easy as possible to understand should formulate it (within the limits of her abilities and preferences) so that the first interpretation to satisfy the hearer's expectation of relevance is the one she intended to convey. An utterance with two apparently satisfactory competing interpretations would cause the hearer the unnecessary extra effort of choosing between them, and the resulting interpretation (if there were one) would not satisfy clause (b).   (Wilson and Sperber 2004: 613–14)

We can illustrate how the procedure works by looking again at three examples:

(73)   George has a big cat.

(74) a.   How are you?
      b.   How are you these days?

As discussed in Chapter 1, a hearer of (73) in a typical present-day situation in London will decide that the speaker is saying that George owns a domestic cat that is big for a domestic cat rather than that he owns a creature such as a tiger or a leopard. If he follows the procedure above, the everyday sense of *cat* is more accessible and so will be arrived at before he thinks of tigers or leopards. Since this is enough to satisfy his expectations of relevance (this is 'relevant enough' if processed in this way), he will now stop searching and assume that the speaker is referring to a large domestic cat.

    As discussed above, one contrast between (74a) and (74b) is that most hearers will assume that the speaker of (74a) is being polite and need not be particularly interested in the hearer's specific health or welfare. This will be arrived at quickly and meets his expectations of relevance. The procedure says, therefore, that he should stop at this point and decide that this is what the speaker had in mind. The extra words in (74b) mean that the hearer cannot stop as soon as he has decided that the speaker is making a polite remark and is not much interested in his health. The extra two words give rise to expectations of increased relevance and so the hearer will go further. In this case, he is likely to assume that the speaker has a greater interest in the details of his well-being around this specific time.

There is one more aspect of the relevance-theoretic account of comprehension which we have not yet discussed: the notion that understanding utterances (and other communicative acts) involves a process of 'mutual parallel adjustment'. This means that the various processes involved in understanding (working out explicit content, accessing contextual assumptions, working out implicit content) happen in parallel and are subject to constant adjustment. This will be discussed more fully in Chapter 4.

3.9   Summary

This chapter has considered the definition of relevance, the different expectations of relevance associated with cognition in general and with ostensive-inferential communication in particular, and the definition of ostensive-inferential communication. We looked at the definition of relevance in terms of positive cognitive effects and processing effort. We looked at the generalisation about cognition represented in the First, or Cognitive, Principle of Relevance. The claim is that in general our cognitive system is geared to maximising relevance, deriving as many effects as possible for as little effort as possible. We then looked at the Second, or Communicative, Principle of Relevance, which claims that acts of ostensive communication give rise to a presumption of optimal relevance. We looked at the difference between maximising and optimising relevance. To maximise relevance is to look for as many effects as possible for as little effort as possible. To optimise relevance is to look for enough effects to justify the processing effort involved in deriving them and to assume that the communicator is being as relevant as possible given their abilities and preferences. We looked at a range of kinds of communication, including those which were not fully ostensive. Now that we know what gives rise to the presumption of optimal relevance, we're ready to go on in the next chapter to use this in explaining particular inferences we make in understanding each other, i.e. to explain how we understand acts of ostensive communication.

Exercise 3.6

As in every chapter, this final exercise asks you to adjust the list of questions you have come up with so far by compiling new questions which have occurred to you while reading this chapter and to think about the kinds of things which might count as answers to any questions you have come up with so far. First, add new questions to your ongoing list. Second, consider all of your questions and think about possible ways of answering them.

3.10   Further reading

For this chapter, the main reading is definitely the book *Relevance*. The more up-to-date version which this book assumes is presented in the 'postface' to the second edition (Sperber and Wilson 1995: 255–79). Earlier discussion of the definition of relevance and its role in communication is in section 3 of the second (1995) edition, pp. 118–71. See also the sources suggested for Chapter 1.

4 Explaining inferences

Topics: pragmatic processes; varieties of inference; explaining inferences

4.1 Overview

We have now looked at how relevance theory developed from a critique of Grice's theory of conversation, at how relevance is defined within the theory, and at the two Principles of Relevance which make predictions about our expectations of relevance in cognition in general and in communication in particular. We can now see how relevance theory explains the inferential processes involved in understanding specific acts of verbal and nonverbal communication. This chapter begins with a reminder of what kinds of pragmatic processes we expect a pragmatic theory to explain. It then considers the nature of inferential processes in general and the kinds of inferences made by humans in thinking and communicating. The first kind of inference discussed is deductive inference. This is the kind of inference captured in formal logical languages. A key feature of deductive inference is that the conclusions generated by a deductive process are guaranteed to be true as long as the initial premises are true. The next section looks at some kinds of non-deductive, or non-demonstrative, inference (the terms 'deductive' and 'demonstrative' are not technically equivalent, but most authors treat these terms and their negative counterparts as synonymous and I will follow that here since nothing important follows from this). Non-demonstrative inferences are generally, but not totally, reliable in that on some occasions when the premises are true, the conclusions will turn out to be false. After looking at a few examples of each kind of inference, the next section considers the kinds of inferences humans tend to make. It is clear that our conclusions tend not to be 100 per cent guaranteed and that this is not simply because we can never be sure of our initial premises. After looking at some more general examples, we consider the kinds of inferences which are made in understanding communication. It seems that some of the inferences we make can be understood as deductive, but not all. The challenge for pragmatics is to see whether we can explain all of the kinds of inferences we make, including those that can occasionally lead us from true premises to false conclusions. Fodor (1983) has argued that this is not possible, and relevance theory can be seen as an attempt to counter Fodor's pessimism. The final section of this chapter shows how relevance theory proposes to explain the inferences we make when understanding ostensive-inferential communication. Sperber and Wilson (1986: 69) suggest that the processes involved in understanding each other can be seen as a kind of 'suitably constrained guesswork', i.e. as a kind of evidence-based inference. This section looks at the kinds of constraints which relevance theory proposes and how these account for examples of linguistic and non-linguistic communication. The key notion here is that addressees follow the relevance-guided comprehension heuristic. We look here at how it aims to explain the interpretation of a range of verbal and nonverbal communicative acts, and at the idea that this involves 'mutual parallel adjustment', i.e. that sub-tasks of the comprehension process are carried out in parallel and constantly adjusted in order to satisfy expectations of relevance. When you have finished this chapter, you should know enough about relevance theory to be able to apply it yourself in explaining specific examples and to understand relatively sophisticated current debates about relevance theory and other approaches to pragmatics. Some of these debates are discussed more fully in Part II.

4.2   Pragmatic processes: what we need to explain

In Chapter 1, we looked at a number of things which pragmatic theories aim to explain. These included contributions to 'direct' meaning, such as disambiguation, reference assignment, recovery of elliptical material, more general enrichment processes, and the recovery of indirectly communicated implications, i.e. implicatures. What unites these processes is that they are inferences we need to make in order to form a hypothesis about what someone intended by an ostensively communicative act. In the case of verbal communication, the starting point for this is the small hint given by the encoded meanings of linguistic expressions. We can communicate nonverbally without using a linguistic stimulus at all, as in Bev's response in (1), or we can produce a linguistic stimulus which provides more or less of a guide as in (2)–(4):

(1)   KEN: Do you fancy going for a stroll around Camden this afternoon?
        BEV: *(spreads arms, raises eyebrows, mimes surprise and disdain)*

(2)   KEN: Do you fancy going for a stroll around Camden this afternoon?
        BEV: On a Saturday?

(3)   KEN: Do you fancy going for a stroll around Camden this afternoon?
        BEV: I never go there when it's busy.

(4)   KEN: Do you fancy going for a stroll around Camden this afternoon?
        BEV: It's really busy on a Saturday and I never go there when it's busy.

While each of the responses in (2)–(4) gives Ken more of a clue than the preceding one, all of them involve an inferential process which is non-demonstrative, i.e. one whose conclusions are evidenced but not totally guaranteed. In (1), Ken has to find an explanation for Bev's nonverbal behaviour. In (2), he needs to work out why she is uttering this preposition phrase with intonational structure consistent with asking a question or being surprised. In (3), he needs to work out how the information that Bev never goes there when it's busy is relevant. In (4), Bev's utterance provides the most help. In fact, Ken can perform a deductive inference based on the two propositions Bev has communicated, i.e. he can infer from this that Bev never goes to Camden on a Saturday. Notice, though, that he needed to make some inferences in order to recover these propositions in the first place and that he still has to work out why it is relevant to have inferred that Bev never goes to Camden on a Saturday.

We expect a successful pragmatic theory to explain how we make inferences based on nonverbal stimuli, how we enrich linguistic content to derive full, directly communicated propositions, and how we go beyond these and infer indirectly communicated propositions. One idea I will develop below is that deductive inferences play a role in this overall process (e.g. inferring that Bev does not go to Camden on a Saturday from the two propositions expressed by her answer in (4) but that these are embedded within a larger and ultimately non-demonstrative process).

4.3   Varieties of inference

As we saw in Chapter 2, one of Grice's main motivations in developing his theory of conversation was to demonstrate that natural languages are not as different from logical languages as some philosophers had previously thought. He aimed to show that natural languages, or at least the meanings of certain linguistic expressions, are similar to those of expressions in logical languages. He suggested that many of the observed divergences between natural and logical languages could be explained as implicatures derived on the basis of underlyingly logical and unambiguous natural language expressions. One of Grice's aims, shared to some extent by post-Gricean pragmaticists, is to consider to what extent the reasoning processes we go through in understanding each other correspond to the kinds of logical processes we find in traditional formal logic. This section explores varieties of inference and considers to what extent they might be involved in human cognition and communication. We begin by considering deductive inference in more detail than we have done so far and then consider some kinds of non-deductive, or non-demonstrative, inferential processes. After that, we will consider to what extent human inferential processes can be seen as deductive and to what extent not.

4.3.1   Deductive inference

So what is **deductive inference?** As mentioned above, one thing which made the ancient philosophers interested in logic was as a way of checking the validity of arguments. If I develop a complex argument, you might debate it by arguing with my initial premises or you might debate it by arguing with the logical steps I have gone through. A clever rhetorician might be able to persuade you to agree with a faulty conclusion even though she began with premises you would agree with. If so, there must be some faulty or misleading steps in the reasoning from her premises to her conclusion. An idea behind classical logic, then, was to make sure that from true premises only true conclusions would follow. This was done by defining a series of valid inferential steps. If an argument only went through valid inferential stages then it was valid overall. The only way a valid argument could lead to false conclusions would be if one or more of the initial premises was false.

A number of logical languages have now been developed, some of them fairly complicated. For our purposes, though, we only need to look at the simplest logical language: the propositional calculus. As we saw in Chapter 2, expressions in propositional calculus consist only of one or more 'propositional variables', one or more propositional operators and, possibly, some brackets to make sure the structure of a particular expression is not ambiguous. Propositional variables are represented by capital letters:

(5)   Propositional variables
         P, Q, R, ...

Operators express relationships between propositions. For now, I won't say anything about what each of these actually mean so that you can think of the structure of expressions before considering meaning. Here are four examples:

(6)   Operators
         &, ¬, v, → ...

As well as these expressions, there are syntactic rules (as for natural languages) which determine what will count as a 'well-formed formula' in the language. Without going into too much detail, here are some well-formed expressions in propositional calculus:

(7)   P & Q

(8)   P & ¬ Q

(9)   P → Q

(10)   P v Q

(11)   P & (P → Q)

And, just to show you that they can be quite long, here's a complicated one:

(12)   (P & (Q → R)) → ((S & R) v (¬ Q → S))

And here are some impossible, because ill-formed, expressions (I'm using the asterisk as in linguistics more generally to indicate 'ungrammaticality'):

(13)   *P Q R

(14)   *P → & R

(15)   *(P v (S

(13) does not work because it simply lists three propositional variables without indicating how they are related. (14) does not work because there is no way of understanding the relationship between the adjacent operators '→' and '&'. (15) does not work because there are two opening brackets which are not followed by closing brackets to indicate the scope of an operator.

Propositional variables are understood as fillers which could represent any proposition. We are interested in finding out such things as that a proposition P would be guaranteed to be true if the conjunction of that proposition P with any other proposition Q (i.e. P & Q) were also true. It does not matter which particular proposition P might represent. There is very little to say about the meanings of these propositional variables (other logical languages, such as predicate calculus, do look at the internal logic of propositions but propositional calculus is only interested in the relationships between propositions). It can be tricky to connect expressions in logical languages with expressions in natural languages, partly because pragmatic processes interfere with 'pure' logical understanding. At the same time, it can help you to understand how they work if you do imagine specific propositions. If you are tempted to think of P, Q and the other variables as representing specific propositions, it is a good idea to keep those propositions as simple and abstract as possible, e.g. think of propositions such as 'the triangle is blue' rather than propositions which you are more likely to entertain in everyday situations and conversations.

The meanings of the logical operators are expressed in terms of 'truth tables' which represent the relationship between the truth or falsity of propositions embedded in a formula and the truth or falsity of propositions expressed by the operators. In this language, meaning is equated with truth or falsity. One of the most influential approaches to linguistic meaning, truth-conditional semantics, develops this idea and proposes to state the meanings of expressions in terms of their **truth conditions**. One way of understanding the thinking behind this is to say that to know the meaning of a proposition is to know what the world would have to be like for it to be true. For now, though, all we need to think about is the relationship between the truth or falsity of propositions and the truth or falsity of more complex expressions which contain them. We'll look now at truth tables for the four operators we have mentioned here. First, here is the truth table for '¬':

(16)   *Truth table for '¬'*

¬	P
F	T
T	F

T and *F* here stand for 'true' and 'false' respectively. The first line says that ¬ *P* is false when *P* is true. The second line says that ¬ *P* is true when *P* is false. While it is risky to think of operators as similar to natural language expressions for the same reasons as it is risky to think of propositional variables as related to actual propositions, you can probably see that the English word most similar to ¬ is *not* and a logician referring to the proposition ¬ *P* in speech would usually say not P. This truth table indicates that when a proposition is true, the negation of that proposition is false and vice versa.

Here is the truth table for '&' (represented in some logical systems as '∧'):

(17)   *Truth table for '&'*

P	&	Q
T	T	T
T	F	F
F	F	T
F	F	F

The first line here says that *P & Q* (i.e. the conjunction of *P* and *Q*, which we can refer to loosely as *P* and *Q*) is true when both *P* and *Q* are true. The other three lines tell us that the conjunction is false whenever at least one of the conjuncts (either *P* or *Q*) is false.

Here is the truth table for '*v*':

(18)   *Truth table for 'v'*

P	*v*	Q
T	T	T
T	T	F
F	T	T
F	F	F

We can think of '*v*' as loosely corresponding to natural language *or*. There is a slight complication, though, when we decide which logical connective is the counterpart of natural language *or* (and similar issues arise for some of the other logical symbols). It is usually assumed that there are two possible terms in logic which could correspond to natural language *or*. One is an 'inclusive' sense where the disjunction of *P or Q* is true as long as at least one of the disjuncts is true.

The other is an 'exclusive' sense where *P or Q* is true if exactly one of the disjuncts is true but false if both are true. This table corresponds to the 'inclusive' sense so the whole disjunction is true given the truth values of *P* and *Q* expressed in each of the first three lines of the table, i.e. as long as at least one of the disjuncts is true then the whole disjunction is true. (On the 'exclusive' sense, the whole disjunct is true so long as one and no more than one of the disjuncts is true.)

Here is the truth table for '→':

(19)   *Truth table for '→'*

P	→	Q
T	T	T
T	F	F
F	T	T
F	T	F

This is the least intuitive of the logical connectives discussed here and students new to logic often find the values in this truth table a bit surprising. In short, the truth table says that $P \rightarrow Q$ is true in every situation except where *P* is true and *Q* is false. This means that $P \rightarrow Q$ expresses a relationship such that the truth of *P* guarantees the truth of *Q*. The intuition we all have which can make the truth table seem questionable is that *if P then Q* (in natural language) suggests some kind of connection between *P* and *Q* such that *P* causes (or, in some cases, provides evidence for) *Q*. However, the logical understanding does not require any such connection. All it requires is that there are no cases where *P* is true and *Q* is false. If we assume *P* and *Q* are any pair of true propositions, say that 'circles are round' and that 'whales are mammals' then a conditional linking these two propositions ('if circles are round then whales are mammals') is true but this might seem like an odd thing to say since we don't know of any connection between these two (unless it is something very general such as that both assume the laws of nature are being followed). Lines 3 and 4 of the truth table can seem even stranger. As long as we assume that *P* is a false proposition, say 'humans are not human', then anything at all, true or false, can come after the conditional connective → and the whole conditional will be true. This means that propositions such as 'if humans are not human then the earth is orbiting the sun' and 'if humans are not human then the earth is not orbiting the sun' are equally true. To grasp this, we need to think of the claim as being about what follows when *P* is true and to say nothing about cases where *P* is false. If there is no claim about the truth of the consequent when *P* is false, then it follows that $P \rightarrow Q$ is consistent with the facts in all cases except where *P* is true and *Q* is false.

The final component of propositional calculus to mention here is a crucial one: the set of inference rules which determine whether or not a particular inference is valid. These are involved in assessing whether particular conclusions do follow from particular sets of premises. There are a significant number of these. Here, with apologies for the classical terminology, we will look at '&-introduction' (pronounced as 'and-introduction'), '&-elimination' (pronounced 'and-elimination'), 'modus ponendo ponens' (also known as 'affirming the antecedent', and often just as 'modus ponens') and 'modus tollendo tollens' (also known as 'denying the consequent', and often just 'modus tollens'). Remember that the aim in each case is make sure that only true conclusions follow from true premises.

(20)   &-elimination
          Premises:
          P & Q
          Conclusions:
          P
          Q

This rule states that if a conjoined proposition *P* & *Q* is true then we can conclude that the proposition *P* is true and that the proposition *Q* is true. There is no possible situation in which *P* & *Q* is true while *P* is false or where *P* & *Q* is true while *Q* is false.

(21)   &-introduction
          Premises:
          P
          Q
          Conclusion:
          P & Q

This rule states that if a proposition *P* is true and a proposition *Q* is true, then we can conclude (as a valid inference) that the conjunction *P* & *Q* is true. There is no possible situation where *P* is true, *Q* is true and *P* & *Q* is not true.

(22)   modus ponendo ponens
          Premises:
          $P \rightarrow Q$
          P
          Conclusion:
          Q

This states that when we know that a proposition of the form $P \rightarrow Q$ is true and we know that the 'antecedent' proposition (the one that comes before the material implication arrow $\rightarrow$) is true, then we can conclude that the 'consequent' proposition (the one that comes after the arrow) is true. There is no possible situation in which $P \rightarrow Q$ is true, *P* is also true and *Q* is false.

(23)   modus tollendo tollens

Premises:
P → Q
¬ Q
Conclusion:
¬ P

This states that when we know that a proposition of the form $P \rightarrow Q$ is true and we know that the consequent proposition is false, then we can conclude that the antecedent proposition is false. There is no possible situation in which $P \rightarrow Q$ is true, Q is false and P is true.

So what does propositional calculus provide us with? A simple and unambiguous language, rules for what can count as a well-formed formula, representations of meaning based on statements of what would make the propositions true and, most importantly for the present discussion, a system of rules which is designed to make sure that only true conclusions follow from true premises. In the next section, we will look at some kinds of non-deductive inference before considering what kinds of inferences humans seem to make.

Exercise 4.1 encourages you to explore the nature of deductive inferences more closely.

Exercise 4.1

- Here are examples of conversational exchanges. See if you can find any examples of deductive inferences being made here.
  - (i)   A: John says that new Seth Rogan film isn't bad.
          B: Do you want to see it?
          A: Not unless somebody else recommends it.
  - (ii) A: There's no rubbish collection this week.
          B: Oh no! That is so annoying.
          A: It's not such a big deal is it?
          B: It is if you're having a party at the weekend.
  - (iii) A: It's bound to rain on Saturday.
          B: The forecast is good.
          A: Yeh, but it always rains when we go camping.
  - (iv) A: Do you want to try the cake I brought?
          B: Does it have nuts in it.
          A: Oh yeh, it does. Sorry.

4.3.2   Non-deductive inference

The previous section was far from a comprehensive discussion of deductive inference. The aim was simply to introduce deductive inference as a 'safe' or 'reliable' process whereby true premises guarantee true conclusions. Similarly, this section is far from a comprehensive discussion of non-deductive inference but aims to make clear that some inferential processes lead to conclusions which are plausible but not 100 per cent guaranteed. Varieties of non-deductive inference include abductive, inductive, probabilistic and statistical reasoning. In this section, we will not distinguish among them, and simply call them **non-demonstrative**. This should serve the purpose of making clear that some inferences which we make naturally and spontaneously are evidence-based and can occasionally lead from true premises to false conclusions.

Often, when people return from a trip abroad they share impressions with their friends when they get home. Here's a typical utterance you might hear from a friend who's just got back from a trip to Istanbul:

(24)   The taxi drivers in Turkey are so nice. Really friendly and helpful.

Another common topic of contemporary conversation is the dangerous driving of other road users. Most of us will have heard an utterance such as (25) before (I've given a selection of options for the subject here):

(25)   Bus drivers/taxi drivers/cyclists are so inconsiderate.

If you ask your friend who went to Istanbul why they think taxi drivers in Turkey are so nice, this conclusion might well be based on very little evidence, maybe even as little as one taxi ride. This is not really enough to justify a general conclusion about taxi drivers in Istanbul, let alone about all of Turkey. Similarly, but arguably less dramatically, the negative opinions of road users about other road users are not usually based on any systematic observation or counting (and 'confirmation bias' can also play a role here, i.e. once an individual has decided that they believe something, they tend to look for examples which support the conclusion rather than assessing equally all relevant evidence). Some of my friends think that bus drivers are dangerous. Others think taxi drivers are the worst. But it is unlikely any of them have actually counted how often they have seen drivers in each group drive in a manner they disapprove of.

What these cases have in common is that the speaker has made a generalisation on the basis of a small number of instances. Perhaps the first thought most people would have on how to make the conclusion more secure would be to look at more instances to back it up. But the problem is more serious than that. Even if the speaker had observed many instances, they could not be sure that the generalisation would be true of all taxi drivers/bus drivers/etc.

Here's another anecdote. When I used to work in a bar, I got used to what regular customers liked to drink and I found that customers would be pleased if I anticipated their usual order and had it waiting for them when they reached the bar. Every now and then, though, a customer would change their mind and decide they'd like something different. On seeing the drink they didn't actually want, the nice ones would say something like:

(26)   Oh, is that for me? I'm really sorry. I thought I'd have a pint of lager for a change today.

The less nice ones would say something less polite such as:

(27)   Who's that for? I didn't order that. Just cos I've had that before doesn't mean I'm going to have it every time I come in!

What this shows is that just because something has happened on more than one occasion, it doesn't necessarily follow that it will ever happen again.

Another context where evidence-based generalisations have been used is in science (for a fuller discussion of the ideas discussed here, see Chalmers 1999). A traditional view of science sees it as beginning with systematic and objective observation and eventually leading to (inductive) generalisations which are then tested by further observation. We can represent this picture as follows:

objective observation → facts acquired → laws and theories → predictions
(based on Chalmers 1999: 54)

Suppose, for example that I am interested in water and how it boils. On this picture, I might begin by observing water being heated on a number of occasions and checking its temperature when it is boiling. I notice that the temperature is always 100 degrees centigrade and so I come up with the generalisation that water boils at 100 degrees centigrade. I can then go on to make predictions based on this about particular bodies of water and so on. The problem with this is that even a huge number of similar observations don't guarantee the truth of the generalisation. Even if I have boiled water a huge number of times and noticed each time that it boiled at 100 degrees centigrade, I cannot know that it will boil at 100 degrees centigrade the next time I try it (for example, if I boil it at an altitude significantly above sea level, it will boil at a lower temperature).

Induction, then, involves observation of patterns and the formation of generalisations based on this. It is clearly something that humans do very often, but it is not a process which invariably leads from true premises to true conclusions. For example, it might well be true that every Turkish taxi driver I have ever met is very friendly and helpful but this does not prevent the next one I meet from being unhelpful and unfriendly.

The main things to notice from this section are that some inferential processes are not deductive and that we seem to make inferences like this spontaneously in a number of contexts. In the next two sections, we'll consider what kinds of inferences we make in general cognition and then what kinds of inferences we make when understanding acts of ostensive communication.

Exercise 4.2 encourages you to explore the nature of non-deductive inferences more closely.

Exercise 4.2

- Here are examples of conversational exchanges. See if you can find any examples of non-deductive inferences being made here.
   (i)   A: Here comes John.
            B: OK. Get ready for fireworks!

(ii)   A: So you've been teaching at Middlesex this year?
       B: Yeh, it's been great fun.
       A: John says the students there are fantastic.
       B: That's right. I forgot he used to teach there.
(iii) A: Did you put salt in that pan?
       B: Yeh, why?
       A: You shouldn't put salt in with beans. It makes them go hard.
(iv)   A: Do you fancy going to that concert on Saturday.
       B: I love bluegrass.

4.3.3   Human inference

So what kinds of inferences do we make in general when under-standing the world? At first glance, it seems clear that they are mainly not deductive. If I see a man approaching a car with keys in his hand, I infer that this man is approaching his own car and that he is about to get into it and start driving. How reliable is my conclusion? Clearly not totally reliable, since it is quite conceivable that the man will walk past the car and get into another, or that he is looking at keys he will not now be using, or that he is going to drive a car that is not his, or that he is going to put something into the boot rather than drive it. And so on. It looks, then, like this inferential process was not a deductive one.

It is possible, though, that deductive rules play a role within a larger process that is not deductive. Simplifying greatly, perhaps we could characterise the conclusion of my initial inference as follows:

(28)   *Premises:*
   a.   That man is approaching that car with the intention of driving off in it.
   b.   That car belongs to that man.
   c.   If nothing prevents him from getting into the car and driving off, then he will get into the car and drive off.
   d.   Nothing will prevent him from getting into the car driving off.
        Conclusion:
        He will get in the car and drive off

Notice that c and d have the form of the modus ponens inference. If we think of *nothing prevents that man from getting into the car and driving off* as *P* and *that man will get in the car and drive off* as *Q*, then line b has the form $P \rightarrow Q$ and line c has the form *P*. So our conclusion can be read as *Q*. This part then could, arguably, be treated as a deductive reasoning process. If this is right, then an inferential process which is not deductive overall nevertheless contains a deductive sub-part. The reason that inferences such as this do not lead to totally reliable conclusions could be argued to be because the premises are not guaranteed rather than because these inferences are not deductive. We could also suggest that the reason they are not guaranteed is because they were not deduced. On this view, we could say that some conclusions are not deduced and some are.

How can we find out whether there is a deductive sub-part in our overall reasoning process? Of course, this is not easy and discussion tends to be both speculative and tentative. Some theorists have argued that human reasoning is not based on fully explicit deductive inference processes. For example, Johnson-Laird (1983; see also Johnson-Laird and Byrne 1991; Johnson-Laird 2004, 2006) has argued that humans use various kinds of 'mental models' rather than fully explicit rules of deductive reasoning. Mental models are representations of possible ways the world could be which are then used in reasoning. Here is a simplified example adapted from a model used by Johnson-Laird (2006: 110–11) in discussing inferences about Agatha Christie's murder mystery *Murder on the Orient Express*. (29) shows the premise that 'If the countess helped then Cyrus helped' and the different possible ways the world could be which would make that premise true:

(29)   *Premise:*
          If the countess helped then Cyrus helped
          Models:
          Countess helped   Cyrus helped
          Countess did not help   Cyrus helped
          Countess did not help   Cyrus did not help

We can see that this model contains three of the four logical possibilities if each person either helped or did not help. The one it rules out is one in which the Countess helped and Cyrus did not help. So what happens if we come to know a new premise, e.g. that the Countess did help. This will lead to a new model based on the conjunction of the two existing models:

(30)   *Premises:*
          If the countess helped then Cyrus helped
          Models:
          Countess helped   Cyrus helped
          Countess did not help   Cyrus helped
          Countess did not help   Cyrus did not help
          New premise:
          The countess helped
          New complete model:
          Countess helped   Cyrus helped

We can see that this is the logical conclusion since we have now ruled out the possibilities in which the Countess did not help. If our new premise was that the Countess did not help, the updated model would look like this:

(31)   *Premises:*
          If the countess helped then Cyrus helped

Models:

Countess helped	Cyrus helped
Countess did not help	Cyrus helped
Countess did not help	Cyrus did not help

New premise:
The countess did not help
New complete model:

Countess did not help	Cyrus helped
Countess did not help	Cyrus did not help

This is logically correct since the new information has not led to any conclusions about whether Cyrus helped or not. So far, the differences between an account based on deductive inference rules and an account based on mental models might not seem very great. There is a significant difference, though. If we have internalised deductive inference rules, then conclusions will follow automatically as soon as we find premises with the properties needed to spark the inference. If we come across a premise of the form *if P then Q* and then we come across *P*, we should automatically derive *Q*. On the mental models approach, this conclusion will depend on the construction of a model and accurate updating of the complete model when we encounter a new premise. One way in which we might find a difference between the two approaches would be in considering what they predict about when we will draw correct conclusions and when we will not. Johnson-Laird and colleagues working on mental models argue that a strength of their approach is that it helps to explain how and why we sometimes get it wrong. Roughly, this follows because conclusions are represented in a model rather than automatically inferred. Sperber and Wilson propose that we do have some real, internalised deductive inference rules which we use spontaneously and propose to explain why we sometimes make mistakes by reference to considerations of relevance.[1]

Sperber and Wilson (1986: 83–103) point out that there are some conclusions which we seem to draw spontaneously and which fit with what we would expect if we have access to deductive rules. If I say to you that:

(32)   If it's raining on Saturday morning, John won't come in to town for your picnic.

and you then discover that:

(33)   It's raining on Saturday morning

you will spontaneously conclude that:

(34)   John won't come in to town for your picnic.

This is easily explained if we assume that modus ponens corresponds to an active rule internalised by humans. To take a slightly more complicated example, if I tell you that:

(35)   If you are over 60 and live in a London borough, you are entitled to a pass for free travel on London transport.

and you know that both (36) and (37) are true:

(36)   John is over 60.

(37)   John lives in a London Borough.

You will conclude that:

(38)   John is entitled to a free pass for travel on London transport.

Here, you have applied '&-introduction' to derive the conjunction:

(39)   John is over 60 and lives in a London borough

and then modus ponens taking (35) and (39) as input to derive (38).[2]

So examples like these can be explained if we assume that deductive rules are part of our cognitive system and spontaneously performed. If we agree with Sperber and Wilson (1986: 83–103) that humans do make deductive inferences, then we might be able to explain some of the inferences we spontaneously make and we might suggest that in cases such as the inference about car ownership and intentions above, there is a deductive sub-part to the overall process. So what is involved in the non-deductive part of inferences such as this? Perhaps this is an 'inductive' (and therefore unreliable) inference based on the number of times in the past when we've seen people approach cars with keys in their hands and the car has turned out to belong to them. If so, it is much harder to explain where the inference comes from. Or it may be an 'abductive' inference (or 'inference to the best explanation') about the intentions that could best explain this behaviour. Jerry Fodor (1983) has suggested that processes such as these are part of our central cognitive system and therefore too complex to be rigorously explainable in scientific terms. The problem, he suggests, is that the domain of possible premises is too great, including every assumption we have previously stored and some others as well, any of which might play a role in non-deductive inference. More generally, Fodor suggests, any central process requires us to access the right assumptions at the right time.

Fodor takes scientific theorising as his example of a central process. He suggested that the evidence we use in developing scientific hypotheses can come from any domain at all, and that because these inferences are unconstrained there is no possibility of explaining how we make them. Fodor also suggested that pragmatic processing is a similarly unconstrained central process, and claimed that a pragmatic theory would, in effect, be 'a theory of everything'. In developing relevance theory, Sperber and Wilson saw themselves as responding to this view by showing that pragmatic processing is a central process where it is possible to make testable claims. We will see in Chapter 12 below that Sperber and Wilson have changed their thinking on this point in important ways; perhaps most significantly, they have developed a view on which pragmatic reasoning and other types of non-demonstrative inference are carried out by modules. We will consider some of the implications of their new thinking in Chapter 12. For now, though, we will focus on how they initially addressed Fodor's challenge while sharing his assumption that pragmatic processing is a central process and therefore has free access to evidence from a wide range of sources, including memories and the outputs of any of the modular input systems.

4.3.4   Human inference in communication

How similar or different are inferences about verbal communication to inferences about the world in general? At first glance, very similar. If you tell me that you are tired of spending Christmas on your own, I might infer that you would like me to invite you to come and spend it with me. But it is quite possible that you think you are simply expressing an attitude and that you have no interest in spending time with me. If I invite you to join me for Christmas, you might think that I am merely being polite and hope that you will say no, even if I insist that I really hope you will come. The openness of the range of possibilities and the risk of misunderstanding suggest that these inferences are not closed deductive processes with guaranteed outputs. So, like general thinking and scientific theorising, utterance interpretation does not look like a deductive inferential process.

Again, though, we might agree that interpreting verbal communication is not deductive as a whole but also suggest that it contains deductive inferences as a sub-part. Sperber and Wilson take this approach and suggest that there is a special feature of interpretations of communicative acts: they are constrained in ways which make them easier to perform and easier to explain. They suggest that utterance interpretation might be quite different from scientific theorising in ways that make it more amenable to theoretical explanation:

> Inferential comprehension ... differs from scientific theorising in a number of relevant respects ... Because the construction and evaluation of a scientific theory may take all the time in the world, the range of hypotheses that can be considered, and the range of evidence that can be taken into account, can be enormous, not just in theory but in practice. By contrast, ordinary utterance comprehension is almost instantaneous, and however much evidence *might* have been taken into account, however many hypotheses *might* have been considered, in practice the only evidence and hypotheses considered are those that are immediately accessible.   (Sperber and Wilson 1986: 66–7)

So Sperber and Wilson believe we can come up with testable hypotheses about the inferential processes involved in utterance interpretation. Utterance interpretation is not a global and unconstrained process but may instead be seen as a process of 'suitably constrained guesswork' (Sperber and Wilson 1986: 69).

They go on to suggest that this 'guesswork' is a form of non-demonstrative inference (a form of evidence-based inference) but that it contains deductive inferences as a sub-part of the overall process. To see how this might work, let's look at an example of utterance interpretation and consider what sorts of inferential processes might be involved. Consider Bev's response in (40):

(40)   KEN: Do you have to cut the grass today?
          BEV: It's raining and I don't have to if it's raining.

This is one place where I need to use a fairly unnatural utterance to illustrate a point. In fact, the unnaturalness actually follows from assumptions about how we interpret utterances (why spell out so much when Ken can understand Bev's intention with a shorter utterance?).

Bev's response here will surely encourage Ken to think that Bev doesn't have to cut the grass today. Ignoring for the moment the inferences Ken needs to make in order to see that the rain is falling now, that *I* refers to Bev, that *I don't have to* means 'I don't have to cut the grass', and so on, we can translate this (again, with some simplification) into propositional calculus formulae. Let's make some very simple assumptions about the propositions. First we'll refer to the proposition that 'It's raining' (at the time of Ken's utterance and where Ken and Bev are located at that time) as P and to 'Bev has to cut the grass' (similarly fleshed out, of course) as Q:

(41)   'It's raining' = P

(42)   'Bev has to cut the grass' = Q

We can now represent the structure of the exchange as something like (43):

(43)   Ken asks whether Q is true

(44)   Bev replies that 'P and (P $\rightarrow \neg$ Q)'

I have transformed Bev's utterance slightly so that it is in the form *P and (if P then not Q)* rather than *P and (not Q if P)* to make clear that this makes available to Ken the input for a modus ponens inference:

(45)   *Input:*
          $P \rightarrow \neg Q$
          P
          Output:
          $\neg Q$

Given this, Ken can automatically infer the conclusion that $\neg Q$, i.e. that Bev does not have to cut the grass. We have seen, then, that this admittedly unnatural utterance is able to generate a set of propositions which enable Ken to deductively infer a relevant conclusion. However, even with an unnatural utterance designed to make a deductive account more likely, this interpretive process can not be seen as wholly deductive. So what are the parts of the process which can not be understood in terms of deductive inference?

Exercise 4.3 encourages you to explore the nature of the deductive and non-deductive inferences involved in utterance interpretation.

Exercise 4.3

- Give as full an account as you can of some of the inferences involved in the following exchanges:
  - (i)   A: Is that chocolate the kids are eating?
          B: Yeh. Their granny gave them two bars each.
          A: Oh boy.
          B: And some sweets.
          A: Hit the panic button.
  - (ii)   A: Have you seen Blue Valentine?
          B: I went with John last week.
          A: Did you cry?
          B: I always cry.
  - (iii) *(Context: Mark Zuckerberg is defending himself against the claim that he 'stole' the idea for the social networking site Facebook from Cameron and Tyler Winklevoss)*
          MARK   You know, you really don't need a forensics team to get to the bottom
          ZUCKERBERG: of this. If you guys were the inventors of Facebook, you'd have
                        invented Facebook.
  (The Social Network, dir. David Fincher 2010)

Parts of the process of interpreting Bev's utterance in (40) which do not seem to be deductive include those in (46):

(46)   Some non-deductive processes involved in understanding Bev's utterance:
  a.   assigning a referent to the pronoun *I*
  b.   understanding that *it* does not refer to an entity in the world
  c.   recognising when and where the raining is taking place
  d.   recognising that *I don't have to* means 'I don't have to cut the grass at the time when it is raining'.

In fact, there are other processes involved in understanding Bev which we have not yet considered. Ken will not simply recover the proposition that Bev does not have to cut the grass and stop interpreting there. In order to satisfy his expectations of relevance, he will surely infer conclusions from the fact that Bev does not have to cut the grass, e.g. that Bev is free this afternoon, that Bev is fortunate, and so on. These will depend on accessing appropriate contextual assumptions such as that Bev will be free if she doesn't have to cut the grass and so on. So we can add two further things which have to be non-demonstratively inferred:

(47)   Further non-deductive processes involved in understanding Bev's utterance:
  a.   accessing appropriate contextual assumptions (e.g. that Bev will be free this afternoon if she does not have to cut the grass)
  b.   deriving further conclusions from the union of these contextual assumptions and propositions expressed/'explicatures' (e.g. that Bev is free this afternoon)

On this view, then, deductive rules play a part in utterance interpretation and the main questions for pragmatics to explain are how we infer the appropriate explicature (for Grice, 'what is said') based on the encoded linguistic meanings of linguistic expressions, how we access the appropriate contextual assumptions, and how we derive implicatures based on explicatures and contextual assumptions.

Now imagine a slightly different exchange:

(48)   KEN: Do you have to cut the grass today?
         BEV: I don't have to if it's raining.

Ken is still likely to decide that Bev does not have to cut the grass but now Ken has to infer more of the interpretation. We can understand Bev here as having uttered $P \rightarrow \neg Q$ and assuming that the hearer can and will infer P (that it's raining) for himself. The challenge for pragmatics is to explain how the hearer knows in a situation like this that what is required is to infer that 'it's raining' in order to use it as a contextual assumption. What makes this even more challenging is that we know there are also contexts in which the hearer might be expected to infer something else, e.g. that it's not raining and that therefore Bev does have to cut the grass (itself based on assuming that the 'if-clause' here represents a 'biconditional', i.e. that Bev has to cut the grass 'if and only if' it's raining). This might follow, for example, if it is a sunny day and Bev looks wistfully out at the sun while speaking. This might in turn suggest that Bev is expressing regret, resignation, and so on.

Another possible exchange is (49):

(49)   KEN: Do you have to cut the grass today?
         BEV: It's raining.

Here, we can think of the speaker as having uttered P and assuming that the hearer can infer $P \rightarrow \neg Q$ ('if it's raining I don't have to') or, of course, $P \rightarrow Q$ ('if it's raining I do have to', which is less likely give standard assumptions about grass-cutting and rain). Thinking in this way, then, we can see part of the hearer's task as being to infer a conclusion. Ultimately, this involves deductive inference. Along the way, though, a number of non-demonstrative steps are required in order to access the appropriate hypotheses about some aspects of the proposition expressed and about which contextual assumptions to use.

The task for pragmatics, then, might be seen as to explain how we infer, non-demonstratively, the propositions communicated directly by utterances, any contextual assumptions required in understanding utterances, and the implicatures of utterances. One part of the explanation might be that we spontaneously perform certain inferences when we have access to the appropriate premises (e.g. we automatically infer $\neg Q$ whenever we access P and $P \rightarrow \neg Q$). A more tricky part is to explain how we manage to access the appropriate contextual assumptions at the appropriate time. And, of course, we need to explain not only how we sometimes get it 'right' but also how we sometimes get it 'wrong', i.e.

how we sometimes access contextual assumptions the speaker did not intend us to use and so make incorrect assumptions about what the speaker intends to convey.

Sperber and Wilson have suggested that what is involved here is 'suitably constrained guesswork'. In the next section, we consider what kinds of constraints relevance theory envisages as doing the job.

4.4   Explaining inferences: principles, presumptions and mutual adjustment

We have seen that we can account for some but not all inferences in terms of deduction. Relevance theory can be seen as (in part) an attempt to explain how we manage to carry out the non-deductive inferences and generally do rather well at it. The answer lies in the presumption of optimal relevance.

4.4.1   Principles and presumptions: constraints on inference

In Chapters 1 and 3, we looked at the two Principles of Relevance and the presumption of optimal relevance which follows from them. Earlier discussion within relevance theory focused on predictions which followed from the presumption of optimal relevance in particular. The presumption of optimal relevance is the presumption that the speaker has in mind an interpretation of her utterance which she thinks will give rise to enough cognitive effects to justify the hearer's effort involved in deriving them and will not put the hearer to any more effort than is consistent with her abilities and preferences.

(50)   KEN: Do you like *Downton Abbey*?
        BEV: I don't like period dramas.

Given that Ken has just asked Bev whether she likes *Downton Abbey*, an interpretation of Bev's utterance which gives rise to enough effects must either communicate an answer to this question or something more relevant, e.g. something with effects which are important enough to eclipse the potential relevance of an answer to the question. As long as there is an easy way to see Bev's utterance as answering Ken's question, and of course a way that is easier to access than any other interpretation, then this is what Ken will decide Bev is attempting to communicate. Let's suppose that Ken knows that *Downton Abbey* is a period drama. In this case, the conclusion that Bev does not like Downton Abbey will be accessed very quickly indeed. There is no need for Ken to look any further for an interpretation, as this easily accessible interpretation clearly satisfies his expectations of relevance.

How does Ken know that this first interpretation is the one intended by Bev? Why does he not think harder and consider whether another interpretation might be intended? Sperber and Wilson (1986: 163–71) claim that this is ruled out by considerations of relevance. If the speaker could have assumed that this interpretation would be the first to occur to the hearer, then she can not have intended for him to discard it and then move on to look for other possibilities. So the first interpretation that satisfies the interpreter's expectations of relevance in a way the speaker could manifestly have foreseen will always be the only one to satisfy these expectations. As we saw in Chapter 1, Sperber and Wilson (1986: 168–71) show this by discussing how example (51) would be interpreted in 'an ordinary situation' (for me, that would be one where it is uttered by a city-dweller in England today):

(51)   George has a big cat.

As we saw, relevance theory predicts that this will be taken to refer to a large domestic cat rather than a tiger or a leopard and the claim is that the presumption of optimal relevance explains why this is so. The most easily accessible sense of *cat* is 'domestic cat', and (51) is relevant enough to justify the effort involved in processing it if we assume that the speaker intends us to believe that George owns a fairly big domestic cat. Even if it occurs to the hearer that (51) would be even more relevant on the assumption that George has a tiger or a leopard, this is ruled out because there are utterances which would clearly have communicated this information while putting the hearer to less effort, such as (52):

(52)   George has a tiger.

The hearer could derive the relevant implications of George's tiger ownership more quickly after hearing (52) than after hearing (51). Therefore (52) would be a more relevant way of communicating it. It would not be rational for a speaker to expect the hearer of (51) first to entertain a readily accessible and relevant interpretation, then to entertain another possibility and discard the first one, particularly given the possibility of communicating the intended interpretation more quickly by uttering (52). As Sperber and Wilson (1986: 169) put it, 'either the first interpretation consistent with the principle of relevance is communicated … or nothing is communicated at all' (the reference to 'the principle of relevance' reflects the fact that the 1986 book presented an earlier version of the theory than the one I am presenting here).

Notice that speakers sometimes playfully exploit the possibility of communicating an interpretation with an utterance which is not optimally relevant. A speaker might utter (50) and then 'correct' herself as in the exchange in (53):

(53)   A: George has a big cat.
            B: Really?
            A: Yes, it's a tiger.

Any humorous effect which A's utterance has here is based on A knowing that B will go for the 'domestic cat' interpretation at first and that the 'tiger' interpretation, while it is a possible interpretation of A's utterance, is not one that any hearer would normally assume. This is an instance of **layering**, where an utterance which is not optimally relevant on one level is used as an ostensive stimulus for a second layer of communication.

Exercise 4.4 encourages you to explore more closely how the presumption of optimal relevance constrains interpretations.

Exercise 4.4

- Suggest an interpretation for B's utterance in each of the following exchanges which is consistent with the presumption of optimal relevance. In each case, also suggest an interpretation which is likely to be less relevant because it would not give rise to enough effects and one which is likely to be less relevant because it would not be accessed first.

    (i)   A: Have you heard about the party?
            B: I've just seen John.

    (ii)   A: That new Terrence Malick film looks weird.
            B: Everybody says it's really good.

    (iii)   A: Did you put salt in that pan?
            B: What if I did?

    (iv)   A (EDINA): Have you eaten something?
            B (PATSY): No, not since 1973.

    (From *Absolutely Fabulous*, BBC TV)

What we have said about the presumption of optimal relevance so far makes it possible to see how it constrains utterance interpretation, making sure that at most there is just one interpretation which will satisfy the hearer's expectations of relevance and is therefore a possible interpretation. In principle, this could be realised by a number of different accounts of how utterances are actually processed. However, this approach presupposes that interpreters look for interpretations in order of accessibility until they find an interpretation which the communicator could have intended to satisfy their expectations of relevance, and then stop looking as soon as they have found one, if they do. As we saw in Chapter 1, more recent discussion (for example, Sperber and Wilson 2002; Wilson and Sperber 2002, 2004) has discussed this process more formally as a 'comprehension heuristic'. The next part of this chapter presents the heuristic and explains how it is seen to constrain utterance interpretation.

4.4.2   Mutual parallel adjustment: what addressees actually do ▬

Wilson and Sperber point out that the task of understanding utterances can be seen as divided into sub-tasks: working out explicatures, working out implicated premises and working out implicated conclusions. They also point out that there is no claim about the order in which these things are worked out, i.e. we do not begin by working out one of these and then move on to another. Instead, hypotheses about each of these are worked out in parallel and are subject to constant adjustment. Rather than working out explicatures first and then working out implicatures based on these, the assumption is that these are derived through a process of **mutual parallel adjustment**. They suggest the lines along which this might work with reference to the following example:

(54)   PETER: Did John pay back the money he owed you?
             MARY: He forgot to go to the bank.

They present a schematic outline of how the comprehension heuristic might be used in working out what Mary intended by her response. They point out that their account is only partial, given the large number of inferential processes involved in understanding any utterance, and present their outline in the form of the diagram in Figure 4.1.

Remembering that we are not assuming that these stages are necessarily ordered in this way in actual online processing, and that we are leaving a significant number of inferences unexplained (Wilson and Sperber point out, for example, that this says nothing about inferences Peter will make about the precise kind of financial institution Mary has in mind), let's now look at each stage of Figure 4.1 to see how the comprehension heuristic is used in each case.

Part (a) simply states that Mary has produced an utterance which encodes a particular incomplete logical form, i.e. a representation with logical properties with gaps which would need to be filled in order for it to be fully propositional and capable of being true or false. (b) indicates that Peter is presuming that the utterance is optimally relevant. (c) is the expectation that Mary will say something which addresses the question Peter has asked. Strictly speaking, (c) depends on more than has been indicated in this context. Peter may have asked this question because he genuinely wonders whether John has paid Mary back, or he may already think that John hasn't and be hoping to find out why not. Another possibility is that this answer has led him to decide that John must not have paid Mary back. The details of this do not matter much here. The key thing is how Peter goes on to infer more.

Part (d) is a key part of the pragmatic interpretation process enabling Peter to understand Mary. If it occurs to Peter that paying Mary back might have depended on going to a particular financial institution, he can then use this to work out the rest of the interpretation. Perhaps the key point here, although not explicitly pointed out by Wilson and Sperber, is that it is not clear how Peter could arrive at an optimally relevant interpretation if he assumed any other intended sense for the word *bank*. We might speculate about the details of the lexical disambiguation process here. We might imagine, for example, that the financial institution sense is considered first and so Peter does not even have to test possibilities for other senses. Or it may be that all possible senses of *bank* are accessed simultaneously and this one leads quickly to further inferences.[3]

(a) Mary has said to Peter, "He$_x$ forgot to go to the BANK$_1$ / BANK$_2$." [He$_x$ = uninterpreted pronoun] [BANK$_1$ = financial institution] [BANK$_2$ = river bank]	*Embedding of the decoded (incomplete) logical form of Mary's utterance into a description of Mary's ostensive behaviour.*
(b) Mary's utterance will be optimally relevant to Peter.	*Expectation raised by recognition of Mary's ostensive behaviour and acceptance of the presumption of relevance it conveys.*
(c) Mary's utterance will achieve relevance by explaining why John has not repaid the money he owed her.	*Expectation raised by (b), together with the fact that such an explanation would be most relevant to Peter at this point.*
(d) Forgetting to go to the BANK$_1$ may make one unable to repay the money one owes.	*First assumption to occur to Peter which, together with other appropriate premises, might satisfy expectation (c). Accepted as an implicit premise of Mary's utterance.*
(e) John forgot to go to the BANK$_1$.	*First enrichment of the logical form of Mary's utterance to occur to Peter which might combine with (d) to lead to the satisfaction of (c). Accepted as an explicature of Mary's utterance.*
(f) John was unable to repay Mary the money he owes because he forgot to go to the BANK$_1$.	*Inferred from (d) and (e), satisfying (c) and accepted as an implicit conclusion of Mary's utterance.*
(g) John may repay Mary the money he owes when he next goes to the BANK$_1$.	*From (f) plus background knowledge. One of several possible weak implicatures of Mary's utterance which, together with (f), satisfy expectation (b).*

Figure 4.1 *Schematic outline of hypotheses formed in interpreting an utterance of* He forgot to go to the bank *(based on Wilson and Sperber 2004)*

In either case, though, relevance theory predicts that Peter will go for the 'financial institution' sense since this is the only one which will lead to an optimally relevant interpretation, and so there is no doubt that it is the first interpretation found to satisfy his expectations of relevance.

(e) simply represents the enrichment of the initial logical form in (a) which follows from the premise assumed in (d). (f) represents the implicated conclusion Peter can now derive from the interaction of (d) and (e). (g) is one of a range of possible weak implicatures which Peter might derive based on the inferences he has made so far. It is a relatively weak implicature since it is possible that Mary did not intend it and possible that Peter will not derive it. However, Mary has given some evidence for it by what she has communicated. It is weaker than (f), which needs to be derived in order for Peter to arrive at an optimally relevant interpretation. (g) is just one possible weak implicature. Other conclusions which Mary has given some evidence for, and which Peter might or might not derive, include assumptions about how reliable John is, how wise it is to lend him money, whether he can be trusted to stick to other kinds of commitments, and so on. The likelihood of inferences such as these is affected by other contextual assumptions, including the kinds of things Peter assumes about John and about Mary, his interest levels in particular kinds of thinking, and so on.

At this stage, you might ask yourself how important implicatures such as (g) are in establishing the relevance of Mary's utterance. Haven't we already shown that it is relevant when we have mentioned (a)–(f)? Isn't the relevance of Mary's utterance that it indicates that John has not repaid her because he forgot to go to the bank and get money he needed to repay her with? To some extent, this is right, but notice that no representations are worth having if nothing follows from them. If Peter asked the question, he must have had a reason for wanting to know whether or not John has paid Mary back. This might have been to do with concern for Mary, to do with how reliable John is, or other things. In other words, something must follow from (f) in order to make this relevant. To the extent that Mary intended to provide evidence for any of these assumptions, they are implicatures and part of the interpretation. It is possible that Peter derives inferences from Mary's utterance which she did not intend and for which Peter does not attribute to Mary an intention to communicate them. In cases where the speaker has no responsibility for a contextually inferred conclusion, these are implications of an utterance but they are not communicated and so not implicatures. We will look at this distinction more closely in Chapters 5 and 7.

We have seen, then, that the key thing which relevance theory claims is that we look for interpretations by following a path of least effort in looking for implications (or other cognitive effects) and stopping when we have enough implications to satisfy our expectations of relevance. Some students and others new to the theory find this unconvincing at first, feeling that it doesn't say very much beyond everyday common sense. However, the question to ask is whether this machinery makes appropriate predictions about a range of interpretations and whether it is possible to develop empirical tests of these predictions. We will look at applications and empirical tests of the theory in more detail below, particularly in Chapter 12. We will conclude this chapter by looking at a number of examples and considering how the comprehension heuristic and the mutual parallel adjustment process explain them. In each case, a key part of the explanation will be showing that the interpretation actually arrived at is the first one which the addressee finds which the communicator could have intended to be optimally relevant.

As mentioned in Chapter 2, Wilson and Sperber (1981: 156–8) pointed out that pragmatic processes seem to be involved in working out what has been said by an utterance such as (55). In particular, they argue, we cannot decide what has been said by the speaker of this utterance until we know which sense of *admit* is intended or the intended referent of *them*:

(55)   Refuse to admit them.

As we have seen, pragmatic processes must be involved in working out the intended sense of *admit* and the referent of *them*. Wilson and Sperber show this by imagining two contexts. In the first, the utterance is produced in response to a question about the other interlocutor's mistakes:

(56)   A: What should I do when I make mistakes?
         B: Refuse to admit them.

In the second, they imagine the utterance produced in response to a question about people with tickets which have expired:

(57)   A: What should I do about the people whose tickets have expired?
         B: Refuse to admit them.

Wilson and Sperber point out that contextual information will guide the hearer in each case and that we could easily develop a Gricean account by pointing out that the utterance in each case would not be relevant and informative enough if we did not select the appropriate sense ('confess to' in the first context and 'allow to enter' in the second) and referent (mistakes in the first context, people with expired tickets in the second).

It is easy to see that the relevance-guided comprehension heuristic makes the right predictions about the interpretation of each of these examples. In each case, the speaker will have produced an utterance with enough effects to justify the processing effort involved only if the hearer chooses the appropriate sense and referent. If the hearer did not find these at first, they should continue to look for an interpretation until they find one which gives rise to adequate cognitive effects. As always, the mutual adjustment process involves performing various tasks in parallel and constantly adjusting them. Finding implicatures which follow from particular decisions about disambiguation or reference assignment provides confirmation for these disambiguations and reference assignments.

There is one component of relevance-theoretic explanations which is necessarily incomplete. We do not have a detailed account of how particular assumptions become more or less accessible while we are communicating with each other. Relevance-theoretic explanations always depend on assumptions about what will be accessible to a particular individual at a particular moment, something which we do not have much independent evidence for. Sperber and Wilson (1986: 170) pointed out that issues such as these are issues for cognitive science in general rather than for relevance theory in particular. However, work in linguistics and cognitive science since 1986 has helped us to know more about such things as the effects of frequency and recency of use.[4] At the same time, the Cognitive Principle of Relevance makes general predictions about the organisation of memory, inference and the perceptual systems which in turn sheds light on questions about the accessibility of contextual assumptions and processing effort.

Discussion of specific cases often involves making specific assumptions about accessibility or focusing on cases where it is fairly clear what is likely to be accessible at a particular moment. Both of these strategies have been used in discussing candidate referents of *them* in these two examples. Given that A in (56) has just asked B about his mistakes, a representation of A's mistakes will be highly accessible. Given that A in (57) has just asked B about people with expired tickets, a representation of people with expired tickets will be highly accessible. An interpreter who is following a path of least effort in looking for candidate referents will find the appropriate ones right away in these situations. The account of the selection of senses of *admit* will closely resemble the account of how Peter decided which sense of *bank* Mary intended in example (54) above. In each case, the appropriate sense is the only one which will lead to an optimally relevant interpretation. We could not, for example, make sense of the idea that B thinks A should refuse to allow his mistakes to enter some physical environment in (56), or that he thinks A should refuse to confess to the existence of people with expired tickets in (57). In both of these cases, we follow the standard relevance-theoretic account. As long as the interpretation we propose is the first one the interpreter comes up with which he thinks the communicator could have intended to satisfy his expectations of relevance, then that is the interpretation he should go for.

Now let's consider the example which Wilson and Sperber used to show that pragmatic processes other than disambiguation and reference assignment are involved in working out what has been explicitly communicated ('what is said', for Grice):

(58)   *(while watching John playing violin)*
          John plays well.

Wilson and Sperber (1981: 158) point out that it will not be enough in this context simply to assign a referent to *John* (let's use the term 'John Smith' to identify the referent) and to decide that *play* refers to the sense related to musical instruments. If that was all we assumed, then we would take the speaker to be explicitly stating ('saying', for Grice) something which amounts to (59):

(59)   John Smith plays some musical instrument well.

Of course, it is clear in this context that the speaker must be intending to communicate something more specific, namely (60):

(60)   John Smith plays the violin well.

Again, it is fairly easy to see that the richer interpretation follows from the relevance-theoretic comprehension heuristic. In fact, there is more than one way in which this account might go. One would say that the 'musical instrument' interpretation is not enough to justify the effort involved in interpreting the utterance. On this view, we would say that an interpretation on which the speaker is communicating merely that John Smith plays some musical instrument well would not give rise to enough effects to justify the effort involved in deriving them, and so the hearer looks further until he comes up with an interpretation which does provide enough effects. We could argue that it is only when the hearer assumes that the speaker is communicating her belief that John Smith plays the violin well that he can derive implicatures such as that the speaker is enjoying John's playing at the moment, that John's violin playing demonstrates that he has worked hard to practise, that he has ability with the violin, and so on. Again, understanding involves mutual adjustment so that the ability to derive appropriate implicatures from this particular enrichment provides support for it.

Another account might point out that the hearer is already thinking about John Smith's violin playing, since a violin is what he and the speaker are watching John play. As a result, an interpretation on which *play* refers to John's playing the violin is highly accessible and will be assumed straight away. This will, of course, be instantly rewarded with cognitive effects (along the lines mentioned above) which are enough to justify the effort involved in deriving them and thus satisfy the hearer's expectations of relevance.

Finally, we might refer to more recent work within relevance theory on lexical pragmatics, which we will consider more fully in Chapter 8. On this view, the interpretation of every word naming a lexical concept involves a pragmatic process of lexical adjustment. Rather than simply accessing a concept {PLAY}, the hearer creates a conceptual representation of {PLAY} appropriate for this context. In this context, the adjusted concept will no doubt refer to violin-playing rather than simply to playing any musical instrument.

All of these accounts assume that the hearer follows the relevance-guided comprehension heuristic, looking for implications (or other cognitive effects) by following a path of least effort and stopping as soon as his expectations of relevance are satisfied.

Another case which demonstrates the nature of relevance-theoretic accounts quite well concerns how we decide the time period referred to by the past tense. In most everyday situations in which I find myself, my addressee is likely to make quite different assumptions about time reference when I utter either (61) or (62):

(61)   I've had breakfast.

(62)   I've been to Tibet.

If I say (61) to my work colleague one day, he is likely to assume that I have had breakfast on the day when I am speaking and probably fairly recently. If I say (62), he is likely to assume that I have been to Tibet at least once in my life and not to narrow down the time scale much at all, apart from assuming that it was not very recently. This follows quite naturally from the relevance-guided comprehension heuristic. Wilson and Sperber (1998) point out that these two examples illustrate what they call the 'interval problem'. They refer to these as cases 'where temporal intervals are left open in the semantics and narrowed down in the pragmatics' (Wilson and Sperber 1998: 11–12). As they point out, use of a simple past tense verb is consistent with a number of different time intervals in which the event described may have occurred. If I say (61), I might have eaten breakfast at any time before the time at which I am speaking. This might have been seconds ago, minutes ago, hours ago, and so on. As Wilson and Sperber point out, there is a logical relationship between different time intervals. If I had breakfast within the last few seconds, then I also had it within the last few minutes, within the last few hours, and so on. So we can think of the hearer's task as being one of narrowing down from a very general characterisation (at some point before this utterance) to something more specific. In most cases, an utterance of (61) will not be relevant unless the speaker has eaten breakfast fairly recently, within the last few hours at least. A hearer following the relevance-theoretic comprehension heuristic will narrow down the representation of the time interval until it gives rise to enough effects to justify the effort involved in driving them. In the case of (61), this will not happen until the represented time interval is quite recent. The cognitive effects which make this utterance relevant might include assumptions such as that the speaker is not hungry at the moment. In (62), by contrast, the utterance is likely to be relevant enough if the speaker has been to Tibet at any time at all. Relevant effects will include assumptions such as that the speaker knows about Tibet, has visited an exciting part of the world, and so on.

As is often the case, pragmatic inferences such as these can be exploited for humorous effects. The exchange in (63) (used in Exercise 4.4) took place in an episode of the television series *Absolutely Fabulous*. The second speaker, Patsy, is a character who drinks vast amounts of alcohol and considers herself to be an exciting and unconventional person.

(63) *(Patsy is holding her stomach in discomfort)*
      EDINA: Have you eaten something?
      PATSY: No, not since 1973.   *(Absolutely Fabulous*, BBC TV, 1994)

The joke here depends on the audience understanding that Edina's question is about whether Patsy has eaten something recently which might explain why she has stomach problems. Patsy's response is humorous because it combines a fairly rational response (*No*) with an indication that she has not only not eaten anything recently but has not consumed anything at all for a very long time. (64) is a much-discussed example (initially mentioned by Bach, 1994b):

(64)   *(to a small child with a cut finger)*
         You're not going to die.

As Bach points out, the speaker here is understood to be communicating that the child will not die in the near future as a result of the cut, rather than that he will never die at any future point. To some extent, this can be thought of as the inverse of the earlier past tense examples. The *be going to* construction merely refers to an indeterminate time later than the time of utterance and the hearer's task is to narrow down the time period. Here, the time referred to has to be in the near future for the utterance to be understood as relevant. However, this alone is not enough for the hearer to have understood the utterance. Clearly, the speaker here intends the hearer to understand that he will not die as a result of the cut rather than just at some near future time. As before, there is more than one way to explain this. We could say that reference only to any future time at all is ruled out because the speaker must know that all humans die eventually. This could result in the hearer narrowing down the time interval to times in the near future. It is not clear, though, how this utterance would be relevant in this context. It is only when the hearer fleshes things out so as to understand that the speaker is saying that the hearer will not die as a result of the cut that the hearer can derive effects which make the utterance worth processing, such as that he should put things in perspective, not be too upset, and so on.

As with the past tense examples just discussed, we might also suggest that the hearer's cut finger is so salient that the hearer will instantly consider the possibility that the utterance relates to the cut. This readily available assumption will give rise to effects along the lines we have just mentioned and the criterion of consistency with the presumption of optimal relevance will be met.

The procedure will work in the same way for examples of nonverbal communication. Consider, for example, Bev's response in the following exchange:

(65)   KEN: How are you today?
         BEV: *(holds up a packet of aspirin)*

A key difference between cases such as this and our previous examples is that there is no code linking the holding up of aspirin with any particular kind of meaning. Bev's action would mean something completely different in a different situation, say in a large chemist's shop where Ken and Bev are scouring the shelves looking for aspirin, or in response to a question about whether Bev has remembered to bring the aspirin on holiday. In the context in (65), of course, Ken will infer that Bev is communicating that she is not very well. How does this work? The relevance-guided comprehension heuristic predicts that Ken will follow a path of least effort in looking for a possible interpretation of Bev's behaviour. In thinking about aspirin, he should be able to access contextual assumptions about when people take aspirin. As long as his first hypothesis treats this as the interpretation which Bev intended (as one which would give rise to enough effects to justify the effort involved in interpreting her behaviour), then he should stop looking for an interpretation.

Note that this does not mean that Ken should stop making inferences. He can continue to work out other things which follow from Bev's behaviour, some of which he might treat as assumptions she intends to communicate (e.g. that she hopes he will be sympathetic towards her) and others which he might not attribute to her (e.g. he might remember that he needs to buy more aspirin to stock up his own bathroom cabinet). However, these further assumptions will follow from the initial conclusion that Bev is indicating that she is not well.

Note also that there are some cases of nonverbal communication where there is an element of encoded meaning. Nodding your head encodes agreement in Britain, for example, but not in all cultures. And there are behaviours with less precise conventional meanings, e.g. rolling your eyes to express something like disapproval.[5]

There are, of course, many different kinds of inference involved in understanding verbal and nonverbal communication. We conclude now by considering how relevance theory explains what goes on when interlocutors fail to understand each other. In most cases, the misunderstanding will arise because the first interpretation which the addressee finds to satisfy his expectations of relevance is not the one envisaged by the communicator. Jokes can be used to illustrate the phenomenon. Here is the joke which 'LaughLab', a research project set up by the psychologist Richard Wiseman, decided was 'The World's Funniest Joke':

(66)   A couple of New Jersey hunters are out in the woods when one of them falls
         to the ground. He doesn't seem to be breathing, his eyes are rolled back in
         his head. The other guy whips out his cell phone and calls the emergency
         services. He gasps to the operator: 'My friend is dead! What can I do?' The
         operator, in a calm soothing voice says: 'Just take it easy. I can help. First,
         let's make sure he's dead.' There is a silence, then a shot is heard. The guy's
         voice comes back on the line. He says: 'OK, now what?'   (LaughLab:
         laughlab.co.uk/)

Clearly, the hunter has made a terrible mistake in interpreting the operator's advice to 'make sure he's dead', acting as if the most important thing was that his partner should be dead rather than that he should make sure he checks whether the worst outcome really has happened. Clearly also, this is an unlikely interpretation. Gurpal Gosali, who submitted this joke to the LaughLab website, said, 'I like the joke as it makes people feel better, because it reminds them that there is always someone out there who is doing something more stupid than themselves.'

Not all misunderstandings depend on someone having been irrational in interpreting an utterance. Some cases arise when there is a mismatch between two individuals with regard to possible senses:

(67)   A: Ozzy Osbourne's coming to dinner.
         B: I'll bring a bat.

To understand B's utterance here, you need to know that one of the things which the rock singer Ozzy Osbourne is known for is biting a live bat's head off during a concert (he didn't realise it was a real bat, by the way). This enables you to access cognitive effects by using the 'flying rodent' sense of *bat* rather than other possibilities such as the 'sports equipment' sense. Wilson and Sperber (1986) have used this example in discussing disambiguation as a pragmatic process and I have used it in class for the same reason. Often, students who do not know this story about Ozzy Osbourne are puzzled by B's utterance. Sometimes, they opt for the 'sports equipment' sense and tell me they have been wondering why on earth B intends to bring a cricket bat to dinner.

Other sources of misunderstanding might include cultural conventions. Among some groups (originally in the United States but now in other groups), (68) is a perfectly normal and friendly way to say goodbye when two friends separate whereas other speakers would expect something fuller such as (69):

(68)   Later.

(69)   See you later, then.

For yet another (British English) group, (70) would be a normal utterance when leaving someone (depending on who the speaker is):

(70)   Laters.

It is quite possible that a hearer unfamiliar with the use of (70) in this way would think another speaker dismissive and slightly rude if they uttered (70) after they have spent some time together.

What unites all of these examples is that there is a mismatch between the speaker's assumptions about which assumptions will be accessible to the hearer and what the hearer does in fact access. A common kind of misunderstanding for me arises when I have forgotten something which someone else has remembered. A typical example would be when I have an important reason to speak to a neighbour. My wife then sees my neighbour is at home and we have an exchange like the following:

(71)   A: Peter's at home just now.
         B: Oh?
         A: You need to speak to him about the party on Saturday.
         B: Oh right, thanks! I'll nip round in a minute.

My wife's initial utterance is intended to implicate that I can speak to Peter now if I go round to his house. These cognitive effects are quite important as they mean I can have the discussion about the party, move on with arrangements, and so on. Having forgotten this, I can only recover a few weak effects from my wife's utterance. When she reminds me that I need to see him, I can see that is a very helpful and significant utterance.

Exercise 4.5 looks at how specific interpretations are constrained by the relevance-guided comprehension heuristic.

Exercise 4.5

• Consider again the same examples you looked at in Exercise 4.4. This time try to explain their interpretation with reference to the relevance-guided comprehension heuristic.

4.5   Summary

In this chapter, we have looked at the two Principles of Relevance, the presumption of optimal relevance, the relevance-guided comprehension heuristic and the mutual adjustment process involved in understanding acts of ostensive communication. We considered relevance-theoretic assumptions made about the nature of the inferential processes involved in the comprehension process. While deductive inferences are assumed to play a role in this, the process overall is seen as non-demonstrative and so leads to conclusions which are plausible but not totally guaranteed. We looked at parts of the process which do not involve deduction. Sperber and Wilson (1986: 69) have described the processes involved in understanding each other as a kind of 'suitably constrained guesswork'. We developed our understanding of the kinds of constraints which relevance theory proposes by thinking about predictions of the presumption of optimal relevance and then looked at the relevance-guided comprehension heuristic which follows from the earlier assumptions. We concluded by looking at how the heuristic can be used to explain the interpretation of a range of verbal and nonverbal communicative acts and at the mutual adjustment process involved in accessing contextual assumptions and in deriving explicit and implicit content. You were invited to practise developing your own explanations in these terms. You should now know enough about relevance theory to be able to apply it yourself in explaining further examples and to understand relatively sophisticated current debates about relevance theory and other approaches. We consider some of these in Part II.

Exercise 4.6

As in every chapter, this final exercise asks you to adjust the list of questions you have come up with so far by compiling new questions which have occurred to you while reading this chapter and to think about the kinds of things which might count as answers to any questions you have come up with so far. First, add new questions to your ongoing list. Second, consider all of your questions and think about possible ways of answering them.

4.6   Further reading

For this chapter, I would recommend the same set of initial readings as suggested for Chapter 1.

PART II

Details and developments

5   Explicature and implicature

Topics: explicit and implicit communication; saying and implicating; the pragmatics of saying; explicature and implicature; alternative approaches

5.1   Overview

One of the key differences between relevance theory and Grice's approach lies in the way that relevance theory sees the distinction between explicit and implicit communication. In common with several other post-Gricean approaches, relevance theory emphasises that pragmatics plays an important role in determining (what Grice would have called) 'what is said' by a communicator. As well as this, the distinction between 'what is said' and 'what is implicated' is replaced within relevance theory by a distinction between explicature and implicature. This chapter explores the new distinctions proposed within relevance theory. It begins with a reminder of Grice's distinction between saying and implicating, and how he drew the distinction between semantics and pragmatics. It then explores some of the problems with Grice's way of drawing these two distinctions and the motivation for the development of the notion of explicature. It spells out how relevance theory distinguishes between explicature and implicature and explores some of the problems in coming up with a definitive way of drawing the distinction. Finally, it considers some alternative ways of accounting for the distinction between explicit and implicit communication.

5.2   Saying and implicating

As we saw in Chapter 2, Wilson and Sperber's (1981) critical discussion of Grice's approach ultimately led to the development of relevance theory. In this chapter, we focus in particular on their new model of the explicit–implicit distinction. The observations about Grice's approach which led to this are about the distinction between saying and implicating, the nature of 'what is said' and the scope of pragmatic principles. Work in relevance theory has also explored issues about the proposed distinction between conventional and conversational implicature, and about the two types of conversational implicature.

These are discussed more fully in Chapter 7 (on types of implicature) and Chapter 11 (on relevance-theoretic semantics).

As we saw, Grice's starting point was a proposed distinction between 'what is said' and what is implicated by an utterance. His motivation was to explain some of the assumed divergences between natural and logical languages and he saw these as being explainable in terms of implicatures. He argued that natural language was not as different from logical languages as had previously been assumed at the level of 'what is said', i.e. that natural language was not as vague and ambiguous as had been supposed. He suggested that some of the differences between natural and logical languages arise because natural language utterances give rise to implicatures. One range of relevant examples is represented in (1)–(4):

(1)   'logical' *and*
        Whales are mammals and crocodiles are reptiles.

(2)   'temporal' *and*
        He ate breakfast and went for a walk in the park.
        implicates: 'first he ate breakfast and then he went to the park'

(3)   'causal' *and*
        The front brakes jammed and he fell off his bike.
        implicates: 'the front brakes jammed and as a result he fell off his bike'

(4)   'locational' *and*
       He cycled to the park and jogged for twenty minutes.
        implicates: 'he cycled to the park and in that place he jogged for twenty minutes'

According to Grice, the word *and* has the same linguistically encoded meaning in (1)–(4) and this meaning can be understood as equivalent to the logical connective &. The perceived differences are due not to the word being ambiguous but to different implicatures which the words give rise to in particular contexts.

In each case, the word *and* encodes the truth-functional meaning shared by the logical connective &. In (1), the intuition is that there is no particular implicature associated with the word *and*, so it is perceived as having the truth-functional meaning of &. In (2), (3) and (4), standard assumptions about the world lead to generalised conversational implicatures about time, cause and place. Of course, because the differences are explained in terms of conversational implicatures, each of these interpretations may or may not arise on particular occasions of use. A context might arise where (1) would implicate something extra about the connection between the two conjuncts. This might arise, for example, in a context where a child is working on a quiz about animal groupings and has just two groupings left to work out. In this situation, there is a sense in which it follows from the child's decision that whales are categorised as mammals that crocodiles must be in the group of reptiles. Similarly, the proposed implicatures in each of (2)–(4) may or may not arise or be replaced by a different one in each case. As they are generalised conversational implicatures, though, the assumption is that these inferences will go through unless there is something particular in the linguistic or non-linguistic context to cancel them. If the suggested implicature in each of (2)–(4) occurred to you spontaneously, that is evidence for Grice's view, since I did not provide any context to help you derive the various implicatures. Grice argued that these implicatures could be cancelled contextually, i.e. when something in the context meant that they would not arise, or linguistically, if the speaker explicitly cancels them. (5)–(7) represent slightly contrived contexts which might change the implicature in each case:

(5)   I don't know much about what he did on the day he disappeared. I know two things he did but I don't know which one he did first. He ate breakfast and went to the park. I know that.

(6)   A: Jane had trouble with her car and her husband on Tuesday. Her car was out of action and her husband had an accident.
          B: Wow! What happened?
          A: The front brakes jammed and he fell off his bike.

(7)   Andy loves walking in the park but he doesn't like to jog outdoors. He does all his jogging on a treadmill in the gym. He combined both things on Wednesday morning. He went to the park and jogged for twenty minutes.

In (8)–(10), the speaker explicitly cancels the possible implicature:

(8)   He jumped on his bike and went to the park. But not in that order.

(9)   The front brakes jammed and he fell off his bike. But not in that order

(10)   He went to the park and jogged for twenty minutes. He didn't jog in the park, though. He prefers jogging in the street.

Grice's approach was seen as an exciting breakthrough, inspiring most subsequent work in pragmatics, suggesting an explanation for the difference between natural and artificial languages, and suggesting one way to explain indirect communication. Relevance theory shares some of the general properties of Grice's approach, but differs in the details of how it explains pragmatic interpretation processes. Here we consider the new model of the explicit–implicit distinction developed within relevance theory.

First, notice that Grice assumes without much discussion a distinction between 'what is said' and what is implicated. As with much of Grice's work, he is careful to acknowledge areas where he has not developed full arguments and this is one of them. He introduces the saying–implicating distinction with an example:

> Suppose that A and B are talking about a mutual friend, C, who is now working in a bank. A asks B how C is getting on in his job, and B replies, *Oh quite well, I think; he likes his colleagues, and he hasn't been to prison yet.*   (Grice 1989: 24)

Grice suggests that A will now be likely to wonder what B is implying. He suggests that the possibilities include:

> such things as that C is the sort of person likely to yield to the temptation provided by his occupation, that C's colleagues are really very unpleasant and treacherous people, and so forth.   (Grice 1989: 24)

He then introduces the term *implicate* and the related nouns *implicature* and *implicatum* 'as terms of art' so as to avoid having to make decisions about which particular verb to use each time he needs a verb like *implicate*. He acknowledges that he needs to begin by relying on our intuitions in understanding what he means by *say* and *implicate*, saying:

> I shall, for the time being at least, have to assume to a considerable extent an intuitive understanding of the meaning of *say* in such contexts, and an ability to recognize particular verbs as members of the family with which *implicate* is associated. I can, however, make one or two remarks that may help to clarify the more problematic of these assumptions, namely, that connected with the meaning of the word *say*.   (Grice 1989: 24–5)

Notice that Grice is identifying a larger issue with the precise meaning of the word *say* than with the word *implicate*. Here is what he says about what he means when using the word *say*:

> In the sense in which I am using the word *say*, I intend what someone has said to be closely related to the conventional meaning of the words (the sentence) he has uttered. Suppose someone to have uttered the sentence *He is in the grip of a vice*. Given a knowledge of the English language, but no knowledge of the circumstances of the utterance, one would know something about what the speaker had said, on the assumption that he was speaking standard English, and speaking literally. One would know that he had said, about some particular male person or animal *x*, that at the time of the utterance (whatever that was), either (1) *x* was unable to rid himself of a certain kind of bad character trait or (2) some part of *x*'s person was caught in a certain kind of tool or instrument (approximate account, of course). But for a full identification of what the speaker had said, one would need to know (a) the identity of *x*, (b) the time of utterance, and (c) the meaning, on the particular occasion of utterance, of the phrase *in the grip of a vice* [a decision between (1) and (2)].   (Grice 1989: 25)

So Grice is acknowledging that this is an 'approximate account'. But what does it suggest about saying and implicating? He sees what is said as 'closely related to the conventional meaning of the words (the sentence)… uttered'. It is not equated with the linguistically encoded meaning but it is also not far from it. Based on the example Grice mentions, the gap between the linguistic meaning and 'what is said' is bridged by identifying the sense of ambiguous expressions ('unable to rid himself of a certain kind of bad character trait' or 'caught in a certain kind of tool or instrument'), identifying the referents of any referring expressions (in this case the referent of *he*), and identifying the time of utterance. From this brief discussion, then, it seems that Grice sees 'what is said' as consisting of 'linguistic meaning plus disambiguation and reference assignment'.

It is not clear whether Grice considered assigning a time to the proposition expressed by an utterance as an aspect of reference assignment, in examples such as the two we discussed in the previous chapter, repeated here as (11) and (12):

(11)   I've had breakfast.

(12)   I've been to Tibet.

As we have seen, one thing we have to do in order to understand these utterances is to decide when the speaker is saying she had breakfast or has been to Tibet. In Grice's terms, the speaker will have said something different if she means that she has had breakfast only at some time in her life rather than within the last few hours. For now, we will assume that this fixing of a time associated with the proposition is one kind of reference assignment process.

Notice that Grice is treating 'what is said' and 'what is implicated' as separate, discrete propositions. Our task in explaining meanings is seen as explaining what proposition a speaker has said and what propositions they have implicated. There is no mention here of the possibility of incomplete or partial propositions being communicated. This might be something to move on to after simpler cases have been dealt with, but it is worth noticing that it is at least conceivable that some utterances will communicate incomplete or partial propositions. These might include questions such as (13), vague responses such as B's reply in (14), vague utterances such as B's response in (15) and the poetic utterance in (16):

(13)   Who ordered the Fiorentina pizza?

(14)   A: Do you like Marjie's cooking?
          B: *(hesitantly)* Well…

(15)   A: How big a Spiritualised fan are you?
          B: Oh, big!

(16)   She walks in beauty like the night (Byron).

The speaker of (13) is likely to be asking for information rather than making a statement and she is not expressing one clear proposition. In fact, she is asking for the hearer to make available a proposition which indicates who ordered this particular pizza. B's response in (14) communicates uncertainty about her response and so does not express one proposition. B's response in (15) indicates that *big* is an appropriate way to describe

B's fandom, but there is no way of saying anything precise about what has been communicated, i.e. about what counts as 'big' here. Byron's line in (16) is hard to paraphrase. It's not clear what exactly it means to 'walk in beauty' or to do so 'like the night'. In what sense does the night walk in beauty? So again it is hard to say what proposition might be being communicated here.

These examples raise important issues for Grice's account. We will put them aside for now and focus on what Grice thinks is involved in determining 'what is said'. The quote above suggests that he thinks that in order to determine 'what is said' by an utterance we need to be able to identify the referent of any referring expressions, when the utterance was said, and what sense of any ambiguous expressions is intended. As we have seen, there are at least three significant problems with this. First, Grice says nothing about how we identify these (nor about how exactly identifying them helps). Second, Grice seems not to have realised that pragmatic processes were involved in working out 'what is said'. Finally, there is more to recovering 'what is said' than just disambiguation and reference assignment.

Of course, Grice was only making an initial proposal about the lines along which a fuller pragmatic theory could be developed, so it might seem reasonable that he did not fill in all of the gaps in his account. At the same time, though, if we do not know how addressees know which senses and referents are intended, we cannot claim to have a full explanation of how utterances are understood. Let's look again at Grice's example to see exactly what is missing in Grice's account.

(17)   He's in the grip of a vice.

According to Grice, we can identify 'what is said' by (17) if we can identify who *he* refers to, when the utterance was uttered and which sense of *in the grip of a vice* is intended. It is clear that we can't take the first step towards explaining an interpretation of (17) if we don't know how exactly these are identified. Even worse, though, it is not clear how knowing the time of utterance will help. Consider another example:

(18)   Belle and Sebastian are playing a gig in London.

Now suppose I tell you that the utterance was produced at 11 a.m. on Wednesday the 4th of April 2012. Is that enough to help you know what I'm saying about the time of the gig? Clearly not, as we can see by imagining the different decisions we would make about this in the following three possible contexts (assuming that the time of utterance does not change):

(19)   *Context 1*
          KEN: Do you fancy coming out for a meal with me and Mike next Saturday night?
          BEV: I'd love to but I can't.
          KEN: Oh, that's a shame. Why not?
          BEV: Belle and Sebastian are playing a gig in London.

(20)   *Context 2*
            KEN: Antoine's bringing his family to stay the weekend before Christmas. He's
                  wondering whether there are any good shows on around then he could take his
                  kids to.
            BEV: Belle and Sebastian are playing a gig in London.

(21)   *Context 3*
            *(Ken and Bev are sitting in the kitchen together, each reading different parts of the
            newspaper. Neither has spoken for around twenty minutes.)*
            Bev: Belle and Sebastian are playing a gig in London.

In context 1, Ken will decide that Belle and Sebastian are playing a gig in
London next Saturday night. In context 2, he will decide they are playing a gig
the weekend before Christmas. In context 3, the assumption will be vaguer,
presumably it will be taken to refer to some time in the not too distant future.
Given how gigs are usually announced, he will probably assume that it could be
at any time in the next year or so. If he is interested enough, he might well ask
Bev exactly when the gig is going to happen. In none of these cases would it be
enough just to know when Bev produced the utterance. The only conceivable
way in which this might work would be if we suggested that 'what is said' here
is simply that the gig is taking place either at the present moment (including a
time before the utterance as the time at which the gig begins) or at some
unspecified time in the future. We would then, presumably, have to say that
any assumption the hearer makes about the time of the gig is an implicature.
This would, of course, be highly counterintuitive.

   To move towards a more explanatory account, then, even assuming that it is
easy to identify the time of an utterance, we need to know how addressees
manage to identify intended senses and referents and what they do with the
information about time of utterance when they've got it. We can move towards
this if we accept Sperber and Wilson's second critical observation about Grice's
approach: that pragmatic processes are involved in recovering 'what is said'.

   The different decisions about the timing of the Belle and Sebastian gig can be
explained as pragmatic inferences about the speaker's intentions. How, for
example, would the utterance in (19) be relevant to a request to go out next
Saturday if the gig was not happening next Saturday?

   Notice that pragmatic theories should also be able to explain how knowledge about time of utterance will be relevant to interpretations. The answer
would seem to be that this knowledge is one part of working out what a
communicator intends. In example (19), it's not enough just to know that
Ken is speaking on the morning of the 4th of April (notice that the precise
time of the utterance is not very important here). We need to know this and
also that the question is about joining in on a social event next Saturday.
With both of these pieces of information, we can infer that the initial invite is
about going out on Saturday the 14th of April and then that Ken's utterance
about the gig must also be about a gig on the 14th of April. In example (20),
we don't even need to know the exact date of the utterance. As long as we

know that the next forthcoming Christmas is the one at the end of 2012, then we can work out that the weekend when Belle and Sebastian are playing is the weekend before Christmas in 2012. Notice, also, that we might well not think about what exactly the date will be. We might decide that knowing it's 'the weekend before Christmas' is accurate enough to understand what Ken intends to communicate.

Notice also that examples (17), (18) and (22) (we discussed (22) in Chapter 2) demonstrate that inferences about time are not all of the same type:

(22)   John plays well.

On one disambiguation of Grice's example (17), we are likely to assume that the person referred to has a part of their anatomy stuck in a particular kind of tool at the time at which the speaker is speaking. On the other disambiguation of (17), we will assume that the person referred to is finding it hard not to indulge in an immoral activity at the time at which the speaker is speaking, although of course they need not be engaged in that activity at this very time. In all three interpretations of (18) which we looked at, the Belle and Sebastian gig will be happening at some time in the future. In (22), we assume that John has the property of being a good player and that this means that when he plays the violin he usually plays it well. This is not the same as saying that John has the property of playing well at the very time of utterance. Typically, to communicate this, a speaker would have said 'John is playing well', which might even suggest that he doesn't usually play well (since the news that he's playing well now would be less relevant if he generally plays well).

Starting from examples such as (22), relevance theorists have explored a wide range of types of inferences which need to be made in order to determine 'what is said' by an utterance. As we saw in Chapter 1, these include disambiguation, reference assignment, the recovery of ellipsed material, narrowing down the intended meaning of vague terms, and deciding whether thoughts represented are being entertained by the speaker or attributed to someone else. There is ongoing debate about the exact variety of types of inference involved here. We will look at some of these debates in more detail below.

Exercise 5.1 focuses on inferences we make in working out what Grice referred to as 'what is said'.

Exercise 5.1

* Spell out some of the inferences involved in working out 'what is said' by B in the following exchanges. Organise your answers into the disambiguation and reference assignment processes which Grice might have envisaged as contributing (although it is not clear whether Grice thought of these as inferential processes) and those which go beyond what Grice envisaged.
  (i)   A: What does John do for a living?
           B: He operates cranes on building sites.

(ii)   A: I really can't face the dishes after all the cooking I did earlier.
          B: Fair enough.
(iii)   A: Any idea what John might want to do after he leaves school?
          B: I don't know. He loves painting.
(iv)   A: I wonder why they're not asking John to look after their house when they're on holiday this year.
          B: He forgot to water the tomatoes last time and they all died.

5.3   The pragmatics of saying

The next two sections consider how relevance theory deals with the distinction between the explicit and the implicit in verbal communication. This section explores the notion that there is considerable pragmatic inference involved in deriving what Grice conceived of as 'what is said' and introduces the notion of **explicature** which replaces 'what is said' within relevance theory. Section 5.4 runs through some examples using the distinction between explicature and implicature, showing how the richer notion of explicature provides an account of a range of phenomena which Grice discussed in terms of his distinction between saying and implicating as well as some phenomena which Grice did not provide an account of. Section 5.5 considers alternative ways of conceiving of the distinctions between explicit and implicit communication and between semantics and pragmatics.

Robyn Carston is the relevance theorist who has worked most extensively on this topic and these sections rely heavily on her work, not only for an account of the relevance-theoretic approach but also for accounts of alternative approaches and their similarities and differences to the relevance-theoretic approach.[1] As we will see in Section 5.5, Carston's ideas have been developed and challenged by a number of authors working within and outside a relevance-theoretic framework. Before looking at some of these arguments in more detail, let's look again at what Grice assumed about the saying–implicating distinction and the adjustments suggested by Wilson and Sperber's early (1981) discussion of this.

As we saw in Chapter 2, Grice made the following assumptions:

(23)   Assumptions made by Grice about the distinction between 'what is said' and 'what is implicated':
    a.   'what is said' is closely related to the conventional, i.e. linguistically encoded, meaning of the utterance
    b.   to get from linguistically encoded meaning to what is said involves disambiguation and reference assignment
    c.   linguistically encoded meanings also contribute to implicature in the case of conventional implicature
    d.   conversational implicatures (generalised or particularised) depend on contextual assumptions and pragmatic principles (maxims of conversation)

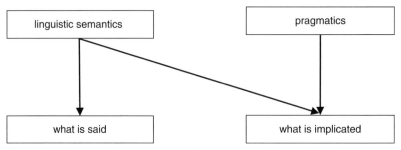

Figure 5.1 *The semantics–pragmatics distinction according to Grice (1975)*

From these assumptions, it follows that linguistic semantics is involved in the recovery of 'what is said' (in all cases) and also in the recovery of 'what is implicated' (in some cases, i.e. in cases of conventional implicature). Pragmatic principles, i.e. the maxims, are involved only in the recovery of (conversational) implicature. As we saw in Chapter 2 above, this leads to the picture of the semantics–pragmatics distinction given in Figure 5.1.

Wilson and Sperber point out that there is more to the recovery of 'what is said' than disambiguation and reference assignment, and that pragmatic principles are also involved in the recovery of 'what is said'. The revised picture they suggest is as shown in Figure 5.2.

We can illustrate the different approaches by referring to the following exchange:

(24)   KEN: Good time last night?
         BEV: Not exactly.
         KEN: What happened?
         BEV: I drank too much, threw up and went home early.

Before going on to discuss this example in more detail, have a go at Exercise 5.2.

Exercise 5.2 asks you to explain what is involved in interpreting utterances from the point of view of a Gricean and a relevance-theoretic approach.

Exercise 5.2

• Suggest an explanation of each utterance in the exchange in example (24) first on a Gricean approach and then on a relevance-theoretic one:

(24)   KEN: Good time last night?
         BEV: Not exactly.
         KEN: What happened?
         BEV: I drank too much, threw up and went home early.

On Grice's view, what is involved in recovering 'what is said' is simply accessing the linguistically encoded meaning, disambiguating any ambiguous

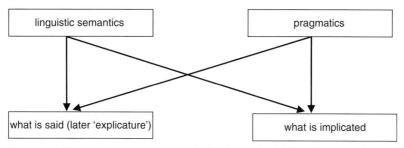

Figure 5.2 *The semantics–pragmatics distinction revised following discussion by Wilson and Sperber (1981)*

terms and assigning a referent to any referring expressions. Assuming that assigning a time reference to a proposition can be included as a form of reference assignment, and assuming that the time of utterance is Wednesday the 4th of April 2012, this means that 'what is said' in each of the utterances in the exchange can be roughly represented as follows:[2]

(25)   KEN: Good time last night?
         What is said: GOOD1 TIME ON THE EVENING OF 3RD APRIL 2012
         BEV: Not exactly.
         What is said: SOMETHING IS NOT EXACTLY SOMETHING
         KEN: What happened?
         What is said: [WHAT] HAPPENED ON THE EVENING OF 3RD APRIL 2012
         BEV: I drank too much, threw up and went home early.
         What is said: BEV DRANK1 TOO MUCH ON THE EVENING OF 3RD APRIL 2012,
                     THREW UP1 ON THE EVENING OF 3RD APRIL 2012 AND WENT TO
                     BEV'S HOME EARLY ON THE 4TH OF APRIL 2012

I have numbered here the concepts derived on the basis of the words *good*, *drank* and *threw up*. This is to reflect the possibility that we might argue that they are ambiguous terms and to indicate that the hearer will assign a sense to them. It is, of course, debatable whether the best way to deal with the range of interpretations which these terms might receive is in terms of linguistic ambiguity. It is possible that *good* is vague rather than ambiguous. An ambiguity account seems implausible since we might need to suggest a very wide range of possible interpretations, perhaps at least one for each noun which it might modify (if we think 'good for a night out' has a different sense from 'good for a knife', 'good for a daughter', and so on). Another problem is that all of the different senses would seem to be associated with words similar or roughly equivalent to *good* in all languages. It would be surprising to find such a similar range of senses for an ambiguous expression across languages. For *drank* (or *drink*), we might suggest that the word has become ambiguous between a sense which refers to drinking alcohol and a sense which refers to drinking anything at all. Again, we might argue that a pragmatic account is preferable. For *threw up*, it seems plausible to suggest that this expression has more than one encoded meaning and that one of them represents the concept of vomiting. For ease of exposition here, I am treating each word as ambiguous for now. Nothing significant follows from this for our current discussion.

What is important here is to notice a range of things which we still need to know in order to understand what the speaker of each utterance in the exchange had in mind. These include:

(26)   Assumptions to be made in understanding the utterances in (24):
    a.   Is the proposition expressed in each case used to represent one of the speaker's own or someone else's thought?
    b.   Is Ken's first utterance a question intended to ask Bev for information about the night before the utterance?
    c.   Is Ken wondering whether someone had a good night, provided a good night, experienced a good night, or something else?
    d.   What does Bev intend to represent as not exactly what in her reply?
    e.   Is Ken asking for information when he says '*what happened*'?
    f.   At what time did the event take place which Ken wants to find out more about by asking '*what happened*'?
    g.   What does Bev mean by '*too much*' when she says she drank too much?
    h.   Who threw up?
    i.   Who went home?
    j.   Where is their home?
    k.   What counts as early?

On the relevance-theoretic approach, the answers to each of these questions will be pragmatically inferred and will count as part of the 'explicit' meaning of the utterance. We can represent the end result of the inferential processes which answer these questions by incorporating them into fleshed out representations of the linguistically encoded meanings. They are highlighted in bold and enclosed in square brackets in this version of the conversation (I've assumed a shared contextual assumption that the exchange takes place on the 4th of April 2012 and that Ken told Bev earlier that he was going to Nicky's party the night before):

(27)   KEN: [**Ken is asking Bev to confirm or deny whether Bev had a**] Good time [**when she went to Nicky's party on the night before this utterance, namely 3rd April 2012**]
    BEV: [**Bev is telling Ken that it would be**] Not exactly [**accurate to say that Bev had a good time when she went to Nicky's party on the evening of the 3rd April 2012**]
    KEN: [**Ken is asking Bev**] what happened [**when she went to Nicky's party on the night before this utterance, namely 3rd April 2012**]
    BEV: [**Bev is telling Ken that Bev**] drank too much [**alcohol at Nicky's party on the 3rd April 2012, that Bev**] threw up [**at Nicky's party on the 3rd April 2012**] and [**that Bev**] went home [**to Bev's house**] early [**i.e. earlier than Bev would normally have expected to go home from Nicky's party on the 3rd April 2012**]

These characterisations are quite loose but they should indicate some of the ways in which relevance theory goes beyond Grice in assumptions about the

extent to which pragmatic processes are involved in recovering explicit meaning. These inferences go far beyond disambiguation and reference assignment,
involving also the recovery of ellipsed material where the absence seems to be
indicated by the nature of the linguistic expressions used, e.g. we know that if
something is *too much*, then it must be too much of something and too much for
something. It is also possible for some of the processes to go beyond what is
strictly required by the nature of encoded linguistic meanings, as we will see in
more detail below. The idea here is that explicitly communicated material is
inferred following the same kinds of processes and constraints as implicit
material. Partly to reflect this, Sperber and Wilson coined the term 'explicature'
to refer to an explicitly communicated proposition. In the next section, we will
look at this notion in a bit more detail by considering how a range of examples
can be handled in terms of a distinction between 'explicature' and 'implicature'.

5.4   Explicature and implicature

As we have seen, relevance theory envisages a greater role for
pragmatics in inferring 'what is said' than was envisaged by Grice. Pragmatic
principles are seen as governing the recovery of **explicatures** as well as
implicatures, and far more has to be inferred at the explicit level than was
envisaged by Grice. Following the initial outline suggested by Sperber and
Wilson, Robyn Carston has developed a fuller account of the range of processes
that are involved in deriving explicatures and implicatures. This section considers how this approach accounts for a range of examples, illustrating some
phenomena which were discussed by Grice and some which were not. We will
begin by considering disambiguation and reference assignment, processes
which Grice recognised were involved in the recovery of 'what is said' but
which he did not explain and which he did not recognise as being governed by
pragmatic principles. We will then look at a number of pragmatic inferences
involved in the recovery of explicature which were not discussed by Grice.
These include 'free enrichment' processes which have been seen as problematic
by some theorists (arguments about this are considered in Section 5.5). We will
then look at how Carston developed a reanalysis of phenomena which Grice
accounted for as examples of generalised conversational implicature. On Carston's analysis, these are not implicated at all but are pragmatically inferred
aspects of explicature. As we will see, in some cases what Grice proposed to
describe as 'generalised conversational implicatures' need not be explicitly
represented at all.

5.4.1   Disambiguation and reference assignment

As we have seen, Grice recognised that in order to understand 'what
is said' by an utterance, addressees need to know the intended sense of any

ambiguous expression and the intended referent of any referring expression. He did not say how these might be determined, did not recognise that pragmatic principles might help, and did not make clear what range of phenomena might be treated in terms of reference assignment. We have seen that the choice of a particular sense of an ambiguous expression might be governed by pragmatic principles. What we have not yet done is to consider the difference between lexical and syntactic ambiguity or the details of the processes which might be involved. It's important to consider exactly how these processes might go so that we can check whether our pragmatic theories do in fact offer an explanation. Let's approach this by considering one example of lexical ambiguity and one of syntactic ambiguity:

(28)   KEN: Do you want to make a note of this?
          BEV: I haven't got a pen.

(29)   KEN: What did you do for the party?
          BEV: I made the cake with the chocolate sprinkles.

Bev's utterance in (28) contains the ambiguous word *pen*. Part of Ken's task in understanding Bev is to decide whether she is saying that she hasn't got a tool for writing with or that she hasn't got an enclosure for animals, or some other sense. Given Ken's question, the 'writing tool' sense is the most likely here. In (29), Bev's utterance is syntactically, or structurally, ambiguous. Part of Ken's task is to decide whether Bev is saying that the cake she made is the one with the chocolate sprinkles or that she made the cake using chocolate sprinkles. Contextual assumptions about cakes and how they are made suggest that the most likely interpretation is that the preposition phrase *with the chocolate sprinkles* is a nominal postmodifier which helps to identify the cake referred to rather than any other possibility (despite the fact that we do sometimes talk about making cakes *with* particular ingredients, which would have the structure consistent with the less likely interpretation here). One of the goals of any account of linguistic communication must be to explain how speakers make decisions like these. As we saw, Grice did not attempt to explain this but Wilson and Sperber have proposed that these are pragmatic processes. This is now a standard assumption within relevance theory and other pragmatic theories.

A natural assumption, then, is that pragmatic principles guide us in making decisions like these. One way to approach this is to make a number of assumptions about the accessibility of particular contextual assumptions, apply our pragmatic principles, and consider what they predict. So we might assume that the 'writing tool' sense is available and consider whether our theory predicts that this will be consistent with the pragmatic principles it proposes, then do the same for the 'animal enclosure' sense and any other possibilities. A Gricean account of (28) might say that the 'writing tool' sense enables Ken to understand Bev's utterance as relevant and informative while other senses would not. If Bev is referring to a writing tool, then we can understand her utterance as implicating that she cannot take a note given that she does not have a tool with which to do this. If we assume any other intended sense, it is hard to see how Bev's utterance could be relevant here. A relevance-theoretic account would involve reference to the relevance-guided comprehension heuristic backed by the presumption of optimal relevance. Together, these predict that the hearer will look for an interpretation which provides enough effects to justify the effort involved in processing the utterance and which the speaker could manifestly have foreseen. For some examples, we need to ask questions about the order in which different interpretations might occur to the hearer. This question is not problematic here since the 'writing tool' sense is the only one which will enable Ken to derive enough positive cognitive effects to justify the effort involved in processing the utterance. As in the Gricean account, these will be implicatures about not being able to take a note because Bev does not have a pen, that it would be useful to know whether anyone else might have a pen, whether there might be other solutions, and so on.

A Gricean account of (29) might begin by noting that there is a significant difference between the two possible structures we have considered, which we might represent with informal labelled bracketing as in (30):

(30) a. $_{NP}$[I] $_V$[made] $_{NP}$[$_{NP}$[the cake] $_{PP}$[with the chocolate sprinkles]]
     b. $_{NP}$[I]$_V$[made] $_{NP}$[the cake] $_{PP}$[with the chocolate sprinkles]

(30a) corresponds to the structure which suggests that [the cake with the chocolate sprinkles] is the one I made. (30b) suggests that it was [with the chocolate sprinkles] that I made [the cake]. Psycholinguistic work on parsing strategies will have implications here, providing evidence about the processing effort involved in deriving each interpretation.

As ever, a relevance-theoretic account will involve the relevance-guided comprehension heuristic backed by the presumption of optimal relevance. Ken will consider possible interpretations in order of accessibility and stop when he finds one that provides enough cognitive effects to satisfy his expectations of relevance. If Ken knows that there is more than one cake at the party, then no individual cake will be quickly accessed until the phrase *with the chocolate sprinkles* is processed, at which point either a representation of a cake with chocolate sprinkles will be accessed, and that will be taken as the referent, or Ken will decide that there must be a cake with chocolate sprinkles which Bev is referring to. An interpretation on which the cake is identified and Bev is saying that she made that cake for the party will be relevant enough to justify the effort involved in processing the utterance without any need to wonder about how the cake was made. Suppose, however, that Ken knows of only one cake present at the party. In this case, that cake will be quite accessible and Ken will presumably assume that Bev is saying she made that cake. If it has chocolate sprinkles on it, then can we take Bev to be saying that she made that cake? If so, we need to ask why we are being told about the sprinkles. We might decide that Bev is proud of the sprinkles or of the nature of her cake. If so, that would seem to be a reasonable interpretation. If the cake does not have chocolate sprinkles, then there are two possibilities: either there is another chocolate-sprinkled cake which Ken did not see but which Bev thinks Ken knows about or Bev is saying that she used chocolate sprinkles to make the cake. The prediction of relevance theory would be for the former. Why? Because Ken is unlikely to have accessible contextual assumptions about cakes with no sign of chocolate sprinkles on them having been made using chocolate sprinkles and for the cake-maker to consider this detail important. Note that this would seem to be a testable prediction. If we create a scenario with one cake and say something like Bev's utterance to someone who knows there is a party, knows of only one cake being there, and can see no visible chocolate sprinkles on it, we can observe whether the hearer responds by saying something like (31) or something like (32):

(31)   Oh, I didn't see a cake with chocolate sprinkles on it?

(32)   Oh, did you use chocolate sprinkles to make it? How did you do it exactly?

Finally, suppose that Ken and Bev are aware of some chocolate sprinkles which need to be used and have been talking about when and how they might be able to use them. This will mean that cognitive effects are quickly accessible when chocolate sprinkles are mentioned. Ken can now infer that the sprinkles Ken and Bev discussed have been used up. In this situation, the interpretation on which chocolate sprinkles were used becomes more likely.

It seems, then, that a pragmatic account of **disambiguation** is plausible. Before moving on, though, we might ask whether we know much about the actual processes involved in disambiguation. In fact, psycholinguistic evidence does tell us some things which seem quite relevant. In particular, there is a significant difference between processes involved in understanding utterances involving **lexical ambiguity** and those involving **syntactic ambiguity**. There is consistent evidence across a number of studies to suggest that we access all senses of ambiguous words when processing utterances, even though we then reject all but the one we use in understanding the utterance (the best-known source for this is Swinney 1979, which we mentioned above). For syntactically ambiguous utterances, we seem much less able to choose between different structures, so it seems plausible to suggest that we go for one structure and that reanalysis involves considerable processing effort (for an initial discussion, see van Gompel 2006). A full account of disambiguation would need to take account of this psycholinguistic evidence and develop an account of exactly how these processes interact with pragmatic processes in arriving at interpretations (for discussion within a relevance-theoretic framework, see Carston 2002a). Relevance theorists have never assumed that disambiguation involves deriving alternative propositions and then using pragmatic principles to make rational choices among them. Rather, processes such as disambiguation and reference resolution are seen as taking place online as part of the mutual parallel adjustment involved in deriving explicatures and implicatures.

There are also a number of things to consider if we aim to develop Grice's account of reference assignment. One general issue concerns the nature of the processes involved in **reference assignment**. Another concerns the scope of the term 'reference assignment', i.e. what range of things do we consider as examples of referring expressions and thus expressions which provide the input to a process of reference assignment?[3] Taking these in order, we will need to develop an account of the linguistically encoded meanings of various types of referring expression. Consider pronouns such as *he*. We cannot claim to have accounted for the interpretation of an utterance containing this word if we do not say something about the linguistically encoded meaning of this and similar expressions. We will need, then, to propose a way of distinguishing the linguistically encoded meanings of (33a–g):

(33) a.　He annoys me.
　　 b.　She annoys me.
　　 c.　It annoys me.
　　 d.　Andy annoys me.
　　 e.　The man in the leather jacket annoys me.
　　 f.　A man in a leather jacket annoys me.
　　 g.　People annoy me.

This is a far from exhaustive list but our list of referring expressions will surely include pronouns such as *he*, *she*, *it* (and others), proper names such as *Andy*, definite noun phrases such as *the man in the leather jacket*, and indefinite noun phrases such as *a man in a leather jacket* and *people* (one thing to account for, which might have already occurred to you, is that some of these expressions can lead to more than one kind of interpretation, e.g. *a man in a leather jacket* could refer to a specific man or a 'generic' interpretation where it is taken to mean that the speaker is annoyed whenever she encounters any man in a leather jacket). As we saw above, Grice said nothing about how referents are assigned to referring expressions but merely suggested that we needed to know the intended referent in order to be able to identify 'what is said' by an utterance. Wilson and Sperber (1981) pointed out that processes of reference assignment must be guided by pragmatic principles. To give an account of how referents are assigned, we also need to give an account of the linguistically encoded meanings of referring expressions such as *he*, *she*, *it*, *Andy* and *the man in the leather jacket*. We will return to this question when we look at the distinction between 'conceptual' and 'procedural' meaning in Chapter 11.

Exercise 5.3 asks you to think in more detail about the actual processes involved in disambiguation and reference assignment.

Exercise 5.3

* Understanding B's utterance in the following exchange involves more than one kind of disambiguation and more than one instance of reference assignment. First, see if you can identify each one. Then propose a Gricean and a relevance-theoretic account.

A: I hear John had an interview at another university last week.

B: Yes. They offered him a chair with a good pension but he didn't take it because of the money.

5.4.2   Other processes

We have seen that disambiguation and reference assignment are pragmatically guided processes involved in the recovery of explicatures. What other processes are involved? One important phenomenon here is **ellipsis**. We need to work out what material needs to be recovered whenever we come across elliptical utterances such as (34a–d):

(34) a.   Andy has too.
      b.   I will if you will.
      c.   Honestly?
      d.   Drives me mad!

In the case of (34a) and (34b), we need to work out the missing verbal material following the auxiliary verbs *has* and *will*. In (34c), we need to recover an entire ellipsed proposition. In (34d), we need to infer the missing subject. In each case, similar arguments to those concerning disambiguation and reference assignment support the view that these are pragmatic inferential processes. In each case, the hearer will look for an interpretation consistent with pragmatic principles. In relevance-theoretic terms, this means that he will look for an interpretation which satisfies his expectation of relevance and stop when he has found one. The constraints on examples such as these seem to be stricter than for other kinds of pragmatic 'gaps'. It would be unusual, for example, to enter a room and say (34a). When would this be reasonable? When contextual assumptions are available to make it possible to work out what needs to be added to complete the proposition. Suppose, for example, that a colleague and I have been wondering whether any other tutors in my department have contacted the maintenance team to report a loss of power in our building. I go to ask two colleagues in other offices and come back to say (34a). Here, it is easy for my colleague to understand that I am saying that Andy has also contacted the maintenance team to report the problem. This fits well with relevance-theoretic predictions about the amount of effort which it is appropriate to expect of a hearer in understanding an utterance. If I am confident that my hearer will work out what Andy has done, I can utter (34a). Of course, a speaker might choose to utter something like (34a) as a kind of playfully challenging opening utterance in order to create a kind of dramatic effect. Understood this way, it will suggest that the speaker is about to make clear what Andy either possesses or has done. I can imagine my daughter coming home from school one day and beginning a conversation like this:

(35)   A: Andy has too!
         B: What?

> A: I can't believe it!
> B: What?
> A: We were saying how weird it is that I've got two sets of grandparents with the same names, and it turns out Andy has as well. Amazing!

Similarly, (34b) is appropriate when there is a highly salient candidate for the thing that I will do if you also do it. This might work, for example, if my friend and I are walking in the countryside and discover an attractive lake we might dive into to cool off. Notice that just this is not enough. It is likely that we need to pause together for a moment looking at it and perhaps exchange a glance. In other words, some coordination is needed to establish that we will both be thinking of the same possibility.

(34c) is unlikely to be uttered without a preceding utterance, say a request for information such as A's utterance in (36):

(36)   A: What do you think of Tim's new partner?
          B: Honestly?

(Notice that prosody is likely to play an important role here. I have suggested a particular way of saying this by including a question mark. An exclamation mark would have suggested different prosody and a different interpretation.) If you have just asked me what I think of Tim's new partner, I can be confident that you will be able to see that this utterance indicates that I am checking whether you are wanting me to answer 'honestly' when I tell you what I think of Tim's new partner. Again, it is very hard to imagine a hearer understanding an utterance like this without some very clear contextual assumptions to guide his inferences.

(34d) is interestingly different from the other cases. Here, the subject pronoun is missing, something which does not occur very often in English. English is usually considered a 'non-pro-drop' language, i.e. a language where subject pronouns need to be explicitly pronounced, unlike 'pro-drop' languages, such as Italian or Spanish, where it is common not to pronounce pronouns explicitly. As this example shows, however, we can produce declarative utterances without a subject in some situations.[4]

As before, a key feature which determines the relative appropriateness of an utterance such as (34d) is the likelihood of the addressee being able to understand what the subject is. As with (34c), an utterance formulated in this way would be an odd initial utterance on entering a room. As with (34c), this could be used for a kind of dramatic effect. This utterance differs from (34c), though, in two ways. First, it would be a slightly odd initial utterance even if the context made clear what it is that drives the speaker mad. I have attempted to come up with scenarios for this, and tested them on a number of people. The only context in which it seems not to give rise to unusual effects is a kind of metalinguistic one where the speaker is checking whether someone has just said 'drives me mad' or something else. Second, even in contexts where it seems appropriate, there is something marked about its interpretation. Compare the following longer utterances:

(37) a.   I can't stand the way these parking people pounce the minute you leave your car for even a second. It drives me mad!
     b.   I can't stand the way these parking people pounce the minute you leave your car for even a second. Drives me mad!

Most people agree that these two utterances would not be understood in exactly the same way. The speaker in (37b) seems to be more angry and more agitated than the speaker in (37a). There are two ways to explain this. One is to say that the utterance with an explicit pronoun is the 'default', 'unmarked' structure in English. Given this, the hearer will notice that (37b) is an unusual form and wonder why the speaker has chosen the non-default structure. A natural explanation is that this follows from her extra irritation and anger. She is so angry and so focused on how mad she is that she doesn't even bother to pronounce the pronoun. One effect of this is that this formulation encourages hearers to imagine the speaker's thoughts and feelings more directly. Like free indirect thought, this formulation seems to invite us to imagine ourselves thinking what the speaker is thinking.

However, a relevance-theoretic account does not need to propose the notion of a default form. Notice that the hearer has to put in more effort in interpreting (37b) than (37a). The missing subject has to be inferred. This extra processing effort has to be rewarded with increased cognitive effects. If not, the speaker has not used the most relevant stimulus consistent with her abilities and preferences and so the utterance will not satisfy the hearer's expectations of relevance. An important question which you might be asking now concerns how we measure processing effort. There is effort involved in inferring what the missing subject must be here, but there is also effort involved in processing the word *it*. So how do we know which is greater? There are two things we might suggest here. First, we might suggest that the effort to process the phonological structure of *it* is not great. This is likely to be backed up by evidence from word frequency, which is often used by psycholinguists as an indicator of processing effort (other things being equal, words used more frequently require less processing effort). However, there are contexts where a small amount of extra phonological processing seems to have a significant effect. Consider, for example, the differences between (38a) and (38b) and between (39a) and (39b):

(38) a.   It's raining.
     b.   It's raining now.

(39) a.   My childhood days are gone.
     b.   My childhood days are gone, gone.

In these pairs of examples, the small amount of extra effort involved in processing *now* and the repeated *gone* seem to have a significant impact on how the utterances are understood. Second, and more importantly, the presence of *it* helps the hearer towards the intended referent so there is some pay-off from processing it. We can see this by considering other forms she could have used here. Compare the following possible utterances:

(40) a.   It drives me mad.
      b.   That drives me mad.
      c.   This drives me mad.

The hearer of each of these will recover slightly different interpretations since (40b) encourages an interpretation in which the speaker is in some sense distanced from what drives her mad and (40c) encourages an interpretation in which she is some sense closer to the source of her irritation. Given this range of possibilities, we can see that *it* helps the hearer in this context. Without the presence of any word at all in subject position, the hearer is not guided in any particular direction in searching for a subject. The hearer then has to find an interpretation which justifies this extra effort. One aspect of the interpretation which several people have reported to me is that utterances such as these suggest that the speaker is assuming that she and the hearer are in very similar cognitive states, almost as if the hearer is 'inside the speaker's head'. This account raises some tricky questions about effort and accessibility. The key thing to notice here is another kind of pragmatic inference which hearers need to make in order to understand what has been explicitly communicated by an utterance.

Exercise 5.4 asks you to consider how to explain the interpretation of some elliptical utterances, including some which illustrate the possibilities for 'pro-drop' in English.

Exercise 5.4

- Propose a relevance-theoretic account of how B's elliptical utterances in the following exchanges might be interpreted:

    (i)   A: John just loves opera. Especially Verdi.
            B: Really? Leaves me cold.
    (ii)   A: When's your exam again?
            B: Friday.
    (iii)   A: You made a right mess of the kitchen yesterday.
            B: Didn't mean to.
    (iv)   A: You don't mind that I ate the last brownie, do you?
            B: Honestly!

An important notion suggested by Wilson and Sperber (1981) and followed up in later work (including Sperber and Wilson 1986; Carston 1988, 1998, 2002a, 2002b, 2004a) is the idea that, in order to satisfy our expectations of relevance, we sometimes continue to flesh out the explicit content of utterances even beyond the stage where we have recovered full propositions, i.e. conceptual representations which could be assessed for truth or falsity.

Relevance theory assumes a number of **free enrichment processes** such as these. Some of them are illustrated, with rough characterisations of the post-enrichment proposition expressed, in (41)–(45):

(41)   *Utterance:*
         The shops are some distance from my house.
         Rough characterisation of the proposition expressed:
         The shops are some considerable distance from my house.

(42)   *Utterance:*
         Everyone doesn't like chocolate.
         Rough characterisation of the proposition expressed:
         EITHER:
         It is not true that everyone in some group likes chocolate.
         OR:
         It is true of everyone in some group that they do not like chocolate.

(43)   *Utterance:*
         Andy ate two of the cakes.
         Rough characterisation of the proposition expressed:
         Andy ate exactly two of the cakes and no more.

(44)   *Utterance:*
         Remember to breathe when you're singing.
         Rough characterisation of the proposition expressed:
         Remember to breathe in the appropriate manner when singing.

(45)   *(responding to a report that Syd Barrett once walked to Cambridge after an evening in London)*
         Utterance:
         That's a walk.
         Rough characterisation of the proposition expressed:
         That is a considerable walk.

The proposed enrichment in each case is predicted by the relevance-theoretic comprehension heuristic. In (41), an interpretation on which the speaker is indicating merely that some distance exists between the house and the shops could not give rise to enough effects to justify the processing effort involved since we assume that the speaker and hearer already assume that there is some distance between them. The hearer must then assume that the speaker intends something more. He will assume that there is something about the distance which does give rise to adequate effects and so that the distance is further than the speaker thinks he would otherwise assume. How far is this? Of course, the details of this depend not only on how far the hearer thinks the shops are likely to be initially, but on how far he thinks the speaker will think that he thinks they are (apologies for the complexity of this!). Suppose, for example, that I have no assumptions about where you live. My initial assumption then is likely to be along the lines of whatever I think is a typical distance for shops to be from where people live. I will then think that the shops are further than that.

How much further? The comprehension heuristic predicts that there is a limit on this. I should assume they are further than I had previously thought but only far enough to give rise to enough effects to justify the effort involved in deriving them. This will mean that I can derive implicatures about the distance being a bit of an inconvenience for you, that this makes your house a less desirable place to live, and so on. I will not go on to wonder whether it's an even further distance because I have already found the first interpretation which satisfies my expectations of relevance. Notice that this account is a bit vague. Notice, however, that it is vague along the same lines as the interpretation itself is vague. So we have the slightly surprising situation of being able to say that relevance theory makes fairly precise predictions about the way in which the interpretation of an utterance such as (41) is vague.

What happens if the hearer decides that the speaker has a mistaken estimate of his initial assumptions? Suppose, for example, that he already knows a little about where the speaker has moved to, including that the shops are on the edge of town and only reachable via a 30-minute walk or a bus journey. Will he assume that the speaker means that they are further than that? No, because he bases his interpretation on what he thinks the speaker thinks about his initial assumptions. The reference to 'abilities' in the presumption of optimal relevance is important here. The hearer has to find an interpretation that makes the utterance not only relevant enough to be worth his attention, but the most relevant one the speaker is willing and able to produce. Since the speaker cannot know about the hearer's assumptions, then she cannot be taken to be assuming this when formulating her utterance. The hearer knows then that 'some distance' is relevant to someone who entertains the assumptions which the speaker thinks the hearer knows. A typical continuation of the exchange in these circumstances might look like this:

(46)   A: The shops are some distance from my house.
            B: Yes, I heard they were on the edge of town.

Here B makes clear that he already has an idea about how far the shops are and indicates agreement that this constitutes a distance which is relevant because it is further than might have been expected.

The accounts of (42)–(45) follow a similar pattern. Exercise 5.5 invites you to propose a relevance-theoretic explanation of a number of examples, including some based on each of these. It explores some of the enrichment processes involved in arriving at the explicatures of utterances.

Exercise 5.5

- Identify some of the inferences hearers need to make in working out the explicatures of B's utterances in the following exchanges and suggest an account of their interpretation from a relevance-theoretic point of view.
    (i)   A: I only made around 20 brownies for the party. Do you think that'll be enough?
           B: Everyone doesn't love chocolate.

(ii)   A: Do you know who ate my chocolates?
        B: John ate two of them.
(iii)   A: Right, I'm off to my singing exam.
        B: Remember to breathe.
(iv)   A: I thought I'd just walk to the beach tomorrow morning.
        B: That's a walk.
(v)   A: I feel funny about inviting John to the party. I always feel awkward around him.
        B: I'm the same.
(vi)   A: Do you think I'm getting too anxious about my dentist appointment?
        B: Well, you're not going to die.

So far, we have seen that relevance theory proposes to replace the Gricean notion of 'what is said' with the notion of 'explicature', how the relevance-theoretic approach aims to explain the pragmatic processes involved in deriving explicatures, and that relevance theory assumes that the range of enrichment processes involved in deriving explicature go beyond the disambiguation and reference assignment assumed by Grice. We have also considered a wider range of 'free enrichment' processes. The general assumption is that the only limits to the kinds of enrichment process which might be involved are those determined by expectations of relevance. The claim that there are free enrichment processes has been challenged and debated from a number of different points of view.[5] We will look at this debate in a little more detail below.

Note that we have only looked at a subset of inferences about explicature so far. One thing we have not yet looked at is how we come to recognise 'higher-level explicatures', i.e. complex communicated propositions which include other explicatures as sub-parts. We can illustrate this phenomenon by considering B's utterance in this exchange:

(47)   A: Did Andy tell you what he thought of *The Artist*?
        B: It's the film of the year.

B's utterance here is not likely to be taken as communicating B's own belief about the film but instead communicating what Andy said about it. B's utterance here is communicating a higher-level explicature which contains another proposition as a sub-part:

(48)   *Utterance:*
        It's the film of the year
        Higher-level explicature:
        Andy said that he thinks that *The Artist* is the film of the year.

(Notice that this higher-level explicature involves two embeddings of the lower-level proposition to reflect that I am assuming the hearer has decided that Andy intended to report his own belief rather than a 'fact' or general assumption.)

Another area we have not discussed is how to account for figurative language, including ironical utterances such as (49) and metaphorical utterances such as (50):

(49)   I just love it when nobody listens to me.

(50)   Your voice is a siren calling me to my doom.

Assuming the speaker of (49) is being ironic and does not love being ignored, then the proposition that the speaker loves it when people don't talk to her is not being communicated here and so is not an explicature. We will need to develop an account of how utterances such as this are understood. In the metaphorical utterance in (50), the speaker does not believe that the speaker's voice actually is a mythical sea creature (the sense of *siren* I am assuming here) so we need to develop an account of utterance such as this.

We will return to consider how we can account for higher-level explicatures in Chapter 6 and how we understand figurative utterances in Chapters 9 and 10.

5.4.3   Reanalysing 'generalised conversational implicature'

One important development within relevance theory has been the reanalysis of two kinds of Gricean implicature. The reanalysis of the notion of 'conventional implicature' was initially proposed and most thoroughly developed by Diane Blakemore (1987, 2002, 2007a) who argued that many of the phenomena which Grice had viewed as 'conventional implicature' were better analysed as examples of 'procedural meaning'. We will look at this in more detail in Chapter 11. Robyn Carston developed the view that many of the phenomena which Grice had treated in terms of generalised conversational implicature should be reanalysed as pragmatically inferred aspects of explicature.[6] Within relevance theory, there is no notion of 'generalised conversational implicature' (or, perhaps more accurately, there is no assumed distinction between generalised and particularised conversational implicatures). Some of the phenomena which Grice envisaged dealing with under this heading are viewed as particularised conversational implicatures. This is discussed more fully in Chapter 7. The remaining cases have been reanalysed in terms of explicature. These are the subject of this section.

The examples we will consider here are associated with the use of the word *and* to conjoin two sentences in English:

(51)   Aberdeen is in Scotland and London is in England.

(52)   He dived into the pool and swam a length.

(53)   He put a new cartridge in and the printer started working.

As we have seen, Grice argued against the view that *and* has multiple senses. Instead, he suggests that *and* always encodes logical '&' and that the differences can be understood as arising because the utterances generate generalised conversational implicatures. Because we have generalised assumptions about diving into pools usually preceding swimming lengths and about printers sometimes coming back to life when an ink cartridge is changed, we make the assumption, a kind of 'default' for Grice, that the diving preceded the swimming and that the change of cartridge caused the printer to start working again. These are not differences in linguistically encoded meanings but in the implicatures which the different utterances give rise to.

How does relevance theory account for these differences? Let's approach this by first remembering how we might interpret single clause utterances such as (54) and (55):

(54)   I've brushed my teeth.

(55)   I've driven a formula one Ferrari.

As we have seen, a relevance-theoretic account of the recovery of explicature will include an account of processes such as disambiguation, reference assignment and more general 'enrichment' processes. If we include time reference as a kind of reference, then one part of understanding these utterances involves making an assumption about when the event described took place. In the absence of any contextual assumptions, we are likely to assume that people we know have brushed their teeth more than once in their lives but not necessarily that they have ever driven a formula one Ferrari. Given this, we would not expect to derive many positive cognitive effects just from the assumption that the speaker has brushed her teeth at least once in her life. On the other hand, we are likely to derive effects from hearing that the speaker has driven a Ferrari even once (for more details on a relevance-theoretic account, see Carston 2002a; Wilson and Sperber 1998). If we assume that the past tense marker indicates that we should assign a time reference at any time prior to the time of the utterance, then a minimally enriched representation of the time at which the event took place will simply be 'at some time prior to the time of utterance', i.e. the explicature will be something like (56):

(56)   [The speaker is communicating her belief that the speaker] has driven a formula one Ferrari racing car [at least once prior to the time of this utterance]

This enrichment makes (55) seem relevant enough, i.e. it gives rise to enough effects to justify the processing effort. A similar development of (54) will not usually be relevant enough, though, so we will need to make stronger assumptions about when this event took place. For the utterance to be relevant, the brushing of teeth will have to be recent enough for something to follow from it in an accessible context. Let's assume two contrasting sets of contextual assumptions as represented in (57) and (58):

(57)   *Contextual assumptions:*
The speaker is Molly, a five-year-old girl whose parents are concerned that she doesn't always remember to brush her teeth before bedtime. It is 7.30pm, which is Molly's bedtime. Molly walks into the living room and says to her parents:
I've brushed my teeth.

(58)   *Contextual assumptions:*
         The speaker is Bev. It is late in the evening. Ken has just asked her if she would like
         a nightcap before bed.
         I've brushed my teeth.

In both of these cases, we will assume that the speaker has brushed her teeth
earlier that evening. There is a slight difference, though, which has to do with
how the utterance gives rise to relevant effects. We might characterise them as
follows:

(59)   *Contextual assumptions:*
         The speaker is Molly, a five-year-old girl whose parents are concerned that she doesn't
         always remember to brush her teeth before bedtime. It is 7.30pm, Molly's bedtime. Molly
         walks into the living room and says to her parents:
         Explicature:
         [Molly is communicating Molly's belief that Molly] has brushed [Molly's] teeth [earlier
         this evening at the appropriate time, which is just before bedtime]

(60)   *Contextual assumptions:*
         The speaker is Bev. It is late in the evening, Ken has just asked her if she would like a
         nightcap before bed.
         Explicature:
         [Bev is communicating Bev's belief that Bev] has brushed [Bev's] teeth [relatively
         recently this evening, as part of Bev's preparations for going to bed]

These explicatures are not vastly different. They are slightly different in a way
that reflects the contrasting sets of implicatures which they will give rise to. For
Molly's parents, the important implicatures are to do with Molly having done
what they want her to do, shown some responsibility, done what is needed in
order to look after her teeth, prepared properly for bed, and so on. For Bev's
partner Ken, the important implicatures have to do with Bev not wanting to
consume something after she has brushed her teeth and before she goes to bed.

How is this relevant to the reanalysis of the kinds of examples which Grice
saw as communicating generalised conversational implicatures? There are two
important things to notice here: first, that this approach assumes that we make
inferences about when or under what circumstances an event is assumed to take
place for most utterances which describe states of affairs, even when they are
not conjoined with another clause; second, that the process of inferring contributions to explicatures in general, including time references, is relatively open-
ended so that the hearer might flesh out the explicature by incorporating content
which is neither linguistically encoded nor required for the derivation of a fully
propositional conceptual representation. This means that we will make assumptions like these for each of the clauses in examples (51)–(53) as part of the
ordinary process of interpreting the utterances. We do not need these inferential
processes to be motivated by the need to derive implicatures or the sense that
there is something special about these clauses in these utterances. One important part of the explanation is the assumption that the process of deriving

explicatures begins as soon as the hearer begins to hear the utterance (at the latest, since he may already be forming hypotheses before the speaker begins to speak) and continues in real time as the utterance unfolds. This means that the hearer will have a representation of the fully fleshed out proposition expressed in the first clause before beginning to work out the proposition expressed by the second clause. The details of the inferences made in deriving explicatures will depend, of course, on what range of contextual assumptions the hearer has accessed. To keep things simple, we will assume that accessible contextual information leads to the following assumptions being used in interpreting these utterances:

(61)   *Some assumptions used in interpreting examples (51)–(53):*
   a.   The speaker is Bev.
   b.   The referent of *he* is Andy.
   c.   The pool referred is the one at London Fields lido.
   d.   The printer is the one in Andy's office.

We will make only loose assumptions about time referents, since this is all we need for this discussion.

Assuming that the hearer accesses and uses these contextual assumptions, here are representations of what the explicatures might look like in each case:

(62)   [Bev is communicating Bev's belief that] Aberdeen is in Scotland [at the moment, has been since the city began to develop, and will continue to be for the foreseeable future] and that London is in England [at the moment, has been since the city began to develop, and will continue to be for the foreseeable future]

(63)   [Bev is communicating Bev's belief that Andy] dived into the [London Fields lido] pool [at approximately 2 p.m. on Saturday 7th of April 2012] and that [Andy] swam a length [of the London Fields lido pool] [immediately after Andy dived into the London Fields lido pool at approximately 2 p.m. on Saturday 7th of April 2012]

(64)   [Bev is communicating Bev's belief that Andy] put a new cartridge in [to the shared printer in Andy office] [at approximately 10 a.m. on Monday the 2nd of April 2012] and that [the shared printer in Andy's office] started working [shortly after Andy put a new cartridge in to the shared printer in Andy's office at approximately 10 a.m. on Monday the 2nd of April 2012] [as a result of the cartridge having been changed]

From these representations, it follows that:

   a.   the order in which we present the two clauses in (62) is not particularly relevant since they both represent propositions which are assumed to be true in general and over a similar and long time scale
   b.   the diving into the pool in (63) preceded the swimming of a length and the swimming took place in the same pool as the diving
   c.   the changing of the cartridge printer in (64) preceded the working of the printer and caused the printer to start working

Most importantly, it is also clear that changing the order of the clauses will have a significant effect for (52) and (53) but not for (51). Finally, and importantly for this account, notice that we do not need to represent separate implicatures about temporal order or causality since these relationships are already indicated in the explicatures derived.

This discussion has shown how Carston's approach reanalyses some of Grice's generalised conversational implicature examples as being about implicitly communicated aspects of explicatures. The next exercise invites you to try the tricky task of outlining how the analysis might apply to other cases which Grice treated as cases of generalised conversational implicature.

Exercise 5.6 asks you to suggest relevance-theoretic explanations of a wider range of cases which a Gricean approach might handle with reference to the notion of generalised conversational implicature.

Exercise 5.6

- In a Gricean approach, B's utterance in each of the following exchanges might be seen as communicating a generalised conversational implicature. Identify the possible generalised conversational implicature in each case and then suggest a relevance-theoretic account of how the utterance is likely to be understood.
  (i)   A: Have you offered Bob a coffee?
          B: He's had three cups.
  (ii)   A: Do you think John's ever tried sushi?
          B: He's been to Japan.
  (iii)   A: Have you spoken to John about his smoking?
          B: I suggested he should cut back a bit and he bit my head off.
  (iv)   A: What do you think of John's new book?
          B: Some of it's pretty good!
  (v)   A: What did you do when you got back home last night?
          B: It was a pretty wild evening! I had a cup of tea and went to bed.
  (vi)   A: Did you finish all the ice cream?
          B: I might have done.

While the details are under constant discussion and revision, Carston's approach can now be considered a kind of 'standard' view within relevance theory. It might be useful to summarise now some of the key differences between Grice's approach and the relevance-theoretic approach. Note that some of these differences (those concerning the notion of conventional implicature) have not been fully introduced yet. These have been discussed mainly in the work of Diane Blakemore and other theorists developing the notion of 'procedural meaning'. This will be discussed in more detail in Chapter 11. With an apology for looking ahead, some key differences between this approach and Grice's approach are shown in Figure 5.3.

Grice's approach		Relevance theory	
a.	distinction between saying and implicating	a.	distinction between explicature and implicature
b.	distinction between conventional and conversational implicature	b.	no conventional implicature (details of this discussed in Chapter 11)
c.	distinction between generalised and particularised conversational implicature	c.	no distinction between generalised and particularised implicatures, i.e. there is only one category of implicature
d.	recovery of what is said involves knowledge of linguistic meaning, disambiguation and reference assignment	d.	recovery of explicature is an open-ended process involving more than disambiguation and reference assignment
e.	recovery of what is said not governed by the maxims	e.	recovery of explicature governed by pragmatic principles
f.	recovery of conventional implicature based on linguistically encoded meanings and not context-dependent	f.	conventional implicature does not exist (see Chapter 11)
g.	recovery of conversational implicature is context-dependent	g.	recovery of all implicature is context-dependent and governed by pragmatic principles
h.	generalised conversational implicatures follow in general from 'saying' a particular proposition; generalised implicatures may be cancelled linguistically or contextually	h.	no distinction between generalised conversational implicatures and particularised conversational implicatures; many phenomena treated by Grice as involving generalised conversational implicature are reanalysed as pragmatically inferred aspects of explicature
i.	particularised conversational implicatures may be cancelled linguistically and arise only given specific contextual assumptions	i.	all implicatures depend on specific contextual assumptions and can be cancelled if contextual assumptions allow this

Figure 5.3 *Differences between Grice's approach and relevance theory*

Carston's approach has been applied in reanalysing a range of phenomena, largely things which Grice and others proposed to account for as generalised conversational implicatures. Before considering alternative views in the next section, we will introduce one of these areas here: the notion of 'scalar implicature'.

As we saw briefly in Chapter 2, **scalar implicatures** are pragmatically inferred conclusions which, it has been suggested, involve a number of logical scales. These are sometimes referred to as 'Horn scales', since Larry Horn was the first theorist to propose an account of these inferences (Horn 1972, 1984, 1989, 2004; see also Levinson 1987a, 1987b, 2000). Perhaps the most well-known and often-discussed examples are inferences which lead from an utterance containing the word *some* to a conclusion which assumes 'not all'. Here are three examples:

(65)   Some of the students enjoyed your lecture.

(66)   Some of your suggestions make sense.

(67)   Some elephants are mammals.

In many contexts, the hearer of (65) will assume that not all of the students enjoyed the lecture and the hearer of (66) will assume that not all of the suggestions make sense. Faced with an utterance of (67), many people will think that it is 'wrong', or even 'false', on the basis that they know that all elephants are mammals. Logically, however, (67) is true given that all elephants are mammals (if it's not true that some of them are, that means that none of them are).

How might we explain this? One option would be to assume that the word *some* linguistically encodes 'some and not all'. It is easy to rule out this possibility. One way is by considering examples where we would not assume 'not all' and another would be to consider cases where we go on to make clear that we mean 'some, in fact all'. Here is an example where the context makes clear that we should not infer 'not all':

(68)   Ken: I really hope all of the students remembered to submit their coursework on time. Do you know if they did?
         Bev: No, I haven't checked. I did check the day before the deadline, though. So I know that some of them were on time.

Here we know that Bev does not know whether all of the students submitted their coursework on time and we know that all of the work she has checked on is in. This rules out the possibility that Bev could be communicating that not all of the students submitted on time. To illustrate the second option, here are all three of the examples just mentioned, with explicit indications that 'some' in this case is consistent with 'all':

(69)   Some of the students enjoyed your lecture. In fact, they all did.

(70)   Some of your suggestions make sense. In fact, they all do.

(71)   Some elephants are mammals. In fact, they all are.

In each case here, the speaker goes on to indicate that all members of the group mentioned have the property referred to. The fact that this does not give rise to a perceived contradiction demonstrates that the word *some* can not linguistically encode 'some and not all'.

Another explanation might be to claim that *some* is ambiguous. On this view, one reading of the word would amount to 'some and possibly all' and the other reading would amount to 'some and not all'. Part of the hearer's task, then, would be to disambiguate and decide which sense is intended in a particular situation. This, of course, is an example of the kind of proposed ambiguity in natural language which Grice's approach was explicitly intended to argue against. Grice aimed to provide an account where we can see *some* as unambiguous and explain the different meanings in terms of an implicature. Arguments against the ambiguity account parallel the arguments against an ambiguity account of other words such as *and* which were discussed in Chapter 2. One argument is that these options seem to exist for the expressions equivalent to *some* in all languages which have such an expression. Another revolves around Grice's 'modified Occam's razor' (Grice 1989: 49) which suggests that 'senses are not to be multiplied beyond necessity'. The idea here is that it is simpler to assume just one sense of the word and to explain different interpretations pragmatically. We should notice however that a methodological starting point could turn out to be wrong. The mind might, for example, be more complicated than it is required to be.

A Gricean account is based, of course, on the maxims of conversation. To see how it works, let's assume that you know that all of my students enjoyed my lecture. If you know this, then you must also know that I will find it relevant and informative if you tell me that they all enjoyed it. You could report this to me by saying:

(72)   All of the students enjoyed your lecture.

If you knew all of the students enjoyed my lecture but nevertheless say to me that:

(73)   Some of the students enjoyed your lecture.

then clearly you would have produced an utterance which is not 'as informative as is required'. Knowing this, I know that if you choose to say (73) this must be either because you know that (72) is not true or because you do not know whether (72) is true. In the latter case, you are prevented from uttering (72) because of the second maxim of quality which says, 'do not say that for which you lack adequate evidence' (ignoring, for the moment, the fact that utterances such as (72) are not often taken strictly literally).

As mentioned in Chapter 2, Larry Horn developed an account for these and related inferences based on the notion of 'scales' and for this reason inferences such as these have become known as 'scalar implicatures'. The scales which give rise to them have become known as 'information scales' or 'Horn scales' (after Larry Horn). Examples of scales include:

(74)   'Informational' or 'Horn scales'
    a.   some, many, all
    b.   possibly, probably, definitely
    c.   tepid, warm, hot
    d.   one, two, three, ...

What Horn pointed out about these was that in each case an item on the scale entails items on that item's left, i.e. 'all' entails 'many', 'many' entails 'some', 'definitely' entails 'probably', and so on. If I ate 'all' of your chocolates, then I must have eaten 'many' of them. If I ate 'many', I must have eaten 'some', and so on. In each case, Horn suggests, uttering a form on a scale will implicate the negation of items on that item's right. If I say I ate 'some' of your chocolates, I implicate I did not eat 'many'. If I say I am 'probably' coming to your party, I implicate that I am not 'definitely' coming, and so on. The notion that numbers form a scale seems self-evident. The idea that they give rise to scalar implicatures is often surprising at first. There are examples which focus on this on the website for this book. The key thing to notice here is that someone who has eaten a certain number of biscuits (for example) had to eat a smaller number on the way, so that someone who has eaten ten has also eaten nine, eight, and so on. If I have three children and you tell me I need to have two children to qualify for a particular benefit, I will assume that I am entitled to the benefit (since three entails two and two is consistent with more than two).

The (neo-)Gricean account of these examples follows similar lines to Gricean accounts of other phenomena. They have generated a considerable amount of interest. In fact, examples such as these might represent the most often discussed kinds of examples in recent pragmatics. The interest focused at first on working out exactly how to deal with them within a Gricean framework and within other approaches which developed from Grice's work. A notion which developed from looking at examples such as these is the idea that there are 'default' inferences associated with the utterance of certain expressions. This idea builds on Grice's idea that generalised conversational implicatures are generated 'by default', in the absence of contextual or linguistic indications which would rule them out. Whenever someone says 'some X' we automatically assume 'not all X', and so on. This approach is, of course, in contrast to the relevance-theoretic approach which rejects the assumption that there are 'default' inferences and, connected to this, that there is a distinction between 'generalised' and 'particularised' conversational implicatures. More recently, the predictions of both kinds of approach have been tested in a number of experimental studies.[7] Both approaches would, of course, be consistent with the response most adult hearers make to utterances of 'some elephants are mammals' (example 67), i.e. for the assumption that this statement is wrong or false. We will look at these examples in more detail in Chapters 7 and 11. In the meantime, we will consider how to account for these examples within a relevance-theoretic approach.

There is more than one way to deal with examples like these within relevance theory. Here we will consider how they might be seen as pragmatically inferred components of explicatures. Given that we envisage **free enrichment processes** as contributing to explicatures, we can envisage enrichments to (65)–(67) along the following lines:

(75)   Some [but not all] of the students enjoyed your lecture.

(76)   Some [but not all] of your suggestions make sense.

(77)   Some [but not all] elephants are mammals.

One advantage of this approach is that it allows for a fairly straightforward explanation of cases where we assume 'some but not all', cases where we assume 'some and possibly all' and cases where we simply assume 'some' and do not consider whether or not this is consistent with 'all' (arguably, of course, this is consistent with 'some and possibly all'; it is clearly not consistent with 'some but not all'). On the Gricean account, by contrast, we will always start from 'some and possibly all' and in some cases move to 'some but not all'. Another advantage of the enrichment approach is that the account of these inferences fits naturally into a relatively well-developed overall framework. However, the account might seem less clear on grounds of intuition and simplicity. Intuitively, there is little evidence to support the assumption that we sometimes incorporate these extra components into explicatures. From a theoretical point of view, we might be concerned that the account being developed here is quite complex. But perhaps the most persuasive argument in favour of this account is based on theoretical simplicity in a different sense. This approach exploits a possibility which is required in order to account for a range of different examples, such as the following:

(78)   The shops are some [considerable] distance from my house.

(79)   That space is too small [for me to be able to park my car in it].

(80)   You're not going to die [from that cut].

What we have been concerned with in this chapter is the way relevance theory distinguishes between explicit and implicit communication. As we have seen, the picture is one where linguistic expressions encode fairly weak semantic representations and considerable inference is needed in order to arrive at interpretations in context. These inferences can be divided into ones which help to flesh out the logical forms encoded by linguistic expressions to derive intentionally communicated propositions, i.e. explicatures, and ones which derive new propositions but are not derived via a similar fleshing-out process, i.e. implicatures. This way of distinguishing explicit from implicit communication is quite different from Grice's saying–implicating distinction. We have seen that this approach can form the basis of the explanation of a wide range of examples. This is naturally taken as an argument in its favour. In the next section, we consider a number of suggested alternative approaches.

5.5   Alternative approaches

We have seen in this chapter that relevance theory sees both what is explicitly communicated and what is implicitly communicated as being pragmatically inferred. The difference between pragmatically inferred expli-catures and pragmatically inferred implicatures is that the recovery of expli-catures begins from a linguistically encoded semantic representation. We flesh out this incomplete logical form in order to arrive at explicatures. As we saw, this account developed from discussion of problems with Grice's way of making the distinction. A number of other theorists also noticed problems with Grice's account and suggested different ways of reconceptualising the explicit–implicit distinction. There is no space here to present alternatives in detail, but this section presents a brief summary of a number of alternative approaches.

There are a number of different ways of grouping the different approaches. Carston (2009a, 2009b, 2010) groups 'post-Gricean' approaches into the following types (not presented here in the order in which Carston presents them):

a. **'contextualist'/'pragmatic' approaches**

Relevance theory is an example of this kind of approach. The gap between what is linguistically encoded and what is explicitly communicated is filled by pragmatic inference in the way we have outlined above. What is encoded is not enough to determine a complete proposition and so pragmatic inference is required before we can arrive at what Grice would have termed 'what is said'. This idea has been referred to variously as 'the underdeterminacy thesis', 'the linguistic underdeterminacy thesis', 'the radical underdeterminacy thesis', 'semantic/semantical underdeterminacy', and so on.[8]

b. **'minimalist', 'literalist' or 'semantic' approaches**

These are approaches which retain the notion of 'semantic content', i.e. approaches which assume that what is linguistically encoded by a linguistic expression is fully propositional and so can be assessed for truth or falsity. Kripke (1977) and Berg (2002) are examples of this approach. As Carston points out, this means that these approaches are no longer treating 'what is said' as something that is necessarily intentionally communicated by the speaker. Consider the following two examples:

(81)   Everybody enjoyed your talk.

(82)   You're not going to die.

On the relevance-theoretic view, both of these expressions fall short of express-ing a complete proposition. To understand what proposition the speaker has expressed, we need to decide the scope of *everybody* in (81) and the circum-stances under which the hearer is not going to die in (82). On the minimalist view, (81) expresses the proposition that everyone in existence enjoyed the talk and (82) expresses the view that the hearer is never going to die. The inter-pretations are then adjusted so that we understand that the speaker in (81) is referring only to people who attended the talk and that (82) is only saying that the hearer will not die from the cut which he is upset about at the moment of the utterance. If (81) is a loose use, the hearer might then decide that *everyone* is not even referring to every single person who attended the talk. As the speaker can not be intending to communicate that everyone in the world enjoyed the talk or that the hearer in (82) will never die, then 'what is said' is not intended in either of these cases. What is arguably even worse for this approach is that it follows from it that no proposition at all is 'said' (in Grice's sense) or asserted for most utterances. This goes against strong intuitions about what has been said by particular utterances. Most people report feeling that there is a marked difference in status between the first suggested 'implicature' represented in (83)–(84) and the other implicatures in each case (I have, of course, over-simplified in representing each of these):

(83)   Everybody enjoyed your talk.
        Said:
        Everybody in existence enjoyed your talk.
        Implicated:
   a.   Everybody who attended your talk enjoyed your talk.
   b.   You should be happy about how your talk went.
   c.   You did a good job of preparing your talk.

(84)   You're not going to die.
        Said:
        You're not going to die at any future time.
        Implicated:
   a.   You're not going to die from that cut.
   b.   You're over-reacting.
   c.   You should calm down.

Stated informally, we have a sense that the (a) implicature in each case is what the speaker 'directly communicated' while (b) and (c) are 'indirectly communicated'. In even looser language, people will tend to think that the speaker 'said' that everybody who attended your talk enjoyed it and was expecting you to infer from this that you should be happy, and so on. As Carston puts it:

> It seems that by treating these as on a par, as … implicatures, not only do we ignore intuitions about directly asserted content, we also lose a distinction that does clear work within an account of communication.   (Carston 2009: 41)

c.   'what is said' plus two levels of communicated content

There is a sense in which this view encompasses aspects of both the 'contextualist' and the 'minimalist' views we have just considered. It assumes a minimalist semantic notion of 'what is said' as well as two levels of pragmatically inferred content, one of which is logically prior (but not necessarily prior in terms of real-time processing) to implicature. The most well-known proponent of this view is Kent Bach (1994a, 1994b, 1997, 2001). Bach suggests that 'what is said' consists of linguistically encoded content with reference assigned to 'pure' indexicals. Pure indexicals are words such as *I*, *you*, *today*. Bach assumes that we can assign reference to these words without pragmatic inference, based simply on facts about speaker, addressee and time of utterance. Pragmatic inference is then involved in deriving two kinds of implicit content: 'implicitures' and 'implicatures' (unfortunately, the choice of a term which only has one vowel differentiating it from the existing term makes it quite tricky to be clear when discussing this approach). Here is a representation of the three levels for (84):

(85)   You're not going to die.
         Said:
         Andy is not going to die.
         Impliciture:
         Andy is not going to die from the cut he is complaining about.
         Implicatures:
   a.   Andy is over-reacting.
   b.   Andy should calm down.

The distinction between impliciture and implicature is similar to the relevance-theoretic distinction between explicature and implicature. However, Bach does not see implicitures as falling on the explicit side of what is communicated. One consequence of this is that there are many cases where nothing is explicitly communicated. Carston (2002a, 2008, 2009a, 2009b, 2010) identifies two main issues with this approach. One concerns indexicals which are not 'pure', i.e. which require pragmatic inference to establish a referent. These are words such as *she* and *that*. We need to make inferences to work out referents of *she* and *that* in a specific situation and the results of these inferences will contribute to Bach's level of impliciture. One thing this means is that 'what is said' includes a representation of whatever constraints are encoded by words such as *she* and *that* and so it will not constitute a fully propositional representation in these cases. Another point made by Carston is that this level of 'what is said' seems to be redundant. As Carston puts it:

> … there doesn't seem to be any role for this conception of 'what is said' that cannot equally well be played by the linguistically encoded expression-type meaning of the sentence, e.g. the logical form of 'You're not going to die', which is the input to any context-dependent pragmatic processes required to recover the intended utterance meaning.   (Carston 2009a: 44)

More generally, we might note that Bach's account introduces one more level of description than the relevance-theoretic account. If we follow the methodological position of always aiming for the simplest possible theory, then Bach's account should only be preferred if we can find a clear justification for the extra theoretical complexity.

d.   semantic content plus pragmatic 'what is said' plus implicatures

This is a different view which sees what is linguistically encoded as minimal but also fully propositional. Proponents of this kind of approach include Borg (2004) and Cappelen and Lepore (2007). Cappelen and Lepore allow for some pragmatic inference to fix indexicals whereas Borg proposes a complete insensitivity to context at this level. Borg's approach does not follow the minimalists we looked at above by assuming that a specific value is encoded by words. Rather she proposes that the semantics of indexicals can be captured by a kind of descriptive constraint. The encoded meaning of (81) and (82) would be something along the lines of (86) and (87):

(86)   There exists a group X such that every member of X enjoyed the talk given by α

(87)   α is not going to die

α in each case should be understood as a singular concept (a concept representing one individual entity) triggered by hearing the forms *your* or *you*. (86) and (87) are intended to be understood as fully propositional representations of semantic content. Such representations are seldom if ever communicated or represented by hearers. Both Borg's and Cappelen and Lepore's approach see 'what is said' as pragmatically inferred, like implicature, and the semantic content they propose is not to be taken as part of what is communicated. Carston (2009a: 46) points out that this means the difference between these approaches and contextualist approaches such as relevance theory is largely a matter of labelling. Both approaches assume that semantic content is linguistically driven and automatically derived and that developments of that content and implicatures are pragmatically inferred. The differences between the two conceptions of what is linguistically encoded are not trivial, though, and so it will be important to explore arguments for or against the different ideas.

There is not enough space here to discuss all of the other approaches and debates around this topic. I will finish this chapter by briefly presenting a few more approaches, some of which overlap to some extent with the relevance-theoretic approach and some which either depart from it or argue explicitly against it.

Jason Stanley and others (see, for example, King and Stanley 2005; Martí 2006; Stanley 2000, 2002; Stanley and Szabó 2000) have argued explicitly against the notion of 'free enrichment' as proposed within relevance theory and argued instead for what has been described as a 'covert indexicalist' account. On their view, any developments of linguistically encoded meanings involved in recovering explicit content must be processes of 'saturation', or 'linguistically mandated completion'. In other words, they suggest that the need for inferential completion must be initiated by the presence of encoded material, in the form of 'covert indexicals', which give rise to the inferences. The covert indexicalists argue that free enrichment would mean that there are no constraints on what can be added to semantic content. Clearly, there are limits on what can be part of explicit content. It seems clear, for example, that we cannot develop the semantic content of (88a) to (88b), from (89a) to (89b), or from (90a) to (90b) (the last two examples are adapted slightly from Hall 2009):

(88) a.   It's raining.
      b.   It's raining and I'm cold.

(89) a.   Everyone likes Sally.
      b.   Everyone$_i$ likes Sally and their$_i$ mum.
            (The subscript i indicates that 'everyone' and 'their' are understood as referring to the same people, so that this means that it is true of everyone that they like Sally and that they like their own mum.)

(90) a.   Every student who chose the syntax option completed the course successfully.
      b.   Every student who chose the syntax option or the pragmatics option completed the course successfully.

Of course, the fuller proposition in each case could be implicated by an utterance expressing the simpler proposition. This would follow, for example, if each example was uttered in the following (slightly odd) exchanges:

(91)   If it's raining, I'll be cold.

(92)   Everyone$_i$ who likes Sally likes their$_i$ mum.

(93)   If every student who chose the syntax option completed the course successfully, then every student who chose the syntax option or the pragmatics option completed the course successfully.

While proposition (b) in (88)–(89) could well be communicated by each utterance (a), it seems they cannot be part of explicit content. The indexicalists suggest that the contextualist view does not make clear why this is so or rule out the inappropriate developments. For this reason, they suggest that any development of explicit content must originate in a 'covert indexical' and that there should be 'unarticulated constituents' of explicit content.

   A natural response from a relevance theorist might be to say that the presumption of optimal relevance, the relevance-guided comprehension heuristic and the nature of the mutual adjustment process rule out certain developments. However, it is important to explain exactly how this is done, particularly since the (b) propositions can be communicated and so contribute to the optimal relevance of an utterance. Hall (2009) explores this argument and suggests that the answer lies in a distinction between what she terms 'local (non-global)' processes and 'global' processes. She suggests that 'enrichment is a local (non-global) process, while complete propositions, arguments and so on, are derived by global inferences, so that the latter are properly inferentially warranted and can function independently as premises or conclusions in inferences' (Hall 2009: 93). Roughly, a 'local' process is one involved in deriving explicatures and a 'global' process is one involved in combining explicatures with contextual assumptions to derive implicatures. Let's combine (92) and (89a) into one exchange:

(94)   KEN: Everyone who likes Sally likes their mum.
         BEV: Everyone likes Sally.

It is interesting that Bev's utterance here sounds slightly unnatural to most speakers. It would be much more natural if Bev began by saying 'Well'. However, it is a possible utterance and it clearly communicates that everyone likes not only Sally but also their own mum, i.e. (95):

(95)   Everyone$_i$ likes Sally and their$_i$ mum.

What stops the hearer from deriving this as an explicature by developing the semantic representation to include this? Hall argues that it is the fact that the weaker, less-developed, proposition (that everyone in the group referred to likes Sally) can be used in interaction with the contextual assumption that everyone who likes Sally likes their own mum to derive the implicature that everyone in the group likes both Sally and their own mum. As soon as the hearer understands the proposition that everyone in the group referred to likes Sally, he can derive the implicature in (95). There is no need to develop the explicature further at this stage. This follows from the relevance-guided comprehension heuristic. A hearer following a path of least effort will be able to derive the implicature which makes this utterance relevant as soon as they have recovered the less developed explicature and there is then no need to develop the explicature further, since his expectations of relevance have already been satisfied. This has, of course, been a brief and simplified discussion, and there are many questions on the details of this which remain to be explored. No doubt this will continue to be an active research area and a source of continued debate.

There are a number of contextualists who do not accept all aspects of the relevance-theoretic view of the explicit–implicit distinction as presented here. These include Travis (1991) and Recanati (1989, 1993, 2002a, 2004) who develop slightly different accounts of the various levels. Purely for reasons of space, we will only consider Recanati here. Recanati follows relevance theory in assuming that pragmatic processes are involved in recovering 'what is said'. He suggests that these processes involve 'saturation' of slots generated by linguistic content (e.g. reference assignment), 'modulation', i.e. adjustment of linguistically encoded concepts, and 'free enrichment' processes. Understanding an utterance of (96a), for example, involves assigning values to *your* and *here*, including deciding what kind of relationship exists between *you* and the house. These are processes of 'saturation'. Sense modulation might involve a decision about exactly what sense of *house* is intended. Free enrichment leads to a conclusion about how far the *some distance* is from the house. The result of these processes is (96b):

(96) a.   Your house is some distance from here.

    b.   The house you own is some considerable distance from the place where I am speaking.

Recanati suggests that the processes involved in enriching the linguistic content in this way are 'associative' rather than inferential, sub-propositional and not accessible to introspection. He terms these 'primary pragmatic processes'. 'Secondary pragmatic processes' are involved in deriving implicatures on the basis of explicatures such as (96b). This contrasts with relevance theory which assumes that the processes involved in deriving both explicatures and implicatures are of one, inferential, type. There are, of course, questions to be explored here about the motivation for distinguishing two types of pragmatic process and claims about the accessibility to introspection of only one variety. This is another area of ongoing debate. For further discussion of this, see Carston (2007), Recanati (2002a, 2002b, 2010).

5.6   Summary

In this chapter, we have looked in more detail at the relevance-theoretic notion of explicature. We have seen how it developed from critical discussion of Grice's saying–implicating distinction, how it handles some of the phenomena which Grice discussed and how it handles some other phenomena. We have looked at issues debated within and outside relevance theory, and at some alternative ways of drawing the explicit–implicit distinction.

Exercise 5.7

As in every chapter, this final exercise asks you to adjust the list of questions you have come up with so far by compiling new questions which have occurred to you while reading this chapter and to think about the kinds of things which might count as answers to any questions you have come up with so far. First, add new questions to your ongoing list. Second, consider all of your questions and think about possible ways of answering them.

5.7   Further reading

The key sources on this distinction are the book *Relevance* (Sperber and Wilson 1986: 176–202) and the development of those ideas in a series of publications by Robyn Carston (beginning with Carston 1988 and most fully developed in Carston 2002a).

6 Types of explicature

Topics: utterances and propositions; words, concepts and the world; higher-level explicatures; strength of explicatures

6.1 Overview

The previous chapter looked at the way in which relevance theory draws the distinction between explicit and implicit communication, and at some of the differing views about how to draw the distinction. This chapter considers some of the properties of explicatures and some of the different kinds of explicatures which might be communicated. First, it considers the proposition expressed by an utterance. This is followed by a discussion of the relationships between words and concepts and between concepts and the world. Within relevance theory, the proposition expressed is the propositional form arrived at by fleshing out a linguistically encoded semantic representation. It is arguably always the case that the lowest-level proposition is embedded under other more complex representations and Section 6.4 looks at these 'higher-level explicatures' in more detail. The chapter concludes by considering the extent to which explicatures can vary with regard to the strength with which they are communicated. This includes considering poetic utterances where some of the details of the proposition expressed are not clear.

6.2 Utterances and propositions

As we have seen in earlier chapters, explicatures can be embedded within other explicatures. Consider Bev's utterance in (1) for example:

(1)   KEN: What are you looking so happy about?
        BEV: It's Friday.

Assuming she is speaking on the 6th of April 2012, Bev may be communicating here all of the following propositions:

(2)   It's Friday on the 6th of April 2012.

(3)   Bev believes that it's Friday on the 6th of April 2012.

(4)   Bev is happy that it's Friday on the 6th of April 2012.

(5)   Bev believes that Bev is happy that it's Friday on the 6th of April 2012.

All of these are explicatures of (1) in that they are derived by developing a **logical form**, or **semantic representation**, encoded by (1). We could represent this semantic representation as (6):

(6)   It is Friday [_____]
                            at some time or in some circumstances

Clearly, (2) is a development of (6) in that it is derived by adding a value in the final slot indicating at what time or in what circumstances *It's Friday* is true (I will ignore, for simplicity, the possibility that the speaker is indicating that some event is taking place on Friday, e.g. in response to a question such as *When's your exam?*). Clearly, (3), (4) and (5) contain (2) as a sub-part and, of course, (5) also contains (4). Relevance theorists refer to these as **higher-level explicatures** of (1) since they are explicatures which contain other explicatures (or, more generally, other propositions) as sub-parts. Of course, these embeddings can be quite complex. We will look at higher-level explicatures in more detail in Section 6.4. The focus of this section is the first propositional completion represented in (2) above. This is referred to as the 'proposition expressed'.

   In simple cases such as (1), the **proposition expressed** is an explicature of the utterance. It is important to notice, though, that this proposition is not always communicated and so is not always an explicature. This is true, for example, in utterances with imperative or interrogative syntax:

(7)   Text me when you're on the way home.

(8)   Are you coming to Andy's party?

In a specific context (and simplifying the representations here), the proposition expressed by (7) might be (9) and the proposition expressed by (8) could be (10):

(9)   Bev texts Ken when Bev is on the way home.

(10)   Bev is coming to Andy's party.

Clearly, the speaker in (7) is not communicating (9) and the speaker in (8) is not communicating (10). Rather, an account of the meanings of imperative and interrogative syntax will help to explain how we understand that (7) will be understood in many contexts as an attempt to get the hearer to text on the way home and (9) as an attempt to find out whether the hearer will be coming to the party. An assumption within relevance theory is that syntactic structures impose constraints which guide interpretation, e.g. declarative syntax makes statement interpretations more likely while interrogative syntax makes question interpretations more likely.

Other cases where the proposition expressed is not communicated include cases of reported speech and irony:

(11)   KEN: What did Andy think Jessie said?
            BEV: It's Friday.

Ken could, of course, understand Bev's utterance here as expressing her own belief that it's Friday. If he takes it as an answer to his question, though, the key higher-level explicature of Bev's utterance will be (12):

(12)   Bev believes that Andy thought that Jessie said that today is Friday.

Notice that we have a nested series of explicatures here:

(13) a.   Bev believes that:
     b.   Andy thought that:
     c.   Jessie said that:
     d.   today is Friday

Humans can represent complex layered propositions with this kind of structure fairly easily, as illustrated in the children's nursery rhyme 'The House that Jack Built' which ends in one version with the utterance:

(14)   This is the farmer sowing the corn that kept the cock that crowed in the morn that waked the priest all shaven and shorn that married the man all tattered and torn that kissed the maiden all forlorn that milked the cow with the crumpled horn that tossed the dog that worried the cat that chased the rat that ate the malt that lay in the house that Jack built.

In ironical utterances, the proposition expressed is again not communicated.

(15)   *(Ken has tried to make the notorious dessert 'chocolate nemesis'. It has gone terribly wrong and it has become a soggy, inedible mess):*
            BEV: Brilliant. This'll be the perfect end to the meal.

The proposition expressed by the second part of Bev's second utterance would be something like (16):

(16)   This dessert will be the perfect end to our meal this evening.

But Bev cannot believe this. Instead, she is dissociating herself from that proposition and expects to be understood as communicating that the dessert will not be a success, that it would be foolish to imagine it could be, and so on (we will look at the details of the understanding of irony in Chapter 10). We might represent one higher-level explicature of Bev's utterance as (17):

(17)   It would be ridiculous to believe that this dessert will be the perfect end to our meal this evening.

This is a fairly typical ironical utterance. There are, of course, a range of kinds of irony, from gently humorous through to fairly scathing rejection or mockery.

For a fairly gentle variety, imagine a situation where Ken wakes up on a Thursday morning and says something like (18):

(18)   I'm really glad it's Friday.

Suppose that Bev then reminds Ken that it is only Thursday. Later, they have the following exchange:

(19)   KEN: I can't believe you're going to that party tonight. It'll finish really late.
        BEV: It's Friday.

A key higher-level explicature would be something like (20):

(20)   Bev is reminding Ken that Ken said and therefore acted as if he believed that today is Friday at around 8am on Thursday the 5th of April 2012.

Here, Bev is making fun of Ken's earlier mistake for a mildly humorous effect.

As we will see in Chapter 10, accounts of irony within relevance theory have assumed that ironical utterances constitute a particular kind of 'echoic' use of language, i.e. utterances which express an attitude to a proposition that the speaker is not asserting but attributing to someone else. This means that they have something in common with reported speech and thought (where the speaker reports someone else's speech or thought). Bev's utterance in (11) above is an example of this. Bev was communicating not that it was Friday but that Andy thought that Jessie said that it was Friday. Bev's utterance in (11) and the two ironic examples (15) and (17) share the property that the speaker is not communicating the proposition expressed.

There are some cases where it is not clear exactly what the propositional content is. Consider (21), which might seem at first glance to be a fairly straightforward utterance:

(21)   I've lived in London for twenty years.

Suppose this is uttered by someone called Ken Young (assuming, for simplicity, that it is uttered at 10 a.m. on the 8th of April 2012, and with the usual caveat that we always use utterances here to represent propositions), we might suggest that the proposition expressed by the utterance is:

(22)   At 10 a.m. on the 8th of April 2012, Ken Young has lived in London for twenty years.

As with previous examples, this is an explicature inferred by a process of 'fleshing out' the linguistically encoded semantic representation. The lower-level proposition also seems to be communicated here, i.e. Ken will be taken to communicate his belief that Ken has lived in London for twenty years. As usual, the overall relevance of the utterance depends on which contextual assumptions are accessed by the hearer. Let's imagine the utterance is part of a larger conversation:

(23)   COLIN: You don't really sound that Scottish, do you?
        KEN: I've lived in London for twenty years.

Ken's utterance communicates the presumption of its own optimal relevance. So Colin assumes that it will provide enough effects to justify the effort involved in interpreting it, that it will provide as many more positive cognitive effects as Ken is willing and able to communicate, and that the speaker was unable (or unwilling) to think of any easier way of conveying these effects. If Colin assumes that *I* refers to Ken and that Ken is saying that Ken has lived in London for twenty years, then he can infer the implicature that:

(24)   Ken's Scottish accent has become much less strong because Ken has lived in London for twenty years.

This will be based on implicated premises such as:

(25)   People who have lived away from their childhood home for more than a few years often lose their childhood accent.

(26)   Scottish people who have lived in London for more than a few years often lose their Scottish accent.

These may, of course, be assumptions that Colin already believes. Even if Colin already believes them, though, they are still implicated premises in that Ken has provided evidence in support of them by producing this utterance in this context. If Ken is communicating (24)–(26), that is clearly enough to justify the effort involved in processing the utterance. Colin might well go on to make further inferences about Ken and other effects of his having lived in London for twenty years, e.g. he might infer that Ken must know London very well, that he must be happy living in London, and so on. Ken's responsibility for any one of these is slightly less than for the previous conclusions and Colin's is slightly more. Colin might even go further and make inferences that Ken did not intend, e.g. he might think negatively about London and people who choose to live there. If he makes assumptions like this, they are implications of the utterance but not implicatures, since Ken did not intentionally communicate them. There are also some implications (assumptions which follow logically from the utterance) where it is harder to decide to what extent they were intended. It is possible, for example, that Ken's utterance implies such assumptions as:

(27)   You should have realised that I've lived here for twenty years.

(28)   It is not surprising that my accent has changed.

(29)   You are not very clever not to have expected my accent to have changed.

There is evidence for these but it is not fully clear that Ken intended them. He might have communicated them inadvertently if the possibility that Colin would derive them did not occur to him. We will look at how the strength of implicatures can vary in Chapter 7 and consider in Section 6.5 of this chapter the possibility that explicatures can also vary in strength.

Now, you might have noticed that I ignored something significant in the discussion of example (23). Am I really suggesting that Ken started to live in

London at 10 a.m. on the 8th of April 1992, i.e. exactly twenty years before the time of utterance? Of course not. The proposition expressed here is less than literal in at least two ways. First, Colin will not understand Ken to be making a precise claim about the amount of time he has lived in London. Second, there is no commitment to Ken having never left London during all of those twenty years. This is an example of 'loose use' or approximation. We might characterise what Ken actually believes as something along the lines of (30):

(30)   Ken has lived in London more or less continuously for approximately twenty years.

Of course, we speak loosely very often. We considered these examples in Chapter 1:

(31)   You've been working on that book for a billion years.

(32)   There were a hundred people at my birthday party.

(33)   Brighton is sixty miles away.

As we said then, the hyperbole in (31) vastly overstates the time period, while the numbers in (32) and (33) are not intended to be exact. If you find out that exactly 97 people or 103 people came to my party, you will not think I have misled you. Similarly, Brighton does not need to be exactly sixty miles away for (33) to be a reasonable and informative utterance.

   Within relevance theory, it has been assumed that loose talk, hyperbole and metaphor have something in common. We say that a hundred people came to the party because that is close enough to the facts of the situation for us to draw relevant conclusions. We say that you have been writing your book for a billion years to indicate that it really is a very long time, knowing that you will not assume that I am communicating literally impossible propositions such as that one thousand million (or one million million) years have passed since you began working on the book. We report numbers loosely trusting hearers not to assume we are being exact. Similarly, in cases of metaphor, we do not assume that the speaker intends to communicate the exact proposition expressed. If you say (34) to me, for example, I will not assume that your teacher flew a military aircraft over your essay and attacked it with a bomb. If you say the more conventionally metaphorical (35), I will not assume that your house has been designed as a place in which to cook food.

(34)   My teacher dropped a smart bomb on my essay.

(35)   My house is an oven.

A final group of utterances to consider are ones where it seems that the propositional content of the utterance is necessarily vague and not resolvable in the context in which the utterance is produced. In these cases, it seems that the speaker does not provide enough linguistic material for the hearer to be able to work out a full proposition. Consider Bev's utterances in (36) (which we discussed in Chapter 5) and (37):

(36)   KEN: What do you think of Marjie's cooking?
              BEV: *(hesitantly)* Well...

(37)   *(Ken and Bev have been working hard, are both tired and are finding that there are lots*
              of different things they need to do at the same time. They meet briefly in the kitchen.)
              BEV: *(sighing)* Oh, life!

In (36), Bev's utterance makes clear that she does not feel incredibly positive
about Marjie's cooking but what exact proposition does she express? She does
not definitely communicate that she hates Magie's cooking but she does make
clear that it's not wonderful. She implicates that she is uncomfortable criticising
it. Perhaps the main motivation for this utterance is to make clear that she does
not want to clearly convey anything very negative. She may even be avoiding
communicating a full proposition so that this can not be held against her.

What exactly does Bev convey in (37)? Clearly it is something about life. But
what exactly? That it is complicated? That it is difficult? Both of these? Perhaps
Bev herself only has a vague idea of what she means to convey? In any case, this
is another example where there is some vagueness about the exact proposition
expressed.

This account does not assume that hearers always work out an exact proposition expressed when processing an utterance, i.e. it is possible to derive
implicatures without constructing full representations of the proposition
expressed or indeed of any explicatures of the utterance. Consider an example
where it is clear what the main point of the utterance is and where this
is conveyed by implicatures communicated by the utterance. Consider, for
example, (38) and (39):

(38)   *(Ken is cooking burgers on a barbecue)*
              KEN: Do you fancy one?
              BEV: I'm a vegetarian.

(39)   *(on a retail company's website in the 'FAQs' section)*
              What can I do if I want to exchange goods after the 30 days deadline?
              Our terms and conditions are clearly stated on the till receipt given at time of purchase.

In (38), it is possible that Ken will derive the key implicatures (e.g. that Bev
does not want a burger) without constructing a full representation of the
proposition that Bev is a vegetarian, including the representation of the time
and circumstances, and so on. What is important, though, is that Bev's utterance
has made this proposition manifest and it is possible for Ken to retrieve the full
proposition later. In (39) (adapted from a real website I discussed with students
in a classroom activity), it is quite possible that the customer will have decided
that a refund will not be possible as soon as she sees that the first sentence in the
response does not directly answer the question. In both cases, it is quite possible
that no representation of the lowest-level proposition expressed plays a role in
processing. However, these propositions are communicated since the speaker
has certainly given evidence to support these conclusions. Even if Ken does not

construct a representation of these at the time of utterance, it is clear that Bev has given evidence to support them and it is quite possible for him to think further about the utterances at any time and arrive at these conclusions. Similar points could be made about higher-level explicatures, which are discussed in Section 6.4.

Exercise 6.1 asks you to consider the range of higher-level and lower-level explicatures conveyed by a range of utterances.

Exercise 6.1

- Identify the some of the higher-level and lower-level explicatures which A is likely to derive in interpreting B's utterance in the following exchanges:
  - (i) *(A and B are in the living-room. B is reading a book)*
    - A: How did you get on at school today?
    - B: I'm reading.
  - (ii) A: What did John's teacher say at the parents evening?
    - B: He's reading at level six.
  - (iii) A: What do you think John told Sue about the party?
    - B: It'll be great fun. She should come.
  - (iv) A: I went to see that experimental theatre group last night. I'm going again tomorrow.
    - B: You enjoyed it?

6.3   Words, concepts and the world

Before going on to consider higher-level explicatures in more detail, this section summarises some key assumptions made within relevance theory about the relationships between words, concepts and entities in the world.

Relevance theory follows a fairly standard view in assuming that content words encode **concepts**. The word *chocolate* encodes the concept {CHOCOLATE}. The word *cheese* encodes the concept {CHEESE}. And so on. When someone hears an utterance containing the word *chocolate* they activate the concept of {CHOCOLATE}. When they hear the word *cheese* they activate the concept {CHEESE}. The difference between (40) and (41) is that the hearer of (40) will activate the concept {CHOCOLATE} while the hearer of (41) will activate the concept {CHEESE}:

(40)   Andy likes chocolate.

(41)   Andy likes cheese.

Another way to talk about the difference is to say that the hearers of (40) and (41) will construct different **conceptual representations**, depending on whether the concept activated by the final word is {CHOCOLATE} or {CHEESE}. These conceptual representations constitute what we have called the propositions expressed and we might represent them (roughly and informally) as follows:

(42)   Andy Adams likes to eat chocolate around 11am on the 29th of March 2012.

(43)   Andy Adams likes to eat cheese around 11am on the 29th of March 2012.

Following Fodor's (1975) assumptions, we can understand our thoughts as conceptual representations (what Fodor would describe as expressions in the 'language of thought'). Any other explicatures or implicatures of the utterance will also be conceptual representations.

Relevance theory assumes that we can explain the meanings of linguistic expressions by describing how they contribute to conceptual representations and that we can explain the meanings of conceptual representations in terms of a version of **truth conditional semantics**. On this approach, the truth conditions of an utterance are determined by the conceptual representations of the propositions they communicate. Following the assumptions of truth-conditional semantics, conceptual representations are semantically interpreted by being put into systematic correspondence with objects, events and states in the world. In Chapter 11, we will see that this account will need to be complicated a little to reflect the fact that not all linguistic expressions encode concepts.

6.4   Higher-level explicatures

In this section, we consider some of the **higher-level explicatures** of utterances. As we have seen, any proposition, such as (44), can be embedded within other, more complex, propositions:

(44)   It's raining.

Typically, these will include descriptions of speech acts (e.g. 'X said that...', 'X asked whether...') or of propositional attitudes (e.g. 'X believes that...', 'X wants to know whether...'). Examples are (45)–(49):

(45)   Ken believes that it's raining.

(46)   Ken wonders whether it's raining.

(47)   Ken thinks that Andy thinks that it's raining.

(48)   Ken wonders whether Andy thinks that it's raining.

(49)   Ken wonders whether Andy wonders whether Ken thinks that Andy thinks that it's raining.

Speakers can choose how explicit they are about each of these levels. I could, for example, communicate the thought expressed in (48) by uttering (50) with rising intonation consistent with asking a question:

(50)   Andy thinks that it's raining.

If I choose (50), I will be trusting you to infer that I am wondering whether Andy thinks that it's raining, rather than expressing my belief that Andy thinks that it's raining. In fact, given the right contextual assumptions, I could utter (40) to communicate the same as any of the utterances in (45)–(49).

Notice that hearers always infer at least one higher level of embedding for any proposition we express. That is, no matter what proposition P I utter (and no matter how internally complex it is), you will always infer one more level under which P is embedded, e.g. 'Ken believes that P', 'Ken wonders whether P', and so on. If I utter (51), for example, you are unlikely to conclude simply that it is raining.

(51)   It's raining.

You will first infer something like (52) or (53):

(52)   Billy believes that it's raining.

(53)   Billy wonders whether it's raining.

If you infer (52), you may accept that it's raining based on the evidence I have provided that I believe it, and come to believe it too. This may be true even if I produce a highly embedded proposition such as (54):

(54)   Andy thinks that Jessie believes that Alan wonders whether Ken knows that Jim told Elsie that it was raining.

On hearing (54), you will still embed the proposition it expresses under a representation of attitude such as 'Ken believes that...' as part of the process of interpreting it.

Higher-level explicatures are an important part of the relevance-theoretic account of linguistic meaning. They play an important role in linguistic semantics in that some linguistic expressions are taken to encode information about higher-level explicatures, and they play an important role in pragmatics in that accounts of utterance interpretation involve assumptions about higher-level explicatures.

We will return to consider linguistically encoded contributions to higher-level explicatures in the discussion of conceptual and procedural meaning in Chapter 11. For now, here are a few examples of linguistic expressions which encode contributions to higher-level explicatures. The cases we will mention briefly here are syntactic structures, words such as *wow* or *goodness*, adverbials such as *luckily* or *seriously*, and prosody.

First, recall how an utterance consisting of just one clause can be understood as expressing one or more higher-level explicatures. (55), for example, could express any of (56)–(58):

(55)   Andy is polite.

(56)   Ken believes that Andy is polite.

(57)   Ken wonders whether Andy is polite.

(58)   Ken is happy that Andy is polite.

Higher-level explicatures such as these might be inferred without any linguistic indication to help the hearer arrive at them. It is arguably not surprising, though, that there seem to be linguistic expressions designed to help us make these inferences. Within relevance theory, a number of expressions have been seen as encoding information about higher-level explicatures.

One area where this has been seen as important is in dealing with the tricky question of what is encoded by different types of sentences. It is clear that (59), (60) and (61) have different meanings but also that they share the property of being about Andy and politeness:

(59)   Andy is polite.

(60)   Is Andy polite?

(61)   Andy, be polite!

It is often suggested that examples such as (59)–(61) share the same propositional content (being about the proposition 'Andy is polite') but differ in some other way (see, for example, Searle 1979). Within relevance theory, we might say that they share a logical form (which is, of course, less than fully propositional) and, in appropriate circumstances, would express the same propositional form. There have been a number of different kinds of attempts to characterise the meaning differences, including accounts based on speech acts and accounts based on a notion of semantic mood (which is less specific than speech act information and leaves more room for inference). Within relevance theory, the proposal has been that they encode different contributions to higher-level explicatures.[1]

One thing to note here is that relevance theory does not take as its starting point the assumption that there exists a well-defined set of 'sentence types' for which we then need to define the linguistically encoded meanings. Many theorists start by assuming that we can divide sentences into declaratives, imperatives, interrogatives, exclamatives, and so on, and that each of these will encode a different kind of meaning. Relevance theory assumes instead a range of different kinds of linguistic features which provide pointers towards the final overall meaning. These include syntactic structures, which we can think of for now as including declarative syntax, imperative syntax, and so on. While they are not usually seen as encoding a contribution to higher-level explicatures, words such as *so* and *then* also seem to help push interpretations in a particular direction (for discussion, see Blakemore 1987, 2002):

(62)   So Andy is polite.

(63)   Andy is polite then.

We'll look at the contribution of words like *so* and *then* in Chapter 11. For now, notice that both of these words seem to make a question interpretation more likely.

Other words which seem to contribute to the derivation of higher level explicatures include *wow*, *goodness*, *seriously* and *luckily*:

(64)   Wow, Andy is polite.

(65)   Goodness, Andy is polite.

(66)   Seriously, Andy is polite.

(67)   Luckily, Andy is polite.

(64) and (65) suggest that the speaker is surprised at Andy's politeness, either at the extent of his politeness or just by the fact that he is polite (for further discussion, see Wharton 2009). Possible higher-level explicatures of these utterances include:

(68)   The speaker is surprised at how polite Andy is.

(69)   The speaker is surprised that Andy is polite.

Seriously in (66) contributes to explicatures about how the speaker is communicating (for further discussion, see Wilson and Sperber 1993). *Luckily* in (67) contributes to explicatures about her attitude to the proposition she is expressing. Possible higher-level explicatures of these utterances include:

(70)   The speaker is saying seriously that (or being serious in saying that) Andy is polite.

(71)   The speaker is saying that Andy is polite and thinks it is lucky that this is the case.

Finally, for now, it has been suggested that prosodic structure can encode contributions to higher-level explicatures.[2] A 'high-rising terminal', for example, can be seen as leading towards a 'question-like' interpretation. An utterance of (72) which ends with high rising intonation (indicated here with the symbol '/' and also, less formally, with a question mark) might well be understood as asking whether Andy is polite rather than saying that he is polite:

(72)   Andy is /polite?

In fact, it is an oversimplification to assume that when a fairly standard Southern British English speaker says 'it's raining' with a falling intonation pattern they are likely to be making a statement and that changing the intonation to a rising one will change it to a question. The context has a big impact here. A fall is quite normal on questions in many contexts and it is fairly common nowadays to make a statement with a high rising tone (a phenomenon often described as 'uptalk'). However, it is definitely true that different intonation patterns make different interpretations more or less likely.

6.5   Strength of explicatures

Inferential conclusions can be more or less strongly evidenced. The more evidence there is to support them, the stronger the individual's belief that they are true. We considered this in Chapter 3 when we looked at different kinds of cognitive effect. We illustrated strengthening as a cognitive effect by considering the situation where an individual thinks they can hear rain outside and then looks outside and sees rain falling. The visual stimulus provided more evidence than the sound and so the assumption that it was raining was strengthened.

Communicated assumptions can vary in **strength** in two ways. There might be more or less evidence to support a particular assumption and the communicator can make their intention to communicate more or less manifest (for discussion, see Wilson and Sperber 2002). We'll consider one example here and then say more on the strength of implicatures in Chapter 7. Consider the following exchange:

(73)   KEN: Are you worried the price of petrol might go up in the budget?
            BEV: I don't have a car.

Bev's utterance here strongly communicates the following assumptions:

(74)   *Explicatures:*
    a.   Bev believes that Bev does not own a car.
    b.   Bev does not own a car.
            Implicatures:
    c.   Bev does not buy petrol.
    d.   Bev is not worried about the price of petrol going up in the budget.

All of these are fairly strongly communicated, since it is hard to see how Bev's utterance would be relevant if she did not intend to communicate them: they are therefore required if the utterance is to satisfy her expectations of relevance. At the same time, there are other possible implicatures of Bev's utterance where there is some evidence that she intended to convey them, but where the evidence is less strong:

(75)   *Further implicatures:*
    a.   Bev does not think she needs to worry about car owners.
    b.   Bev disapproves of people who own cars.
    c.   Bev cares about the environment.

These may not be implicatures which Bev specifically intended to communicate but they would follow from her utterance given appropriate contextual assumptions, and she has provided some evidence to support them. These are, then, weaker implicatures than (74c–d).

Similarly, explicatures can vary in strength. An important distinction to make here is between degrees of explicitiness and strength of explicatures. Bev's possible responses in (76) vary with regard to how explicitly they communicate the proposition that Jess has a French exam the day after the exchange:

(76)   KEN: What's up with Jess? She seems really stressed.
            BEV: a. French tomorrow.
                 b. French exam tomorrow.
                 c. She's got a French exam tomorrow.

Differences in the strength of explicatures may follow fairly straightforwardly from the context in which the utterance is produced. Consider, for example, (77) and (78):

(77)   *(after trying a mouthful of a new dish prepared by Ken)*
        BEV: I don't like this.

(78)   *(to Ken, after serving a new dish to their dog Toby and watching him sniff it unenthusiastically)*
        BEV: He doesn't like it.

Clearly, Bev has less evidence for the assumption that Toby does not like the new dish in (78) than she does for her own response in (77). (77) will be taken as an expression of Bev's own belief that she does not like the dish and so Ken will take this as quite strongly evidenced. With (76), Ken is likely to think that Bev's belief is a conclusion she has drawn based on the evidence of Toby's behaviour. So this is less strongly evidenced. Note, however, that both of these propositions are quite strongly communicated since Bev's intention to convey them is quite strongly manifest.

Explicatures may come with even less evidence than this. (36) and (37) above, repeated here as (79) and (80), are cases where the speaker does not supply enough linguistic material for the hearer to identify one clear propositional form:

(79)   KEN: What do you think of Marjie's cooking?
        BEV: *(hesitantly)* Well...

(80)   *(Ken and Bev have been working hard, are both tired and are finding that there are lots of different things they need to do at the same time. They meet briefly in the kitchen.)*
        BEV: *(sighing)* Oh, life!

We said above that these utterances might be treated as cases where there is no clear proposition expressed. Another way to respond to these cases would be to say that they give some evidence for each of a range of propositions without making it possible for the hearer to decide for certain whether each one is actually intentionally communicated. Part of the range in each case is represented in (81) and (82):

(81)   *Candidate explicatures for Bev's utterance of 'well...':*
   a.   Marjie's cooking is less than wonderful.
   b.   I do not enjoy eating Marjie's food.
   c.   I find it hard to comment on Marjie's food.

(82)   *Candidate explicatures for Bev's utterance of 'Oh, life!':*
   a.   Life is difficult.
   b.   Life is complicated.
   c.   Life continues to challenge me.
   d.   I am constantly overwhelmed by the challenges of life.

Bev has given some evidence for each explicature in (81)–(82) but she has not given decisive evidence that she intends to convey any particular one of them, and indeed it seems reasonable to conclude that her informative intention itself was vague. Part of the effect of these utterances comes from the fact that the hearer has to run through a range of candidate propositions, each of which has been weakly communicated.

There are utterances similar to the examples we have just considered where the communication of a range of weak explicatures contributes to the sense that the utterance has poetic or literary effects (for discussion of examples such as this, see Dogan 1992). Consider, for example, this famous haiku:

(83)   Sick and feverish
        Glimpse of cherry blossoms
        Still shivering.   (Ryunosuke Akutagawa 1892–1927)

There is no way for the reader of (83) to know who is sick and feverish, glimpsing the cherry blossoms, and so on.[3] This means that there is no way to fill in all of the gaps in the corresponding semantic representation. We cannot decide who is entertaining these thoughts. We can, of course, imagine some of the possibilities and derive effects from them, e.g. I might imagine that I am the speaker and imagine a particular kind of sick, feverish feeling, and so on. However, no particular set of propositions which I might derive can be thought of as *the* intended interpretation. Part of the poetic quality of utterances like this arises because of these uncertainties. The lyrics of pop songs also constitute cases where utterances give rise to **weak explicatures**. When The Beatles sing the lines in (84):

(84)   You say you've lost your love
        Well she told me yesterday
        It's you she's thinking of
        And she told me what to say
        She says she loves you   (The Beatles, 'She Loves You', 1963)

the listener can entertain the words as being sung by the character represented by the singer addressing them to the listener, by the listener to someone else, by someone else to the listener, and so on (for discussion of the effects caused by this, see Durant 1984: 202–9). The fact that utterances such as these give rise to a range of weak explicatures means, in turn, that they give rise to a range of **weak implicatures**. We consider the notion of weak implicature in Chapter 7 and consider how they arise in metaphorical utterances in Chapter 9.

Exercise 6.2 asks you to consider a range of examples which vary in terms of the strength of the range of explicatures they communicate and to consider the effects these give rise to.

Exercise 6.2

- Identify explicatures likely to be communicated by B's utterance in each of the following exchanges. How strong is each explicature? What kinds of effects do these explicatures give rise to?

  (i)   A: Where's the salt and pepper?
        B: On the table.

  (ii) A: Did you give the students their coursework exercise?
        B: It looks really difficult! There's so many questions! I haven't studied all of this? Why's the deadline so soon?

  (iii) A: What's your favourite poem?
        B: Shall I compare thee to a summer's day?

6.6   Summary

This chapter built on the previous one by considering some of ways in which explicatures can vary. We looked at the notion of the 'proposition expressed', contrasting that with higher-level explicatures which contain the proposition expressed or other propositions as a sub-part. We saw that utterances can convey a number of explicatures embedded within each other and that the relevance of some utterances depends mainly on the communication of higher-level explicatures. Finally, we saw that explicatures can be communicated with more or less strength and that poetic and other effects can follow from the fact that utterances convey a range of weak implicatures. In the next chapter, we consider the different kinds of implicatures which utterances can convey.

Exercise 6.3

As in every chapter, this final exercise asks you to adjust the list of questions you have come up with so far by compiling new questions which have occurred to you while reading this chapter and to think about the kinds of things which might count as answers to any questions you have come up with so far. First, add new questions to your ongoing list. Second, consider all of your questions and think about possible ways of answering them.

6.7   Further reading

For this chapter, I would recommend the same set of initial sources as the previous chapter. There is some discussion of higher-level explicatures in *Relevance* (Sperber and Wilson 1986: 224–54) and in two papers published shortly after the book (Wilson and Sperber 1988, 1993). Both of these papers are reprinted in Wilson and Sperber's more recent book (2012). See also Carston (2002a: 116–34).

7　Types of implicature

Topics: implications and implicatures; implicated premises and implicated conclusions; deriving implicatures; strength of implicatures

7.1　Overview

In the last chapter, we looked in more detail at the relevance-theoretic notion of explicature and the different types of explicature which can be communicated. This chapter looks in more detail at the notion of 'implicature'. We start, in the next section, by considering the difference between implications and implicatures. Implications are conclusions which follow logically from one or more premises. Implicatures are intentionally communicated implications. This means that, for any utterance, its implicatures constitute a subset of its implications and so the task of interpreting an utterance can be understood either as finding the implications intended by the communicator or as deciding which of a range of implications of an utterance constitute its implicatures. Section 7.3 looks at the difference between implicated premises and implicated conclusions. Implicated premises are inferred so that they can then act as the input to further inferential processes. Implicated conclusions are inferred through the interaction of implicated premises with other assumptions, including explicatures of the utterance. Separating implicated premises and implicated conclusions is not easy, particularly since any conclusion worth having is worth having because it enables us to make further inferences based on it. This section also explores the relationship between contextual assumptions and implicated premises. Complications arise here because contextual assumptions may need to be inferred for the first time in understanding an utterance (in which case they are clearly implicated premises) or they may already be manifest to the hearer (in which case, I will suggest, they are still implicated premises, since the speaker has provided evidence of an intention to make them more manifest by producing the utterance whose interpretation required them). Section 7.4 looks in more detail at the process of deriving implicatures and Section 7.5 considers how implicatures can vary in strength. A number of factors combine to determine the relative strength of implicatures and in some cases it is difficult to know exactly how much responsibility a communicator takes for conclusions we might draw. The idea that some utterances give rise to a wide range of weak implicatures is important in accounting for some aspects of style and for the 'poetic' effects of some utterances. This section also considers cases where interpreters might not know whether a particular conclusion is or is not an implicature of the utterance and what determines the extent to which we are aware of, or consciously think about, this question.

7.2   Implications and implicatures

In many areas of the study of language, terms used technically and with precise definitions are also used more loosely, and often with more than one meaning, in everyday contexts. As mentioned in Chapter 1, it is important to distinguish technical senses of 'infer' from everyday usages. In discussing conclusions which addressees infer, Grice proposed to use the terms 'implicate' and 'implicature' consistently as technical terms both for clarity and also to avoid having to make decisions each time about exactly which more common verb or noun (such as *imply*) to use. This section considers the definitions of these terms and the difference within relevance theory between implications and implicatures.

What is an implicature? For Grice, it is an intentionally communicated conclusion. For some later pragmatic theorists, any communicated proposition which is not part of what is said is an implicature. Sperber and Wilson formalised the notion that the *-icature* and *-icate* endings signify intentional communication when they formulated their own notion of explicature:

> On the analogy of 'implicature', we will call an explicitly communicated assumption an *explicature*. Any assumption communicated, but not explicitly so, is implicitly communicated: it is an *implicature*. By this definition, ostensive stimuli which do not encode logical forms will, of course, only have implicatures.   (Sperber and Wilson 1986: 182)

So Sperber and Wilson define **implicatures** as communicated assumptions which are not explicitly communicated. As we have seen, an important difference between the two approaches lies in the different ways that they understand what it means to be 'explicitly communicated'. We will see that there are differences within the understanding of implicature as well, most notably that there are no conventional implicatures and no generalised conversational implicatures within relevance theory. Implicatures can be organised into types in other ways (implicated premises or conclusions, stronger or weaker) but there is no notion of encoded ('conventional') implicatures and no notion of 'default' or 'automatic' ('generalised') conversational implicatures. Notice that one consequence of Sperber and Wilson's definition is that nonverbal communication (which, by definition, does not involve encoded 'logical forms') conveys only implicatures. An alternative might be to consider the term 'implicature' as one which applies only to indirectly communicated assumptions associated with verbal communication. In this case, we would need another term for assumptions communicated nonverbally.

As we have seen, any utterance will carry some implications which the communicator has not intended to communicate and so we need to have terminology which distinguishes what is intentionally communicated from what is not. Within relevance theory, the term **implication** is a logical term describing assumptions which are inferred from any type of stimulus (a sight, a sound, a thought, an utterance) and are among the cognitive effects which contribute to its relevance. An implication may or may not have been intentionally conveyed and may or may not have been communicated at all. This means that all implicatures are implications but not all implications are implicatures.

Here is a fairly straightforward example of the kind often used to illustrate implicature:

(1)   KEN: Do you want me to give you Jessie's number?
        BEV: She texted me yesterday. I've got it on my phone.

It is clear from Bev's utterance that she does not want or need Ken to give her Jessie's number. This is clearly a strong implicature of Bev's utterance. It is required in order to see that her utterance is relevant and Ken's expectations of relevance will be satisfied if he derives this implicature. Even in this simple case, though, there are other things which Ken can infer from Bev's utterance but which do not contribute to the relevance of the utterance. These might include assumptions which Ken is already entertaining, such as those in (2):

(2) a.   Bev knows how to use a phone.
    b.   Bev is happy to talk to Jessie.
    c.   Bev is happy to talk to Ken.

There might also be things which follow from Bev's utterance which she could not have envisaged. Suppose that Ken had suspected that Bev and Jessie had fallen out and not been in touch with each other recently but that Bev does not know this. Ken will now be able to conclude that:

(3)   Ken was wrong when he thought Bev and Jessie had not been in touch with each other recently.

The assumptions in (2) and (3) are implications of Bev's utterance (because they logically follow from it) but not implicatures (because she did not intend to communicate them and they do not contribute to the relevance of her utterance to Ken).

For any utterance, there will be implications which are not implicatures. Consider an utterance of (4) said by a stranger on a train platform:

(4)   The train's been cancelled.

This utterance will provide evidence for a large number of conclusions. Let's assume that the utterance is said by a stranger to me on platform one at Finsbury Park station and that I have access to the following set of contextual assumptions, among others:

(5) a.   It is 0755 on Monday 2nd of April 2012.
   b.   I am waiting for the 0800 train to Moorgate on Monday 2nd of April 2012.
   c.   Trains for Moorgate leave Finsbury Park every fifteen minutes.
   d.   The trip from Finsbury Park to Moorgate on these trains takes around ten minutes.
   e.   Trains on this line are cancelled fairly often.
   f.   When one train is cancelled, it is sometimes connected with a larger problem and other trains are late or cancelled.
   g.   It is possible to travel by underground from this station.
   h.   The underground trip from here to Moorgate will involve changing trains once and should take around twenty minutes.
   i.   I have an appointment in an office five minutes' walk from Moorgate at 0830.
   j.   I had thought of taking the 0745 train or even the 0700 but decided the 0800 would be fine.

What is the most likely explicature of the stranger's utterance? On standard relevance theory assumptions, we would assume that the stranger knows that the train I am waiting for is the 0800 to Moorgate and that I will assume that this is the train she is referring to. This would suggest an explicature such as (6):

(6)   [A stranger has told me that] the 0800 train from Finsbury Park to Moorgate on Monday 2nd of April has been cancelled.

If I believe her, the following conclusions follow (among others):

(7) a.   My journey will be delayed.
   b.   The earliest train from Finsbury Park to Moorgate which I can catch will leave at 0815.
   c.   If I take the next train, I will arrive at Moorgate at 0825.
   d.   If I arrive at Moorgate at 0825 and move quickly, I might just make it in time for my appointment.
   e.   If I wait for the 0815 I might be a little late for my appointment.
   f.   If I wait for the 0815 and it is late or cancelled, I will miss my appointment.
   g.   If I take the underground, I should arrive at Moorgate at around 0820 and should be able to arrive a few minutes early for my appointment.
   h.   I am more likely to make it to my appointment on time if I take the underground train.
   i.   I would have been in good time if the 0800 had not been cancelled.
   j.   I would have arrived in very good time if I had taken the 0745 train.
   k.   I would have arrived in very good time if I had taken the 0700 train.

All of these seem like relevant conclusions to derive (they are 'positive cognitive effects' of the utterance). How many of them could the stranger have intended to communicate to me? Only (7a–c) are plausible candidates, since all of the others depend on assumptions about me and my appointment which the stranger could not have had access to. So all of (7d–k) are implications of her utterance (they logically follow from it, given the appropriate contextual assumptions) but not implicatures (they are not intentionally communicated). It is quite likely, in fact, that only (7a) is a fairly strong implicature of the stranger's utterance since she can envisage that deriving this will make the utterance relevant to me and may not have anything further in mind.

This illustrates the important point that the borderline between implicatures and mere implications is not always definite and clear. The vagueness around this borderline has important social implications. In this case, not much follows from whether (7b–c) are implicatures or mere implications. The relevance of the stranger's utterance depends on her having communicated something from which I can derive enough positive cognitive effects to justify the effort involved in processing the utterance. It is clear that I can do this whether or not (7b–c) are implicatures. There are some implicatures about our social relationship which I can derive either way, such as (8) and (9):

(8)   The stranger has passed on helpful information to me.

(9)   The stranger has shown consideration for me.

These assumptions seem to be important in accounting for social aspects of human interactions, including accounting for what motivated the stranger to tell me about the cancellation. What would be the difference between the stranger's utterance here and an utterance which seems at first glance to convey only implications and not implicatures? A typical and often discussed example is where two people who don't know each other meet on the street and one of them asks the other for the time. Suppose I ask a stranger what time it is and she replies:

(10)   Ten past ten.

Assuming the time and date as indicated, the explicature of her utterance will be something like:

(11)   It is ten minutes past ten on Wednesday the 4th of April 2012.

Are there any implicatures? We would usually assume not since she does not have access to any contextual assumptions about me which would be required to derive new conclusions. The implications for me might include:

(12) a.   It will be at least twenty past ten before I can arrive at the lecture room.
     b.   I'm going to be over twenty minutes late for my lecture.
     c.   I'd better not go to the lecture at all.

The stranger has no knowledge of my lecture or its timing so she has no responsibility for any of these conclusions. There are some implicatures of her utterance, though, such as those indicated in (8) and (9) above. So it turns out that even an utterance which seems at first to have only implications and not implicatures does in fact communicate important implicatures about social relationships. One area where this is significant is in developing an account of 'phatic communication', communication which seems to be mainly about developing or maintaining social relationships.[1] Before leaving our two strangers, there is one more difference between them we should note. The stranger on the train platform took it upon herself to tell me about the cancellation whereas the stranger on the street was merely answering a question. So there is a slight difference in the implicatures about social relationships. One part of accounting for this might be to say that the stranger on the train platform implicated (13)–(14) while the stranger on the street implicated (15)–(16):

(13)   The stranger has chosen to pass on some helpful information to me.

(14)   The stranger has made a decision on her own part to show consideration to me by sharing information.

(15)   The stranger has passed on some helpful information to me in response to a request.

(16)   The stranger has shown consideration to me by sharing information in response to a request.

Arguably, the stranger on the rail platform has been more sociable than the stranger on the street. The difference, though, is fairly small and both kinds of behaviour seem like fairly common ways for humans to interact. I think, though, that most people would be more offended by someone who refused to answer when asked what time it is than by someone who heard a train was cancelled but didn't announce it to anyone else.[2]

A clearer illustration of how implicatures play a role in social relationships comes from cases where there is a contrast between a hurtful implication and a hurtful implicature. Suppose, for example, that Ken has tried to pass his driving test several times and always failed. A new acquaintance, Sandra, is chatting to Ken and Bev and they exchange the following utterances:

(17)   KEN: Do you drive?
        SANDRA: Yes, I just passed my test actually. It turned out it was really easy.
        BEV: Yes, any fool could pass, couldn't they, Ken?

One of the implications of Sandra's utterance is (18):

(18)   Sandra found something easy that Ken found difficult.

One of the implications of Bev's utterance is (19):

(19)   Bev thinks negatively about Ken because he hasn't passed his test.

(18) is an implication of Sandra's utterance since Sandra does not know anything about Ken's driving test history. Ken will not be happy about the contrast between Sandra and himself but he cannot think that Sandra intended to communicate something negative about him in particular. (19) is an implicature of Bev's utterance since Ken's driving test history is mutually manifest and tagging Ken's name to the utterance makes it more salient that she is intentionally

communicating this to him. Other things being equal, the negative implicature will be more hurtful than a mere implication since it is clearly intended to hurt Ken. Of course, it may be that he is not so sensitive and that this is intended as a less serious kind of banter. The details of this will depend on details of the relationship and the set of mutually manifest assumptions.

We can think of the task of an addressee as being to work out which members of the set of implications of an utterance are implicatures (intentionally communicated) and which are not. In Section 7.5 below, we will see how the extent to which this is clear affects the strength of individual implicatures and in Chapter 9 we will see how this is involved in the relevance-theoretic account of metaphor and other kinds of creative language use. We'll conclude this section by considering the implication that follows from every utterance that the speaker or writer is alive (at the time of speaking or writing). This follows for any utterance but it is usually unlikely to be considered as a possible implicature of an utterance, even though there are contexts where it is an important implication, such as when there is concern over whether someone is alive or not. An exception in a fictional example occurs near the end of the Walt Disney film *The Jungle Book*. Baloo the bear has been fighting the dangerous tiger Shere Khan to save the life of the young human Mowgli. Baloo lies lifeless on the ground and Mowgli and Bagheera the leopard assume he is dead. Bagheera makes a speech about how noble Baloo has been, even going so far as to lay down his life for his friend. Mowgli is crying. As Bagheera is speaking, Baloo begins to speak. Here is the relevant part of the script:

(20)   MOWGLI: (*to the unconscious Baloo*) Baloo, get up. Oh, please get up.

        BAGHEERA: Mowgli, try to understand.

        MOWGLI: Bagheera, what's the matter with him?

        BAGHEERA: You've got to be brave, like Baloo was.

        MOWGLI: You... you don't mean... Oh, no. Baloo.

        BAGHEERA: Now, now. I know how you feel. But you must remember, Mowgli. Greater love hath no one than he who lays down his life for his friend.

        (*Baloo starts to wake up, not noticed by Bagheera and Mowgli*)

        BAGHEERA: Whenever great deeds are remembered in this jungle, one name will stand above all others: our friend, Baloo the bear.

        BALOO: (*sniffing*) He's cracking me up.

        BAGHEERA: The memory of Baloo's sacrifice and bravery will forever be engraved on our saddened hearts.

        BALOO: Beautiful.

        BAGHEERA: This spot where Baloo fell will always be a hallowed place in the jungle, for there lies one of nature's noblest creatures.

        BALOO: I wish my mother could have heard this.

        BAGHEERA: It's best we leave now. Come along, Man Cub.

        BALOO: Hey, don't stop now, Baggy. You're doing great! There's more, lots more!

                       (*The Jungle Book*, Walt Disney Productions, 1967)

In this context, the implication that Baloo is alive does seem to be an implicature of each of Baloo's utterances. Notice, by the way, that we are 'eavesdroppers' on this scene, as are all viewers and readers of fiction. We are looking and listening to the characters here and making inferences about their inferences. There is more than one layer of communicative intention which we consider when watching the film. The film-makers are communicating with us and also showing us communication among the characters. When Baloo first speaks (*He's cracking me up…* etc.) the film-makers are showing us (implicating) that Baloo is alive. When Baloo speaks to Bagheera and Mowgli (*Hey, don't stop now, Baggy…*) he is implicating to Bagheera and Mowgli (and us) that he is alive.[3]

The account of phatic communication developed by Zegarac and Clark (1999) is based on looking at similar variation in certain implications of every utterance, such as:

(21)   The speaker is communicating with me.

(22)   The speaker is willing to engage in conversation with me.

For many utterances, these are mere implications and the main relevance of the utterance lies elsewhere. In some contexts, such as when there is a question over whether or not a particular person is willing to communicate with another, the evidence that the communicator is willing to communicate can be an important source of the relevance of the utterance.

Exercise 7.1 asks you to consider the difference between implications and implicatures and some of the social and other effects which follow from the implications and implicatures communicated by particular utterances.

Exercise 7.1

- Consider B's utterance in each of the following exchanges. Make a list of conclusions which A might derive from each one. Decide for each one whether it is an implicature or a non-communicated implication. Indicate where it is not clear how to categorise a particular conclusion and consider how variations in the accessibility of particular contextual assumptions affect the status of the conclusions:

  (i)   (*A and B live together. B usually leaves for work at 8 a.m.*)
        A: Do you want me to bring you up a coffee?
        B: It's ten past eight.

  (ii) (*A and B live together. A and B had a major argument and have not spoken for two weeks.*)
        A: Do you fancy a cuppa?
        B: I'd love one.

  (iii) A: Did you see the end of the test match?
        B: I don't really watch sports.

  (iv) A: Do you recycle cardboard?
        B: I think it's really important to think about what we do to the planet.

7.3   Implicated premises and implicated conclusions

There is an interesting pattern which repeats itself in many examples of indirect communication, dating from Grice's work and running through the work of all pragmaticists since. It is illustrated in (23):

(23)   KEN: Do you fancy a cup of coffee?
         BEV: Actually, I'm avoiding caffeine just now.

Most people will realise straight away that Bev is communicating that she doesn't fancy a cup of coffee and that the reason for this is that she doesn't want to consume anything with caffeine in it. Depending on the context, there might be further implicatures about other drinks Ken could offer or other things he could do. Usually, the representation of this would look something like this:

(24)   *Explicature:*
         Bev is avoiding drinking or consuming things with caffeine in them.
         Contextual assumptions:
         Ken has asked Bev whether Bev would like a cup of coffee.
         Coffee contains caffeine.
         Implicatures:
         Bev would not like a cup of coffee.
         Bev would not like a cup of coffee because it contains caffeine.

The account is based on assuming that coffee contains caffeine, and that both Ken and Bev know that Ken has just asked Bev whether she would like a cup of coffee. When Bev says that she is avoiding caffeine, Ken can combine this with the existing contextual assumptions to derive the implicatures which make the utterance relevant enough to be worth processing. The indirectness is justified because it enables Bev to communicate not just that she doesn't want coffee but also why, which means that it is easier for Ken to know what to think of doing or saying next. This removes the risk of social embarrassment or impoliteness which might have arisen if Bev had simply replied 'no'. It is also helpful since Ken now knows about a number of other things which Bev will not want to drink. All of this can be captured by suggesting further implicatures, such as:

(25) a.   Bev has a reason for not wanting coffee.
     b.   Bev is not turning Ken down because of any negative reason such as that Bev does not like Ken.
     c.   Bev might want to drink something that does not contain caffeine.
     d.   Bev will not want to drink anything else which contains caffeine.
     e.   Bev will not want to drink tea.

At first glance, this example looks quite different from an exchange such as (26):

(26)   KEN: Do you fancy a cup of coffee?
         BEV: Actually, I'm avoiding drinks with tannin in them at the moment.

Suppose that Ken does not know in advance that tannin is present in coffee. In this case, Bev has given evidence by her utterance that (she believes that) coffee contains tannin. Our representation of the inference process might look like this:

(27)   *Explicature:*
          Bev is avoiding drinking or consuming things with tannin in them.
          Contextual assumptions:
          Ken has asked Bev whether Bev would like a cup of coffee.
          Implicated premise:
          Coffee contains tannin.
          Implicatures:
          Bev would not like a cup of coffee.
          Bev would not like a cup of coffee because it contains tannin.

The key difference here is that we have treated the assumption that coffee contains tannin as an implicature rather than as a contextual assumption. It is labelled an **implicated premise** because it is then used in deriving further implicatures, i.e. **implicated conclusions**.

We can come up with even clearer examples by creating concepts which no-one has heard of before. In an early discussion of relevance theory, Levinson (1987c: 722–23) gives the following example about a fictional car called a Zorda:

(28)   KEN: Would you drive a Zorda?
          BEV: I wouldn't drive ANY expensive car.

This would be accounted for as involving the following assumptions:

(29)   *Explicature:*
          Bev would not drive any car that is expensive.
          Contextual assumptions:
          Ken has asked Bev whether Bev would drive a Zorda.
          Implicated premise:
          A Zorda is (believed by Bev to be) an expensive car.
          Implicatures:
          Bev would not drive a Zorda.
          Bev would not drive a Zorda because Bev considers it expensive and would not want to drive anything expensive.

Levinson points out that the assumption about Zordas being expensive is one that anyone would infer and it cannot be something already known since a Zorda is a fictional car invented for the purpose of this example. In responding to Levinson's point, Sperber and Wilson (1987b: 749) suggest that the derivation of this implicated premise can be explained if we assume a heuristic which means that 'on presentation of assumptions of a certain form, one considers whether one has evidence for assumptions of a related form'.[4] Following this heuristic, the hearer accesses the assumption that Zordas are expensive and considers whether there is any evidence to support it. The fact that it is the most easily accessible assumption which leads to a plausible interpretation of this utterance is, of course, evidence which supports this conclusion.

Another kind of example makes clear that we can use assumptions more generally that we did not have access to before the speaker began to speak. Sperber and Wilson (1986: 43–4) discuss an example where Peter and Mary are hill-walking. Mary points to a building on an opposite hill and says:

(30)   I've been inside that church.

If we suppose that Peter was not aware before Mary spoke that the building was a church, this fact will not cause Peter any difficulty in understanding Mary's utterance. The fact that she has spoken in this way makes it clear to him that Mary knows it is a church. We can say that it was manifest to Mary before she spoke, but not to Peter, that the building is a church. Mary's utterance makes manifest to Peter that the building is a church and also makes this mutually manifest to both of them. The relevance of the utterance here is to show that contextual assumptions used in understanding an utterance need not be known to the hearer before the utterance is produced.

There are two questions about this account which we should discuss now. One is about the distinction between contextual assumptions and implicated premises and the other is about the distinction between implicated premises and implicated conclusions. I will suggest here that we should not draw any theoretically significant distinction between contextual assumptions and implicated premises and suggest that the distinction between implicated premises and implicated conclusions is tricky in ways that resemble difficulties involved in distinguishing implicatures from implications.

We have seen that contextual assumptions are sometimes things that the hearer knew before the utterance (e.g. that coffee contains caffeine) and sometimes become known to the hearer as part of interpreting the utterance (e.g. that coffee contains tannin, that Zordas are expensive, that that building over there is a church). The question to consider now is how much theoretical weight to attach to a possible distinction between implicated premises and contextual assumptions. The simplest option is to say that we should not attach any theoretical weight to this at all. We could simply say that communicators provide evidence for a number of assumptions and that some of these (implicated premises) are used to derive others (implicated conclusions). The fact that addressees are sometimes already aware of some of these assumptions does not affect the fact that the communicator has provided evidence for them. This has the advantage of simplicity and there is one more reason for adopting this view: communicators provide some evidence for any assumptions required for arriving at a satisfactory overall interpretation even if addressees were already aware of them.

Consider (26) again, repeated here as (31):

(31)   KEN: Do you fancy a cup of coffee?
            BEV: Actually, I'm avoiding drinks with tannin in them at the moment.

There are three possible scenarios with regard to Ken's knowledge about tannin in coffee before hearing Bev's utterance. Ken might know that coffee contains tannin; Ken might not know that coffee contains tannin; finally Ken might suspect or have some evidence that coffee contains tannin. If Ken knows that coffee contains tannin, he will simply use this as an implicated premise in understanding Bev's response. If Ken does not know that coffee contains tannin, he will assume this now and use it as an implicated premise alongside other assumptions to derive the implicature that Bev does not want coffee (similar to the 'Zorda' example mentioned above). What if Ken has some evidence that coffee contains tannin but is not certain? In this case, Bev's utterance will provide more evidence and lead to a strengthening of Ken's belief. Strengthening is, of course, one kind of cognitive effect which can contribute to relevance and so this would clearly count as an implicature. Just as implicated conclusions are a subset of the implications of the utterance, implicated premises are a subset of its contextual assumptions – those the hearer was expected to use in arriving at a satisfactory overall interpretation. Relevance theory sees communication as involving making assumptions 'manifest or more manifest'. When an assumption is already manifest, it becomes more manifest to the extent that it becomes more accessible. Implicated premises are not those *used* in deriving implicatures, but those that are *required* for arriving at a satisfactory interpretation.

Now let's think again about what it means to 'know' that coffee contains tannin. Since we can never be certain about the factual status of our assumptions about the world, to 'know' must mean to entertain with a strong conviction. It is not obvious that there is ever a situation where we would describe 'knowledge' as an absolute such that the assumption can never be strengthened or contradicted. (Do you believe coffee contains tannin? What would you think if you read a newspaper report tomorrow stating that this was something people had believed until recently but that new research shows that there is no tannin in coffee and the evidence for the presence of tannin had been misinterpreted?) Given these considerations, I think it is reasonable to say that Bev's utterance provides confirming evidence that coffee contains tannin, and so leads to a slight strengthening of the assumption even here. For reasons such as this, it seems reasonable to think of all contextual assumptions required for deriving implicatures (or, more generally, for arriving at a satisfactory overall interpretation) as implicated premises.

Now what about the distinction between implicated premises and implicated conclusions? Is this clear-cut in this example? I would argue not, for two reasons: first, the relevance of any assumption depends on what implications it carries; second, there is a sense in which any assumption which is communicated is a conclusion. Consider the implicated premise that coffee contains tannin. This may be relevant as it strengthens an existing assumption. That assumption is relevant because it follows from this that Bev does not want coffee. The assumption that Bev does not want coffee is relevant because it follows from this that Ken should not make coffee for Bev. And so on. If any assumption is relevant, this must be because something follows from it. It follows, then, that any relevant assumption is potentially the premise for another inference. Consider the evidence that supports the assumption that coffee contains tannin. We might represent it as follows:

(32) a.   Bev has said that Bev is avoiding tannin.
     b.   Bev knows that I know that I have just asked whether Bev wants coffee.
     c.   If coffee contains tannin then Bev will not want coffee.
     d.   So Bev must think that coffee contains tannin.

(32d) is the result of an inferential process, which means it also has the status of an implicated conclusion.

So how do we make a clear distinction between implicated premises and implicated conclusions? One way is to say that **implicated conclusions** are inferred from the explicatures of the utterance plus contextual assumptions, and that **implicated premises** are inferred from the presumption of relevance plus the fact that the utterance has been made. In the case of (31), then, we might characterise some of the communicated assumptions as follows:

(33)   *Utterance:*
    a.   Actually, I'm avoiding drinks with tannin in them at the moment.
          Explicature:
    b.   Bev is avoiding drinks with tannin in them.
          Implicated premise:
    c.   Coffee contains tannin.
          Implicated conclusion:
    d.   Bev does not want to drink coffee.

(33d) follows from the explicature (33b) and the implicated premise (33c). (33c) follows from the presumption of relevance and the fact that Bev has said (33a). It is inferred (made manifest or more manifest) because it is required in order to infer (33d) and satisfy the hearer's expectations of relevance. In the next section, we look in a little more detail at how implicatures of all varieties are derived.

7.4   Deriving implicatures

This section considers how we derive implicatures based on the relevance-guided comprehension heuristic and the mutual adjustment process. In deriving implicatures, just as in every other aspect of utterance-interpretation, hearers will follow a path of least effort and stop when they find an interpretation which satisfies their expectations of relevance. How does this work in practice? Here, we'll consider four different situations: one where there is a very clear candidate implicature or set of implicatures at the earliest possible stage of the process, i.e. before the speaker begins her utterance; one where there are no clear candidates in advance but where candidates soon emerge; one where things are more complicated because the initial path turns out to be incorrect; finally, one where it is hard to identify an implicature at all.

First, consider a case where the hearer has an expectation before the utterance begins. Consider, for example, Bev's utterance here:

(34)   KEN: You won't want a coffee, will you?
          BEV: I never touch caffeine.

Here (simplifying as usual), Bev communicates the following implicated premises and implicated conclusion:

(35)   *Implicated premises:*
          Coffee contains caffeine.
          If Bev is avoiding caffeine, Bev will not want a coffee now.
          Implicated conclusion:
          Bev does not want a coffee.

Ken will follow a path of last effort in considering possible interpretations. In this case, Ken is already thinking that Bev does not want coffee and may already know that this has to do with avoiding caffeine. Clearly, Ken's utterance suggests that the implicated conclusion is already in his mind before Bev speaks. All Ken has to do is to connect the response with the appropriate contextual assumptions and derive the implicature. If Ken is already thinking that Bev does not drink coffee because Bev does not consume anything containing caffeine, then Ken is already entertaining all of these assumptions and Bev's utterance serves only to confirm them. If any alternative interpretation occurs to Ken, it will be ruled out because it is more effortful than the interpretation Ken has already arrived at, given that Ken assumes that this is what Bev will have assumed that Ken will assume (apologies for the complexity of this, but this complex embedding is crucial for an accurate description).

Suppose that Ken does not know that it is because of caffeine that Bev does not drink coffee. In this scenario, Ken is already entertaining the implicated conclusion and only needs to derive and make connections with these implicated premises to arrive at this interpretation. If Ken knows that coffee contains caffeine, then this assumption will be highly accessible as it is part of the encyclopaedic information, or background knowledge, which Ken already has linked to this concept. If Ken does not already know this, then Bev's utterance provides evidence for the assumption. To some extent, this is similar to examples (28) (*Would you drive a Zorda?*) and (30) (*I've been inside that church*) discussed above. Given that Ken already assumes that Bev does not want coffee, Ken will already have a strong expectation that Bev is about to confirm that she does not want coffee. When he hears Bev say that she's avoiding caffeine, Ken will already be thinking that this must be intended to communicate that Bev does not want coffee. Ken simply needs to ask himself whether Bev could reasonably have intended this interpretation. Of course, the answer is yes. Now Ken has evidence for all of the implicated premises listed above and for the conclusion that Bev does not want coffee.

Now let's consider a situation where the hearer does not have any expectations about what Bev might be about to communicate. Suppose that Ken does not know anything about Bev's preferences and does not know that coffee contains caffeine. Ken offers Bev a coffee and the response is as follows:

(36)   A: Do you fancy a coffee?
            B: I'm off caffeine at the moment.

What will Ken do in following a path of least effort here? He will begin by assuming that Bev is communicating either that she does want a coffee or that she does not want one. What will make one line of reasoning more accessible than the other? There are several things which will encourage the line of reasoning which leads to the conclusion that Bev does not want coffee. First, the formulation *I'm off …* makes clear that Bev is avoiding something. It is surely less effortful to develop a line of reasoning such as (37) than a line of reasoning such as (38):

(37) a.   Bev is avoiding caffeine at the moment.
     b.   If coffee has caffeine in it, Bev will be avoiding caffeine.
     c.   So Bev might not want coffee because of its caffeine content.

(38) a.   Bev is avoiding caffeine at the moment.
     b.   Maybe coffee doesn't have caffeine in it but something else does.
     c.   If so, then maybe Bev is making a contrast between coffee and other things.
     d.   If so, then maybe Bev is intending to communicate that she wants coffee because it doesn't have caffeine in it unlike other things which do.

This is a slightly long-winded way of saying that the negative aspect of Bev's utterance invites a negative inference about coffee. Suppose, however, that Bev's formulation did not indicate a positive or a negative direction. Imagine, for example, Bev responded as in (39) (adapted from an example discussed by Sperber and Wilson 1986: 11, 56):

(39)   KEN: Fancy a coffee?
            BEV: Coffee would keep me awake.

In this context, Ken's interpretation will begin in the same way as before, i.e. Ken will start from the assumption that Bev's utterance will communicate either an acceptance or a rejection of the offer of coffee. The direction of the interpretation depends partly on the relative accessibility of the two assumptions in (40):

(40) a.   *Contextual assumption favouring acceptance interpretation:*
            Bev wants to stay awake.
     b.   *Contextual assumption favouring rejection interpretation:*
            Bev does not want to stay awake.

Of course, this will depend on whether anything has happened to make Ken think either that Bev does or that Bev does not want to stay awake. This could follow from something Bev has said previously or from other general assumptions, e.g. assumptions about what time of day it is, what people tend to want to do in particular situations, and so on. In a relevance-oriented cognitive system, memory will be organised so that more strongly evidenced assumptions will tend to be more accessible in general, since they are likely to make a greater contribution to relevance.

Of course, it is not only which assumption comes to mind first which determines Ken's interpretation. Ken is looking for an interpretation which Bev could manifestly have intended to communicate, given Bev's abilities and preferences. If, for example, it occurs to Ken that Bev looks tired and should have an early night, this will not necessarily mean that Ken decides that Bev is rejecting the coffee because she wants to go to bed. Ken might decide instead that Bev wants to keep herself awake in order to be sociable and is over-riding her desire for sleep for this reason. If so, Ken might go on to refer to this and encourage Bev to go to bed.

What happens if Ken has no expectations at all about whether Bev wants to stay awake or not and has no access to contextual assumptions which will help. In this case, relevance theory predicts that Ken will not be able to decide and will perhaps ask for clarification. Notice, however, that speakers will not tend to ask for clarification in a 'neutral' way, e.g. by asking (41):

(41)   So does that mean you do or you don't want one?

It is far more likely that Ken will check by asking a 'biased' question such as (42) or (43):

(42)   So you'd rather just get off to bed, would you?

(43)   Is that a yes, then?

Why should this be? One motivation for this is that there is a risk of one or more negative implications if Ken makes clear that he doesn't know how to interpret Bev's utterance. One implication is that Ken and Bev are not as close as they would be if Ken understood straight away. An even more negative implication would be that Ken is irritated to some extent by the indirectness of Bev's reply. By indicating that he has tentatively moved in one direction, as in (42) or (43), Ken tries to make himself seem closer to Bev's line of reasoning. At the same time, of course, this is a risky strategy since it will have the opposite effect if Ken makes the wrong guess. If Bev intends to accept the coffee and Ken thinks the opposite, the implication is, of course, that Ken and Bev do not understand each other very well.

There is another thing we might point out about examples like this. It is fairly common to turn down a request indirectly for reasons of politeness. Work in conversation analysis, originating in the work of Schegloff and Sacks

(1973) has shed light on this phenomenon with reference to the notion of 'adjacency pairs' and 'preferred responses'. Briefly, adjacency pairs are pairs of utterance types which often go together in conversation, e.g. a question is often followed by an answer. In some cases, there is more than one option for the second member of a pair. Questions may be followed either by answers or by a disclaimer. Offers may be followed by acceptance or non-acceptance. And so on. The response which the first utterance seems to expect is described as the 'preferred response'. When we produce a dispreferred response, we often try to reduce the negative implications of this, e.g. by giving a reason for not offering the preferred response. At the same time, it is common when inviting someone to a social event not to ask them directly, which runs the risk of being met by an explicit refusal, but to begin by asking about an aspect of the context which will be relevant to whether they can accept. Suppose, for example, I call you up to ask whether you might want to come to the cinema with me on Friday night. I might ask you the question in (44) rather than the one in (45):

(44)   Are you doing anything on Friday night?

(45)   Do you fancy going to see a movie on Friday night?

One reason for this is that it is easier to turn me down politely by saying (46) before you've even been asked out than by having to say (47) afterwards:

(46)   I've got a family thing on then, actually.

(47)   Oh, I'd've loved to. I'm afraid I've got a family thing on then, though. What a shame.

(44) and (45) represent a kind of conversational sequence. (44) counts as a 'pre-request' which comes before an actual request such as (45). The pre-request checks whether one of the conditions for accepting the actual request is met. If it is, the actual request can follow. Turning down a pre-request has fewer negative implications since the speaker has not explicitly turned down a request but simply provided some information relevant to a request they haven't heard yet. Turning down an actual request has negative implications, raising the possibility that the speaker does not enjoy the hearer's company and so on. Of course, even the 'pre-request'-rejection sequence has negative implications, partly because we are used to such sequences and know that the person who is about to be invited might realise that a request is coming and, in effect, be turning down that request pre-emptively. Still, the fact that this is less manifest makes the utterance less likely to be perceived as impolite.

   In some cases, the initial path taken by the hearer turns out to be incorrect. Consider again, for example, (39), repeated here as (48):

(48)   KEN: Fancy a coffee?
        BEV: Coffee would keep me awake.

It is, of course, quite possible for Ken not to have access to some of the assumptions needed to arrive at the intended interpretation. Let's imagine the following set of contextual assumptions are accessed by Ken:

(49) a.   Ken and Bev are flatmates.
     b.   It is 11.30 p.m. on a Tuesday night.
     c.   Bev usually gets up at 6.30 a.m. every day.
     d.   Bev likes to go bed around midnight.

Let's also imagine that Ken has not paid enough attention to earlier conversations, or forgotten them, and that Bev thinks Ken will also access the following assumptions:

(50) a.   Bev has an essay due in on Wednesday.
     b.   Bev has decided that she has to stay up into the night so that she can finish her essay.
     c.   Bev told Ken earlier about the essay and her plans.

Clearly, Ken is likely to make an incorrect assumption here. If she does not remember the earlier conversation or consider it worth checking, there will be a misunderstanding. Ken is likely not to make a coffee for Bev and this will either lead to a clarifying conversation or to a disgruntled Bev and a less good relationship between Ken and Bev. The explanation for this has to do with the range of manifest assumptions, the degree of their manifestness, including what Ken and Bev assume about their manifestness to each other, and whether they are actually accessed and used by Ken in interpreting the utterance. In relevance-theoretic terms, this all depends on the nature of Ken and Bev's **mutual cognitive environment** (a notion we mentioned in Chapter 3).

Finally, of course, it is possible that the hearer simply cannot see how to derive implicatures from an utterance. Consider, for example, the following exchange:

(51)   KEN: Would you like a coffee?
        BEV: I've just had some cereal.

Here, Ken might well not be able to see what Bev is getting at with this response. The only way Ken could understand would be if Ken had access to a contextual assumption such as (52), which would suggest accepting the offer, or (53), which would suggest turning it down:

(52)   Bev likes a cup of coffee after she has had her cereal in the morning.

(53)   Bev does not like drinking coffee after she has finished her cereal.

If Ken cannot access either of these assumptions, he is likely to give up and ask for clarification.

Cases where the hearer gives up can be seen as related to certain kinds of creative language, such as jokes, 'poetic' or literary language. Here is a playful example:

(54)   (Ken and Bev are watching TV. Ken is sitting in front of Bev.)
        KEN: Am I in the way?

BEV: Yes, but don't worry. At least you're not old.

KEN: What?

BEV: Well, being in the way is a problem, but being 'old and in the way' is what you
       really want to avoid.

Ken is confused at first by Bev's utterance. Bev eventually clears it up by
indicating a jokey reference to a well-known cliché about people being old
and 'in the way' of younger people. Part of the comic effect comes from the fact
that Ken does not understand at first and has a kind of 'aha!' moment when
recognising Bev's intention.

'Poetic' or literary language can achieve effects partly based on a particular
kind of difficulty associated with deriving the intended meaning. There are
countless examples. To take just one, consider the following extract from
Wallace Stevens's poem 'The Man With The Blue Guitar':

(55)   The man bent over his guitar,
            A shearsman of sorts. The day was green.
            They said, 'You have a blue guitar,
            You do not play things as they are.'
            The man replied. 'Things as they are
            Are changed upon a blue guitar.'
            And they said then, 'But play, you must,
            A tune beyond us, yet ourselves,
            A tune upon the blue guitar
            Of things exactly as they are.'   (from Wallace Stevens, 'The Man with
              the Blue Guitar', in *Selected Poems*, 1953, Faber and Faber, London: 52)

What exactly is the poem communicating here? What contextual assumptions would we use to try to understand it? What implicatures should we
derive? How can we check whether we are on the right path? Of course,
answering questions such as these about a literary text can take a long time.
In many cases, the ongoing search for a possible interpretation, or interpretations, is the thing which makes readers enjoy literature. What Stevens's
poem and the playful communicator in (54) have in common is that they
begin by confusing their audience. A difference is that the puzzle in (54)
is cleared up fairly quickly while the 'puzzle' or puzzles posed by Stevens
can be engaged with over a very long period of time. Some literary readers
continue to think about the interpretation of particular texts for a lifetime.
Part of this process involves considering what evidence there is for particular implicatures which a text might be implicating. A key notion used
within relevance theory to account for poetic effects is the notion that
implicatures come with varying degrees of strength. We will look at this
in Section 7.5.

Exercise 7.2 asks you to consider the derivation of particular implicatures in
particular contexts and how the relative accessibility of particular assumptions
affects interpretations.

Exercise 7.2

* Suggest an account of how B's utterances will be understood in the following exchanges. In each case, make clear how the relevance-guided comprehension heuristic gives rise to the interpretation and how the interpretation depends on the accessibility of particular contextual assumptions.

  (i)   *(A and B have spent the evening together. At the end of the evening they approach B's home.)*
       B: Do you want to come up for a coffee?
       A: I don't drink coffee.
       B: I haven't got any!
            (from the film *Brassed Off*, 1996, dir. Mark Herman)

  (ii) A: I'm just going to make some coffee. Do you want some?
       B: The kettle's just boiled.

  (iii) A: What's Marjie's house like?
       B: Hard to say. What do you think of china dogs and garden gnomes?

  (iv) A: How did your exam go?
       B: [*starts to whistle the humorous song* 'Always Look On The Bright Side Of Life']

7.5   Strength of implicatures

A final observation about implicatures is that they come with varying degrees of strength. We saw in Chapter 6 how explicatures can be more or less strong. In fact, there has been more discussion on the relative strength of implicatures within relevance theory and much less on the strength of explicatures. We'll consider the relative *strength of implicatures* here, beginning with the following example:

(56)   *(at a summer garden party, Ken is cooking over a barbecue grill.)*
          KEN: Would you like a burger?
          BEV: I'm a vegetarian.

Bev clearly implicates here that she does not want a burger and that this is because she is vegetarian. We might partly explain this by suggesting that Bev has communicated the following assumptions:

(57)   *Proposition expressed/explicature:*
          Bev is a vegetarian.
          Implicated premises:
          Vegetarians do not eat meat.
          The burgers contain meat.
          Anyone who is a vegetarian will not want to eat a burger.
          If Bev is a vegetarian, Bev will not want a burger.
          Implicated conclusion:
          Bev does not want a burger.

This seems to characterise the main aims of Bev's utterance. However, we can ask of any act of indirect communication why the speaker chose to be indirect. One part of the answer here is that the indirectness allows Bev to communicate not only that she does not want a burger but also why she does not want one. This pre-empts a possible follow-up question and also might reduce possible negative implications associated with turning down a request (as mentioned above). Another thing the indirectness does is to provide evidence for further inferences. Some of these we can be quite sure of, such as the assumptions in (58):

(58) a.   Bev will not eat anything with meat in it.
     b.   Bev will not want a steak.
     c.   Bev will not want a sausage containing meat.

We might go on to consider other possibilities for which her utterance provides less evidence. We might, for example, wonder why Bev is a vegetarian and consider various possible reasons, e.g. for reasons of morality or religion. If we know that Bev is an atheist and therefore rule out the possibility that religion is the source of her vegetarianism, we might go on to consider a range of possible associations with non-religious vegetarianism. Each of the assumptions in (59) might occur to us:

(59) a.   Bev has ethical objections to eating meat.
     b.   Bev takes ethical considerations seriously.
     c.   Bev is interested in environmental issues.
     d.   Bev is more left-wing than right-wing.
     e.   Bev thinks negatively about globalisation.

While each of the assumptions in (58) and (59) follow from Bev's utterance and specific contextual assumptions, Bev's intention to convey the assumptions in (59) is much less manifest than her intention to convey those in (58). The assumptions in (58) (or similar assumptions) are required in order to arrive at a satisfactory overall interpretation. The assumptions in (59) might marginally increase the relevance of the utterance and so fall under the second clause of the presumption of optimal relevance (the speaker making her utterance as relevant as her abilities and preferences allow). So the assumptions in (58) are more strongly communicated than those in (59). We can see that Bev's utterance provides some evidence to support them (i.e. that they must be at least implications of the utterance) by considering how Ken might respond if asked who among his friends might, for example, be interested in environmental issues. If Ken knows little else about Bev and doesn't know many people interested in the environment, it is possible that he might think of Bev on the basis of her vegetarianism. More generally, we tend to form impressions of people based on whatever information we have about them. Still speaking generally, we create impressions of ourselves and of our identity by what we reveal to others about ourselves. Bev's vegetarianism contributes to our impression of Bev. We can see that the conclusions in (59) are not strongly communicated because we could imagine Bev going on to say that she has no interest in the environment or something which contradicts any of the other assumptions.

Another thing to notice here is that Bev's intentions themselves may be vague. Rather than the speaker having a precise intention which the hearer can only partly identify, it may be that the speaker's intentions themselves may be vague, i.e. she may be intending to convey a certain drift or to steer the inference process in a certain direction rather than to convey a fairly precise set of assumptions.

One way to discuss the contrast between the assumptions in (58) and those in (59) is to say that Bev's utterance provides more evidence that she intends to convey the former than the latter. In relevance-theoretic terms, the assumptions in (58) are stronger implicatures than those in (59). Relevance theory assumes that implicatures come in varying degrees of strength ranging from very strong implicatures through to very weak ones, which shade off into entirely unintended contextual implications. As with other assumptions, the degree of strength of an individual implicature depends on how much evidence the speaker provides that she intends to convey it. The strongest implicatures are those which need to be recovered in order to arrive at a relevant-enough overall interpretation. In (56), the implicated premise that (Bev thinks that) the burgers contain meat and the implicated conclusion that Bev does not want a burger because it contains meat are very strongly communicated, since Ken could not arrive at a satisfactory overall interpretation of Bev's utterance without making them. By contrast, assumption (59c), that Bev is interested in environmental issues, is quite weakly communicated, if at all, since, although Ken is encouraged to look for some such implications given the way Bev has chosen to formulate her utterance, there is no need for Ken to think of this particular one, and we could easily imagine saying that Ken has understood Bev's utterance perfectly well, even if he never entertains this particular assumption. The weaker the implicature, the wider the range of possible implications, such as those in (59). At the weakest end of the spectrum, there is a grey area where it is hard to be sure where weak implicatures shade off into unintended contextual implications.

Perhaps the clearest examples of weak implicature occur in 'poetic' or literary language. Sperber and Wilson (1986: 237) illustrate this by discussing Flaubert's comment on the poet Leconte de Lisle that:

(60)   His ink is pale. (Son encre est pale.)

Sperber and Wilson point out that we cannot think Flaubert means literally to say something about the colour of the ink Leconte de Lisle uses to write with. Instead, we assume a less than literal interpretation, which might carry implications along the following lines:

(61) a.   Leconte de Lisle's writing lacks contrasts.
     b.   Leconte de Lisle's writing will not last.

c.   Leconte de Lisle's writing is unemotional.

d.   Leconte de Lisle does not pour his soul into his writing.

e.   Leconte de Lisle's writing has little impact on readers.

We could go on coming up with others. A key thing to notice is that no individual one of these implications needs to be recovered by an interpreter in order for us to say that he has understood the utterance. This utterance achieves its effects not by giving rise to evidence that the communicator intended to convey one strong implicature, or a small set of strong implicatures, but rather by marginally increasing the manifestness of a very wide range of weak implicatures. This is assumed to be typical of many kinds of poetic or literary language.[5] We will return to look at these kinds of effects in more detail when we discuss metaphor in Chapter 9.

Exercise 7.3 asks you to consider how the relative strength of implicatures varies according to which contextual assumptions are accessible in particular situations and at some of the effects which arise because of variation in strength of implicatures.

Exercise 7.3

• Consider again example (56):

(56)   *(at a summer garden party, Ken is cooking over a barbecue grill.)*
       KEN: Would you like a burger?
       BEV: I'm a vegetarian.

Look at the list of possible implications and implicatures suggested in the chapter. First, consider whether you agree that these are possible conclusions which Ken might derive. Consider any others which might occur to him. For each one, consider how Bev might have adjusted her utterance to make that conclusion more likely or less likely to be derived as an implicature.

7.6   Summary

In this chapter we have looked at the kinds of assumptions which can be communicated indirectly and how they are recovered. We looked at the distinction between implications and implicatures, noting that the latter are a subset of the former and that there is not always a clear cut-off point between them, i.e. there are cases where it is hard to decide whether or not a particular implication which follows logically from an utterance together with contextual assumptions is one which the communicator intends to convey. We looked at the distinction between implicated premises and implicated conclusions, noting that this distinction can be hard to draw in some cases. In the same section, we looked at the overlap between contextual assumptions and implicated premises. I suggested that contextual assumptions will count as implicated premises to the extent that they are required to arrive at a satisfactory overall interpretation.

We looked at how implicatures can vary in strength and how utterances can vary in terms of how many relatively strong and how many relatively weak implicatures they give rise to. This is important in accounting for some 'poetic' or literary effects and is also exploited in accounting for figurative language, as we will see in Chapter 9.

Exercise 7.4

As in every chapter, this final exercise asks you to adjust the list of questions you have come up with so far by compiling new questions which have occurred to you while reading this chapter and to think about the kinds of things which might count as answers to any questions you have come up with so far. First, add new questions to your ongoing list. Second, consider all of your questions and think about possible ways of answering them.

7.7 Further reading

Again, *Relevance* is the key initial source (Sperber and Wilson 1986: 193–224). Work by Adrian Pilkington (particularly Pilkington 2000) develops the application of the notion of 'weak implicature' in accounting for creative language use.

8   Lexical pragmatics

Topics: words and concepts; words and inference; inferring concepts: broadening and narrowing; 'ad hoc' concepts

8.1   Overview

This chapter considers recent work on lexical meaning developed within relevance theory which has been described using the term **lexical pragmatics**. This work focuses on how words are understood in context. The central idea here is that the contribution of words with conceptual meanings involves more than simply accessing the concepts encoded by the words and slotting them into semantic representations. Comprehension also routinely involves adjusting the encoded concepts to reflect specific meanings intended by communicators. Work in this area has been carried out not only by relevance theorists but also by a number of linguists, philosophers and cognitive scientists. A starting assumption for many theories is that regular content words contribute to utterance meanings by encoding concepts. The chapter begins with a brief discussion of this and an illustration that understanding some words involves making inferences about exactly how they are being used on a specific occasion. Section 8.4 considers recent thinking on how 'conceptual' meaning is understood in context; in particular, it looks at processes of concept adjustment in the form of 'broadening' and 'narrowing'. Section 8.5 considers the more radical assumption that human cognition and utterance interpretation involve the regular creation of unlexicalised concepts, i.e. concepts which are not the encoded meaning of any word, and are created as and when required as part of the processes involved in understanding each other and the world. This means that there is another kind of inference involved in deriving explicatures on the basis of linguistically encoded meanings, beyond the processes discussed in Chapters 5 and 6. The ideas discussed in this chapter have also played an important role in recent discussion of how metaphorical utterances are understood within relevance theory and so they are involved in the discussion of metaphor in Chapter 9.

8.2   Words and concepts

As discussed in Chapter 6, relevance theory assumes that content words contribute concepts to conceptual representations derived in understanding utterances. The difference between (1) and (2) is that (1) contains a word which encodes {CHOCOLATE} while (2) contains a word which encodes {CHEESE}.

(1)   Billy likes chocolate.

(2)   Billy likes cheese.

Traditional semantic theories would say that the word *chocolate* 'denotes' the concept {CHOCOLATE} and that anyone who believes the proposition that Billy likes chocolate knows that Billy likes any entity which falls within the scope of that denotation. So words like these denote objects of a certain type. Other words denote events or properties. If we understand the contributions words make to conceptual representations, we can explain the conceptual representations derived from understanding utterances and we can account for the meanings of conceptual representations by providing semantic interpretations which state their truth conditions.

Before looking at more recent work on lexical pragmatics, one thing to notice is that there are some words whose precise denotations have to be adjusted in context as part of the comprehension process, i.e. where there is more to understanding their contribution than simply activating the concepts they encode. A typical example is the word *tired* which names the gradable concept {TIRED}:[1]

(3)   I'm tired.

If I say (3) to you, part of the process of understanding my utterance is to make an inference about how tired I am. If I say it to you in the middle of the morning, you might have a different understanding than if I say it to you late at night. You might think differently again if I say it to you after I have just played a game of tennis.

Sperber and Wilson (1998) consider how an utterance of (3) might be interpreted if uttered by Mary after Peter has asked whether she would like to go to the cinema. Clearly, in this context, Mary must mean that she is tired enough not to want to go to the cinema. As Sperber and Wilson point out, not just any degree of tiredness would be enough to mean that Mary does not want to go to the cinema. Peter's expectations of relevance lead him to enrich the notion of tiredness until it has enough effects to satisfy them. In this context, that means providing evidence for an answer to the question he has just asked. One way to see this is to consider how differently Peter would understand Mary's utterance if she said it on arriving home from work and before Peter had mentioned the possibility of going to the cinema. Here, Peter's expectations of relevance would be satisfied as soon as he enriched his understanding of Mary's tiredness far enough for him to derive effects such as that she is more tired than she usually is when she comes home. This may or may not be consistent with her wanting to go to the cinema.

As always, this involves a process of mutual adjustment. Peter adjusts the explicit content of Mary's utterance until it enables him to derive enough implicated meaning to satisfy his expectations of relevance. As soon as he has done this, he stops. He will not carry on enriching his understanding of how tired Mary is beyond what is necessary to satisfy his expectations, whether that means deriving enough effects to suggest an answer to his suggested cinema visit or a less precise interpretation.

As the rest of this chapter makes clear, recent work assumes that pragmatic processes similar to these take place in understanding not only words which encode gradable concepts but in a much wider range of cases. In fact, Sperber and Wilson suggest that processes like these, which adjust the denotations of concepts encoded by words, regularly take place as part of the process of understanding utterances.

8.3   Words and inference

We know that understanding each other often involves making inferences and we know that this is often about the meanings of words, or the concepts they are used to convey on particular occasions. Here are some examples:

(4)   Billy says he doesn't like chocolate now.

(5)   She's a bib.

(6)   Everybody loves your cooking.

In understanding an utterance of (4), we need to make an inference about which of the people or things in the world named *Billy* is being referred to and to decide whether *he* refers to Billy or someone else. If *he* is someone else, then we need to work out who. We need to decide whether *chocolate* means chocolate in the form of chocolate bars, chocolate drinks, chocolate flavour, all of these or something else. And we need to decide what time period *now* refers to. In (2) we need to decide who *she* refers to and in what sense she is *a bib*. We could be in a fantasy or fairytale context where she is an item of clothing used to catch drips when babies are feeding, in a sports context where two teams are competing and one team wearing coloured vests to identify team membership, or perhaps we need to access some kind of metaphorical interpretation, perhaps based on the first notion of a *bib* as something grownups attach to babies when they are eating to keep food from spilling onto their clothes. In (5), we need to decide what *everybody* refers to, i.e. which group is the one of which every member loves your cooking. While *your cooking* has an obvious most likely referent ('the things that you cook'), we infer this rather than other possibilities where *your x* could be an x associated with *you* in several different ways (e.g. 'the cooking you spoke about', 'the cooking you said you liked').

As we saw in Chapter 2, Grice envisaged only two processes intervening between 'conventional' (linguistic) meanings and 'what is said': disambiguation and reference assignment. Each of the processes we have described for (4)–(6) can be seen as falling into one of these categories. We could say that disambiguation is involved in working out the intended senses of *chocolate* and *bib* and that reference assignment is involved in working out the intended referents of *Billy*, *he*, *now*, *she*, *everybody* and *your*. Other inferences, such as deciding that an utterance is intended metaphorically, would be seen by Grice as part of 'what is implicated' rather than 'what is said'. We have seen that there are a number of other kinds of inferences which we need to make in order to work out what propositions have been expressed by utterances and that there are other kinds of word meanings which require inference on the part of interpreters. Some of these are illustrated in (7)–(9):

(7)   You're not going to die.

(8)   He plays well.

(9)   Is this painful?

In (7), we need to decide whether the speaker is saying that the referent of *you* is immortal or something less surprising, e.g. that a specific injury will not kill them. In (8) the hearer needs to decide not only which sense of *play* is intended but also possibly to enrich the sense to refer to playing a particular kind of object, e.g. we might infer that it refers to playing the violin if said while watching someone play the violin. In (9), the hearer needs to decide what exactly will count as *painful* in this context. The inferences just mentioned for (7) are explained in relevance theory as aspects of explicature which go beyond disambiguation and reference assignment. Examples (8) and (9) are more relevant to discussion in this chapter as they have been explained with reference to the notion of 'lexical pragmatics'. The next section introduces this by considering two ways in which we sometimes adjust word meanings in context: narrowing them so that they apply to a smaller set of entities and broadening them so that they are more inclusive.

Exercise 8.1 focuses on some of the inferences involved in understanding words in context.

Exercise 8.1

- Consider the words in bold in each of the following examples. Describe the concept which you think this word usually encodes and then explain how it is likely to be adjusted to have a particular sense in this context.
    (i)   A: Here, I brought you a coffee.
             B: You're an **angel**.

(ii)   A: I really tried to annoy John yesterday but nothing I said bothered him.
        B: I know. He's a **sponge**.
(iii)   A: I lent John another fiver yesterday. He still owes me ten quid from last time.
        B: I know. He's a **sponge**.
(iv)   A: I finished two articles this week and prepared the talk for next week's conference.
        B: Wow, you're **flying** right now.
(v)   A: Fancy meeting up next week sometime?
        B: Sure. I'll see if I've got any **windows** and get back to you.

8.4   Inferring concepts: broadening and narrowing

So far, we have assumed that there is a fairly straightforward relationship between 'conceptual expressions' (i.e. words that encode concepts) and the concepts they encode. When we look at this more closely, however, things are less clear. First, we could ask what exactly is the nature of the encoding relationship. In thinking about this, it helps to remember that relevance theory assumes Fodor's (1983) modular view of mental architecture, as discussed in Chapter 3.

At this stage of our discussion, perhaps the most significant claim Fodor makes is that there is a 'module' specialised to deal with linguistic input. This module takes transduced sound or visual representations as input and provides semantic representations as output. As outlined above, we assume that these semantic representations fall far short of determining the propositions which we take to be communicated by acts of verbal communication. We have looked at a number of ways in which they fall short above, including the presence of ambiguous expressions, referring expressions, ellipsis, required enrichment processes, and so on. But what about the content supplied by words which encode concepts? On the Fodorian view, a natural assumption is that the language module will automatically access whichever concept is named by a particular word and this concept will then constitute part of the incomplete logical form which is the semantic representation of the linguistic expression uttered.

In line with this, the account of word meaning presented in the book *Relevance* (Sperber and Wilson 1986: 83–93) suggests that word meanings should be understood in terms of encoding. On hearing the sequence of sounds which correspond to a particular word, the language module will automatically activate the associated concept and make it available as a possible component of an utterance's semantic representation. Where a word is ambiguous, all possible senses will be made available and one task for pragmatics will be to decide which sense must be intended in this case. So what exactly is the nature of the conceptual material which is made available? The assumption is that a concept is a kind of 'address' in memory which provides access to three kinds of 'entry', containing three types of information: lexical, logical and encyclopaedic. The lexical entry provides access to linguistic information about the word, e.g. word class and pronunciation. The logical entry provides access to logical information, understood as licensing inferences which will follow from propositions containing that concept. The encyclopaedic entry provides access to information about objects, events or properties which fall under the concept, which comes from background knowledge and an individual's own experience of the world. Inferences can be drawn based on encyclopaedic entries just as they can from logical entries. The main difference is that encyclopaedic information will vary from individual to individual while logical entries should be relatively stable across speakers. Here is a simplified, informal and partial representation of lexical, logical and encyclopaedic entries for the concepts {BARE} and {BEAR}, based on my personal understanding of (one sense of each of) the words and (partial understanding of) the concepts and so reflecting my own pronunciation, with /e/ representing a monophthong and /r/ always pronounced at the end of the word:

(10)   {BARE}
         lexical entry:
         adjective
         pronounced / b e r /
         logical entry:
         property of a certain kind
         encyclopaedic entry:
         wearing no clothes
         with no accompaniments
         simple
         straightforward

(11)   {BEAR}
         lexical entry:
         noun
         pronounced / b e r /
         logical entry:
         animal of a certain type
         encyclopaedic entry:
         no longer exist in the wild in Scotland
         found in the wild in North America
         dangerous for humans
         attracted by food scraps
         a black bear once appeared in my aunt's back yard

Perhaps the first thing which will strike readers unfamiliar with this approach is that there is so very little listed under the logical entries here and that some of the things we think of as key aspects of the meanings of the words appear as encyclopaedic entries.[2] The idea which I have tried to capture by formulating the entries in this way is that a concept is linked in various ways to different kinds of information. If an individual knows a word in her language she will know how to pronounce it and where to position it in an utterance, she will draw certain inferences automatically whenever she hears the word uttered, and other inferences will be made in certain contexts but not others. Lexical and logical entries will be shared by almost all individuals who share the same language while encyclopaedic entries will vary from individual to individual.

One of the key ideas developed in and since Wilson and Sperber's (1981) critique of Grice is that we do not always activate and deploy the concept associated with a word without modification. In particular 'enrichment' processes often adjust the specific sense of a word, such as when understanding example (12), which was mentioned in Chapter 2:

(12)   *(watching John Smith play the violin)*
         He plays well.

As we have seen, the hearer of (12) will not only disambiguate the word *play* and decide that John Smith plays a musical instrument well. He will go further and decide that John Smith plays the violin, in particular, well. This shows that we sometimes adjust our understanding of words beyond simply disambiguating and accessing the concept they name. Here we adjust the sense of *play* to mean 'playing the violin'. A number of theorists in recent years, including relevance theorists, have developed the view that making inferences such as this, and adjusting our understanding of the concepts named by words, is something we regularly do when understanding utterances.[3]

Here are some other examples:

(13)   She's a bib.

(14)   That's not a knife. Now THAT is a knife!   (*Crocodile Dundee*, dir. Peter Faiman, 1986)

(15)   He was upset but he wasn't upset.

(13) could be used during a football training session to mean that the referent of *she* will be playing in the team which will be wearing coloured bibs to identify them. One way to explain this would be to say that the hearer adjusts the sense of *bib* to mean that it refers to a person who will be wearing a bib during this training session. On another occasion, (13) could be a metaphorical utterance intended to communicate that the referent of *she* is someone who deals with difficult situations so that other people don't have to have their lives affected by them. Here, we have to do more work in adjusting our understanding of the term *bib*. We will look at metaphorical utterances such as this in more detail in Chapter 9.

(14) is an utterance produced by the character Mick 'Crocodile' Dundee when confronted by a mugger in the film *Crocodile Dundee*. Here is the full exchange:

(16)   *(Dundee and Sue are walking at night. A young man steps out from the shadows, followed by other young people.)*

> YOUNG MAN: You got a light, buddy?
> DUNDEE: Yeah, sure, kid.
>   *(He reaches for his lighter. The young man produces a switchblade.)*
> YOUNG MAN: And your wallet.
> SUE: Mick, give him your wallet.
> DUNDEE: What for?
> SUE: He's got a knife.
> DUNDEE: That's not a knife.
>   *(He produces a huge Bowie knife.)*
>   Now THAT'S a knife!
>   *(Dundee slashes the youth's jacket and looks into his eyes.)*
> YOUNG MAN: Shit!
>   *(Young man runs away.)*

How do we explain this exchange? Clearly, Dundee is using the word *knife* in such a way that the mugger's switchblade does not count as an example. When Sue says that the mugger has a *knife* the concept she names is broad enough to include the switchblade. When Dundee uses the term, only something as large as his Bowie knife will count. Again, we need to adjust our understanding of the concept named by the word *knife* on this occasion to understand what Dundee is saying.

Example (15) is discussed by Carston (2002a: 324). This utterance was produced by the witness Kato in the trial of O. J. Simpson, who was charged with murdering his wife and her friend. Kato was a friend of Simpson's who had seen him on the day of the murders. His utterance here is clearly intended to use the word *upset* in two different senses. He judges that Simpson was upset in one sense but not the other. As Carston says:

> The utterance looks contradictory on the surface, but, in the context of a witness being questioned about Simpson's state of mind on the day when his wife was murdered, it was understood as communicating that he was in a certain kind of upset state of mind, but that he was not in another (more intense, perhaps murderous) mental state. The word 'upset' was understood as expressing two different concepts of upsetness, at least one, but most likely both, involving a pragmatic strengthening of the more general lexical concept UPSET.   (Carston 2002a: 324)

Carston suggests then, that at least one of the senses of *upset* in this context is strengthened to mean a more intense kind of mental state than might be intended in other uses. This is similar to Mick Dundee's use of the term *knife* in example (14)/(16).

Based on examples such as this, Carston (1997), Sperber and Wilson (1998) and others have suggested that working out the meanings conveyed by particular uses of words *always* involves inference. Carston (1997, 2002a: 320–75) developed this idea most fully, beginning by considering two processes: **broadening** (or 'loosening') and **narrowing**. The adjustment of the encoded concept {PLAY} to refer to playing the violin rather than just any musical instrument is a case of narrowing. One way of thinking of recent developments is to see that broadening is also involved. The following examples illustrate how these processes work:

(17)   Holland is flat.

(18)   My friend Sally is moving to London. Do you think you could introduce her to some men?

(19)   Thelma's a princess.

In interpreting (17), we will not assume that Holland is literally flat but assume that flat has been loosely used to pick out a more general property appropriate to describe countries which have relatively few hills or areas of raised land. In interpreting (18), we will not assume that Sally will want to meet absolutely any men we know but that she is interested in meeting heterosexual men of a roughly similar age who might be interested in spending time with her with a view to developing a romantic relationship. In interpreting (19), we will not assume that Thelma is a member of a royal family and at the same time we may well assume that she has some qualities which are not necessarily shared by all princesses (e.g. being a bit spoilt, with a strong sense of self-importance, and so on). If we interpret (17)–(19) in the ways I have in mind, then (17) illustrates concept broadening, (18) illustrates concept narrowing and (19) illustrates simultaneous broadening and narrowing. In the next section, we will consider the more recent view on which understanding uses of words in any utterance involves processes such as these and even that every time we hear a concept-naming word, we create a new 'ad hoc' concept for the purpose of interpreting the specific utterance. In fact, the general idea, based on ideas suggested initially by Dan Sperber (1994a, 2001) goes even further and suggests that we create an ad hoc concept every time we perceive any object or represent any concept.

Exercise 8.2 asks you to explore examples which involve concept broadening and narrowing.

Exercise 8.2

- Consider the emboldened word in each of the following exchanges. Describe how you think the encoded concept will be adjusted in understanding this utterance and decide whether this counts as a case of narrowing, of loosening, or of both simultaneously.
    (i)   A: I looked for George in the canteen but I couldn't see him. Which table does he usually sit at?
           B: The **round** one in the corner.
    (ii)   A: Did you see that outfit Robbie was wearing? Talk about bling!
           B: I know. He's a **rock god**.
    (iii) A: Did you pick up a copy of that new novel you were talking about?
           B: No, they didn't have any with a **hard** cover.
    (iv)   A: Did you read John's thesis?
           B: Yes, it was interesting, but what a lot of **holes** in the argument!

8.5   'Ad hoc' concepts

The starting point for recent work in lexical pragmatics within relevance theory is the notion that the concepts named by words are inferentially adjusted when we process utterances. As Wilson and Carston (2007: 230–1) point out, the more general starting point is the work of the psychologist Lawrence Barsalou (1987, 1993) who focused on 'protoypical narrowing' in understanding concepts and who is usually credited as the source of the description of these processes as involving **'ad hoc' concept formation**. Later work by Glucksberg, Manfred and McGlone (1997) showed that concept adjustment could involve broadening as well as narrowing. As Wilson and Carston suggest:

> This opens up the possibility of a unified account on which lexical narrowing and broadening (or a combination of the two) are the outcomes of a single interpretive process which fine-tunes the interpretation of almost every word.   (Wilson and Carston 2007: 231)

Carston (1997, 2002a) discusses a range of examples, showing how we can account for the interpretation of a large number of utterances by assuming that both broadening and narrowing occur every time we interpret a word in context. Here is how this account will deal with (17)–(19).

This approach assumes that concepts are always adjusted when accessed in context. Adjusted concepts are conventionally represented with a star after them. The encoded concept FLAT is represented as FLAT* when understood in context in an utterance of (17). When we need to refer to two different adjusted concepts, we add another star, so that FLAT** is understood as an adjusted concept different from FLAT*, and so on. When we hear (17), we adjust the concept FLAT to FLAT*, which we might think of as roughly equivalent to 'fairly flat in terms of its landscape when compared to countries in general'. The key thing about FLAT* is that this is a broader sense than FLAT since it applies to things which are not absolutely flat. What is important in context is that this utterance allows us to derive implicatures such as (20)–(22):

(20)   Holland is not mountainous.

(21)   The views in Holland will be those of a relatively flat landscape.

(22)   It would be relatively easy to cycle around Holland.

One thing to notice about the concept FLAT is that it represents something we will strictly speaking never encounter in real life, since no surfaces are absolutely flat. Every time we hear it, we make particular assumptions about exactly what concept it represents. Another concept, FLAT**, will be understood if we talk about a 'flat-screen television', another when we talk about a 'flat tyre', and so on.

In the case of (18), the concept MEN* which the speaker will be understood to have in mind is a narrowed sense, referring as we have said to men of a type we imagine that Sally will be hoping to meet. Here, the key features are to do with the potential of these men to become romantic partners for Sally. In another utterance, say in (23), the relevant features might be to do with being grown-up, able to face difficulties. In another, such as in (24), the focus might be on showing compassion. And so on.

(23)   Some boys seem to take forever to become men.

(24)   Don't think we have no feelings. We're men, not robots.

It could be argued that there is more than broadening going on in the comprehension of *flat* in (17) and more than narrowing in the comprehension of *men* in (18). We might say that FLAT* is looser than an absolute sense of FLAT but that it is not only loosened to mean 'flattish'. We also need to think about exactly what kind of 'flatness' is appropriate for a country, which is different from that associated with a TV, and so on. A bit less clearly, we might say that MEN* is narrower than simply meaning male adult humans, but also that there could be some looseness about exactly what kinds of people will count. Example (19), however, clearly involves both broadening and narrowing. As Carston (1997, 2002a) points out, it is easy to imagine contexts in which it is mutually manifest that Thelma is not actually a member of a royal family. This means that the communicated concept PRINCESS* is broader than the encoded concept. At the same time, we would expect the hearer to make inferences about exactly what kind of 'princess' Thelma is. We will pick out some properties shared by all princesses, such as (25) and (26):

(25)   Thelma is an important person.

(26)   Other people are expected to treat Thelma with great respect.

At the same time, we are likely to make inferences about Thelma which are based on stereotypical properties not necessarily shared by all princesses:

(27)   Thelma is spoilt.

(28)   Thelma is demanding.

(29)   Thelma thinks everyone else should do whatever she wants.

Not all princesses have these properties so the understood sense of *princess* here is narrowed as well as broadened. Inferences such as these are based on information stored in the encyclopaedic entries of activated concepts. Accessing them is of course guided by the relevance-guided comprehension heuristic and the mutual adjustment process with the most easily accessible implications derived first.

The notion is then that understanding uses of words in context always involves 'ad hoc' concept formation. The formation of these concepts can involve broadening or narrowing of the encoded concept, and in some cases both broadening and narrowing are involved. This new approach is significant in many ways, including in the account of various kinds of figurative language, which we will look at in Chapters 9 and 10. It suggests a different way of dealing with utterances which are not understood as literal.

Relevance theorists have always assumed what is sometimes called 'the continuity hypothesis' on which loose, hyperbolic and metaphorical utterances are not different in kind, or processed in significantly different ways, from literal utterances. On this view, literalness is a matter of degree and utterances may be more or less literal. Full literalness is not the norm but an exception at one end of the range of possibilities. In earlier relevance-theoretic accounts, a non-literal utterance would be assumed to express a literal proposition which was not communicated but which was used to derive relevant implicatures, based on the encyclopaedic entries of the encoded concepts. On this account, (17) would express the proposition that Holland is literally flat. In understanding this utterance, addressees would not pause to consider whether the utterance was intended to be literal, but just start to derive implications and stop when they had enough to satisfy their expectations of relevance in a way the speaker could manifestly have foreseen. Any interpreter would of course rule out the possibility that the speaker is communicating that Holland is completely flat since this is both generally implausible and mathematically impossible. Instead, they will start deriving relevant implicatures such as those mentioned above:

(30)   Holland is not mountainous.

(31)   The views in Holland will be those of a relatively flat landscape.

(32)   It would be relatively easy to cycle around Holland.

This account seems to work, but it is slightly counterintuitive in that it suggests that speakers do not assume that the speaker of (17) is communicating the proposition expressed. On the more recent approach, the proposition expressed by (17) includes an adjusted concept FLAT*:

(33)   Holland is FLAT*.

With the concept adjusted in this way, we can now say that the proposition contextually inferred using the semantic representation of this utterance is, in fact, communicated and the relevant implicatures are derived from this proposition.

One question we might ask about this is how precisely the adjusted concepts can be characterised in each case. In Chapter 6 above we considered the notion that we might not always be able to characterise the content of explicatures precisely. The examples we discussed there were haikus and pop songs where it might not be easy to identify the exact intended referents of all referring expressions. On this view, it seems that there will also be cases where not all of the features of an adjusted concept will be clear. In the next chapter, we will see how this might apply in accounting for metaphorical utterances.

Exercise 8.3 asks you to compare ad hoc concept accounts of lexical meaning with earlier relevance-theoretic accounts.

Exercise 8.3

- Consider B's utterance in each of the following exchanges. First, propose an account based on the earlier relevance-theoretic account, which assumes a less than literal relationship between the proposition expressed and the speaker's thought. Then propose an account based on the more recent 'ad hoc concept' approach.

  (i)   A: What do you think of the new version of the script?
          B: It's OK, but it's a bit flat.

  (ii)   A: Did you crucify John for being late?
          B: I'm not a dalek.

  (iii)   A: I hear they've invited Pauline and Peggy to the party.
          B: Fasten your seat belts. It's going to be a bumpy night.

  (iv)   A: What did Flaubert say about that other guy's writing?
          B: His ink is pale.

8.6   Summary

In this chapter, we have looked briefly at the new field of lexical pragmatics which explores the inferences involved in understanding words in context. Relevance-theoretic accounts of word meaning now assume that there is more to understanding uses of words than simply accessing the concepts they encode. Rather, pragmatic processes create 'ad hoc' concepts derived by modifying the encoded concepts in order to find interpretations which satisfy their expectations of relevance. This has a number of implications for semantics and pragmatics, including the suggestion of a new account of non-literal utterances. This account will be explored further in the next chapter, where we consider how relevance theory accounts for figurative language.

Exercise 8.4

As in every chapter, this final exercise asks you to adjust the list of questions you have come up with so far by compiling new questions which have occurred to you while reading this chapter and to think about the kinds of things which might count as answers to any questions you have come up with so far. First, add new questions to your ongoing list. Second, consider all of your questions and think about possible ways of answering them.

8.7   Further reading

The relationship between words and concepts is discussed in *Relevance* (Sperber and Wilson 1986: 83–93) but the ideas developed there really took off in later work, including one key paper by Sperber and Wilson (Sperber and Wilson 1998) and further developments by Robyn Carston (e.g. Carston 1997, 2002a). Wilson and Carston (2007) is a useful recent discussion.

9   Figurative language: metaphor

Topics: literal and non-literal language; descriptive and interpretive representations; Grice's account of metaphor; metaphor and weak implicatures; metaphor and ad hoc concepts

9.1   Overview

This chapter and the next one consider how relevance theory aims to account for two varieties of figurative language: metaphor and irony. There is a wide range of kinds of figurative language (for discussion, see Gibbs 1994; Glucksberg 2001) but these are by far the most extensively studied. This chapter begins by considering the traditional distinction between literal and non-literal language. Work in relevance theory rejects the traditional view on which there is a sharp distinction between utterances which are literal and utterances which are non-literal. It also rejects the assumption that there is a clear distinction between these phenomena and other kinds of utterances. Instead, they assume that 'metaphorical' and 'ironic' utterances (or utterances we label as such) exploit features which occur in a range of utterances, and that utterances can be more or less metaphorical or ironic depending on how they exploit these features. Given these assumptions, it is possible for some utterances to share some of the features of metaphor or irony without being clearly classifiable as metaphorical or ironic. One way to express this is to say that neither metaphor nor irony are 'natural kinds'. Partly as a result of the work discussed in the previous chapter, the relevance-theoretic approach to literalness has changed over the years. Section 9.2 briefly considers Grice's account of non-literal language and points out some problems with his approach. Section 9.3 considers the distinction between descriptive and interpretive representations and shows how relevance theory exploits these two modes of representation in accounting for a variety of utterances. The next three sections present three approaches to metaphor: Section 9.4 briefly presents Grice's approach; Section 9.5 presents the relevance-theoretic approach developed in the book *Relevance* (Sperber and Wilson 1989); Section 9.6 presents a more recent account based on work on lexical pragmatics in general and on the notion of ad hoc concept formation in particular.

9.2   Literal and non-literal language

The traditional assumption about literalness has been that literal uses of language are different in kind from non-literal uses. This is the view taken by Grice who saw the examples in (1)–(4) as blatant violations of the maxim of quality at the level of 'what is said':

(1)   *(Grice contextualises this as: 'X, with whom A has been on close terms until now, has betrayed a secret of A's to a business rival. A and his audience both know this')*
X is a fine friend.

(2)   You are the cream in my coffee.

(3)   *(Grice's contextualisation: 'Of a man known to have broken up all the furniture')*
He was a little intoxicated.

(4)   Every nice girl loves a sailor.   (examples from Grice 1989: 34)

Grice suggests that the speaker in each of (1)–(4) has said (or 'made as if to say') something which is blatantly false and that this inspires the hearer to infer an implicature which is true and so preserves the assumption that the speaker's utterance as a whole has observed the Cooperative Principle. (1) is an example of irony, which Grice treats as communicating the opposite of what is said. (2) is an example of metaphor, which Grice treats as communicating a simile related to what is said. (3) is understatement ('meiosis') where we infer a stronger version of what is said. (4) is overstatement where we infer a weaker version. For Grice, there is a marked difference between non-literal utterances such as (1)–(4) and literal utterances such as (5)–(8):

(5)   *(in the same context as Grice envisaged for the ironic version and mentioned in (1) above)*
X is a terrible friend.

(6)   You are very special.

(7)   *(in the same context as Grice envisaged for (3) above)*
He was very drunk.

(8)   Many nice girls love sailors.

(4) is of course an outdated example, no doubt used playfully by Grice as an echoic allusion to the song 'All The Nice Girls Love A Sailor'. I assume Grice would have recognised something like (8) as a reasonable non-hyperbolic paraphrase.

Grice's approach suggests, then, that understanding a non-literal utterance involves first accessing and rejecting a literal interpretation, and then looking for a more appropriate non-literal one. This means that literal utterances are understood in a way quite different from non-literal utterances.

There are several problems with this approach. Some are specific to the accounts of irony and metaphor. Others apply to Grice's approach to non-literal language more generally. First, it's not clear that the implicatures suggested here do characterise what is communicated by these utterances. Our intuitions surely do not suggest that (1) in this context communicates only (5), that (2) communicates only (6), and so on. If this were so, we could just as easily utter the literal versions and, arguably, there would be no reason ever to use the non-literal utterances. In other words, it's not clear on this view why non-literal language should exist. If a speaker intended to communicate that someone is not a fine friend, why not simply say (5) rather than (1) so that the hearer can access the intended meaning directly? It's not clear what is gained by asking hearers to go through the extra step of first accessing and then rejecting the literal interpretation. Within Grice's approach, there is a more specific problem. The non-literal utterances count for Grice as cases of 'flouting' a maxim. But there is something quite unusual about these cases of flouting. In general, when a speaker flouts (blatantly violates) a maxim, this causes the hearer to infer an implicature which will justify the violation. A Gricean account of Bev's utterance in (9), for example, would suggest that it violates the maxim of quantity by not providing enough information (or that it violates the maxim of relation by not being relevant):

(9)   KEN: Have you finished that essay yet?
        BEV: The weather is really weird these days, isn't it?

Ken infers that Bev has said something uninformative or irrelevant because she does not want to talk about the essay. Taking what is said together with what is implicated, the utterance as a whole is informative and relevant. In examples (1)–(4), by contrast, the implicature *replaces* what is said, confirming that what is said does indeed violate the maxims. There is no 'what is said' in any of (1)–(4). This seems to undermine Grice's notion that the Cooperative Principle and maxims are grounded in rationality. In these cases, we might argue that the speaker has been *irrational* in communicating in this way.

Another specific problem is that it's not clear on this picture how we know what to infer in each case. When a speaker blatantly violates the maxim of quality, she may be doing so in order to communicate the opposite of what is said, a related simile, a stronger version of what is said or a weaker version. It's not clear how the hearer will identify which of these is appropriate in a particular case.

Related to this, Grice's account seems not to fit with some of his aims in developing the notion of implicature. In particular, Grice (1975: 50) suggested that implicatures should be calculable. He said:

> The presence of a conversational implicature must be capable of being worked out; for even if it can be intuitively grasped, unless the intuition is replaceable by an argument, the implicature (if present at all) will not count as a conversational implicature: it will be a conventional implicature.
> (Grice 1975: 50)

For Grice, then, conversational implicatures should be capable of being worked out and not simply follow by some automatic procedure whose stages can not be spelled out clearly. Blakemore (1987: 35) points out that Grice's general working out schema for conversational implicatures 'is not recognisable as a standard logical argument' (Blakemore 1987: 35). She points in particular to a stage in the schema which can not be understood as deductive. This is step (c) in the schema as represented below:

(10)   *Working out schema for conversational implicatures*
   (a)   The speaker (S) has said that p.
   (b)   There is no reason to think that S is not observing the maxims.
   (c)   S could not be doing this unless he thought that q.
   (d)   S knows (and knows that the hearer (H) knows that he knows) that H can see that he thinks that the supposition that he thinks that q is required.
   (e)   S has done nothing to stop H from thinking that q.
   (f)   S intends H to think, or is at least willing to allow H to think, that q.
   (g)   And so, S has implicated that q.
                                                (Blakemore 1987: 35: after Grice 1975: 50)

As Blakemore points out, (c) is the key stage where the content of the implicature is introduced but it is not clear where that content comes from. She suggests that this outline 'seems to assume that the hearer has already identified *q*, the conclusion simply being that it was intended as part of the speaker's message' (Blakemore 1987: 35). The problem is even worse in the case of non-literal language since stage (c) follows from the recognition of non-literalness and different kinds of assumptions are required for different varieties. Here is the working out schema adapted for non-literal utterances:

(11)   *Working out schema for non-literal utterances*
   (a)   The speaker (S) has said that p.
   (b)   There is no reason to think that S is not observing the maxims.
   (c)   p is literally false and so the speaker could not be communicating p.
   (d)   S could not be observing the maxims unless he thought that q.
   (e)   q is a 'closely related proposition' to p.
   (d)   S knows (and knows that the hearer (H) knows that he knows) that H can see that he thinks that the supposition that he thinks that q is required.
   (e)   S has done nothing to stop H from thinking that q.
   (f)   S intends H to think, or is at least willing to allow H to think, that q.
   (g)   And so, S has implicated that q.
                                           (after Blakemore 1987: 35: after Grice 1975: 50)

The relevant steps in this representation are (d) and (e). Here Grice suggests that the hearer moves from a recognition that *p* is false to a stage where he looks for a 'closely related proposition' to *p*. This is quite far from a clearly calculable step. Even worse, the nature of the closely related proposition will vary depending on whether the non-literal utterance is metaphorical, ironic, an understatement, an approximation, hyperbole, and so on. How will the hearer work out which proposition is the one intended on a particular occasion? And how can we understand this as clearly calculable?

Finally for now, it's not clear how Grice's approach could be extended to deal with rough approximations or 'loose talk' such as the following examples:

(12)   The lecture was a bit of a mess. A hundred students turned up.

(13)   Aberdeen is five hundred miles north of London.

The speaker in (12) may well not have counted the exact number of students who turned up at the lecture and the hearer is unlikely to assume that the exact number is known. Instead, it is likely that the hearer will assume that around one hundred students turned up. The point of the utterance is surely to suggest that a larger number arrived than were expected, with negative consequences such as over-crowding, shortage of handouts, and so on. In (13), there are two ways in which this is less than accurate. First, the distance between Aberdeen and London is not exactly five hundred miles (and it is of course not clear where the distance is taken to begin and end, nor that we could ever measure an exact distance of five hundred miles). Second, the direction is not exactly north (true or magnetic). Instead, the hearer will assume that the distance is around five hundred miles and that the direction is roughly northwards. It is not clear that hearers have a sense that the speaker in (12) or (13) is diverging from a norm of literalness. It is even more dubious to assume that hearers then move on to infer an implicature which the speaker is intending to communicate by use of a non-literal utterance.

Finally, notice that this approach suggests that understanding non-literal utterances of all varieties involves an extra step which is not involved in understanding literal utterances, i.e. the stage of rejecting the initial literal interpretation and replacing it with a non-literal one. Our intuitions on this are not necessarily reliable but they do not straightforwardly fall into line with this assumption. This has also been taken to suggest that non-literal utterances will take longer to process than their literal counterparts. Experimental work has not confirmed this (see Gibbs 1994, 2001, and further references in these sources).

For reasons such as these, relevance theorists have rejected the view that speakers aim to follow a norm of literal truthfulness. These reasons are discussed more fully in a number of sources (including Wilson 1995; Wilson and Sperber 2002).

Accounts of literal and non-literal uses of language within relevance theory have evolved over the years. What has remained constant is that literalness in verbal communication is not assumed to be a norm occasionally departed from for specific purposes. Earlier accounts were based on the idea that hearers could see the relevance of utterances without assuming they were literal. Suppose I utter (12) in a context where we both know that I expected around fifty students to attend my lecture and that I am booked into a classroom which holds seventy. You will infer conclusions such as the following:

(14)   More people turned up at the lecture than expected.

(15)   There were not enough handouts to go round.

(16)   There was not enough room for everyone to sit down.

Notice that (14)–(16) follow from the assumption that around one hundred people turned up as well as from the assumption that exactly one hundred people turned up. There is no need, then, for the hearer to make a decision about whether or not the utterance is literal.

More recently, accounts within relevance theory have been based on the approach to lexical pragmatics outlined in the previous chapter where concepts are adjusted, or ad hoc concepts created, in the course of interpretation as part of the mutual adjustment process. On this view, then, part of the interpretation of (12) will involve creating an ad hoc concept of ONE HUNDRED* which will be broader than the encoded concept and include numbers on either side of 100 as well as exactly 100. This approach has also led to a new account of metaphor. Before looking at these two approaches in more detail, the next section looks at two kinds of representation envisaged within relevance theory: descriptive and interpretive representation. We will then move on to look at ways in which relevance theorists have used these notions in accounting for metaphor and irony.

Exercise 9.1 asks you to consider Grice's account of non-literal utterances and some problems with the Gricean approach.

Exercise 9.1

- Consider the metaphorical and 'loose' uses of language in the following exchanges. How might they be handled on Grice's approach? To what extent does each example raise problems for Grice's approach?

    (i)   *(B is about to sing a solo in front of a large audience for the first time)*
         A: Are you nervous?
         B: My legs are jelly.

    (ii) A: Do you think John will be nervous before the match on Saturday?
         B: Of course! He'll be playing in front of fifty thousand people.

    (iii) A: Do you know anybody who's been around long enough to know why we started having staff meetings on Wednesday afternoons?
         B: John should know. He's been here since the beginning of time.

    (iv) A: I asked John whether he knew how to use an interactive whiteboard and he went ballistic!
         B: I think you've upset him.

9.3   Descriptive and interpretive representations

Utterances are not used only to communicate information about the world. When we speak, we also express our own beliefs, opinions or attitudes. An utterance such as (17) could express my belief about the bedroom it refers to:

(17)   This bedroom is really disgusting.

It could also be used to report what someone else has said in a context such as the one suggested in (18) or to suggest what someone else might be thinking in a context such as the one in (19):

(18)   KEN: What did Jess say?
            BEV: This bedroom is really disgusting.

(19)   *(Ken walks into Bev's bedroom and Bev notices that he looks like he disapproves of what he sees.)*
            BEV: I know what you're thinking. This bedroom is really disgusting.

(20)   *(Ken walks into Bev's bedroom and looks at the messy room.)*
            KEN: This bedroom is really disgusting.
            BEV: *(pulling a face and mimicking in an exaggerated style)*
                 This bedroom is really disgusting!

In each case, of course, these interpretations are partly encoded and partly inferred. In (18), Bev could be ignoring Ken's question and choosing to comment on the disgusting bedroom rather than reporting what Jess said. In (19), Bev could be stating her own view rather than attributing the thought to Ken.

One way to account for this is to say that the utterance could be used either to state the speaker's own belief about the bedroom or to represent someone else's utterance or thought. Within relevance theory, this involves a distinction between descriptive and interpretive representation. A descriptive representation is treated as a true or in some way evidenced representation of a state of affairs in the world. An interpretive representation is treated as a more or less faithful representation of some other utterance or thought which it resembles in content (that is, with which it shares logical and contextual implications). If uttered as a straightforward descriptive use of language, then (17) would be understood as representing the speaker's own belief that the bedroom is 'really disgusting' (with some inference to be made about exactly what *really* means here, of course). In (18), if taken as a report of speech, the same sentence would be understood as a more or less faithful report of Jess's utterance. In (19), it is a more or less faithful interpretation of Ken's thought. As an ironic utterance in (20) it is a more or less faithful interpretation of Ken's utterance, which resembles that utterance through sharing logical and contextual implications with it. These last three examples are interpretations of other people's thoughts or utterances. Descriptive uses of language represent states of affairs by expressing propositions which we can judge as true or not. Interpretive uses of language represent thoughts or utterances (or other representations with a conceptual content) by sharing logical or contextual implications with them, which means that we can judge them by how closely they resemble the thought or utterance they represent, or how 'faithful' an interpretation they present. Sperber and Wilson (1986: 224–31) suggest that interpretive representation is a sub-type of a more general notion of representation by resemblance. A drawing of a person can represent that person by resembling the person visually. An utterance can represent another utterance not only by resembling it in content, but also by resembling it in form (as happens in mimicry, direct quotation or parody). Interpretive representations crucially exploit resemblances in content. Consider, for example, (21) as a summary of the plot of *Hamlet* or (22) as a summary of a business meeting:

(21)   He can't decide whether to avenge his father or not and then everybody ends up dead.

(22)   We have to work harder or there's going to be redundancies.

(21) is a one-sentence summary of the plot of a five-act play which takes several hours to perform. (22) is a summary of a meeting which might have taken a few minutes or considerably longer. In each case, the speaker has produced an utterance which provides evidence for some of the conclusions which could be derived from the original. Part of the act of interpretation is deciding which of the many conclusions derivable from the original are ones the speaker should aim to provide evidence for in his or her own utterance.

The distinction between description and interpretation is key to understanding how thoughts and utterances can be relevant. It is illustrated in Figure 9.1. Perhaps the most striking thing about this diagram initially is that it suggests that all utterances are interpretations of a thought of the communicator. All utterances resemble a thought of the communicator by sharing conceptual and logical properties with that thought. I could represent my thought about your bedroom by uttering (17) or by uttering (23) or (24):

(23)   Disgusting.

(24)   Yuck!

(17), (23) and (24) could be seen as three ways of interpreting the same thought. We will see in Section 9.4 how this interpretive relationship is involved in the relevance-theoretic account of degrees of literalness and the idea that full literalness is not any kind of norm in verbal communication.

Given that all utterances are interpretations, then, it is in distinguishing two kinds of mental representation that the distinction between description and interpretation plays its most significant role. A thought which is a description will be taken to be true of the state of affairs it represents. If I think that whales are mammals, then I am entertaining a thought expressing the proposition that the set of whales is included in the set of mammals and treating it as true in the world which I live in. A thought which is an interpretation will represent another thought or utterance by sharing logical or contextual implications with it, i.e. by resembling it in content to some degree.

The bottom of Figure 9.1 suggests that the thought interpreted by an utterance can itself be one of four kinds of representation: (a) an interpretation of an actual (e.g. attributed) representation; (b) an interpretation of a desirable (e.g. relevant)

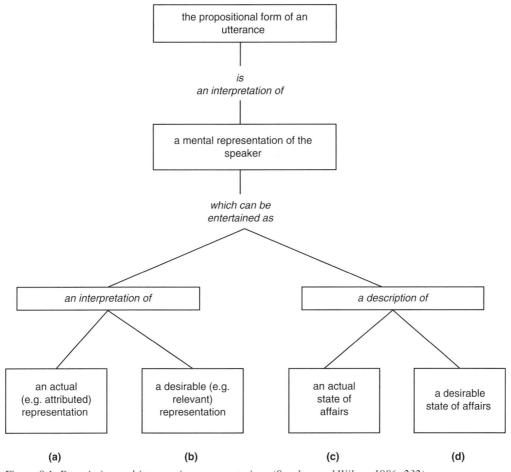

Figure 9.1 *Descriptive and interpretive representations (Sperber and Wilson 1986: 232)*

representation; (c) a description of an actual state of affairs; or (d) a description of a desirable state of affairs. We will not consider (b) and (d) here as they are significant for dealing with other phenomena (such as the encoded meanings of interrogative and imperative syntax) but not for figurative language.

(c)   descriptions of actual states of affairs

Descriptions of states of affairs are, of course, the most familiar of the four categories since they include the most typical kind of utterance in which a speaker commits herself to the truth (or probable truth) of the proposition expressed, i.e. where she states her own belief. Of course, while declarative sentences are the most common form used for expressing this, not all utterances with declarative syntax do express the speaker's own belief. Jokes, fiction, suppositions and attributions are obvious exceptions:

(25)   *Opening of a joke:*
          A man walks into a bar …

(26)   *Opening of a novel (Dickens's* Tale of Two Cities*):*
            It was the best of times ...

(27)   *Supposition:*
            You find yourself stranded on a desert island ...

(28)   *Attributed thought:*
            You're enjoying your new school.

The most obvious way to deal with these within relevance theory is to assume
that they all involve the embedding of the proposition expressed under another
kind of description, such as:

(29)   *Opening of a joke:*
            [In the fictional joke world] A man walks into a bar ...

(30)   *Opening of a novel (Dickens's* Tale of Two Cities*):*
            [In the fictional world of the book] It was the best of times ...

(31)   *Supposition:*
            [Suppose that] You find yourself stranded on a desert island ...

(32)   *Attributed thought:*
            [I think you're thinking that] You're enjoying your new school.

Declarative syntax seems to be specialised for the representation of beliefs.
However, it is not clear exactly what might be the encoded meaning of declarative syntax or of the indicative mood.[1]

(a)   interpretations of actual representations

There are several ways in which a thought can be an interpretation of
an actual representation (that is, an actual thought or utterance). Perhaps the
most obvious is the case where it is an interpretation of a thought attributed to
someone else. This might occur when I think about what you are thinking.
Suppose, for example, that we are eating a meal together and I notice that you
keep glancing at a box of chocolates I have left on the kitchen table. I might
decide that you would like me to offer you some. If so, I am representing
thoughts which I think you might be having. Examples in speech include cases
where the speaker is understood to be reporting what someone else has said or
thought, such as (17) above where *this room is disgusting* was taken to represent
a thought or utterance attributed to someone else.

It is also possible for the thought or utterance represented to be attributed to
the speaker herself, usually not one she is entertaining at the time of utterance.
Suppose, for example, that I am planning a party and I say to you:

(33)   Ken's always fun to have around.

Later, Ken turns out to have been a terrible guest, moping around sulkily, picking
pointless arguments and causing a number of difficult scenes. Later, I might say:

(34)   Ken's always fun to have around!

Here I am representing (or 're-presenting') my own earlier utterance and making clear that I think it was very foolish. If I invite Ken without discussing my idea as in (33), i.e. if there is no previous utterance which it alludes to, then (34) might be a way of representing and ridiculing my earlier thought. We'll see in Chapter 10 that the relevance-theoretic account of irony is based on the idea that we can attribute thoughts in this way and implicitly communicate our attitudes to those thoughts.

Other examples of interpretive representation include reports, summaries such as (21)–(22) above, translations and newspaper headlines. In each of these cases, the speaker or writer produces an utterance which is intended to resemble the original closely enough for the hearer or reader to be able to get an accurate enough idea of what it said or implied. Of course, what counts as 'enough' varies from context to context. *There will be spending cuts* might be close enough as a one-sentence summary of a much longer budget statement. The translation of a novel into a new language needs to be much closer and translators will work very hard trying to adjust their translation to be as accurate as possible, while knowing, of course, that full accuracy is not possible (for discussion of translation within a relevance-theoretic framework, see Gutt 1991).

Exercise 9.2 asks you to consider examples which illustrate the distinction between descriptive and interpretive interpretation.

Exercise 9.2

- Consider B's utterance in each of the following exchanges. Decide whether the utterance is likely to be understood as representing a thought which is a description or an interpretation. In some cases, you might decide that both options are likely. Explain what makes each one likely to be descriptive, interpretive, or vague between the two:
  (i) A: What did John say when you told him they'd asked you to work overtime at the weekend?
       B: Not to do it.
  (ii) A: Did you say John's refusing to help?
       B: He's tired after a long day at work.
  (iii) A: They're saying we should coach students directly on specific exam topics now.
        B: Fantastic. What a great idea.
  (iv) A: That actress we were talking about has pulled out of filming to go on a meditation holiday.
       B: It's not easy being the nation's sweetheart.

9.4 Grice's account of metaphor

Metaphor has been accounted for in two ways within relevance theory. Before looking at these, we will remind ourselves of how Grice attempted to account for metaphor and some of the problems associated with his account. First, here are some fairly straightforward examples of metaphor to make sure we agree on the kind of utterance we are discussing:

(35)   John's a lion.

(36)   Sally is a block of ice.

(37)   Robert is a bulldozer.

(35)–(37) are metaphorical given that John is a human being and not a lion, Sally is not literally a block of ice and Robert is not literally a bulldozer. To explain these utterances we need to account for the intuition that they are not literal and to explain how they are understood. When considering the non-literalness of metaphors, we also need to recognise that they are often felt to be different from other non-literal utterances such as the loose uses in (38) and (39):

(38)   *(The speaker did not count the guests so does not know the exact number.)*
          There were a hundred people at the party.

(39)   *(The speaker lives just outside the official city border of Paris.)*
          I live in Paris.

Here are questions which we will expect an adequate account of metaphor to answer:

(40)   Questions about metaphor:
   a.   How is metaphor understood?
   b.   What is the relationship between metaphorical and literal utterances (e.g. an utterance of (35) which is informing us about the name of a lion)?
   c.   What is the relationship between 'dead' or conventional metaphors and more creative metaphors?
   d.   What is the relationship between 'loose' or approximate uses and metaphor?
   e.   What is the relationship between hyperbole and metaphor?
   f.   Why are some metaphors perceived as more creative than others?

As we saw above, Grice suggested that metaphor and hyperbole (as well as irony and understatement) involve a blatant violation of the maxim of quality. The hearer notices that what is said is blatantly false and looks for a related implicature which is true. Grice's initial example of metaphor is:

(41)   You're the cream in my coffee.

In this context, the speaker cannot mean to communicate the proposition that the hearer literally is the cream in her coffee, which is clearly false. So the hearer looks for a related true proposition which the speaker could be implicating and decides that the speaker must be implicating the proposition that:

(42)   You're like the cream in my coffee.

Hyperbole is seen as exploiting the same mechanism:

(43)   That's the best essay I've ever read.

The difference here is that the related proposition which is implicated is a weaker version of (43), e.g.

(44)   That's one of the best essays I've ever read.

Several problems with this approach have been pointed out. First, it's not clear why it is rational to say something false in order to implicate something true. Grice's account presupposes that speakers are rational and that it is rational to produce utterances formulated as they are. If the intention is to communicate that you are like the cream in my coffee, why not just say that? Second, it's not clear how the hearer knows which proposition is being implicated. If metaphor, hyperbole, understatement and irony (which we'll be discussing again below) all involve the speaker saying something false in order to implicate something different, how does the hearer know when to derive an implicature which is the opposite of what is said, when to derive something similar, when to derive something weaker and when to derive something stronger. Third, some metaphors are not clearly false:

(45)   John's no lion.

(46)   Be an angel.

(47)   Is John an angel?

(45) is true if John is a human being. It's not clear how imperatives such as (46), interrogatives such as (47) and other non-declaratives could be understood as true or false so the maxim of quality cannot be involved in explaining them. Fourth, it's not always clear that we can understand what a metaphorical utterance conveys as involving a related simile. Consider (48) and (49) produced as comments on another speaker's conversation which seems to be heading towards controversial conversational territory:

(48)   He's close to the edge there.

(49)   Don't do it! Step back!

If I produce utterances such as these in order to communicate that some aspect of another person's conversation is risky, e.g. because it might make another person angry and lead to a scene, it's not clear what related simile could capture this. Perhaps it would be along the lines of 'the social risk he's taking by talking like this is similar to the physical risk he'd be in if he were standing near to the edge of a cliff or precipice of some kind'. This is, of course, quite complicated and again it raises questions about the plausibility of an account which suggests that we first run into a kind of processing dead-end, then realise that we need to try another track, then wonder what 'closely related proposition' is being communicated, and finally come up with this rather complex and in many ways not very closely related proposition. Fifth, it's not clear that Grice's approach could be extended to deal with rough approximations:

(50)   The party was a disaster. A hundred people showed up.

(51)   Aberdeen is five hundred miles north of London.

Assuming that we do not think the speaker counted the number of people at the party, (50) does not communicate that exactly one hundred people showed up. Nor does it communicate that fewer or more than one hundred people showed up. It communicates that somewhere around one hundred people showed up. (51) is an approximation in two ways. Five hundred miles is an approximation similar to that in (50) in that Aberdeen is somewhere around five hundred miles from London. The direction 'north' is also an approximation. It is not intended to mean 'due north' or 'magnetic north' but 'roughly north'. Both are strictly speaking false. It's not clear how they fit into Grice's account. It might just about be possible to argue that they each communicate a related simile or explicitly approximate statement ('it was like one hundred people showed up', 'Aberdeen is close to five hundred miles and roughly due north from London') but this would suggest then that (50) and (51) function in the same way as metaphors and it is clear that we do not perceive either example to be metaphorical. Finally, experimental evidence does not confirm Grice's approach. If hearers first access a literal interpretation and then move on to a metaphorical interpretation when required, we might expect this to be reflected in processing times. Experiments carried out over several years by Ray Gibbs, Sam Glucksberg and others (for discussion, see Gibbs 1994, 2001; Glucksberg 2001, 2004) suggest both that there is no significant difference in processing times for metaphorical as opposed to non-metaphorical interpretations (or, more generally, for non-literal as opposed to literal ones) and that hearers often begin by testing a metaphorical interpretation.

We'll now move on to consider two approaches to metaphor developed within relevance theory. They have in common that they are 'deflationary' (Sperber and Wilson 2008) in that they do not assume that metaphor involves a departure from a norm of communication but instead assume that it exploits general properties of communication shared by many utterances. They differ with regard to the nature of the proposition expressed by utterances. The second approach we'll look at, developed more recently, assumes that lexical pragmatic processes, and ad hoc concept formation in particular, are involved in understanding metaphorical utterances. First, we'll consider the earlier account which is based on the idea that we do not begin by assuming that the speaker is committed to the truth of all the implications which would follow if the utterance were literally understood.

9.5   Metaphor and weak implicatures

There are two main ways in which metaphor has been treated within relevance theory. First, Sperber and Wilson (1986, 1990) developed an account based on the assumption that the process of developing the semantic representation of an utterance into the proposition expressed did not involve the use of 'ad hoc' concepts. Instead, hearers would start deriving appropriate inferential conclusions from the encoded concepts without assuming that the utterance is a literal interpretation of the speaker's thought. This account explains metaphor in the same way as it explains loose talk and approximations. One way of thinking about this is to say that in general, the proposition expressed by a loose, hyperbolic or metaphorical utterance is not an explicature (because it is not part of what is communicated). Later accounts (Carston 1997, 2002a, 2002b; Sperber and Wilson 1998, 2008; Wilson and Carston 2006) argue that understanding utterances involves adjustments to lexically encoded concepts, or the creation of 'ad hoc' concepts, which then figure in the proposition expressed. Both accounts share the assumption that loose use, hyperbole and metaphor work in the same way, and that literal truthfulness is not a 'norm' which is departed from in these cases.

The first account assumes that hearers begin not by wondering whether a speaker is being literal or not, but simply by moving on to derive conclusions which the speaker might have intended to communicate and which would make their utterance relevant in the expected way. In interpreting the approximation in (50), for example, the hearer does not wonder whether exactly one hundred people turned up to the lecture but simply begins to derive relevant implications such as those in (52):

(52) a.   More people showed up than were expected.
     b.   There was not enough space for everyone.
     c.   There was not enough food.
     d.   There was not enough drink.

These conclusions would follow whether exactly or approximately one hundred people turned up. The hearer will not derive all of the implications which follow from (50) but only those which the speaker could clearly have intended and which help to make the utterance relevant enough.

The interpretation of a metaphor such as (35), repeated here as (53), follows exactly the same pattern. Again, the hearer does not wonder whether John is literally a lion but simply begins to derive relevant implications, such as those in (54):

(53)   John is a lion.

(54) a.   John is brave.
     b.   John is to be feared.
     c.   You should be careful around John.

This account of non-literal uses of language is centred around the interpretive relationship at the top of Figure 9.1, i.e. the relationship between the proposition expressed and the speaker's thought. The assumption is that the proposition expressed by every utterance is an interpretation of a thought of the speaker's. It resembles the speaker's thought because it shares certain logical properties with that thought. Literal utterances are those where the thought represented is identical to the proposition expressed (so that all of the implications of the proposition expressed are also implications of the thought represented). In cases of loose use or metaphor, only certain implications of the proposition expressed are shared by the thought. As long as the hearer can arrive at the intended implications, then communication will be successful. The underlying assumption is that utterances are not direct externalisations of thoughts but are understood as interpretively representing those thoughts (and hence as resembling them to a greater or lesser degree). Let's begin by considering a fairly straightforward response to a request for information:

(55)   KEN: When were you born?
        BEV: 1960.

In this context, Ken will decide that Bev is communicating her belief that she was born in 1960, i.e. after midnight on the 31st of December 1959 and before midnight on the 31st of December 1960. Bev has provided evidence for any proposition which follows logically from this proposition, including all of the assumptions in (56):

(56) a.   Bev was born more than fifty years ago.
     b.   Bev is over 50 years old.
     c.   Bev is over 40 years old.
     d.   Bev was born in a leap year.

Bev does not of course necessarily intend to communicate all of these propositions but she has given evidence for them all and Ken can feel safe in assuming that he has evidence for them based on Bev's utterance. We can say that the proposition expressed by Bev's utterance is a literal interpretation of Bev's thought, which shares all of its logical implications. Now consider a different example:

(57)   I was born fifty years ago.

What exactly is the proposition expressed here? That Bev is exactly 50 years old? To the second? To the day? Or more loosely? All of these are, of course, possible. And because fifty is a round figure, we can even imagine someone who is 49, 51 or 52 uttering (57). There is more than one way of explaining this. Sperber and Wilson's (1986) suggestion is that the proposition expressed by (57) is that the speaker is 50 years old but that we do not necessarily assume that the speaker is committing herself to exactly that proposition. Rather, we use the proposition to derive logical implications and, as ever following considerations of relevance, we select from this set those implications which we think the speaker intends to communicate (i.e. those which would make the utterance optimally relevant). These might include the propositions in (58):

(58) a.   The speaker is an adult.
     b.   The speaker is not a young person.
     c.   The speaker is middle-aged.

d. The speaker has had experience of life.

e. The speaker is not naive.

As long as the speaker can trust us to recognise the intended implications and not to derive any which are clearly not intended, e.g. that the speaker has the properties of someone around the age of 50, then (57) can be uttered by someone who is slightly younger or slightly older than 50 years. Of course, there are contexts in which (57) could be intended to mean more specifically that the speaker is over 49 and under 51, e.g. in response to a question about age when filling in an official form. The key thing on this view is that we do not begin by assuming that the proposition expressed is a literal interpretation of the thought it represents, but simply go ahead and begin to derive enough implications to satisfy our expectations of relevance. The same kind of consideration will apply to loose uses such as (50) and (51).

So this approach assumes that metaphors exploit the possibility of producing an utterance which is a less than literal interpretation of the thought it represents. The propositional form of the thought represented is relatively far from the proposition expressed and the utterance may give rise to a relatively wide range of relatively weak implicatures. Very creative or poetic metaphors are cases where the utterance gives rise to a particularly wide range of weak implicatures.

Let's consider again the very standard example (35), repeated again here as (59):

(59)   John's a lion.

Once we have identified the referent of *John*, decided which sense of *lion* is intended (let's assume that this refers to a particular species of large wild cat), and made assumptions about the time and circumstances (e.g. that this is true of John as a general property rather than in specific circumstances, say when he is playing football or in his workplace), here are some logical or contextual implications of the claim that John is a lion:

(60) a. John is an animal of a certain type.

b. John is a member of the cat family.

c. John is a kind of creature who hunts without weapons, killing and eating his prey.

d. John is brave.

e. John is to be feared.

f. You should be careful around John.

The hearer will understand the utterance correctly as long as he can recognise the implications which the speaker intends to convey, such as (60d–f), and does not assume that the speaker intended to communicate any of the non-intended implications, such as (60a–c). Understanding this utterance as a metaphor, then, means selecting implications such as that John is brave while not making assumptions such as that John is a member of the cat family.

Perhaps the first thing to notice about this account is that it treats metaphor as involving exactly the same mechanisms as are involved in understanding non-literal approximations. Notice also that hyperbole (overstatement) will be treated in exactly the same way. Suppose I say (43), repeated here as (61):

(61)   That's the best essay I've ever read.

Logical and contextual implications of (61) include the following:

(62) a.   I have never read an essay as good as this one.
   b.   Every other essay I've read is worse than this one.
   c.   This is a very good essay.
   d.   I am very impressed by this essay.
   e.   I am far more impressed by this essay than is usual for me.
   f.   I think very highly of the student who wrote this essay.

Provided the hearer can easily identify implications such as (62c–f) as part of what I intended to communicate and does not include any that I do not necessarily intend to imply, such as (62a–b), then this may be an optimally relevant way to communicate my thought. So hyperbole is explained in the same way as approximations and metaphor. There is no special interpretive mechanism associated either with hyperbole or with metaphor.

   Here, then, are some key features of this account:

a.   The explanation of how hearers understand metaphors is the same as the one which explains how they understand approximations and loose talk.
b.   Literalness is not seen as a norm but rather as a limiting case at one end of a continuum along which utterances regularly vary.
c.   Literalness is defined in terms of how closely the proposition expressed by an utterance resembles the thought of the speaker which it (interpretively) represents (the more implications are shared by the proposition expressed and the thought represented, the more literal the utterance).
d.   Perceptions of metaphor as 'deviant' or 'abnormal' do not arise. The non-literalness of metaphor is a feature shared with non-metaphorical utterances.

A question which this raises, and which we will return to below, is where the perceptions of metaphor as 'deviant' do come from. How is metaphor special? Part of the answer on this account has to do with the strength of implicatures.

   As we saw in Chapter 7, implicatures come with varying degrees of strength. We illustrated this with example (63):

(63)   *(standing over a barbecue at a summer garden party)*
       KEN: Would you like a burger?
       BEV: I'm a vegetarian.

A relatively strong implicature of Bev's utterance is:

(64)   Bev does not want a burger.

Weaker implicatures include:

(65) a.   Bev thinks it is wrong to eat meat.
   b.   Bev is relatively idealistic.
   c.   Bev is interested in environmental issues.
   d.   Bev has relatively left-wing political views.

As an example of an utterance which conveys a wide range of relatively weak implicatures, we looked at Flaubert's remark about the poet Leconte de Lisle represented in (66):

(66)   Son encre est pale.
           (= His ink is pale)

This weakly implicates conclusions such as these:

(67) a.   Leconte de Lisle's writing lacks passion.
   b.   Leconte de Lisle does not throw himself fully into his work.
   c.   Leconte de Lisle's work is relatively feeble.
   d.   Leconte de Lisle's work will not last.

This utterance illustrates the idea in relevance theory that relatively poetic or creative metaphors give rise to a range of weak implicatures rather than strongly implicating a small number of conclusions. This open-endedness is a key feature of relatively poetic metaphors. One thing which follows from this characterisation is that hearers might spend a considerable amount of time thinking about exactly what range of implicatures are evidenced by a particular utterance. This fairly sustained interpretive process is, of course, typical of literary interpretation. So this account gives a fairly natural account of how literary interpretations might be generated by particular kinds of utterances.

   Exercise 9.3 asks you to consider some literal and less-than-literal utterances and account for them based on the approach on which the hearer's task is to identify the communicated implications of an utterance without first considering whether the utterance is to be understood as literal.

Exercise 9.3

* Explain as fully as you can how B's utterance is likely to be understood with reference to the account of literal and non-literal interpretation just presented in this chapter:
   (i)   A: Are you pleased that your partner is pregnant?
          B: I'm over the moon.
   (ii)   A: Are the Cheeky Monkeys still your favourite band?
          B: Nobody likes them any more.
   (iii) A: Did you say you and John don't understand each other very well?
          B: My signal breaks up every time I speak to him.
   (iv)   A: What did Flaubert say about Leconte de Lisle?
          B: His ink is pale.

Before we move on to look at relevance-theoretic accounts of irony (Chapter 10), we will look at a more recent approach to metaphor developed within relevance theory. This second approach shares most of the properties of the account we have just outlined. A key difference is that encoded concepts are adjusted as part of the interpretation process and so the proposition expressed in metaphorical utterances is communicated and is therefore an explicature.

9.6   Metaphor and ad hoc concepts

A more recent account of metaphor has been developed based on the ideas about how words are understood in context which we looked at in Chapter 8, i.e. on ideas about lexical pragmatics. As we saw, the idea here is that the concept communicated by a word in a particular context need not be identical to the concept encoded by that word. Lexical semantics explores what is encoded by words. **Lexical pragmatics** explores what they communicate in particular contexts. Here are three examples (from Carston 2002a: 324ff.):

(68)   There's a rectangle of lawn at the back of my house.

(69)   This steak is raw.

(70)   Jim's bedroom is a rubbish dump.

In (68), an adjusted concept {RECTANGLE*} is constructed to denote the less than fully rectangular shape intended. In (69) the steak has been exposed to some cooking heat and so an adjusted concept {RAW*} is understood. (70) is an example of metaphor. Andy's room is not literally a place where people come to deposit their rubbish. An adjusted concept {RUBBISH DUMP*} is constructed in understanding this utterance. On this new account, there is still continuity between what are intuitively perceived to be literal and non-literal utterances. One very significant change is that the proposition expressed by a metaphorical utterance will now contain an adjusted concept, and may be part of what the speaker intends to communicate.

Here is how this approach accounts for hyperbole and metaphor. We will start by considering the hyperbole in (71):

(71)   I'm starving.

If we assume that the concept STARVING encoded by the word *starving* applies to people who are dying because of malnutrition then this is the concept that will be communicated by a literal utterance of (71). Assuming it is intended hyperbolically, as an overstatement, then the speaker does not mean to communicate that she is dying but merely that she is very hungry, hungrier than we would usually expect her to be, etc. On the earlier account, this would be explained by saying that the hearer treats some but not all of the implications of (71), represented in (72), as implicatures.

(72) a.   The speaker is very hungry.
   b.   The speaker is far hungrier than we would usually expect the hearer to be.
   c.   The speaker is dying from malnutrition.
   d.   If we don't do something to help her soon, it may be too late.

By contrast, (72c) and (72d) would not be treated as implicatures. If (72c) and (72d) occur to the hearer, he will rule them out on grounds of relevance. The utterance will satisfy the hearer's expectations of relevance once implications (72a) and (72b) have been derived. So a hearer who is following the relevance-guided comprehension heuristic will stop looking for an interpretation as soon as he has accessed them and will not consider (72c) and (72d). A speaker who intends to communicate (72c) and (72d) will need to formulate her utterance differently to make clear that these are intended conclusions.

The new approach, by contrast, adopts the idea that utterance interpretation involves the inferential derivation of 'ad hoc' concepts, created for the purposes of a specific interpretation after accessing the encoded concept as a starting point. The concept encoded by *starving* will be inferentially adjusted and we will represent the new, adjusted, 'ad hoc' concept as STARVING*. The explicature of (71), then, will be (73):

(73)   The speaker is STARVING*

This new adjusted concept is broader (more general) than the encoded concept which applies only to things actually dying through malnutrition. The broadened concept also applies to things in a state of significant but not life-threatening hunger. With this new adjusted concept in the explicature, assumptions such as (72c) and (72d) can no longer be derived. Implications which follow from this adjusted concept are all made manifest by the speaker and the hearer will access enough of them to satisfy her expectation of relevance and then stop.

It is worth emphasising that this new account is not different with regard to the set of implications which will be derived. These will be exactly the same implications, but in the course of the mutual adjustment process, the encoded concept will be adjusted so as to properly warrant these implications. The key difference is that ad hoc concepts can figure in the proposition expressed.

To see how this approach accounts for metaphor, we will consider the first example mentioned above, repeated here as (74):

(74)   John's a lion.

As we saw above, the earlier approach would treat this as expressing but not communicating the proposition that John is a lion. This proposition will give rise to the following implications about John in a context containing stereotypical assumptions about lions:

(75) a.   John is brave.
   b.   John is to be feared.

    c.   You should be careful around John.

    d.   John is a member of the set of feline creatures.

    e.   John likes to hunt without weapons, killing and eating his prey.

This earlier approach explained the metaphor without appealing to ad hoc concepts, by suggesting that the hearer does not necessarily assume that the speaker is committed to all of the implications of the proposition that John is (literally) a LION. As long as he can identify which ones the speaker intended to communicate, such as (75a–c), and not derive those which he could not have intended to communicate, here (75d–e), then the metaphor will be successful.

On the new approach, the proposition expressed – which in this case will also be an explicature of the utterance – will contain a modified 'ad hoc' concept LION*, a concept adjusted so that its implications include (75a–c) but not (75d–e). The implications of the metaphor on the new account will be identical to those arrived at on the earlier account, but the fact that the proposition expressed is now an explicature makes it fall into line with other, non-metaphorical utterances. This is the key difference between the earlier and the later account. They share the ideas that metaphorical utterances are not 'deviant', that they exploit mechanisms also used by other utterances, and that literal truthfulness is not a norm, maxim or convention that speakers are expected to convey. The only difference is the introduction of ad hoc concepts and the idea that they can figure in the proposition expressed. One thing to notice is that hearers might not identify one definite ad hoc LION concept here. As Carston (2002a: 358) puts it, in discussing example (37) ('Robert is a bulldozer'): 'There may be quite a range of subtly different concepts licensed by an utterance of, for instance, 'Robert is a bulldozer'... No specific one is strongly communicated and the hearer's construction of any one of them is good enough for the communication to have succeeded.'

One question which a number of theorists (including some relevance theorists) have been focusing on recently is the intuition that there is still something special about metaphor, a phenomenon which Carston (2010), referring to work by Camp (2008), describes as the 'lingering of the literal'. Carston and Camp point out that that there is an intuition shared by many speakers that the original encoded concept in a metaphorical utterance is not completely dropped but that hearers continue to be aware of it while developing their interpretation.[2] This is further reinforced by the reported intuition for many metaphors that interpreters are aware of a visual image generated by the encoded concept. Consider an utterance such as (76):

(76)   Bev is an iphone.

Hearers report that they continue to think of an actual iphone when understanding utterances such as this, even while they are aware that Bev is not understood literally to be an iphone. They also report an intuition that they are aware of an image of an iphone when thinking of this utterance. These intuitions are not

shared, or not shared as strongly, when interpreting less novel, possibly conventionalised, metaphors such as:

(77)   He's a rat.

The assumption here is that this sense of *rat* is a conventionalised or 'dead'
metaphor so that a new sense, along the lines of EVIL/UNTRUSTWORTHY
PERSON, has replaced the original sense. There is an interesting contrast,
pointed out by Sperber and Wilson (1985, 1990) between (78) and (79):

(78)   Tidy your room, you pig.

(79)   Tidy your room, you piglet.

There is a clear intuition that (79) is more creative and gives rise to more, and
different, effects than (78). If these were similar metaphorical utterances, the
differences would only follow from the fact that the hearer is associated with a
younger pig in (79) than in (78). But (79) is perceived as more 'lively' and as
giving rise to a wider range of effects than (78). We can explain this by
assuming that the sense of *pig* involved in understanding (78) is a conventionalised, 'dead' sense while the sense of *piglet* used in (79) is a more creative
metaphor. As pointed out by Carston (and also discussed by Stöver 2011a,
2011b), these effects are more easily explained if we think that there is a
proposition expressed by (79) which contains the encoded concept PIGLET, or
an adjusted concept PIGLET* which refers to certain properties of the animal,
while (78) encodes a different, conventionalised sense of *pig* which does not
provide access to thoughts of animals or where the implications of having pig-
like qualities are not pursued very far.

The newer approach differs from the earlier one that, on this view, the
proposition expressed is capable of being communicated by both metaphorical
and non-literal utterances. This strengthens the claim that metaphorical and
other non-literal utterances are not different in kind from literal utterances.
The previous account and the new account share the feature that they follow
from existing assumptions about what is involved in utterance interpretation and
do not require any special piece of theoretical machinery.

An important topic in recent discussions of metaphor has been how to
account for what have been termed **emergent features**. These are properties
which 'emerge' as part of the process of utterance interpretation but are not
encoded by any of the linguistic expressions used. A much-discussed example
(see, for example, Carston 1997; Sperber and Wilson 2008; Vega Moreno 2004,
2005, 2007; Wilson and Carston 2007) is (80):

(80)   My surgeon is a butcher.

An informal account of this utterance might say that it communicates negative
assumptions about my surgeon, e.g. that he or she is callous about patients,
treating them as no more significant than pieces of meat, and so on. A more

formal account will point out specific properties communicated by the utterance. A traditional account will say that the hearer rules out a literal understanding of the proposition expressed as it does not fit with our real-world background assumptions and we then look for something else that could be communicated.[3] In the previous relevance-theoretic account, the key thing is for the hearer not to reject propositions which logically follow from (80) but which the speaker manifestly could not have intended to communicate. Let us assume that the implications of (80) include those in (81) (of course, not all of these will necessarily be derived by all people):

(81) a.   My surgeon prepares and sells meat.
      b.   My surgeon is professional in working with meat.
      c.   My surgeon is skilled with a knife.
      d.   My surgeon takes a detached attitude to the things he cuts up.
      e.   My surgeon does not empathise with the things he cuts up.
      f.   My surgeon gives no thought to the feelings of what he cuts up.

Presumably, the hearer rejects (81a–b) but might decide that (81c–f) are communicated. Does something along those lines sound like an accurate account of what (80) communicates? I would guess not until you add assumptions specifically about patients, e.g. those in (82), and some of the salient negative implications about the surgeon such as those in (83):

(82) a.   My surgeon does not care about the feelings of his patients.
      b.   My surgeon treats all patients the same.
      c.   My surgeon enjoys operating on people.

(83) a.   My surgeon is incompetent.
      b.   My surgeon deserves to be struck off.
      c.   Nobody should be treated by my surgeon.
      d.   My surgeon is insensitive.
      e.   My surgeon has little regard for human life.

I don't know how plausible each of these sounds to you. However, they are possible conclusions which the hearer of (80) might be expected to derive and so we need to explain how they are derived. Note, however, that none of these follow from the statement that someone is a butcher. There is no information along these lines associated with the concept BUTCHER. Therefore, they cannot arise simply from choosing which encyclopaedic properties of the concept BUTCHER the speaker is intending to attribute to my surgeon. They have been termed 'emergent features' because they seem to 'emerge' during the process of interpretation rather than already being associated with a concept expressed in the utterance. So where do they come from? It has been suggested (for example by Romero and Soria 2007) that an inferential account, such as the relevance-theoretic one, cannot explain how these assumptions arise (alternatives which might be seen as doing a better job of accounting for emergent properties might include associationist accounts such as that of Recanati 2002b or work within the general framework of cognitive linguistics, such as the 'blending' theory developed by Fauconnier and Turner 2002). However, Wilson and Carston (2007) and Sperber and Wilson (2008) suggest that emergent properties can be accounted for fairly straightforwardly in an inferential account. Vega Moreno (2007) goes even further, suggesting

> that the reason why modern theories of metaphor cannot provide an explanation for the emergence problem, and so cannot provide a successful account of metaphor interpretation, is partly that they lack an inferential comprehension procedure.   (Vega Moreno 2007: 105)

In other words, she suggests that emergent properties are problematic for non-inferential approaches precisely because these approaches are not inferential. She also points out that emergent properties do not arise only for metaphorical utterances. She cites Hampton (1997) who observes that people tend to associate properties such as 'failure' with the phrase 'Oxford graduate factory worker' and 'confused' with the phrase 'rugby player who knits' even though neither of these notions are associated with the terms combined in the larger phrases.

The account suggested by Vega Moreno, by Carston, and by Wilson and Carston[4] argues that emergent features arise naturally as part of the usual process of working out an interpretation that satisfies the hearer's expectations of relevance. Wilson and Carston (2007: 251–52) discuss how this might go with reference to example (84), slightly adapted from (80) above:

(84)   That surgeon should be dismissed. He's a butcher.

The claim, as they summarise it, is that 'emergent properties are analysable as genuine contextual implications which emerge in the course of the mutual adjustment process based on contextual premises derived from several sources' (Wilson and Carston 2007: 251). They suggest that understanding the second sentence here will involve constructing an adjusted ad hoc concept BUTCHER* based on the encoded concept BUTCHER. This will be based on encyclopaedic assumptions about butchers, including assumptions about how they handle meat. From the proposition that the person in question is a BUTCHER* who handles meat in this way and the proposition that he is a SURGEON, it follows quite straightforwardly that this person is not performing his surgical duties in an appropriate manner. These assumptions will be readily accessed and the hearer will be able to see how they lead to an optimally relevant interpretation. A similar account will be possible for more straightforward utterances such as (80) above, repeated here as (85):

(85)   My surgeon is a butcher.

The hearer will look for implications which would make the utterance relevant. Encyclopaedic information about surgeons includes the information that they treat human patients by operating on them with scalpels and other equipment, that this requires a huge amount of care, that a good surgeon will show some sensitivity to the people they are operating on, and so on. Encyclopaedic information about butchers will include the assumptions about how they handle meat with knives mentioned above. It is easy to see that it will be relevant to know that a surgeon who is a BUTCHER* (i.e. who deals with the human forms they operate on in the way that butchers handle meat) is not a good surgeon, that patients may suffer, and so on; so assumptions such as this are cognitive effects which contribute to the relevance of the utterance.

What about the emergent properties of non-metaphorical utterances such as (86) and (87)?

(86)   He is an Oxford graduate factory worker.

(87)   He's a rugby player who enjoys knitting.

Understanding (86) will involve accessing assumptions about Oxford graduates, including that we expect them to be able to find well-paid and prestigious jobs, and assumptions about factory workers, including that their jobs are relatively lowly paid and relatively unprestigious. It follows then that the person referred to here has been less successful than we would expect for an Oxford graduate. So it is quite easy to see how the emergent property of being a failure will be inferred here. The case of (87) seems less straightforward to me. If we assume that rugby players don't usually take part in activities of certain types and knitting is one of them, then we can see that this person is not a stereotypical rugby player. This can then lead to assumptions such as that the person is confused. This is less straightforward than the account of the previous example since the property of being 'confused' is less likely to be inferred on hearing (87) than the property of being a 'failure' on hearing (86). Accessing these assumptions can then be seen as contributing to the construction of relevant ad hoc concepts in each case, e.g. of a SURGEON with a disregard for human life etc., of a BUTCHER* who is insensitive, and so on. A question which we might want to explore in more detail is how exactly an account in terms of contextual implications and an account in terms of adjusted ad hoc concepts overlap. This is one thing which Exercise 9.4 asks you to consider.

Exercise 9.4 asks you to account for a number of examples with reference to the notion of ad hoc concept construction, to compare these accounts with earlier relevance-theoretic accounts and accounts based on other approaches, and to consider possible ways of accounting for 'emergent properties' in understanding metaphorical and non-metaphorical utterances.

Exercise 9.4

- First, consider the examples from the previous exercise. Explain how these would be handled on the ad hoc concept account.
- Now compare the three accounts we have looked at so far (Grice's approach and the two relevance-theoretic accounts). Identify any problems the examples raise for each account and consider which account seems to handle each example most successfully.

9.7   Summary

In this chapter, we looked at how relevance theory accounts for the distinction between literal and non-literal uses of language in general and how we understand metaphor in particular. We looked at two approaches to metaphor within relevance theory: an earlier approach, based on the assumption that literalness is not a norm and that we do not always assume that the proposition expressed by an utterance is communicated; and a later approach based on the idea that we construct ad hoc concepts as part of the process of understanding the way words are used in context. We compared this approach with Grice's more traditional account. To sum up, then, there are now two ways of accounting for metaphorical uses of language within relevance theory, each of them capable of explaining how they are understood. They share the assumptions that:

a.   Literalness is not 'privileged'; literal interpretations are not accessed and assessed before we go on to derive non-literal ones.
b.   There is no maxim or convention of literal truthfulness.
c.   Loose uses, approximations, hyperbole and metaphor are explained in a similar way.

They differ in that the newer account appeals to ad hoc concepts which may figure in the proposition expressed. On the newer account, the proposition expressed may be explicated in cases of both literal and non-literal utterances. There is debate about the extent to which relevance-theoretic approaches can account for so-called 'emergent features' which 'emerge' as part of the process of utterance interpretation.

Exercise 9.5

As in every chapter, this final exercise asks you to adjust the list of questions you have come up with so far by compiling new questions which have occurred to you while reading this chapter and to think about the kinds of things which might count as answers to any questions you have come up with so far. First, add new questions to your ongoing list. Second, consider all of your questions and think about possible ways of answering them.

9.8   Further reading

Ideas on figurative language, including the distinction between descriptive and interpretive representation, are presented in *Relevance* (Sperber and Wilson 1986: 217–43). There is a wide range of useful work on figurative language from a relevance-theoretic point of view. Good starting points include Carston (2002a) and papers collected in Wilson and Sperber (2012), including Sperber and Wilson (1990, 2008). On 'emergent features', see Vega Moreno (2007) and Wilson and Carston (2006).

10 Figurative language: irony

Topics: irony as echoic; Grice's traditional approach; irony as pretence; data from other sources

10.1 Overview

This chapter begins, in Section 10.2, by presenting the relevance-theoretic account of irony, which sees it as involving echoic use. In Section 10.3, we consider Grice's account, which takes what can be thought of as a traditional view, where ironic utterances are understood to be expressing the 'opposite' of what the speaker actually intends. Section 10.4 considers an alternative to the relevance-theoretic view which has its origins in discussion by Grice. On this view, irony is seen as involving a kind of pretence. Finally, Section 10.5 very briefly considers evidence from developmental studies and studies involving subjects with conditions such as autistic spectrum disorders. This evidence suggests that metaphor and irony should be seen as distinct kinds of phenomena.

10.2 Irony as echoic

We will now look at and compare three accounts of irony. This time we will approach things from a different direction, beginning with the relevance-theoretic account and then looking at two alternative approaches: Grice's proposed account which is based on the idea that ironical utterances blatantly violate the maxim of quality and accounts based on the notion of pretence.

Within relevance theory, both attributed thoughts and irony are dealt with in terms of the interpretive relationship lower down in the diagram presented in the previous chapter as Figure 9.1. The relationship at the top of the diagram, between the proposition expressed by the speaker's utterance and the thought which it interpretively represents, is not important in determining whether or not an utterance is ironic. This relationship may be close or distant when we attribute thoughts or produce ironical utterances. It is fairly close, for example, if I say ironically that an unappetising dish we have just eaten is delicious. It is quite far if I say ironically that someone I don't like is 'the light of my life'. What is key is that the thought being represented does not describe a state of affairs but instead is in turn an interpretive representation of another thought or utterance. The term 'interpretive use' has been used to refer to an utterance which is not only interpretive in the way in which all utterances are, by interpreting a thought of the speaker, but where the speaker's thought interpreted by the utterance is itself an interpretation of another thought. Bev's utterance in (1) can be interpreted in two ways, one of which is an example of interpretive use:

(1)   KEN: What did Andy say?
         BEV: You've got coffee on your shirt.

Bev here could be seen as responding to Ken's question and letting Ken know what Andy said, or she could be taken to be ignoring that question for now and simply letting Ken know about the spilt coffee. If Bev is reporting Andy's utterance then this is a case of interpretive use. Bev's utterance is not intended to describe a state of affairs in which coffee is on Ken's shirt but to attribute to Andy an utterance with a similar content. Here is how we might analyse the utterance when understood in this way:

(2)   *A summary of how Bev's utterance is understood by Ken:*
  a.   The proposition expressed by Bev's utterance
  b.   is an interpretation of Bev's thought
  c.   which is an interpretation of Andy's utterance
  d.   which said that
  e.   Ken has coffee on Ken's shirt.

To make clear that the interpretive relationship at the top of Figure 9.1 is not important here, we can consider attributed thoughts which are relatively loose or informal. Consider, for example, (3) and (4):

(3)   KEN: What did Andy say?
         BEV: A hundred people came to the party.

(4)   KEN: What did Andy say?
         BEV: You're the brightest star in the sky.

Bev's utterance in (3) could be understood as a loose approximation or as communicating an accurate figure based on careful counting. Bev's utterance in (4) is likely to be understood as a metaphor. In both cases, the literalness or non-literalness of Bev's utterance has no bearing on whether or not it is understood as representing an attributed thought.

   Verbal irony involves more than just interpretive use, though. Wilson and Sperber suggest that irony involves a sub-category of interpretive use which they term 'echoic'. An utterance is echoic if it is intended to be understood as implicitly attributing a thought or utterance with a similar content to someone else (or to the speaker at a different time) and also as implicitly conveying the speaker's attitude to that thought or utterance. Sperber and Wilson (1986: 239) illustrate this by considering the following two scenarios (I've adapted them slightly here):

(5)   *Ken and Bev are talking in the morning and Ken says:*
        KEN: It's a lovely day for a picnic.
        They go for a picnic and the weather is indeed beautiful. Bev says:
        BEV: It IS a lovely day for a picnic.

(6)   *Ken and Bev are talking in the morning and Ken says:*
        KEN: It's a lovely day for a picnic.
        They go for a picnic and the weather is dreadful. Bev says:
        BEV: It IS a lovely day for a picnic.

In both (5) and (6), Bev can be understood as echoing Ken's earlier utterance and implicitly communicating her own attitude to it. In (5), the attitude is positive, suggesting that Ken was absolutely right to suggest that it was a lovely day for a picnic. In (6), the attitude expressed is negative, suggesting that Ken was wrong or even ridiculous in suggesting that it was a lovely day for a picnic. Bev's utterance in (6) is, of course, an example of verbal irony. Her utterance in (5) is not ironic since she is implicitly endorsing rather than rejecting the opinion she is echoing.

Sperber and Wilson claim that the two defining features of verbal irony are that the utterance is tacitly attributive (interpretive use) and that it tacitly expresses a negative (mocking, contemptuous) attitude to the thought represented. To demonstrate this, Wilson (2006) considers possible responses in the following scenario (again, slightly adapted):

(7)   *Ken and Bev have just played a game of tennis, watched by their friend Andy. Bev won easily. After the game, Ken says (seriously) to Andy:*
        KEN: I nearly won.
        Bev says one of the following:
   a.   The poor fool thinks he nearly won.
   b.   He's a fool if he thinks that.
   c.   He thinks he nearly won.
   d.   He nearly won.

Bev's potential reply (a) explicitly indicates both that Bev is attributing the thought to Ken and that she thinks it is foolish. Reply (b) explicitly indicates her negative attitude to the thought. Reply (c) explicitly attributes the thought to Ken leaving her negative attitude implicit. Reply (d) merely represents the proposition that Ken nearly won while leaving implicit both the fact that this is being attributed to Ken and that Bev thinks it's a foolish thought. Example (d) is the only one which Wilson and Sperber claim is standardly classified as ironic, and in this case both the attribution to Ken and the negative attitude are implicitly communicated. Here it is easy to see that many other types of utterance have something in common with irony, and the approach just outlined can explain why.

Exercise 10.1 asks you to suggest accounts of a number of examples based on the assumption that irony involves interpretive use which is implicitly attributive and which expresses an implicitly dissociative attitude.

Exercise 10.1

- With reference to the approach which treats irony as involving attributive use, propose an account of B's utterance in each of the following exchanges (assuming that it is taken to be an ironic utterance):

  (i)   (*A has just spilled red wine on B's carpet.*)

  A: I'm really sorry. I hope you're not too upset about it.

  B: I'm not upset at all. I love it.

  (ii)   A: What do you think if I invite Robbie on Friday?

  B: I'd say that's the best idea you've ever had.

  (iii)   A: I hope you're not offended that I didn't make it to your party last week?

  B: Not at all. Only the very best people have the courage to behave like that.

  (iv)   A: I'm going to make myself a cuppa. Make one yourself if you fancy one.

  B: Hooray! The age of chivalry is not dead.

The next two sections briefly compare the relevance-theoretic account to two alternative accounts. In Section 10.5, we will consider other relevant sources of data, including from developmental work (looking at how children develop particular abilities and understanding), work on metarepresentational abilities, and work on the nature of autistic spectrum disorders.

10.3   Grice's 'traditional' approach

Grice's approach to irony resembles the 'classical' or 'traditional' view that ironical utterances are ones where the speaker says the opposite of what she means. He suggests that a speaker blatantly violates the first maxim of quality ('do not say what you believe to be false') and implicates a related proposition, in this case one which is the opposite of what she said. Grice's example is (8):

(8)   (*said of John who has betrayed the speaker*)
John's a fine friend.
What is said:
John is a fine friend.
What is implicated:
John is not a fine friend.   (Grice 1989: 120)

In this context, where it is clear to the hearer that the speaker cannot think that John is a fine friend, the speaker has openly violated the first maxim of quality. But the hearer assumes that the maxims must be being obeyed 'at some level' and so looks for a 'related implicature' which does express something true. In this case, he decides that the speaker must be communicating the opposite of what is said. As a result, he derives the implicature that the speaker is communicating that John is not a fine friend.

This fairly simple and intuitive account does suggest an explanation for how ironical utterances are understood. However, there are serious problems with this account which suggest that it cannot be right. We'll mention some of them here.

The first problem is one that is common to Grice's account of all cases where the speaker is seen as flouting the first maxim of quality (irony, metaphor, overstatement and understatement). On this account, the speaker turns out not to be 'saying' anything in Grice's sense, since he is not intending to communicate the proposition expressed. Grice describes the speaker of an ironical utterance as 'making as if to' say something. When the hearer realises that what is being communicated is the opposite of what is said, this would seem to confirm that the speaker has violated the first quality maxim rather than helping to see how it has been obeyed. In example (8), for example, the conclusion would seem to be that the speaker has indeed spoken falsely when saying that 'John is a fine friend'. In other cases, the derivation of an implicature helps to preserve the idea that the speaker has observed the Cooperative Principle and the maxims. In (9), for example, the derivation of the implicature makes it possible to see that the speaker's utterance is relevant since the hearer can use what is said to derive a relevant implicature.

(9)   KEN: Would you like a burger?
        BEV: I'm a vegetarian.
        What is said:
        Bev is a vegetarian.
        What is implicated:
        Bev does not want a burger.

The assumption that Bev is a vegetarian is not clearly relevant at first glance. Once Ken has accessed the appropriate implicated premises or contextual assumptions and the implicature that Bev does not want a burger, we can see that what is said is relevant in helping Ken to work out the implicatures.

The situation with (8) is quite different. Here, the derivation of the implicature that John is not a fine friend would seem to confirm that what the speaker has said is indeed false and so to confirm the assumption that the speaker's utterance does not conform to the maxims of conversation and the Cooperative Principle. On the relevance-theoretic account, by contrast, the speaker is communicating higher-level explicatures about the proposition expressed, attributing it to someone else and expressing a dissociative attitude to it. All of this follows because the hearer is following the relevance-guided comprehension heuristic. At every stage, the hearer is looking for an interpretation that satisfies his expectations of relevance and this is consistent with relevance-theoretic pragmatic principles.

Second, it's not clear on this account how the hearer knows which proposition to assume is the one being implicated. Grice suggests that irony, metaphor, hyperbole and understatement are all cases where the speaker says something which is clearly false in order to implicate a 'related' true proposition. In the case of irony, what is communicated is the opposite of what is said; in the case of metaphor, it is a related simile; in the case of hyperbole, a weaker proposition; in the case of understatement, a stronger proposition. How does the hearer know which proposition to derive? When hearers misunderstand irony, they do not tend to interpret it as a metaphor. So this account will not really explain ironical interpretations unless it includes an account of how the hearer knows which path to go down. On the relevance-theoretic account, the hearer infers that the speaker is echoing a thought attributed to someone else, and implicitly dissociating herself from it, by following the same pattern of interpretation which accounts for other utterances.

Third, not all ironical utterances are blatantly false. In some cases, an utterance is understood as ironic even though it is literally true, e.g.:

(10)   That's not the wisest decision you've ever made.

If I have just done something which is obviously very unwise, you might say (10) and intend it as an ironical understatement. In this context, though, (10) is true. On the relevance-theoretic account, this issue does not arise since recognising that the utterance is echoic and dissociative does not depend on the proposition expressed being false. The speaker can dissociate herself for other reasons, e.g. because it would be inappropriate to have this thought or to express it in this way.

Fourth, not all ironical utterances communicate the opposite of the proposition expressed. (10) does not communicate (11):

(11)   That's the wisest decision you've ever made.

In some cases, it's hard even to see what would count as the opposite of what was said. Suppose you light a firework and tell me it will produce the most amazing display I've ever seen, and the firework gives a very feeble effect, makes it only a few inches off the ground and falls straight down to earth with no sound effects. I might exclaim (12) loudly and intend it ironically:

(12)   Woo hoo!

There is no clear proposition along the lines of 'not woo hoo!' which I could plausibly be taken to communicate. This relates to more general problems with the first maxim of quality suggested by Wilson and Sperber (2002). They argue with reference to a wide range of examples (including loose talk and approximations) that relevance is more important than literal truthfulness in communication. (12) is not problematic on the relevance-theoretic account, which does not assume that communicators are generally expected to tell the literal truth. What matters is that we can see how the utterance is intended to be seen as relevant. In this case, the relevance of the utterance comes from the fact that it highlights a contrast between the promised spectacle and what has actually happened.

Finally, it's not clear why irony should exist at all on Grice's account. If all I intend to communicate is that John is not a fine friend, why not simply say this rather than saying the opposite of what I mean and expecting you to work out what I actually intend?

The relevance-theoretic account argues that speakers are simply exploiting possibilities which are generally exploited in other kinds of communication. A particular combination of possibilities leads to what are traditionally regarded as cases of verbal irony. Like other pragmatic theories, relevance theory does not agree with Alice that speakers should always say exactly what they mean and never expect hearers to make inferences to work out intentions.

A final problem, noticed by Grice (Grice 1989: 53), is that it is not possible to be ironic simply by saying something which is blatantly false. Grice presents the following example:

> A and B are walking down the street, and they both see a car with a shattered window. B says, *Look, that car has all its windows intact.* A is baffled. B says, *You didn't catch on; I was in an ironical way drawing your attention to the broken window.*   (Grice 1989: 53)

As Wilson and Sperber point out:

> B's utterance meets all of Grice's conditions for irony ... but it would not normally be understood as ironical.
>
> (Wilson and Sperber 2012: 127)

Overall, then, it seems clear that Grice's account is not adequate, even though it accords with what seem to be quite natural intuitions. In fact, as Wilson and Sperber (2012) go on to point out, Grice makes a comment about his problematic example which can be taken as pointing towards the account developed by Sperber and Wilson, in that he suggests that what is missing from his account might be to do with the expression of a negative attitude to the proposition represented.

Exercise 10.2 asks you to consider how Grice's account might explain the previous examples, some of which raise problems for his approach.

Exercise 10.2

- Consider B's utterance in each of the exchanges in Exercise 10.1. Consider how Grice's account would explain their interpretation and identify any problems they raise for his approach.

10.4   Irony as pretence

Here, we will consider approaches to irony based on the idea that it involves a kind of pretence. Pretence theories are usually thought of as the main contemporary competitors to the echoic account developed within relevance

theory. On this view, irony is understood in terms of pretending to say something which the speaker does not actually intend to communicate, Pretence
theories can be understood as alternatives to Grice's approach, and as attempts
to deal more adequately with the data, avoiding some of the problems mentioned above. At the same time, they can be seen as building on Grice's
approach, since Grice also mentioned that ironical speakers could be understood
as 'pretending to say' something other than what they intend to communicate.
He suggested that:

> To be ironical is, among other things, to pretend (as the etymology sug-
> gests), and while one wants the pretence to be recognised as such, to
> announce it as a pretence would spoil the effect.   (Grice 1989: 54)

This idea was developed by a number of researchers.[1] On this view, the speaker
of an ironical utterance is not actually making a statement but merely pretending
to. She expects the addressee to recognise that she is pretending and that she
holds a negative attitude to what she is pretending to say, e.g. because it would
be ridiculous to say such a thing.

It might seem that there is not much difference between the pretence account
and the echoic/attributive account proposed by relevance theorists. On one
view, the speaker is pretending to say something which it would be ridiculous
to say, and expressing an implicitly negative attitude to anyone who might say
it. On the other view, the speaker is attributing a thought to someone else and
expressing an implicitly negative attitude to that thought. Wilson and Sperber
(2012) consider similarities and differences, arguing that the relevance-theoretic
echoic approach is more successful. Their main claim is that echoing and
pretence are distinct mechanisms, and that while all ironic utterances are echoic,
only some of them involve pretence. Finally, they point out that pretence
theories do not in fact explain Grice's problematic example.

The pretence approach involves the assumption that a speaker is not 'saying'
anything in Grice's sense, but pretending to say something, in order to dissociate herself from what she is pretending to say. In some cases, it will be clear
who the speaker is pretending to be, for example when the ironic utterance
clearly responds to something someone else has just said. Consider, for
example, (13):

(13)   KEN: Do you fancy some nuts?
          BEV: What an excellent idea for someone with a nut allergy.

Here, Bev is clearly being ironic and expressing a negative attitude to Ken's
suggestion. On the pretence view, she is pretending to be someone who believes
Ken, and clearly expressing a negative attitude to anyone who would speak as
he has just done. Sometimes, there is no clear target or source for the attitude the
speaker pretends to adopt, as in (14):

(14)   *(on a rainy day)*
          What a beautiful day!

On the pretence view, she is pretending to express the idea that it's a beautiful day in order to dissociate herself from it.

Wilson and Sperber (2012) argue that there are some cases where echoing and pretence can combine, and one might talk of 'ironic pretence'. There definitely seems to be pretence involved when a writer produces a parody of someone else, whether a specific or a more general target is intended. The writer Craig Brown has produced a large number of pieces like this over the years. Some of his writing parodies a specific individual, such as this parody of President Barack Obama at the breakfast table, presented as a diary entry:

(15)   January 1st
            These cornflakes are real and they are everywhere. And I tell you this, Michelle, I say. The packet may have been shaken, but the flakes will recover. So it is with profound gratitude and great humility that I accept my breakfast cornflakes.   (Craig Brown *The Lost Diaries*. 2010. Fourth Estate, London).

Clearly, Brown is pretending here to be President Obama discussing his breakfast cereal in a style which resembles the style of his political speeches and other kinds of political address. In other cases, Brown mimics not a real person but a person of a particular type, as in this extract from a piece purporting to be written by Brown's fictional newspaper columnist, Bel Littlejohn, defending the progressive school Summerhill:

(16)   OK, so maybe the kids can't read or write – but when's that ever been the point of school?   (Craig Brown writing as 'Bel Littlejohn', *The Guardian*, cited at: www.guardian.co.uk/books/2010/oct/02/craig-brown-lost-diaries-parody)

Here, Brown is pretending to be an invented character with opinions that he intends to ridicule. There is clearly a sense in which Brown is pretending in both of these pieces with the aim of making fun of the writers he is pretending to be. These cases are also clearly echoic, in that not only the form but also the content of the utterances he is imitating are being mocked.

While pretence plays a role here, it is important to note that parody is not identical to irony. Sperber (1984) discusses the difference with regard to Clark and Gerrig's (1984) proposed pretence theory. Wilson and Sperber (2012) follow Sperber in suggesting that 'parody is related to direct quotation as irony is related to indirect quotation'. Both Sperber (1984) and Wilson (2011) suggest that parody can be understood as ironic where speakers or writers can be understood as attributing a thought they wish to dissociate themselves from, i.e. when they fit the echoic account. However, they point out a significant feature of spoken parody, which is that there are restrictions on the intonation patterns involved. In particular, it seems that the tone of voice generally recognised as characteristic of irony is quite distinct from the parodic tone of voice. The 'ironic tone of voice' has been described as a 'flat, deadpan' tone of voice when producing a parody, and is discussed by Ackerman (1983), Rockwell (2000) and Bryant and Fox Tree

(2002). There are issues about how exactly to define it but for now we can think of a way of speaking with relatively low pitch level and few prosodic contrasts. Sperber explains the difference between parody and irony as follows:

> Imagine that Bill keeps saying, 'Sally is such a nice person', and that Judy totally disagrees. Judy might express a derogatory attitude to Bill's judgement on Sally in two superficially similar, but quite perceptibly different, ways. She might imitate Bill and say herself, 'Sally is such a nice person!' with an exaggerated tone of enthusiasm or even worship. Or she might utter the same sentence but with a tone of contempt, so that there will be a contradiction between the literal content of what she says and the tone in which she says it. The first tone of voice is indeed one of pretence and mockery. The second tone of voice is the ironic tone, the nuances of which have been described by rhetoricians since classical antiquity.   (Sperber 1984: 135)

As this suggests, a 'flat, deadpan' tone of voice would not be consistent with a parodic utterance but it is perfectly acceptable for irony. Wilson and Sperber (2012) spell out the implications of this:

> When a parodic utterance is used to convey a derogatory attitude to an attributed thought, it could indeed be appropriately described as a case of ironical pretence. By contrast, use of the flat, deadpan 'ironical tone of voice' described in the literature would instantly betray the pretence and make it pointless. If Grice's comment that 'while one wants the pretence to be recognised as such, to announce it as a pretence would spoil the effect' adequately explains why an ironical utterance cannot be prefaced with the phrase *To speak ironically*, it also seems to exclude use of the flat, deadpan 'ironical tone of voice'.   (Wilson and Sperber 2012)

Consider, now, two ways of understanding Bev's utterance in (17):

(17)   *(Ken, Bev and Jess are eating together)*
          KEN: Broccoli's delicious.
          BEV: *(to Jess)* Broccoli's delicious.

For present purposes, we'll ignore the possibility that Bev is endorsing Ken's comment and assume that Bev's aim is to dissociate herself from it. We could claim here that Bev is pretending to be Ken, or mimicking him. If we do, it is still clear that she is attributing the thought that broccoli is delicious to Ken and dissociating herself from it. Alternatively, we could claim that she is echoing Ken's utterance without mimicking him (as she could, for instance, in reporting his speech to someone else). That is, we could claim that she is echoing the thought he expressed and implicitly dissociating herself from it without making any claims that pretence or mimicry is involved. The crucial difference between the two cases will depend on whether Bev seems to be mimicking Ken's speech patterns or not. If she does seem to be imitating Ken, we can understand her utterance as involving pretence and mockery, which we might describe as a kind of parody. If she does not seem to be imitating Ken's speech patterns, the utterance would be echoic without involving any pretence. Pretence theories, of course, claim that all irony involves pretence.

Going back to examples (15) and (16), one thing which makes clear that these involve pretence is that the parody involves imitation of the style of the victim of the parody and not merely the content. We are expected to laugh at Craig Brown's representation of the way Barack Obama speaks and the language of Bel Littlejohn as well as the content. The way in which the content contributes is different in (15) and (16). In (15), part of the humour comes from Obama's elevated rhetorical style being associated with something relatively trivial. In (16), the idea expressed (that reading and writing are not really the point of school) is itself ridiculous.

What all of this suggests is that pretence may well be involved in some ironical utterances, but it is not present in all cases and there is a clear difference between parody, where the communicator is mimicking the speech of another person, and irony, where the speaker is implicitly attributing and dissociating herself from another person's thought. These two features are what make the utterances echoic, and Wilson and Sperber suggest that all cases which fit the pretence approach also seem to be echoic. At the same time, they argue that not all cases of irony have to be seen as involving pretence.

There are, in fact, two versions of the pretence account. One of these assumes an echoic element and one does not (e.g. Clark and Gerrig 1984). One point to mention before moving on is that pretence theories with no echoic element do not succeed in explaining Grice's problematic example, i.e. why we cannot always say something which is patently absurd and be taken to be ironic. If a car has a broken window, it would be absurd to say that all of its windows are intact. Pretence accounts do not explain why a speaker cannot pretend to be someone who thinks they're broken in order to dissociate herself from such an absurd idea. This might, of course, be possible if we introduce some extra pragmatically derived assumptions. On the echoic account, the explanation is quite straightforward. In cases where we can identify a person or a type of person who has expressed or might express this absurd thought, the utterance will work as an example of irony. Suppose, for example, that Ken keeps telling Bev how safe his neighbourhood is and guarantees that she will never see a car there with a broken window. Later, Ken and Bev are walking down the street and she points to a car with a broken window and says:

(18)   Look, that car has all its windows intact.

In this context, Bev will be understood quite straightforwardly as ironically echoing Ken's claim that she will never see a broken car window in his street. Suppose, on the other hand, that Ken keeps telling Bev that his neighbourhood is very dangerous and that all the windows in all the cars in his street are always broken. Later, Ken and Bev are walking down the street and she points to a beautiful shiny new car, gleaming in the sunlight with all its windows intact and says:

(19)   Look, another car with a broken window.

Here, she will be seen as ironically referring to Ken's claim that the car windows in his street are always broken.

This relates to another observation often made about irony, which is that it is much more common to comment ironically on a state of affairs where things have gone wrong than to comment ironically on a state of affairs where everything has gone right, i.e. (20)–(22) are much more likely to be ironical than (23)–(25):

(20)   Lovely weather!

(21)   That's a great idea!

(22)   How graceful!

(23)   Terrible weather.

(24)   That's a terrible idea!

(25)   How clumsy!

On the echoic account, there is a natural explanation for this. If I tell you that it's going to be lovely weather one morning and then it rains heavily, you might utter (20), expecting me to recognise that you are ironically echoing my previous thought which turned out to be very wrong. If I tell you that it's always terrible weather where we live, after which the sun breaks through and it's a lovely day, you might utter (23) as a way of reminding me of how wrong I am. But what if there is no previous utterance to echo? In this case, we might understand the speaker as ironically echoing past hopes or expectations that have been disappointed. It is quite normal for humans to hope that things will go well. Positive utterances such as (20)–(22) are much more likely to be thoughts we hope to express than negative ones so (20)–(22) are more natural examples of this kind of utterance than (23)–(25). Possibly, it is also more typical of human nature to laugh at things that have gone wrong than at things which have gone well.

A final argument which Wilson and Sperber make in favour of the straightforward attributive approach is that it is theoretically more simple than a pretence approach with an echoic element. They suggest that, 'if the attributive-pretence account makes the same predictions as the echoic account, wouldn't it be simpler to bypass the pretence element entirely and go directly to the echoic account?' (Wilson and Sperber 2012).

Exercise 10.3 asks you to consider how a pretence account might explain a range of examples, some of which raise problems for this approach.

Exercise 10.3

- Consider B's utterance in each of the following exchanges. Consider how a pretence account would explain their interpretation and identify any problems they raise for this approach:
  - (i)   A: Get your car out of my driveway right this minute! I don't care how ill your father is!

B: Thanks so much for your consideration.

(ii)   A: This is the day you've got that double dentist appointment.

B: Hooray! My lucky day!

(iii)   *(Based on a reported utterance by Dorothy Parker)*

A: The President has passed away.

B: How could they tell?

(iv)   *(B is a police officer)*

A: I hear you arrested four people this morning and scared off some burglars from a jewellery store.

B: That's right. Another boring day at the office.

10.5   Data from other sources

This final section considers some further evidence about the nature of irony and, in particular, how it differs from metaphor. If a traditional or Gricean account were right, then metaphor (and hyperbole) and irony (and understatement) would be very similar phenomena. Both involve the speaker saying something which is clearly false with the aim that the hearer will realise that she must be implicating something which is true. In the case of metaphor, the hearer decides that the speaker is implicating a related simile. In the case of irony, she is implicating the opposite of what she said. And so on. If relevance-theoretic accounts are right, then metaphor and irony are significantly different. Recognising metaphor involves a particular relationship between the proposition expressed by the utterance and the thought of the speaker's that it represents (the nature of the relationship being slightly different depending on whether we are using ad hoc concepts or not). Recognising irony involves a relationship between the proposition expressed and another thought or utterance which is attributed to someone else (or to the speaker in another situation). With reference to Figure 9.1, metaphor is about the interpretive relationship at the top of the diagram between the proposition expressed and a mental representation of the speaker, while irony is about the interpretive relationship at the bottom of the diagram between the proposition expressed and an attributed thought or utterance. Ironic utterances do not simply describe states of affairs; they represent other thoughts or utterances (which may in turn describe states of affairs).

This proposed difference between metaphor and irony should suggest different predictions about how they are understood and also raises the possibility that we might be able to find particular empirical tests of the theory. This has indeed been found in two areas in particular: developmental studies and studies involving subjects with conditions such as autistic spectrum disorders. Briefly, the key findings are that children begin responding to metaphorical utterances in similar ways to grownups earlier than they begin to respond to ironical utterances in a similar way, and that people with autistic spectrum disorders find ironical utterances more difficult to understand than metaphorical utterances. These findings are predicted by the relevance-theoretic account which sees ironical utterances as necessarily involving doubly interpretive representations.

An important paper exploring these differences is Francesca Happé's (1993) paper which showed correlations between metaphorical understanding and performance on 'first-order false belief tasks' and between ironical understanding and performance on 'second-order false belief tasks'. To understand this work, we need to know what the false-belief tasks involve. The most well-known test of false-belief abilities is the 'Sally-Anne task', developed by Wimmer and Perner (1983). In classic versions of this task, subjects are introduced to two dolls, 'Sally' and 'Anne'. Sally has a basket. Anne has a box. Sally puts a marble into her basket and then leaves the scene. While she is away, Anne moves the marble from Sally's basket into Anne's box. Subjects are asked where Sally will look for her marble when she returns. Subjects with typical adult abilities will expect Sally to look in the basket where she left the marble. Subjects who have difficulties representing what might be in the minds of others sometimes expect Sally to look in the box. These subjects include young children under the age of 4 and people with autistic spectrum disorders. What kinds of false-belief abilities are involved in this? Wilson (2011: 4) presents the following range of representations to illustrate:

(26)   The ball is in the box.

(27) a.   Sally thinks the ball is in the box.
     b.   Sally thinks the ball is in the basket.
     c.   Anne thinks Sally thinks the ball is in the box.
     d.   Anne thinks Sally thinks the ball is in the basket.

As Wilson explains, (27a–d) are interpretive metarepresentations of other people's thoughts while (26) is a descriptive representation of a state of affairs. Someone who cannot represent the thoughts of others as inconsistent with their own beliefs can only represent (26), (27a) and (27c). Someone who can represent thoughts of others which may be inconsistent with their own beliefs would be able to represent (27b). This means they can manage 'first-order' false-belief tasks. Someone who can represent thoughts of others which in turn represent thoughts of others which may not be consistent with their own beliefs can also represent (27d). This means they can be successful in 'second-order' false belief tasks. A number of studies have found that younger children and people with autistic spectrum disorders can have difficulties with different kinds of false-belief tasks. Most significantly for the present discussion, it has been suggested that success with metaphorical comprehension goes alongside success with first-order false-belief tasks while success with ironical comprehension goes alongside success with second-order false-belief tasks.[2] There is only space here to present this idea very briefly, and the details of different kinds of 'mind-reading' abilities are complex, but the key thing to notice here is that there is considerable evidence to suggest that metaphor and irony involve different kinds of processing and that this is predicted by the relevance-theoretic account of the two kinds of comprehension. Wilson (2011a) considers some of these questions in more detail, including a discussion of accounts which assume that different kinds of mental module are involved in comprehension.

10.6   Summary

In this chapter, we considered the relevance-theoretic approach to understanding irony. We compared this echoic account with Grice's traditional account and to approaches based on the idea that irony involves pretence. We concluded by briefly considering evidence from other sources which suggests that metaphorical and ironic comprehension involve different kinds of processing and are associated with different kinds of mind-reading ability. The developments discussed here and in the previous chapter can be seen as demonstrating at least two things: first, that metaphor and irony are complex and interesting phenomena which continue to raise interesting questions even after they have been studied by a wide range of researchers; second, that there has been ongoing discussion and revision of ideas within relevance theory, with some ideas still being revised and developed.

Exercise 10.4

As in every chapter, this final exercise asks you to adjust the list of questions you have come up with so far by compiling new questions which have occurred to you while reading this chapter and to think about the kinds of things which might count as answers to any questions you have come up with so far. First, add new questions to your ongoing list. Second, consider all of your questions and think about possible ways of answering them.

10.7   Further reading

See the suggestions at the end of the previous chapter on figurative language in general. Useful sources on irony include Wilson (2006) and the paper 'Explaining irony' which is available in Wilson and Sperber's more recent book (Wilson and Sperber 2012).

11 Linguistic semantics

Topics: semantics and pragmatics; representation, translation and interpretation; from words to the world: two kinds of semantics; concepts and procedures: two kinds of meaning

11.1 Overview

While relevance theory is often thought of as a theory of pragmatics, many of its most important applications have been within the domain of linguistic semantics. This chapter begins by considering the relationship between semantics and pragmatics. One thing that this book assumes is that there is a significant two-way relationship between work in semantics and work in pragmatics. On the one hand, it is not possible to make significant progress in semantics without having at least some idea of the kind of pragmatic theory which the semantic analyses will interact with to determine interpretations in context. At the same time, it is not possible to explain how interpreters move from linguistically encoded meanings to contextually inferred meanings without having some idea of what kinds of meanings are linguistically encoded. Progress in semantics depends on assumptions about pragmatics and progress in pragmatics depends on assumptions about semantics. The powerful pragmatic theory provided by relevance theory makes it possible to see how very general semantic analyses can form the basis for a wide range of interpretations in specific contexts, This chapter looks at the general picture of the semantics–pragmatics distinction assumed by relevance theory and at some of the kinds of linguistically encoded meanings which have been proposed within this approach. Section 11.2 explores general assumptions about the relationship between semantics and pragmatics. Section 11.3 considers three important notions in the consideration of linguistic meaning: representation, translation and interpretation. Section 11.4 considers how relevance theory makes connections between linguistic expressions and entities in the world. The overall picture proposed by relevance theory assumes that there are two kinds of semantics: a translational linguistic semantics for the sentences of a natural language provides the input to pragmatic processes which contributes to mental representations and guides hearers in developing them; an interpretational semantics of mental representations accounts for the meanings of our thoughts.

Section 11.5 looks at another important distinction proposed within relevance theory: the distinction between conceptual and procedural meaning.

11.2   Semantics and pragmatics

In Chapters 1 and 2, we looked at the way relevance theory draws the distinction between semantics and pragmatics, and contrasted this with Grice's approach. Relevance theory starts from the assumption that has become known as the **underdeterminacy thesis**, the idea that the meanings of linguistic expressions radically underdetermines the propositions they express. Typical examples which demonstrate this include:

(1)   Here.

(2)   It's the same.

(3)   You're too late.

(4)   You're going to die.

The linguistically encoded meaning of (1) does not tell us whether the speaker is stating that something is in a place indicated by the word *here*, drawing the hearer's attention to something which is in a place indicated by the word *here*, or something else from a wide range of possibilities. It also does not tell us what place is indicated by *here*. Example (2) does not say what is the same as what nor in what way it is the same. Example (3) does not say who *you* refers to (not as obvious as 'you' might think) nor what they are too late for. Example (4) might simply be stating the obvious fact about someone that they will die one day or it might refer to a specific time ('you're going to die in the next few minutes') or circumstances ('you're going to die from the wound you've just received', 'you're going to die if you eat that mushroom'). And so on.

Relevance theory assumes not only that any utterance is likely to communicate some assumptions indirectly but also that a considerable amount of inferential work is involved in working out what proposition has been expressed and what attitude is being expressed to that proposition (represented in higher-level explicatures, as we saw in Chapter 6). For example, each of (1)–(4) could be seen as asking a question, making a statement, issuing a request, and so on. This can be understood in terms of the attitude the speaker has to whatever proposition we assume they are expressing.

Relevance theory claims that pragmatic processes are involved in every stage of the process of comprehension and that linguistically encoded meanings are no more than clues to the intended overall interpretations, i.e. it assumes the 'underdeterminacy thesis'. In making this claim, there are a number of assumptions which relevance theory rejects. First, it rejects the idea that linguistic semantics is about a coding relationship between linguistic expressions and propositions; second, it rejects the Gricean view that pragmatics is only about what is implicated, rather than what is said; third, it rejects the view that anything pragmatically inferred must be an implicature.

A very wide range of pragmatic processes are involved at every stage of the process of utterance interpretation. In example (1), this will include:

(5)   Inferences required in understanding an utterance representing the word *here*:
   a.   which word has been uttered (*here* or *hear*)
   b.   what is the referent of *here*
   c.   what is in the location being referred to
   d.   whether the speaker is making a statement, asking a question or something else
   e.   what the speaker is implicating by this utterance

A similar range of inferences will need to be made in understanding (2)–(4).

Exercise 11.1 asks you to explain as many of the inferences involved in understanding (1)–(4) as you can, and to consider how the likelihood of each of these inferences is affected by contextual assumptions.

Exercise 11.1

- Consider each of (1)–(4). Imagine a situation where they might be uttered and suggest a set of contextual assumptions which might be accessed by someone interpreting each one. With reference to the relevance-guided comprehension heuristic, propose as full an account as you can of how you think an utterance of each one might be interpreted given these assumptions.
  (i)   Here.
  (ii) It's the same.
  (iii) You're too late.
  (iv) You're going to die.
- Now suggest a different set of contextual assumptions for each one and propose an account of how the utterance might be interpreted given these new assumptions.

There is no claim about these processes happening in any particular order. As we have seen, they may be happening in parallel, with overlap, or even not be carried out in full. A first summary of the relevance-theoretic position can be given in Figures 11.1 and 11.2, which are designed to contrast relevance-theoretic assumptions with those of Grice.

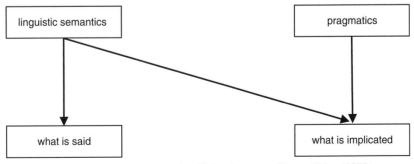

Figure 11.1 *The semantics–pragmatics distinction according to Grice (1975)*

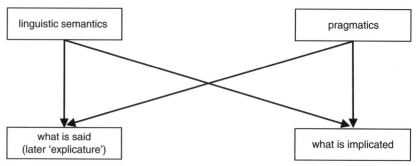

Figure 11.2 *The semantics–pragmatics distinction according to Wilson and Sperber (1981)*

These figures represent differences between Grice's view and Wilson and Sperber's (1981) view. The main difference represented here is that Wilson and Sperber propose that, in Grice's terms, 'pragmatics is involved in recovering what is said'. When they first developed this idea, Wilson and Sperber did not take issue with Grice's proposed category of conventional implicatures, i.e. of linguistically encoded implicatures. In later work, relevance theory rejected the notion of conventional implicature as understood by Grice (see discussion by Blakemore 1987, 2002). In more recent work, the representation of the semantics–pragmatics distinction has developed considerably. It can be represented in Figure 11.3.

We will look at ideas represented in specific parts of Figure 11.3 later in this chapter. First, here is a brief trip through the diagram with reference to one example:

(6)   *Contextual assumptions: Ken and Bev are going to a dinner party at Andy's house tomorrow evening. Bev has just asked Ken whether she should call Andy to let him know that she is a vegetarian.*
       KEN: He knows.

The first part of the diagram represents the relationship between linguistic expressions and their encoded semantic representations. Within relevance theory, these semantic representations have been referred to as 'logical forms'. This reflects the fact that these representations have logical properties but are less than fully propositional, and have to be developed into fully propositional forms before they can be regarded as true or false. A logical form which can be evaluated for truth or falsity is a fully propositional form. The semantic representation of (6) can be represented as follows:

(7)   [_____] knows [_____][_____]
              referent of *he*   something   at some time or under some circumstances

This representation explicitly indicates that an interpreter will need to infer the referent of *he*, what the referent of *he* knows, and when the referent of *he* knows it. There are a number of other things which this representation says nothing

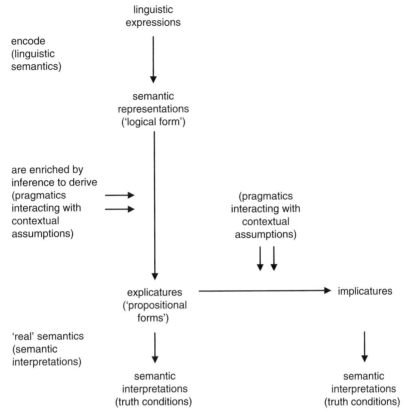

Figure 11.3 *The semantics–pragmatics distinction within relevance theory*

about, including who entertains the proposition expressed or whether it is entertained as a belief, a hypothesis or something else.

On the basis of the linguistically encoded semantic representation in (8), we can then move on to infer a propositional form by filling in the gaps indicated there. In this context, we are likely to infer the following proposition:

(8)   Andy knows that Bev is a vegetarian.

As ever, (9) is not a full proposition but simply another utterance. We need to think of a particular Andy, a particular Bev, and to make an assumption about when *he* knows this. Understood in this way, as a proposition communicated by Ken's utterance, (8) is an explicature. We can than flesh out the explicature further to derive higher-level explicatures. In this case, a key explicature is:

(9)   Ken believes that Andy knows that Bev is a vegetarian.

This contains the proposition expressed (8) as a sub-part and is a pragmatically inferred development of the logical form (7).

So far we have seen that the underspecified logical form linguistically encoded by (7) is pragmatically developed to recover explicatures, which may include the proposition expressed, and further higher-level explicatures which include lower-level explicatures as sub-parts. The next part of the diagram represents the derivation of implicatures from the interaction of explicatures with other contextual assumptions. In this case, Bev will be likely to infer the following proposition as the strongest implicature of Ken's utterance:

(10)   Neither Ken nor Bev needs to call Andy to inform him that Bev is a vegetarian.

This is a strong implicature for which Ken's utterance provides strong evidence and for which Ken takes responsibility. This follows because it is hard to see how Ken's utterance would be optimally relevant if it did not communicate this. Bev is likely to go a little further than this and infer implicatures such as the following:

(11)   There was no need to ask Ken whether Andy needed to be informed about Bev's vegetarianism.

(12)   Ken and Andy have spoken about Bev's vegetarianism.

These are relatively strong implicatures for which Ken takes a significant amount of responsibility. Bev may go beyond this and infer other implicatures for which she takes more responsibility, such as:

(13)   Bev should have known that Ken would have made sure that Andy knows about her dietary requirements.

(14)   Ken is a bit upset that Bev did not assume he would have made sure Andy knew she was a vegetarian.

It is less clear to what extent Ken is responsible for these. They are consistent with other inferences made on the basis of Ken's utterance and they may have occurred to Ken. At the same time, they may be contradicted by other contextual assumptions and they may not have occurred to Ken when he made his utterance. If they did occur to Ken and he did not intend Bev to derive them, then he may well have reformulated his utterance to make them less likely. He might, for example, have said something like:

(15)   Oh, sorry. I forgot to mention that I'd spoken to Andy. I told him you're a vegetarian so no worries there.

The final part of the diagram concerns the relationship between the explicatures and implicatures derived by Bev and states of affairs in the world. The idea here is that propositional representations (i.e. thoughts), whether entertained as the result of utterance interpretation or from other sources, represent possible states of affairs in the world – the ones that make, or would make, them true. At the moment, the best candidate for accounting for this is some form of truth-conditional semantics (for discussion, see Fodor 2008; Margolis and Laurence 1999). The picture we have developed so far is developed further in the next four sections.

11.3   Representation, translation and interpretation

What does it mean for something to mean something? This question is considered at the start of most courses on linguistic meaning and most studies of linguistic meaning. It has been suggested (e.g. by Bialystok 1987, 1991, 2001) that this is something children need to understand before they can grasp details of the particular languages they learn. At the same time, there is a sense in which children already know what it is to mean since they understand how to infer the intentions of others from a very early age (see, for example, discussion by Tomasello 2005). In any case, to understand the relevance-theoretic account of linguistic meaning, we must begin by thinking about what it means for something to have a meaning. There are three key notions involved in the relevance-theoretic account: **representation, translation** and **interpretation**.

Relevance theory follows Jerry Fodor and other cognitive scientists in assuming that the mind is representational and computational (Fodor 1975) and it adopts a version of his modularity thesis (Fodor 1983) which assumes that the mind contains modules understood as **input systems**. Fodor assumes that cognitive processes can be understood as involving mental representations and computations involving those representations (this general approach is sometimes described as the 'computational theory of mind'). We could say that to hold the belief represented in (16) is to entertain a conceptual representation of a state of affairs, namely that Ken is a member of the set of vegetarians, and accept that representation as true, or probably true.

(16)   Ken is a vegetarian.

If this belief is combined with other contextual assumptions then we might derive other beliefs (**conceptual representations**) which we can also accept as true, or probably true. We might, for example, have access to the contextual assumption in (17):

(17)   If Ken is a vegetarian, he won't want to eat the stew I have made.

If so, we will be able to infer the conclusion in (18):

(18)   Ken will not want the stew I have made.

One way to talk about this is to say that we have performed a computation which took (16) and (17) as input and delivered (18) as output. Of course, this particular computation has the form of a 'modus ponendo ponens' inference as discussed in Chapter 4:

(19)   Modus ponendo ponens
          Premises:
          P → Q
          P
          Conclusion:
          Q

So we can think of the mind as a system of representations and of computations which take representations as input and provide other representations as output. Fodor (1975) develops the idea further and suggests that we can think of the conceptual representation system as a language, the 'language of thought', since our thoughts have a semantics (they are 'about' states of affairs in the world) and a syntax (they have a structure which allows them to act as the input to computations).

What is the relationship between language and thought? One common view is that language is essentially communicative. On the 'language-is-for-communication' view, we start from the assumption that the function of language is to enable us to communicate, and we might then conclude that thinking is a matter of 'speaking to oneself'. The alternative view is that our internal conceptual representation system is a language whose function is to enable us to think, and then see languages like English or Sanskrit as enabling us to externalise our thoughts. Sperber and Wilson (1986: 173–4) express this view, comparing our use of language as a means of communication with an elephant's use of its trunk to pick things up. They follow Fodor in defining language as 'a grammar-governed representational system' but argue that there is no systematic link between language and communication:

> Our point is ... that the property of being a grammar-governed representational system and the property of being used for communication are not systematically linked. They are found together in the odd case of human natural languages, just as the property of being an olfactory organ and the property of being a prehensile organ, though not systematically linked in nature, happen to be found together in the odd case of the elephant's trunk.   (Sperber and Wilson 1986: 173)

They go on to suggest that language understood in this way must exist 'not only in humans but in a wide variety of animals and machines with information-processing abilities' and go on to suggest that:

> The great debate about whether humans are the only species to have language is based on a misconception of the nature of language. The debate is not really about whether other species than humans have languages, but about whether they have languages which they use as mediums of communication... The originality of the human species is precisely to have found this curious additional use for something which many other species also possess, as the originality of elephants is to have found that they can use their noses for the curious additional purpose of picking things up. In both cases, the result has been that something widely found in other species has undergone remarkable adaptation and development because of the new uses it has been put to. However, it is as strange for humans to conclude that the essential purpose of language is to communicate as it would be for elephants to conclude that the essential purpose of noses is for picking things up.   (Sperber and Wilson 1986: 173)

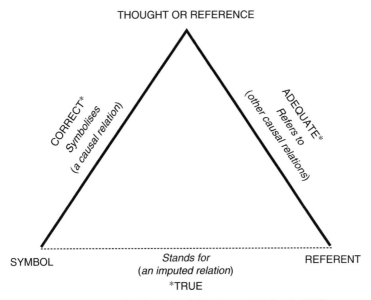

Figure 11.4 *The 'triangle of meaning' (Ogden and Richards 1923)*

Sperber and Wilson suggest, then, that a 'language' is a representational system with both a syntax and a semantics. Humans are not unique in possessing a language but their language is different from that of other creatures. One way in which it is different is that we have developed ours for use in ostensive-inferential communication.

What is a **representation**? Clearly, any representation must be a representation of something. Fodor (1987, 1990, 1994, 2008) has developed a causal theory of content on which our thoughts represent particular states of affairs in the world because of a causal relationship between those thoughts and the states of affairs that make, or would make, them true. My belief that the temperature has dropped, for example, is caused by changes in the world that cause me to construct a conceptual representation of this state of affairs and treat it as true, or probably true.

Of course, semanticists and pragmaticists are not only interested in relationships between our thoughts and the world. We also want to know about the relationships between linguistic expressions and the world. The standard view is that these are mediated by thought. This view has perhaps been most famously represented in the idea proposed by Ogden and Richards represented in what has been referred to variously as 'the triangle of meaning', the 'semiotic triangle' or the 'triangle of reference' (Ogden and Richards 1923: 11). Figure 11.4 presents it in a simplified form. Simplifying very much, we can think of 'thought or reference' at the top of the diagram as corresponding to concepts, 'symbol' at the bottom as corresponding to words, and 'referent' at the bottom as corresponding to entities in the world. The triangle suggests that there are direct causal relations between 'symbols' and 'thought or

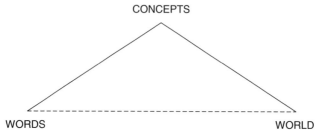

Figure 11.5 *Words, concepts and the world (adapted from Ogden and Richards 1923)*

reference' and between 'thought or reference' and 'referent', but only 'an imputed relation' between 'symbol' and 'referent'. As Ogden and Richards put it:

> Between the symbol and the referent there is no relevant relation other than the indirect one, which consists in its being used by someone to stand for a referent. Symbol and Referent, that is to say, are not connected directly (and when, for grammatical reasons, we imply such a relation, it will merely be an imputed, as opposed to a real, relation) but only indirectly round the two sides of the triangle.   (Ogden and Richards 1923: 11–12)

Figure 11.5 offers a simplified version of the triangle using the terms 'words', 'concepts' and 'world'. On this view, then, there are direct relationships between words and concepts and between concepts and the world, but only an indirect relationship between words and the world. In fact, relationships between words and the world must be mediated by relationships between words and concepts.

Many semantic theories, including relevance theory, fit in with this adjusted version by assuming that linguistic expressions are linked to mental representations which in turn represent states of affairs in the world. David Lewis (1970) famously attacked this approach. He had in mind in particular the work of Katz and Fodor (1963) and of Katz and Postal (1964) who were aiming to develop a semantic theory within a broadly Chomskyan approach. Katz and Fodor proposed that words and other linguistic expressions encoded structured sets of concepts which they called 'semantic markers'. Lewis made the point that this was essentially a process of translation from one language to another. Katz and Fodor were translating from natural languages into the language of semantic markers, which Lewis termed 'markerese'. This would tell us no more about the actual meanings of the expressions than would have been achieved by translating into any other language, say Latin or French. If I tell you that the English word *table* 'means' the Latin word *mensa*, you will naturally ask me what *mensa* means and you won't know what *table* or *mensa* mean until you know what entity or entities in the world they represent. Lewis suggested that translation into 'markerese' or any other language only helps to account for meaning if we already know the meanings of expressions in the target language. A theory of meaning requires not mere translation into other languages but **semantic interpretation**, which relates expressions to entities or states of affairs in the world.

Some approaches to semantics, particularly formal approaches, go against Ogden and Richards's view by suggesting that there is indeed a direct link between linguistic expressions and entities in the world. The referent of the expression *the first female British Prime Minister* just is the human being we can also refer to as *Margaret Thatcher*. One such approach is 'Montague grammar' named after the logician Richard Montague (Montague 1974; for an introduction, see Dowty, Wall and Peters 1980). If you take this view, you solve the problem of 'markerese' by providing semantic interpretations but you fail to explain the role of human minds in the story and you fail to account for the connections between words and concepts or concepts and the world. Other approaches such as Jackendoff's (2002) approach, propose a 'conceptualist semantics' which focuses on the relationship between linguistic expressions and concepts. On this view, the reality of the world outside is less relevant than the workings of human minds which represent it.

Relevance theory assumes that our thoughts can be explained in terms of truth-conditional interpretations. It accepts Lewis's point about 'mere translation' not being the same as 'interpretation' and therefore that we have not fully accounted for the meanings of linguistic expressions until we have also accounted for what thoughts represent. Nevertheless, it assumes that the first step in accounting for the meanings of linguistic expressions is to say what mental representations they give rise to. The relationship with the world is then to be accounted for by providing a semantic interpretation of our mental representations. Relevance theory proposes, then, two kinds of semantics: linguistic semantics which translates linguistic expressions into conceptual representations (as represented at the top of Figure 11.3) and the semantics of the language of thought which accounts for the meanings of those conceptual representations (as represented at the bottom of Figure 11.3). This approach is the topic of the next section.

11.4   From words to the world: two kinds of semantics

Relevance theory takes seriously Lewis's comments on the deficiencies of a purely translational semantics but still proposes that one step in accounting for linguistic meanings involves translating linguistic expressions into mental representations. A later step accounts for the relationship with the world by providing semantic interpretations of representations in the 'language of thought' (Fodor's 1975 term for the system we think in). As relevance theory also argues for the **underdeterminacy thesis**, the linguistically encoded semantic representations are not full propositions but logical forms which need to be fleshed out before they express complete propositions. These complete

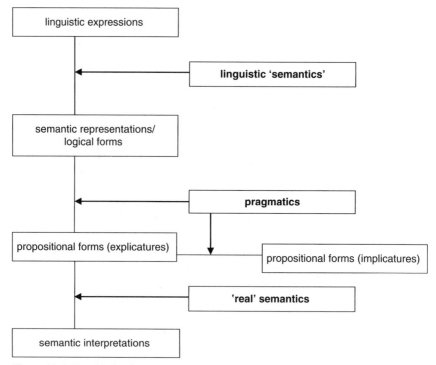

Figure 11.6 *Two kinds of semantics*

propositions can then be interpreted semantically. At the moment, the best candidate for this task is some form of truth-conditional semantics.

There is no space here to explain fully what is involved in **truth-conditional semantics**. The key notion is that thoughts represent actual or possible states of affairs: those states of affairs that would make them true. Given this, then we could say that to know the meaning of an expression is to know what the world would have to be like for that proposition to be true. We can know the meaning of an expression without knowing whether it is true because we do not always know what the world is like. The overall relevance-theoretic picture is presented in Figure 11.6, a simplification from Figure 11.3 above. Remembering, of course, that this is not intended to represent any kind of sequenced relationship in actual real-time processing, the first stage in this picture is the relationship between linguistic expressions and 'logical forms', the incomplete conceptual representations encoded by linguistic expressions. They are termed 'logical forms' to reflect the fact that they have logical properties even though they do not express full propositions. An utterance such as (20) might represent the logical form represented informally in (21) and in a different form in (22):

(20)   He's a vegetarian.

(21)   Whoever *he* refers to has the property of being a vegetarian at some time or under some circumstances.

(22)   [_____] is a vegetarian [_____]
              referent of *he*   at some time or under some circumstances

As we have seen in previous chapters, we cannot say whether this is true or false, or what state of affairs in the world it represents, until we know the answers to a number of questions. We need to know who *he* refers to, whether the speaker is expressing a belief of her own, attributing it to someone else, asking whether it is true, hoping that it might be true, or something else. And so on.

Despite these gaps, we can still make some inferences based on the logical form represented in (21) and (22). We can conclude (23)–(25), for example:

(23)   There is at least one vegetarian.

(24)   The referent of *he* does not eat meat.

(25)   There is at least one person who does not eat meat.

This shows that even a semantically incomplete representation can have logical properties.

Starting from this logical form, we can infer the proposition being expressed and any higher-level explicatures. Assuming we can identify a referent of *he*, say Andy Adams, we might infer the proposition expressed in (26) (which in this case will be an explicature) and the higher-level explicatures (27) and (28):

(26)   Andy Adams is a vegetarian at 10 a.m. on the 2nd of April 2012.

(27)   Ken is expressing his belief that Andy Adams is a vegetarian at 10 a.m. on the 2nd of April 2012.

(28)   Ken believes that Andy Adams is a vegetarian at 10 a.m. on the 2nd of April 2012.

On the basis of these explicatures and appropriate contextual assumptions, other propositions can be inferred. These, of course, are implicatures and implications. Here are some possible implicatures:

(29)   Andy Adams will not want to eat meat when he comes to Bev's party on the 6th of April 2012.

(30)   There will be at least one vegetarian at Bev's party on the 6th of April 2012.

(31)   There will be at least one person who does not want to eat meat at Bev's party on the 6th of April 2012.

(32)   Bev is wrong to think that she doesn't need to cater for vegetarians at her party on the 6th of April 2012.

These might follow given the contextual assumptions (33)–(35):

(33)   Ken has just asked Bev how she's going to cater for vegetarians at her party on the 6th of April 2012.

(34)   Bev has said that there are no vegetarians coming to her party on the 6th of April 2012.

(35)   Andy Adams is one of the guests who will be coming to Bev's party on the 6th of April 2012.

Assuming that each of these really expresses a full proposition (and not that we're simply translating into English as we are in fact doing) then we can develop semantic interpretations of them. Most approaches to this task are based on some version of truth-conditional semantics.

To sum up, then, there are two kinds of **semantics** within relevance theory. A translational first step decodes linguistic input and provides incomplete **representations** in the **language of thought** as output. These logical forms fall short of expressing full propositions. Pragmatic processes are involved in fleshing these out (i.e. 'developing' them) until they are fully propositional, in working out further explicatures and in deriving implicatures. The meanings of fully propositional forms can then be given by means of **semantic interpretations** which can be provided by what Lewis would call 'real' semantics (i.e. the semantics of mental representations). The assumption is that some form of truth-conditional semantic theory is the best currently available for this.

There is one inaccuracy in the story we have looked at so far. We have assumed so far that all linguistic items encode contributions to conceptual content. We will now consider exceptions to this by considering expressions which encode **procedural meanings**.

11.5   Concepts and procedures: two kinds of meanings

This section considers one of the most influential and widely applied notions to be developed within relevance theory: the distinction between conceptual and procedural meaning. The idea of making this distinction arose from discussion of Grice's proposed category of 'conventional implicature', and was first developed extensively in the work of Diane Blakemore (1987, 2002). This section begins by sketching the distinction, before seeing how it emerged in Blakemore's work and how it has come be seen as applying to a wider range of linguistic expressions.

11.5.1   Two kinds of meanings

The distinction between conceptual and procedural meaning relates to the distinction outlined above between two phases of interpretation: a decoding phase and an inferential phase. In the decoding phase, linguistic expressions are translated into semantic representations, i.e. logical forms which vastly underdetermine the speaker's meaning. The inferential phase takes these semantic representations as input and develops them into fully propositional forms: that is, conceptual representations which represent states of affairs in the world and are capable of being true or false. This process involves interaction with accessible contextual assumptions and eventually leads to the set of (higher- and lower-level) explicatures and (stronger or weaker) implicatures which constitute the overall interpretation of an utterance.

To understand the conceptual–procedural distinction it is important to understand that logical forms, semantic representations, explicatures and implicatures are all seen as couched in the 'language of thought'. **The language of thought** is a conceptual representation system whose constituents are **concepts**. This means that the logical forms recovered by linguistic decoding, the explicatures derived by fleshing them out, and the implicatures derived from the interaction of explicatures with contextual assumptions are all understood as conceptual representations. The conceptual–procedural distinction is based on the assumption that not all linguistic expressions encode conceptual material. One way to illustrate the distinction between conceptual and procedural meaning (based on discussion by Blakemore 2002: 89–98) is to consider how we interpret an utterance consisting of two sentences such as (36):

(36)   It's raining. I'm going for a walk.

To understand this, we need first to know what is linguistically encoded by the utterance, which we might represent, very simply/simplistically, as follows:

(37)   Semantic representation of (36):
           It is raining [at time or in circumstances to be inferred]
           [referent of *I*] is going for a walk [at time or in circumstances to be inferred]

The word *rain* is seen as encoding the concept RAIN, which figures directly in the proposition expressed, and is therefore described as having conceptual meaning. To work out what is intended by a particular utterance of (36), we need to make inferences about who *I* refers to, when the rain is happening, and so on. We also need to make an inference about the connection between the two propositions expressed. There are a number of possibilities, including:

(38) a.   It is raining. [It follows from the fact that it is raining that] I am going for a walk.
     b.   It is raining. [Despite the fact that it is raining] I am going for a walk.
     c.   It is raining. [Evidence for the fact that it is raining comes from the fact that] I am going for a walk.
     d.   It is raining. [It is also true that] I am going for a walk.

All of the above possibilities might be inferred by a hearer of (36). At the same time, we might help our hearer to arrive at the intended connection between the propositions by including a linguistic expression which makes one of the connections more likely to be inferred than the others, as in the examples in (39):

(39) a.   It's raining. So I'm going for a walk.
     b.   It's raining. But I'm going for a walk.
     c.   It's raining. After all, I'm going for a walk.
     d.   It's raining. Moreover I'm going for a walk.

The claim is that the encoded linguistic meanings of expressions such as *so*, *but*, *because*, *moreover*, and others such as *therefore*, *however*, *nevertheless*, guide the hearer by making one of the possible inferential connections more salient than the others. We'll look at the possible meanings of these expressions in more detail below. Here are rough characterisations for now:

(40) Tentative semantic representations for *so*, *but*, *after all*, *moreover*:

a.   P *so* Q:
  Q follows from P

b.   P *but* Q:
  Q contradicts a assumption suggested by P

c.   P *after all* Q:
  P follows from Q

d.   P *moreover* Q:
  Q is further evidence for something suggested by P

We will look below at some of the reasons for thinking that these characterisations are too simple. Meanwhile, the following exercise asks you to consider some examples so that you can understand some of the reasons for thinking along these lines to begin with.

Exercise 11.2 asks you to consider some examples containing expressions which have been thought to encode procedural meanings.

Exercise 11.2

- All of the following expressions have been considered to encode procedural meanings. For each one, consider what you think the encoded procedure might be. What kinds of evidence can be seen as confirming or disconfirming the view that their meanings are procedural? How might you find out more?
  (i)   *this*
  (ii) *however*
  (iii) *well*
  (iv) *oh*
  (v)   falling and rising tones (as in the contrast between *You don't want coffee* said with a falling or a rising prosodic contour)

The notion of **procedural meaning** has been applied to a wider range of examples than those so far discussed. Pronouns such as *he*, *she* and *it* have been seen as encoding procedural meanings which help hearers to infer intended referents. Prosody, syntactic structures and interjections have also been seen as encoding procedural meanings. To take one example, the utterance in (41) encodes a semantic representation along the lines of (42):

(41) That's good.

(42) [the referent of *that*] is GOOD [at some time or in some circumstances]

Let's imagine that (41) is uttered by Bev in the following exchange:

(43)   KEN: It looks like over a hundred people will be coming to the party.
           BEV: That's good.

This might lead Ken to infer the explicature and implicatures in (44), among others:

(44)   *Explicature:* Bev believes that it is good that over a hundred people are coming to Ken's party on Saturday evening.
           Implicature: Bev believes that Ken will be pleased that over a hundred people are coming to Ken's party on Saturday evening.
           Implicature: Bev believes that Ken must be looking forward to the party.

Suppose that Ken has been expecting around sixty people to come to the party, has prepared for around sixty guests, and has been worrying that he might not have enough food, drink and space to accommodate everyone. In this context, the thought that a hundred people will be coming is not a good one. Ken's interpretation will depend, though, on whether he thinks Bev knows that he's worried about the possibility that more than sixty people will come. If he thinks she doesn't know, he will still be likely to infer the explicature and implicatures in (44), and he might go on to say something like (45):

(45)   No, it's terrible. I've been planning for around sixty people.

If he thinks Bev knows that he's been planning for sixty people, he might infer what amounts to an ironic interpretation, as represented by the explicature and implicatures in (46):

(46)   *Explicature:* Bev believes that it would be silly to think that it is good that over a hundred people are coming to Ken's party on Saturday evening.
           Implicature: Bev believes that Ken will be worried that over a hundred people are coming to Ken's party on Saturday evening.
           Implicature: Bev believes that Ken must be dreading the party.

Another possibility is that Bev doesn't know what Ken has been expecting and so she is wondering whether the possibility of a hundred people coming is a good or a bad thing. If Ken recognises this, he might infer the following explicature and implicatures:

(47)   *Explicature:* Bev is wondering whether Ken thinks that it is good that over one hundred people are coming to Ken's party on Saturday evening.
           Implicature: Bev would like to know whether Ken is pleased or worried to think that over one hundred people are coming to Ken's party on Saturday evening.
           Implicature: Bev isn't sure how to react to Ken's statement about one hundred people possibly coming to the party.

To summarise, there are at least three ways in which Ken might understand Bev's utterance. He might decide that she is stating her belief that this is a good thing. He might decide that she is ironically suggesting that this is a bad thing. He might decide that she is asking whether he thinks this is a good thing. And of course there are other possibilities. The notion of procedural meaning arises from the observation that there are linguistic expressions which can help hearers to follow the intended inferential path. Here are two alternative utterances which Bev might have produced:

(48) a.   Wow! That's good!
     b.   So that's good then.

(48a) is likely to suggest that Bev believes that the possibility of a hundred guests is a good thing. (48b) is likely to suggest that she is wondering what Ken thinks about it (this is not the only possibility, of course, and different contextual assumptions will make different interpretations more or less likely). Different prosodic patterns such as variations in intonational structure might also provide clues (for discussion of prosody within a relevance-theoretic framework, see Wilson and Wharton 2006). A rising pitch on *good*, for example, might suggest a question interpretation. A high falling pitch might suggest a positive attitude. And so on. For the ironic interpretation, there are two possible intonation patterns which might help. One is a kind which has been described as a 'flat, deadpan' pitch pattern (mentioned in Chapter 10), another is a stylised 'positive' pitch pattern (for discussion, see Ackerman 1983; Rockwell 2000; Bryant and Fox Tree 2002). While neither of these will determine an ironic interpretation, and there are acknowledged problems with defining either pattern clearly, both of them will make one more likely.

11.5.2   From conventional implicatures to procedural meanings ▨

The term 'procedural meaning' was not used in initial discussion of this idea, including in the best-known source for the idea, namely the book by Diane Blakemore (1987) which first developed the idea in a critical discussion of Grice's notion of 'conventional implicature'. Grice's notion was intended to account for cases where he considered that implicatures were 'conventionally', i.e. linguistically, encoded. Grice discussed the following example:

(49)   Bill is a philosopher and he is, therefore, brave.

Grice suggested that what is said by an utterance of (49) would be identical to what is said by (50):

(50)   Bill is a philosopher and Bill is brave.

He suggested that the effect of the word *therefore* here is to communicate the implicature in (51):

(51)   The fact that Bill is brave follows from the fact that Bill is a philosopher.

For Grice, (51) is an implicature rather than part of 'what is said':

> Now I do not wish to allow that, in my favoured sense of 'say', one who utters [(49)] will have *said* that Bill's being courageous follows from his being a philosopher, though he may well have said that Bill is courageous

> and that he is a philosopher. I would wish to maintain that the semantic
> function of the word 'therefore' is to enable a speaker to *indicate*, though
> not to *say*, that a certain consequence holds.   (Grice 1989: 121)

For Grice, then, the speaker of (49) is *saying* that Bill is a philosopher and that
Bill is brave, while simultaneously *indicating* that his bravery follows from his
being a philosopher. He can be seen, then, as performing two utterances (Grice
would say 'speech acts') at the same time.

What does Grice mean by this? It's usually assumed that he intends 'what is
said' to be understood as the truth-conditional content of the utterance and that
'what is indicated' is a conventional implicature. So what kind of thing is an
'indicated' conventional implicature? To explain this, Grice suggests a distinction between two kinds of 'speech act' involved in utterances: a 'central', or
'ground-floor', speech act and a 'non-central', or 'higher-order', speech act.
Discussing a different example, he says:

> One part of what the … speaker … is doing is making what might be called
> ground-floor statements … at the same time as he is performing these
> speech-acts he is also performing a higher-order speech-act of commenting
> in a certain way on the lower-order speech-acts.   (Grice 1989: 362)

Grice suggests that a speaker who says (49) where there is no consequence
relation between being a philosopher and bravery will not have said anything
false. Rather they will have 'misperformed' a higher-order speech act. This
misperformance will not affect the truth value of 'what is said':

> while a certain kind of misperformance of the higher-order speech-act may
> constitute a semantic offense, it will not touch the truth-value … of the
> speaker's words.   (Grice 1989: 362)

What Grice suggested, then, was that a word such as *therefore* linguistically
encodes an implicature so that the speaker of an utterance such as *X and*
therefore Y is simultaneously communicating *X and Y* and *Y follows from X*.

As conventional implicatures are linguistically encoded, i.e. they fall under
the scope of linguistic semantics, there are two ways in which they are significantly different from conversational implicatures, whether generalised or particularised. First, they do not depend on the maxims, i.e. on pragmatic inference.
Every single utterance of (49) will communicate the assumption that Bill's
bravery follows in some way from his being a philosopher. The second, related,
difference is that conventional implicatures are neither contextually nor linguistically cancellable. We cannot imagine a context which would prevent the
consequence implicature of (49) and if we try to cancel it explicitly, our verbal
behaviour will seem odd. In fact, it will seem that we are contradicting
ourselves:

(52)   Bill is a philosopher and he is, therefore, brave. I don't think his bravery has anything to
         do with him being a philosopher or anything, though.

There is something odd about an utterance such as (52), suggesting either that the speaker does not understand what *therefore* means or that they are confused in some other way. The situation is different with the conversational implicatures associated with examples such as (53) and (54):

(53)   I broke a finger yesterday.

(54)   I'm a vegetarian.

The generalised conversational implicature associated with (53) is that the speaker broke one of her own fingers which is biologically attached to her hand. Grice sees this as generalised since it arises in all normal contexts where (53) is uttered and does not depend on any idiosyncratic contextual assumptions. Particularised conversational implicatures depend, of course, on a specific context so we need to provide one in order to know which particular implicature might follow from an utterance of (54). Assuming that I have just offered you a burger, then one implicature will be that you do not want a burger. Both of these implicatures can be cancelled contextually, i.e. there are contexts in which they do not arise (strictly speaking, hearers may have access to sets of contextual assumptions which do not give rise to them). For (53), if we imagine that the speaker makes porcelain items for a living, and that many of these are hands, then we might assume she broke a porcelain finger rather than one of her own. For (57), we simply need to imagine a burger-free context, or perhaps a context where some other food has been offered. If, for example, it is uttered in response to the offer of a hot dog, then it will implicate that the speaker does not want a hot dog. The other way to cancel implicatures is to rule them out explicitly. Here are attempts to do this for each implicature:

(55)   I broke a finger yesterday. Not my own, though. I was in a wrestling match and I broke the other guy's finger.

(56)   I'm a vegetarian. But I do break the rules sometimes and they look tasty. OK, I'll have one.

These might not sound terribly natural, but they do demonstrate that the speaker can cancel the implicature in each case without confusing the hearer or seeming confused herself.[1]

The picture Grice developed, then, involves a distinction between 'what is said' and 'what is implicated', a distinction between conventional and conversational implicatures, and a distinction between generalised and particularised conversational implicatures. We saw in Chapters 5 and 7 that there is no distinction within relevance theory between generalised and particularised conversational implicatures. We will now see how the notion of 'conventional implicature' has disappeared, and how these examples have been reanalysed within relevance theory.

Blakemore's (1987) development of the notion of procedural meaning, originally conceived of in terms of **semantic constraints**, began with a critical discussion of Grice's account. Blakemore and others (e.g. Bach 1999) identified a number of problems with Grice's account but perhaps the most important for a relevance-theoretic account is simply that it does not fit within this framework as neatly as the procedural meaning account does. Before exploring this further by looking at the procedural meaning account in more detail, we will point out two issues with Grice's approach. First, there is something odd about the label 'conventional implicature'. What is the definition of an 'implicature'? If it means something that is inferred, then conventional implicatures do not seem to count, since, by definition, they are linguistically encoded and not inferred. If it means 'not part of what is said', then it is not clear how well-motivated this term is and it begins to look as if 'conventional implicature' is more of a label than an explanatory account. Why and how should such a phenomenon emerge? Second, there is reason to doubt the extent to which the semantic analyses proposed will be able to account for the range of data here. Taking the word *but*, for example, one thing we might point out straight away is that there is still no agreed semantic analysis for this word. Why should this be? If the word simply encodes an implicature, why can't semanticists simply state what that implicature is? Instead, it seems that every proposed semantic analysis runs into counterexamples, leading to an endless series of revisions. On the one hand, language users do not have serious problems in understanding utterances containing words such as *but*; on the other hand, linguistic semanticists find it almost impossible to work out what on earth this word might mean. It is far from clear that any account has solved these problems and come up with an adequate proposed semantic analysis. However, if the meanings of expressions such as *but* are internalised procedures which we do not have conscious access to, then this would help to explain why it is so difficult to explicate what they encode. In fact, as we will see below, one of the tests which has been proposed for identifying cases of procedural meaning is that procedural meanings are expected to be difficult to paraphrase. When a word encodes a concept, that concept can figure directly in our thoughts, and when it does figure in our thoughts, we should have no difficulty understanding it. Procedural meanings are linked to procedures that do themselves figure directly in our thoughts. If Blakemore and other procedural semanticists are right, then Grice's account amounts to an attempt to express in conceptual terms something which is not conceptual.

11.5.3   From non-truth-conditional meaning to procedural meaning

As we saw above, the main advantage of approaches to meaning based on truth conditions is that they make it possible to characterise the relationship between representations and states of affairs. A weakness with many approaches is that they assume that the bearers of truth conditions are linguistic expressions. We looked at a range of examples above, in fact throughout this book, which demonstrate that there is a significant gap between linguistically encoded meanings and truth conditions. Grice's notion of 'conventional implicature' can be seen as an attempt to account for one variety of non-truth-conditional meaning.

Wilson and Sperber (1993) consider and contrast approaches to linguistic semantics based on a distinction between truth-conditional and non-truth-conditional meaning with approaches based on a distinction between conceptual and procedural meaning. They consider whether it might be possible to reduce one approach to the other or to systematically relate them, and conclude that this is not possible. In order to understand Wilson and Sperber's argument, we need first to make sure we agree on what the two distinctions involve.

Wilson and Sperber (1993) suggest that in linguistics, the truth-conditional/ non-truth-conditional distinction tends to be seen as applying to linguistic expressions, while the conceptual/procedural distinction is cognitively motivated. The former contrasts two kinds of expression, those which contribute to the truth-conditional content of the utterance in which they occur and those which do not, while the latter is a contrast between two kinds of processing. For Wilson and Sperber, the truth-conditional content of an utterance is typically determined by the proposition expressed. For Grice, the truth-conditional content of an utterance seems to equate with 'what is said'. We can illustrate this with some of Grice's own examples. The example Grice used to illustrate what he meant by 'saying' is (57):

(57)   He's in the grip of a vice.

As we've seen, Grice suggested that we will know 'what is said' here once we know the referent of *he* and the sense of *in the grip of a vice*. If the referent is John Smith, the speaker will have said either that John Smith is 'unable to rid himself of a certain kind of bad character trait' or that 'some part of [John Smith]'s person' is 'caught in a certain kind of tool or instrument' (Grice 1989: 25). Here are three examples where Grice discussed what is implicated as well as 'what is said', with approximate characterisations in each case of 'what is said' and an implicature suggested by Grice:

(58)   Bill is a philosopher and he is, therefore, brave.
         'what is said':
         Bill is a philosopher and Bill is brave.
         (conventional) implicature:
         Bill's bravery is a consequence of Bill's being a philosopher.

(59)   I broke a finger yesterday.
         'what is said':
         There exists a finger which the speaker broke yesterday.
         (generalised conversational) implicature:
         The broken finger is one of the fingers biologically attached to the speaker's own hand.

(60)   War is war.
         'what is said':

War is war.
(particularised conversational) implicature:
You shouldn't be surprised at the behaviour of people involved in the war we are discussing.

It seems from Grice's discussion that he is assuming that 'what is said' is the location of truth-conditional meaning and anything else communicated is an implicature. Implicatures might be linguistically encoded (conventional implicature) or dependent on aspects of the context (generalised conversational implicatures or particularised conversational implicatures). If this is right, then to ask whether the conceptual–procedural distinction corresponds to, or can be reformulated as, the distinction between truth-conditional and non-truth-conditional meaning is to ask whether conceptual expressions (i.e. linguistic expressions which encode conceptual meaning) always contribute to 'what is said' and procedural expressions (i.e. linguistic expressions which encode procedural meaning) always contribute to 'what is implicated'. If we only consider Blakemore's early work on connectives such as *so*, *but*, etc. this might seem plausible, since Blakemore showed how these can be seen as constraining the range of possible implicatures of an utterance. We can see this by considering the examples in (39) above, repeated here:

(61) a.   It's raining. So I'm going for a walk.
      b.   It's raining. But I'm going for a walk.
      c.   It's raining. After all, I'm going for a walk.
      d.   It's raining. Moreover I'm going for a walk.

In (61a), *so* constrains possible inferences in such a way that that the speaker's going for a walk is seen as following from the fact that it's raining. In (61b), two implicatures are that we wouldn't expect the speaker to go for a walk in the rain and that the fact that she is going for a walk contradicts and denies this expectation. In (61c), the speaker's going for a walk is evidence for the fact that it is raining. In (61d), the speaker's going for a walk is to be taken as supporting one or more inferential conclusions which also follow from the fact that it is raining. In each case, then, we can understand the contribution of the expression with procedural meaning as being to constrain the range of possible implicatures of the utterance.

However, Wilson and Sperber (1993) point out that more recent work has identified cases where procedural meanings contribute to 'truth-conditional meaning', or to the proposition expressed, and cases where conceptual meaning contributes to non-truth-conditional meaning. Wilson and Sperber frame their discussion around the diagram in Figure 11.7.

Wilson and Sperber discuss all of the distinctions in this diagram. However, we only need to consider the bottom part of the diagram to understand the point about the conceptual–procedural distinction we are considering here.

As Figure 11.8 makes clear, there are six possible kinds of expression based on a two-way distinction between conceptual and procedural encoding and a

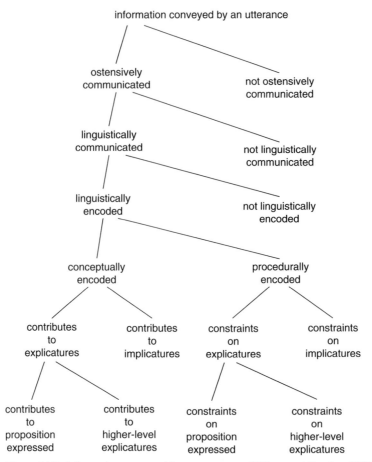

Figure 11.7 *Information conveyed by an utterance (Wilson and Sperber 1993)*

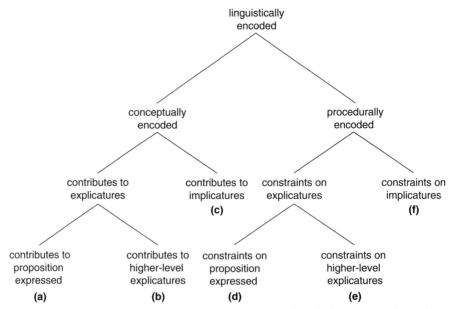

Figure 11.8 *Conceptual and procedural meaning (adapted from Wilson and Sperber 1993)*

three-way distinction between proposition expressed, higher-level explicatures and implicatures. Wilson and Sperber point out examples of linguistic expressions corresponding to five of these six possibilities. The one logical possibility for which they do not suggest any examples is the possibility of conceptually encoded contributions to implicatures. Following suggestions by Scott (2010, 2011), we will consider below whether there are also candidates for membership of this slightly problematic category. We will now run briefly through each of the six categories, providing examples of all of them. We won't look at evidence for categorising the examples in this way yet but will return to this when considering possible tests for procedural meaning in Section 11.5.5.

(a)   Conceptual contributions to the proposition expressed

This is perhaps the least problematic category since all approaches assume that some linguistic expressions contribute conceptual components of conceptual representations. So, for example, the word *play* encodes a number of senses, one of which is to take part in a sport, and the word *watch* encodes a number of senses, one of which is to look at something with the intention of understanding what it involves, the word *football* encodes a number of senses, one of which is a sport, and the word *tennis* encodes a number of senses, one of which is another sport. We can explain the meanings of these words partly by saying that they encode these concepts. Knowing which concepts these words encode contributes to an explanation of how we understand the similarities and differences between the following utterances:

(62)   I'd rather play football than watch it.

(63)   I'd rather watch football than play it.

(64)   I'd rather play tennis than football.

(65)   I'd rather watch tennis than football.

(b)   Conceptual contributions to higher-level explicatures

As we saw above, including in Chapters 5 and 6, relevance theory assumes that explicatures can contain propositions embedded under other descriptions. We can illustrate this by considering the following three utterances:

(66)   It's raining.

(67)   Ken thinks it's raining.

(68)   Andy says that Ken thinks it's raining.

The proposition expressed by (66) is that it is raining at some particular time or in some situation. (67) says that Ken thinks that this proposition is true. (68) says that Andy says that Ken thinks that it is true. We could, of course, carry on embedding (66) as long as our minds can cope with the complexity and remember the overall proposition expressed. Notice that some of these markers of attributed speech or thought could be omitted if we trust the hearer to infer them. I might simply say (66), for example, if you ask me:

(69)   What did Andy say Ken thinks?

Also, even a simple utterance of (66) will be understood as conveying a representation indicating who entertains it and what they entertain it as. If I say (66), you might, for example, understand what I am communicating as:

(70)   (I am expressing my own belief that) it's raining.

In this case, (70) represents a higher-level explicature of (66).

There are linguistic expressions which seem to contribute conceptual material to higher-level explicatures. Adverbials such as *honestly* or *frankly*, for example, seem to contribute to higher-level explicatures. (71), for example, would lead to a higher-level explicature such as (72) and (73) would lead to a higher-level explicature such as (74) (for discussion, see Ifantidou 2001, 2005a, 2005b, 2005c):

(71)   Honestly, it's raining.

(72)   I am telling you honestly that it's raining.

(73)   Frankly, I don't think that top suits you.

(74)   I am saying frankly that I don't think that top suits you.

Words such as *honestly* and *frankly*, then, contribute conceptual material to higher-level explicatures. We could also suggest that verbs which represent thinking, saying, etc. contribute to higher-level explicatures:

(75)   John thinks it's raining.

(76)   John says it's raining.

(77)   John knows it's raining.

(c)   Conceptual contributions to implicatures

Wilson and Sperber do not propose any candidates for this kind of meaning. At first, it is hard to think of any possible candidates. There is no a priori reason why any such expressions should exist and it would not necessarily be problematic for this approach if such cases did not exist. Cases which have been discussed seem to have more to do with pragmatics than linguistic coding. Kate Scott (2010, 2011), for example, considers the following pair of possible utterances:

(78)   John went into town for his lunch. He was late back to the office.

(79)   John went into town for his lunch. The rascal was late back to the office.

What is the difference between how we understand (78) and (79)? Scott suggests that (79) asks us to 'do more work' in processing *the rascal* than is involved in processing *he* in (78). While the referent in each case is clear and easily accessible, finding a referent for *the rascal* involves forming a representation of a specific rascal. As part of this process, Scott suggests, we are likely to derive (80) as an implicated premise:

(80)   John is a rascal.

The motivation for this implicated premise is the fact that the concept {RASCAL} is encoded by the word *rascal*. While there is a sense in which a conceptual meaning contributes indirectly to an implicature here, this is a matter of pragmatics and depends largely on the presence of the procedural expression *the*. There are no clear cases of conceptual meaning communicating directly to implicature.

(d)   Procedural constraints on the proposition expressed

Pronouns are usually assumed to contribute to the proposition expressed not by naming a concept which contributes to the proposition but by constraining the hearer's search for a referent. The word *she* in (81) does not name a particular person but it does affect the process of finding a referent so that an utterance of (82) in the same context will be understood differently, due to the use of *he* rather than *she*:

(81)   Do you know whether she's awake?

(82)   Do you know whether he's awake?

Thus pronouns affect the truth-conditional content of utterances, but by constraining the reference assignment process rather than by encoding concepts which figure directly in the proposition expressed.

(e)   Procedural constraints on higher-level explicatures

There are several candidates for constraints on higher-level explicatures. We looked at one case earlier when we considered the interjection *wow*. The presence of *wow* at the start of (84) means that it is more likely to lead to a higher-level explicature such as (85) than an utterance such as (83) which does not include *wow*:

(83)   It's raining.

(84)   Wow, it's raining.

(85)   The speaker is surprised that it's raining.

Of course, (85) might well be derived purely inferentially on the basis of an utterance of just (83), depending on the accessibility of particular contextual assumptions, but (84) makes the speaker's intention more manifest and its derivation more likely. Another thing which might influence the interpretation is prosody and several theorists have suggested that certain kinds of prosodic meaning can be seen as procedural.[2]

(f)   Procedural constraints on implicatures

Of course, we have already looked at examples of expressions (*therefore*, *but*, *so*, *after all*, *moreover*) which are assumed to constrain the derivation of implicatures. Here is another example with the word *so*:

(86)   Ken's coming to the party. We won't be seeing Mary.

(87)   Ken's coming to the party. So we won't be seeing Mary.

The word *so* makes more manifest to the hearer that the proposition that we won't be seeing Mary is being presented as a conclusion, in this case derived from the proposition that Ken is coming to the party. As Blakemore (1987: 86) points out, *so* can also be uttered at the start of a discourse, as in (88):

(88)   *(seeing the hearer walk in with lots of bags filled with shopping)*
       So you've spent all your money.

It is hard to see how Grice's approach would account for discourse-initial uses of words such as *so*. On Blakemore's approach, the procedure encoded by *so* presents the proposition it introduces as a conclusion. The hearer infers what this conclusion follows from and there is no difficulty caused by the lack of preceding uttered material.

This range of examples makes clear that, as Wilson and Sperber suggest, the conceptual–procedural distinction is not reducible to a distinction between truth-conditional and non-truth-conditional meaning. The notion of procedural meaning has been applied to a number of areas, including the analysis of prosody, different syntactic structures and nonverbal communication.[3] In Section 11.5.5 below, we will look at some specific features of, and questions about, procedural accounts.

Exercise 11.3 asks you to consider a range of examples, focusing on the contribution of particular expressions with conceptual and procedural meanings.

Exercise 11.3

*   Propose an account of how B's utterance might be understood in each of the following exchanges. In proposing your account, identify which terms you think have encoded procedural meanings.
    (i)   A: I've asked John to be careful driving home tonight.
           B: But he won't.
    (ii)   A: Will it rain tonight, do you think?
           B: Oh I doubt it.
    (iii)   A: Do you want to go and find John? He's out walking in the field behind the house.
           B: In these shoes? I don't think so.
    (iv)   A: John seems happy enough watching telly while we all slave away in here.
           B: Don't let's start that again. Please!

11.5.4   Further questions about procedural meaning

While the notion of procedural meaning has been used extensively within relevance-theoretic work on linguistically encoded meanings, there is still considerable work to do in developing our understanding of the nature of procedural meaning and our methodology in developing accounts of particular kinds of procedural meanings. Questions that might be raised include:

- What kinds of procedural meanings are there?
- How are procedural meanings acquired?
- How do procedural meanings change over time?
- What constraints are there on developing procedural analyses?

While all of these questions, and others, are both interesting and challenging, we will consider only the final one here.

One answer to the question will simply be that a procedural analysis is justified when it provides the best available account of how a particular expression is understood. That is, we will adopt a procedural analysis when it does a better job than any alternative analysis. At the same time, though, there has been some discussion of whether we might develop tests which provide evidence for or against the decision to suggest a procedural analysis and whether there are constraints on the nature of procedural meanings. These can be understood as sub-questions implicit in the question about what constraints there are on developing procedural analyses.[4]

Blakemore (2002: 82–8) points out a number of properties which we might expect an expression with procedural meaning to have. She says:

> If we recall what has been said about procedural encoding so far, we will see that we seem to know more about what procedural meaning is not than what it is... However ... we can draw certain conclusions about what properties we can expect an expression which encodes procedural meaning to have.   (Blakemore 2002: 82)

The properties which Blakemore identifies as likely to be associated with procedural expressions are: they are difficult to paraphrase; they are difficult to translate; they lack synonymous conceptual counterparts; they are not compositional; they are interpreted differently from conceptual expressions in fragmentary utterances. We will briefly consider each of these in turn.

Procedural meanings are difficult to paraphrase

It might be obvious from having looked at a few examples that it is hard to say exactly what procedural expressions encode. As Blakemore points out, this is corroborated when we ask native speakers to explain what particular terms mean. If we ask a native speaker what *tree* means, the answer might be along the lines of (89):

(89)   A big plant with a wooden trunk and branches. Some of them have fruit or berries you can eat.

If you ask a native speaker about the meaning of *but,* you are more likely to receive answers such as (90) or (91):

(90)   It's like '*however*'.

(91)   Sort of a contrast or something.

Notice that (90) is referring to another procedural expression which has a slightly different meaning. One clear piece of evidence that *but* is not synonymous with *however* is that there are contexts where *but* sounds perfectly fine but *however* sounds odd. Blakemore (2002: 116) gives the following pair of examples:

(92)   *(speaker, who is in shock, has been given a whisky)*
            But I don't drink.

(93)   *(speaker, who is in shock, has been given a whisky)*
            ??However I don't drink.

As Blakemore points out, *however* sounds strange at the beginning of an utterance where the speaker is responding to something nonverbal.

Procedural meanings are difficult to translate

Closely related to the previous point is the fact that it is often difficult to translate expressions with procedural meanings. In some cases, it is fairly straightforward to identify a procedural equivalent in another language, e.g. French *mais* seems to be easily translatable as English *but* in examples such as (94) and (95):

(94)   Je suis bien fatiguée mais je vais lire encore un peu avant aller au lit.

(95)   I'm really tired but I'm going to read a bit more before bed.

However, it is much less clear that (96) and (97) are equivalent:

(96)   Mais oui!

(97)   But yes!

Similar issues occur with conceptual words such as *love,* but there is a particular issue with procedural expressions, related to the difficulties with paraphrasing just mentioned. When we discuss possible translations, once again we find it much harder to formulate the nature of the issue when discussing procedural expressions than when discussing conceptual expressions.

Procedural meanings do not have synonymous conceptual counterparts

Blakemore points out that some expressions which do not contribute to the truth conditions of an utterance on some occasions seem to have synonyms which are truth-conditional on other occasions. The example she gives is *seriously* in examples such as (98) which seems to be synonymous with the use of *seriously* in (99):

(98)   Seriously, you will have to leave.

(99)   He looked at me very seriously.

As Blakemore points out, we can understand the concepts encoded by *seriously* as the same in these two cases. However, it seems that *well* in (100) is not synonymous with *well* in (101):

(100)   A: What time should we leave?
            B: Well, the train leaves at 11.23.

(101)   You haven't ironed this very well.

Procedural meanings are non-compositional

Blakemore points out that procedural expressions do not combine with each other to form constituents of propositions in the same way as conceptual expressions do. She presents some examples of conceptual composition, including (102) and (103):

(102)   In total, absolute confidence, she has been promoted.

(103)   Speaking quite frankly, I don't think people ever ask themselves those kinds of questions.

As she points out, the phrases *in total, absolute confidence* and *speaking quite frankly* involve the combination of the individual words into a more complex expression. It does not seem to be possible to modify *however* in a similar way:

(104)   ??Tom likes pop art. Totally however, Anna prefers Renaissance art.

Blakemore mentions Rouchota's (1998) examples which show that a kind of combination of procedural expressions is possible but that it is different in kind from the ways in which conceptual expressions combine:

(105)   The cat left footprints all over the manuscript of my book. But after all, he can't read.

(106)   The exam scripts are covered in mud. So he must have walked over them too.

The main difference here is that it seems that the two procedural expressions in these examples each give rise to procedures but that they do not combine with each other to give rise to complex procedures.

Procedural fragments are not interpreted in the same way as conceptual fragments

Finally, Blakemore considers the possibility of producing a fragmentary utterance consisting only of procedural expressions. She presents (107) as an example of a conceptual fragment and (108) and (109) as examples of procedural fragments (I have slightly simplified the contextual information here; (109) was originally discussed in Blakemore 1997):

(107)   Coffee.

(108)   *(after talking about the 'trials and tribulations' of having to spend a whole summer writing a book)*
          But still.

(109)   *(said by a university lecturer after hearing an explanation for non-submission of student coursework)*
          Nevertheless.

Blakemore points out that neither (108) nor (109) are to be thought of as uttered with rising intonation which suggests incompleteness. She suggests that (107) is interpreted in a different way from (108) and (109). (107) is likely to be fleshed out to give rise to explicatures including the encoded concept {COFFEE} such as (110) or (111):

(110)   It is time to have a coffee break.

(111)   The speaker believes that we need to buy coffee.

The range of propositions which might be communicated based on the fragmentary procedural expressions is much wider and since no element of them is linguistically encoded, they cannot be understood as explicatures. For (108) they might include (112) and (113):

(112)   It is worth putting time in to writing the book.

(113)   Writing the book is something the speaker cares very much about.

For (109) they might include (114) and (115):

(114)   The student could have handed in some of the work.

(115)   The student has not tried hard enough.

As Blakemore points out, there is nothing in these propositions which corresponds to the procedural expressions uttered. The procedural expressions do not contribute material to any communicated proposition. Rather, they indicate the way in which the utterance might be relevant and so make particular ways of processing more salient.

    None of these features is so strongly associated with procedural encoding that it can be considered a criterion for determining when an expression's encoded meaning is procedural. So finding that an expression has one of these properties would not, on its own, mean that we can conclude that its meaning is procedural. The one definite criterion, of course, is that the expression is non-truth-conditional in the sense that it never encodes a constituent of the proposition expressed.

11.6   Summary

In this chapter, we have reviewed the relevance-theoretic picture of linguistic semantics and the proposed relationship between linguistic semantics and pragmatics. On this view, there are two varieties of 'semantics': 'linguistic semantics' is concerned with the linguistically encoded meanings of linguistic expressions while 'real semantics' (the semantics of mental representations) is concerned with the relationships between conceptual representations and the world. Linguistically encoded meanings are partly translational, involving a translation from public language to conceptual representations, and partly procedural, encoding material which affects the processes involved in interpreting utterances. It is assumed that 'real' semantics will refer to truth conditions. The meanings of our thoughts can be understood in terms of relationships between conceptual representations (in this case our thoughts) and possible states of affairs.

We have now worked through a fairly comprehensive account of the relevance-theoretic framework overall. The next chapter considers a range of ways in which the theory has been extended, developed and applied in recent years.

Exercise 11.4

As in every chapter, this final exercise asks you to adjust the list of questions you have come up with so far by compiling new questions which have occurred to you while reading this chapter and to think about the kinds of things which might count as answers to any questions you have come up with so far. First, add new questions to your ongoing list. Second, consider all of your questions and think about possible ways of answering them.

11.7   Further reading

There is discussion of relevance-theoretic semantics in *Relevance* (Sperber and Wilson 1986: 172–93) but most sources on linguistic semantics focus on the meanings of particular expressions. Carston (2002a: 48–64) also discusses the general picture. Blakemore (1987) is the key starting point for work on the conceptual–procedural distinction. See also: Blakemore (2002, 2007a), Wilson and Sperber (1993 – also available in Wilson and Sperber 2012), and the papers collected in Escandell-Vidal, Leonetti and Ahern (2011).

12 Conclusion: applications and recent developments

Topics: testing pragmatic theories; kinds of data; linguistic and pragmatic development; pragmatics and the mind; words and beyond; competitors and challenges; other views; what's next?

12.1 Overview

The aim of this book has been to present the key ideas of relevance theory and to consider how it accounts for a range of linguistic and non-linguistic phenomena. Along the way, we have looked at some ways in which the theory has been developed, applied and challenged. This chapter briefly considers some of these topics. The theory has been applied in a large number of areas and tested and challenged in a number of ways, so that this chapter cannot hope to come close to providing a comprehensive overview. Instead it indicates a number of important areas and gives a brief indication of the issues involved. Relevance theory has not yet suggested solutions to all of the questions discussed here but we would expect an adequate cognitive and pragmatic theory to contribute to all of them.

12.2 Developing the theory

No theory stands still and of course we expect developments and revisions to take place as theorists interrogate and work with the theory. There have been a number of developments since what might be thought of as the 'classic' version of the theory was presented in the book *Relevance* in 1986. This section mentions a number of these, some of which have been mentioned in earlier chapters, and some areas for future research.[1] I hope that this helps to give you a sense of a developing theoretical approach, how it has evolved over the years, and how it might develop in future.

One key source which suggested important developments was the 'postface' to the second edition of the book *Relevance* (Sperber and Wilson 1986, 2nd edition 1995). This section presents four developments in the theory mentioned there.

12.2.1   Two Principles of Relevance

In earlier versions of the theory, what we have been referring to here as 'The First, Cognitive, Principle of Relevance' was not described as a principle. It was described as a law-like generalisation but not awarded the status of a principle. What we have been referring to as 'The Second, Communicative, Principle of Relevance' was simply referred to as 'The Principle of Relevance'. In the 1995 postface, Sperber and Wilson proposed to refer to both generalisations as **Principles**. This was partly intended to make clearer that both generalisations had the same status while referring to different aspects of human behaviour (cognition and communication respectively). It was also designed to help keep assumptions about **maximising relevance** (looking for as many effects as possible for as little effort as possible) separate from assumptions about **optimising relevance** (looking for an interpretation that makes the ostensive stimulus at least relevant enough to be worth processing, and moreover the most relevant one compatible with the communicator's abilities and preferences). Several commentators, students, and others new to the theory mistakenly assumed that relevance theory claimed that interpreters of acts of ostensive communication were entitled to look for as many effects as possible for as little effort as possible: that is, for maximal relevance. In some cases, the fact that this does not seem to happen was taken as a drawback with the theory.

12.2.2   Defining relevance

In this book so far, we have assumed that a stimulus or other phenomenon is relevant to an individual to the extent that it has **positive cognitive effects** for that individual and to the extent that the effort involved in deriving them is small. Previously, the theory had made reference to 'contextual effects' rather than 'positive cognitive effects'. Why this change? First, to reflect that the effects we are looking at take place within a cognitive system. The term 'contextual effects' suggests that we might be discussing other kinds of systems, including logical or abstract systems. Of course, we might discuss such contextual effects but this is not the main concern of relevance theory.

The addition of the term 'positive' to qualify the cognitive effects is also significant. This is designed to recognise the possibility that some effects derived on the basis of false assumptions might be disadvantageous and, in fact, lead to a stimulus being less relevant rather than more. More specifically, Sperber and Wilson have in mind here the idea that the human cognitive system is fallible, and that what seems to us from the inside like a relevant update to our system may in fact turn out to make it correspond less well to how the world actually is. In that case, it will have *seemed* relevant to us without actually *being* relevant, since it does not bring about an improvement in our representation of the world. Imagine, for example, that you are on the way home and you notice two things: first, that thick smoke is rising from your house; second, that your front door is ajar. The smoke might lead you to think that there is a fire in your house. The open door might lead you to think that someone has broken in to your house. If true, both of these thoughts are highly relevant. However, if the smoke is caused by your partner playing with a smoke machine in the garden, then the smoke is less relevant than if it is caused by an actual fire. If the door has been left open by your partner as he has popped to the letter box on the corner, then this is less relevant than it seemed. The way in which you process the stimuli will not be affected by the facts of the matter, but the relevance of the stimuli will be.

In Chapter 3 we looked at two scenarios discussed in the 1995 'Postface' to show that 'positive cognitive effects' can follow from either false or true initial assumptions, so that the relevance of a stimulus does not depend on every assumption it gives rise to being true. One scenario involved Peter correctly guessing that his wife was talking on the phone to a man and wrongly guessing that she had a lover. The other scenario involved Peter wrongly guessing that she was talking to a man and correctly guessing that she had a lover. This showed that the degrees of relevance which each assumption had were not determined by whether they were true but by whether they had 'positive cognitive effects'.

12.2.3   The presumption of optimal relevance

A third change discussed in 1995 was to the **presumption of optimal relevance**. As we have seen, the new version says that:

(1)   Presumption of optimal relevance
    (a)   the ostensive stimulus is relevant enough for it to be worth the addressee's effort to process it
    (b)   the ostensive stimulus is the most relevant one compatible with the communicator's abilities and preferences.

Here is an earlier version:

(2)   Presumption of optimal relevance (earlier version)
    (a)   the set of assumptions I which the communicator intends to make manifest to the addressee is relevant enough to make it worth the addressee's while to process the ostensive stimulus
    (b)   the ostensive stimulus is the most relevant one the communicator could have used to communicate I.

The reference to 'a set of assumptions I' in these clauses is not a very significant difference from the later formulation. The first clause in the later version is simpler than the previous version largely for reasons of economy. It is shorter and simpler and makes clear that the stimulus must make it possible to derive enough ('positive cognitive') effects to justify the effort in processing the utterance. A more significant change was the introduction in the second clause of explicit reference to the communicator's 'abilities and preferences'.

As Sperber and Wilson point out, the discussion of the presumption of optimal relevance always did make reference to the communicator's abilities and preferences, but these were not referred to explicitly in the presumption itself.

12.2.4   The relevance-guided comprehension heuristic

A fourth change which we have been assuming was not discussed in the postface: the development of the **relevance-guided comprehension heuristic** which we have been assuming throughout the book. While the heuristic was not named as such, the basic idea it represents was present in the first edition of *Relevance*.[2] Presenting the heuristic as such, along with developing discussions of the mutual adjustment process, have helped to make it clearer exactly what kind of processing is envisaged in developing interpretations.

12.3   Testing pragmatic theories: kinds of data

An assumption made by scientific enquiry in general, and approaches to linguistics and pragmatics in general, is that there is no way of knowing in advance what data might be relevant to testing a theory. No source of data can be ruled out as irrelevant in advance. Nevertheless, in any area of enquiry, research often focuses on a specific kind of data. For example, linguistics in general was once seen as dividing into two camps: those who focused on intuitions and those who looked at corpus data. Now, both linguistics in general and pragmatics in particular focus on a wider range of data sources. Before going on to look at work in specific areas, this section considers some of the kinds of data used in investigating topics in pragmatics and considers some of the methodological and other issues associated with each kind of data.

12.3.1   Intuitions

Since the work of Chomsky in the late 1950s, linguists have used intuitions as data and we have, of course, used intuitions in considering examples throughout this book. When Chomsky first proposed the use of intuitions as data, this was resisted by many linguists. Some considered introspection to be unscientific since it was seen as a move from an objective to a subjective approach. Others considered intuitions to be too far removed from the 'real' data of actual language use. Despite all of the difficulties, intuitions are now routinely used by many linguists and psychologists in a wide range of areas (for critical discussion of issues about the use of intuitions and suggestions for how linguists should approach this kind of data, see Birdsong 1989 and Schütze 1996). Alongside increased confidence in intuitions, the use of other kinds of data has also increased. Naturally, finding evidence to support a conclusion from more than one source increases confidence in the results.

A key problem, of course, is that intuitions vary not only from speaker to speaker but for the same speaker at different times. Nevertheless, Chomsky showed that there is clear evidence of consistent cross-speaker intuitions in some cases. While many cases are questionable and intuitions unclear, Chomsky suggested that we should begin by focusing on examples where intuitions are clear and build our theories on them. A classic example used by Chomsky (1965) is the contrast between the pairs in (3) and (4):

(3) a.   John is easy to please.
    b.   It is easy to please John.

(4) a.   John is eager to please.
    b.   It is eager to please John.

Speakers of English agree that (3a) and (3b) mean much the same thing if uttered in the same context and are understood as referring to the same *John*. (4a) and (4b) might seem to have the same structure on the surface but (4b), while an acceptable utterance, can not mean the same as (4a). More specifically, the pronoun *it* in (4b) must refer to some entity which is eager to please John while the pronoun *it* in (3b) does not refer to any entity in the world. Both (3a) and (3b) tell us something about John and how easy it is to please him. (4a) tells us about how eager John is to please people in general while (4b) can only be telling us about how eager some specific entity is to please John. Despite all the variability among speakers in general, these intuitions are consistently reflected across the vast majority of speakers. It seems, then, that this provides evidence of a cross-speaker phenomenon which we should want to explain.

This example is assumed to reflect an aspect of grammar. Similar consistencies exist with examples which demonstrate aspects of our pragmatic abilities and knowledge. Here is one example (this book is full of others!):

(5)   KEN: Time for a treat, Would you like cake or a chocolate biscuit?
       MOLLY: Cake and a biscuit.
       KEN: You can have cake OR a biscuit.

Ken's first utterance here could be intended as an 'inclusive' or an 'exclusive' disjunction. On an inclusive reading, Molly can choose both cake and a biscuit or just one of the options. On an exclusive reading, Molly can have one or the other but not both. It seems that the English word *or* is consistent with either reading. Molly responds in a way consistent with the inclusive reading. Ken's response to this makes clear that an exclusive disjunction is intended by stressing the word *or*. Ken does not say this explicitly but Molly can infer his intention pragmatically, partly based on the contrastive stress on *or* and partly because of the repetition in a context where Molly has just asked for both.

Pragmaticists are used to using intuitions as data, but there are a number of issues which need to be borne in mind when using them. Some of these apply to the use of intuitions in general and some are specific to their use in looking at pragmatic processes. We have already mentioned the variability of intuitions and this arises with regard to pragmatics as much as to other areas. Strategies to deal with this include focusing on clear examples, carefully considering the nature of variability, sometimes by looking at other relevant data, and the use of other kinds of data alongside evidence from intuitions.

Birdsong (1989) and Schütze (1996) discuss issues around the use of intuitions in studying grammar. They use the term 'metalinguistic performance' to refer to what people do when considering their intuitions. This highlights the fact that using intuitions is different from using language and not something we are used to doing. It also reflects the gap between behaviour on a specific occasion ('performance') and an underlying system of linguistic 'competence'. It is important to bear similar issues in mind when using intuitions as data for pragmatic theories. When I ask you to consider (5) above, I am asking you to do something quite different from what is being done by an actual person having a conversation such as the one in (5). At each stage, Ken and Molly will derive implications, work out what they think the other person's utterance means and act on that. When we consider (5), we imagine what Ken and Molly are likely to do. So we can think of this as a kind of 'meta-' task, i.e. one taking place at a metaphorically higher level than in actual conversation. We are imagining what might happen in such an exchange and, of course, this involves making some assumptions about what might be in the minds of Ken and Molly as they are having the conversation. We might refer to the use of intuitions in pragmatics as **metapragmatics**.

Another key difference has to do with access to contextual assumptions. In an actual context, any individual has an infinite number of thoughts available or potentially available to them at any time. In interpreting an utterance, an individual has to construct a context, starting with immediately accessible assumptions that seem likely to contribute to relevance, and adding contextual assumptions in order of accessibility until they arrive at what they take to be the intended interpretation. In 'metapragmatics', by contrast, we imagine what might be available to an individual and of course our model of the relevant set of contextual assumptions is radically impoverished compared to what is available to an actual individual at a specific time. When we say something like, 'Molly will assume that Ken means that Molly can have either cake or a biscuit but not both', we really mean 'our best guess based on simplifying assumptions about what cognitive resources would be available to Molly in a situation such as this is that Molly will assume ...'.

Recanati (1989) has suggested what he refers to as the 'Availability Hypothesis' as a kind of heuristic for theorists to follow in developing pragmatic theories:

(6)   Availability Hypothesis:
         In determining whether a pragmatically determined aspect of utterance meaning is part of what is said, that is, in making a decision concerning what is said, we should always try to preserve our pre-theoretic intuitions on the matter.   (Recanati 1989: 310)

This suggests that we should try to come up with theoretical accounts which respect the 'pre-theoretical intuitions' of speakers. What does this mean exactly? It could be interpreted as little more than a statement of a general approach which linguists and pragmaticists follow, i.e. that we use intuitions as data and therefore would reject accounts which seem not to be consistent with our intuitions. However, we need to be aware that intuitions can be misleading. Within grammar, there are many examples of intuitions not directly reflecting underlying competence.

Recanati's focus was on determining the contents of what Grice called 'what is said'. At first glance, this might seem unproblematic. Gibbs and Moise (1997) carried out a number of experiments which, they claimed, supported the relevance-theoretic approach to the 'saying–implicating' distinction since subjects faced with a choice tended to pick more 'enriched', 'explicature-like' paraphrases of utterances such as (8a) rather than more minimal paraphrases which are closer to the Gricean idea of 'what is said' such as (8b):

(7)   We have two footballs.

(8) a.   We have at least two footballs and perhaps more.
    b.   We have exactly two footballs.

However, Nicolle and Clark (1999) showed that the choice of paraphrase was affected by the context. Speakers would pick more minimal paraphrases when these seemed more relevant and would even choose implicature paraphrases in some contexts. Nicolle and Clark suggested that subjects were, in effect, choosing the paraphrase which would make the best alternative utterance in the same context, i.e. the one which would be most likely to give rise to a similar interpretation. Despite these issues, the work of Gibbs and Moise, and of Nicolle and Clark, shows that subjects have fairly consistent shared intuitions, which makes it possible to develop further tests in this area. Further examples of experimental work are discussed in Section 12.5.3.

12.3.2   Corpora

Traditionally, the most common alternative to intuitions in studying language is the use of corpora. A corpus simply means a collection of examples of language use which has been annotated and organised in some way. In recent years, more and more corpora make use of computer and internet technology. It has become much easier to create large databases which are searchable in a variety of ways. There are many corpora available now, some of them available online.[3] Two corpora of English which are available online with samples available for free are the British National Corpus (www.natcorp.ox.ac.uk/) and the International Corpus of English (http://ice-corpora.net/ice/index.htm). There are, of course, many other corpora of English and of other languages. Perhaps the most striking use of internet resources is 'WebCorp' (www.webcorp.org.uk/), an online tool which aims to treat the whole of the web as one big corpus.

There has been considerable disagreement over the years about how useful corpus data can be. At its most extreme, there have been linguists who reject outright the relevance of particular kinds of data. Some linguists in the Chomskyan tradition have suggested that corpora cannot provide relevant data since they present only 'performance', i.e. language in use, rather than providing more direct evidence about 'competence', i.e. the underlying linguistic system. On the other hand, some linguists have suggested that intuitions are worthless compared to the 'naturally occurring data' found in corpora. However, if we take seriously the idea common in scientific work that any data can in principle be relevant, and that the key thing is how clearly we can show that it is relevant to the hypothesis we are investigating, then we should consider for each case how useful particular data are, whether they come from corpora, from intuitions, or from some other source. This is often tricky since so many factors are involved in producing data of any kind. More recently, linguists in general are more open to using a range of kinds of data and judging each particular piece of data-based research on its own merits. This has been reflected in growing interest in corpus data in pragmatics in general and in work in relevance theory in particular.[4]

One significant relevance-theoretic project which uses corpus data is the project titled 'A Unified Theory of Lexical Pragmatics' carried out by a team of researchers at University College London (www.ucl.ac.uk/psychlangsci/ research/linguistics/lexicalpragmatics/). Among other methods, this work used corpus data from the Bank of English (www.titania.bham.ac.uk/) and WordNet (wordnet.princeton.edu/) to test and develop hypotheses about lexical pragmatics (see Chapter 9 above). In particular, the corpus data provided evidence about how particular words are used by speakers. One example is the word *boiling* which can be used in the phrase *boiling water* to convey a concept with the following range of encyclopaedic properties, among others:

(9)   Encyclopaedic properties of different ad hoc concepts which might be
         communicated by the phrase *boiling water*:
   a.   SEETHES AND BUBBLES, HIDDEN UNDERCURRENTS, EMITS VAPOUR, etc.
   b.   TOO HOT TO WASH ONE'S HANDS IN, TOO HOT TO BATHE IN, etc.
   c.   SUITABLE FOR MAKING TEA, DANGEROUS TO TOUCH, etc.
   d.   SAFE TO USE IN STERILISING INSTRUMENTS, etc.
                                        (based on Wilson and Carston 2007)

The corpus data is mainly used here to find examples of the range of ways in which the term *boiling* is used in actual conversations.

12.3.3   Experiments

One of the most significant developments in methodology in recent years has been an increase in experimental approaches to pragmatics. This has been seen as especially important for relevance theory, since early work was largely based on data from intuitions and there was considerable discussion of whether and how it might be possible to develop other kinds of empirical tests. As Sperber and Noveck (2004) point out, the use of intuitions is not in itself problematic. However, they suggest, the reliance on intuitions

> has meant that preference for one theory over another is justified not in terms of crucial empirical tests but mostly on grounds of consistency, simplicity, explicitness, comprehensiveness, explanatory force, and integration with neighbouring fields. The development of experimental work has meant that there can be more directly empirical grounds for choosing one theory or approach over another.   (Sperber and Noveck 2004: 8)

Jorgensen, Miller and Sperber (1984) was an early example of experimental work on pragmatics. Since the 1990s, a large number of experimental studies have been carried out (for overviews, see Sperber and Noveck 2004 and Noveck and Sperber 2007). As we saw above, Gibbs and Moise (1997) and Nicolle and Clark (1999) carried out tests to explore intuitions about explicature and implicature. There have also been a number of developmental studies (see suggestions for further reading below) and some work exploring central notions of the theory, i.e. predictions which follow from the two Principles of Relevance.[5]

An early test of the central notions of relevance theory was Sperber, Cara and Girotto's (1995) paper on the Wason selection task (Wason 1966). In this task, subjects are asked to select from a number of items the ones which are relevant to testing a hypothesis. Here is a classic formulation of the task:

Here are four cards. Each has a letter on one side and number on the other side. Two of these cards are with the letter side up and two with the number side up:

| A | G | 7 | 8 |

Indicate which of these cards you need to turn over in order to judge whether the following rule is true:

if there is an A on one side, there is a 7 on the other side

Most subjects faced with this task suggest that the cards to turn over are the card with the A visible and the card with the 7 visible. In fact, though, the logically correct answer is that subjects should turn over the card with the A and the card with the 8. Subjects are right to turn over the A card, since anything other than a 7 on the other side would show that the hypothesis is false. They are also right not to turn over the G card as there is no claim about what is on the other side of cards with a G on one side. Turning over the card with a 7 is not relevant. If there is an A on the other side, that is consistent with the hypothesis. If there is anything else on the other side, that is also consistent since the hypothesis is about cards with an A. The card with an 8 should be turned over since an A on the other side would invalidate the hypothesis by showing that some cards with an A on one side do not have a 7 on the other side.

One way to summarise the selection task is to say that it is about presenting a hypothesis which has the logical structure of a conditional of the form *if P then Q* and then showing subjects four cards corresponding to *P*, *not P*, *Q* and *not Q*. A correct response is one which selects the card corresponding to *P* and the card corresponding to *not Q*. This is because evidence which would invalidate the hypothesis would be in the form *P and not Q*. Since Wason first discussed the task, there has been a huge amount of research on the selection task and factors which contribute to success in the task. Sperber, Cara and Girotto developed versions of the task designed to explore the possibility that relevance-theoretic assumptions could explain what makes some versions of the task easier than others. In particular, they claimed that versions where the 'correct' response was made more relevant (by reducing effort and increasing effects) would be easier than versions where the 'correct' response was less relevant (relatively hard to process and yielding relatively few effects). The results confirmed the hypothesis. Subjects did best on versions of the task where 'correct' responses were low in effort and high in effects, did worst on versions where these were effortful and low in effects. For 'high effort, high effects' and 'low effort, low effects' versions, the success rates were somewhere in the middle. There has been further discussion of this work (see, for example, Fiddick, Cosmides and Tooby 2000; Sperber and Girotto 2002, 2003) but the key thing to stress here is that this work showed that it is possible to develop tests which explore predictions following from central tenets of relevance theory.

Another area where there has been a significant amount of research has focused on scalar implicature and the question of whether inferences such as (11) are generated by default (i.e. automatically and immediately) when interpreting utterances such as (10) (for a summary of work in this area, see Noveck and Sperber 2007):

(10)   Some of the students enjoyed the lecture.

(11)   Not all of the students enjoyed the lecture.

Levinson (2000), for example, claims that (11) follows from (10) by default, i.e. that hearers of an utterance containing the term *some* automatically access an implicature such as (11) at the outset, which they may later reject if this is clearly not consistent with other contextual assumptions. To take a very simple example, this might occur in the following exchange:

(12)   KEN: I really hope at least some of the students enjoyed the lecture.
          BEV: I looked at the feedback sheets. They all said that they enjoyed it. So you can be absolutely sure of it. Some of the students enjoyed the lecture.

On the relevance-theoretic approach, there is no assumption of a default inference. Addressees will start from the encoded meaning of *some* (as 'more than one') and make further assumptions depending on the contextual assumptions available to them at the time. Noveck and Sperber (2007: 196) summarise different predictions made by 'GCI theories' ('generalised conversational implicature theories') such as Levinson's and those of relevance theory. Since GCI theories assume default enrichment followed by contextual cancellation in some contexts, then we might expect a 'literal' interpretation in such a context to take longer than a 'non-literal' interpretation where default enrichment is not cancelled. Since relevance theory assumes that enrichment takes place only when it is contextually motivated, then literal interpretations should be faster and non-literal interpretations slower.

A large number of experiments have tested these predictions. Noveck and Sperber suggest that the evidence so far lends more support to the relevance-theoretic approach by showing that scalar implicatures are not immediately accessed, but take time to develop. However, further research is ongoing and they point out that, even if we accept that the evidence is, so far, more for than against relevance theory:

> Does this mean that relevance theory is true and GCI theory is false? Of course not ... we do not expect readers to form a final judgement on the respective merits of GCI theory and relevance theory on the basis of the experimental evidence presented. What we do hope is to have convinced you that, alongside other kinds of data, properly devised experimental evidence can be highly pertinent to the discussion of pragmatic issues, and that pragmaticists – and in particular students of pragmatics – might greatly benefit from becoming familiar with relevant experimental work and from contributing to it (possibly in interdisciplinary ventures).
>
> (Noveck and Sperber 2007: 209–10)

12.3.4   Texts

Another source of data comes from example texts. Looking at particular texts could be thought of as a variety of corpus work but I have decided to discuss these separately since different methodology is involved in analysing particular texts as distinct from looking at collections of utterances and investigating trends across them. Here, the technique involved can be focused in two directions. Some approaches will focus on explaining how a text works by applying ideas from pragmatic and/or other theories. Others will focus on testing predictions of theories by looking at the extent to which particular texts conform to them. Since relevance theory considers and makes predictions about all kinds of ostensive communicative acts, the texts to be considered can include nonverbal and 'mixed mode' texts, i.e. texts which combine verbal and nonverbal material.

Another important area which can be thought of in this way is the application of ideas from relevance theory to stylistic analysis. We will discuss this kind of work again in Section 12.6.2 below. It might be worth noting, however, that we are looking at 'texts' every time we consider an example of any type. There is, of course, a difference between looking at a constructed example dreamt up by a theorist to make a point and an actual utterance produced naturally in order to communicate something. Note, however, that literary and other fictional texts have a slightly unusual status with regard to this. They are 'natural' in that actual human beings produce them. They are 'unnatural' in that they are created for literary or other effects, not always spontaneous, and often intended to represent something which someone else might say or have said rather than being simple spontaneous utterances produced by speakers in 'natural' contexts.

12.3.5   Misunderstandings and meaning disputes

Related to other kinds of work focusing on texts, another interesting though not much developed kind of test and application of relevance theory involves looking at cases where there are disputes about meanings. This often involves someone expressing unhappiness or taking offence at someone else's utterance. The response will often be to deny that the original speaker intended the meaning taken by the offended party. This can be illustrated by artistic examples where an artist or performer is accused of causing offence and denies this intention, such as John Lennon's famous utterance (13), which he later apologised for, saying of the pop group The Beatles:

(13)   We're more popular than Jesus now.

In apologising, Lennon explained that he was not aiming to make a comment on the Beatles particularly but more about how interest in religion was less strong than previously among young people. In one discussion, he suggested that:

(14)   If I'd said television is more popular than Jesus, I might have got away with it.

Pragmatic theories might be expected to discuss the details of Lennon's original intention, how it was interpreted and what evidence there was for what he later claimed was his intended interpretation.

An interesting, though slightly different, example is the response given by the film-maker Luis Buñuel when asked about the meaning of his film *Un Chien Andalou*. He replied that it was:

(15)   Nothing more than a desperate, passionate appeal to murder.

Clearly, Buñuel's response is partly informed by an awareness of more typical kinds of debate about artistic intention and poses the problem that we do not know what exactly he means by this.

Finally, of course, misunderstandings occur frequently in everyday conversation. These include relatively trivial examples which are easy to clear up such as (16):

(16)   (*Ken is standing in the kitchen holding a kettle*)
            KEN: Did you remember to pay the gas bill?
            BEV: Thanks. Yes, I'd love a cup.

Here, Bev has not really paid attention to Ken's words but made an inference mainly based on visual evidence. It is clear what has gone wrong and it will be quite easy for Ken to ask again and for both Ken and Bev to see how the misunderstanding arose.

A more subtle example involves the use of first names with the intention of seeming friendly, something which might easily backfire. I was once asked the following question by a car salesman soon after he had asked me my name:

(17)   Have you ever driven a Nissan before, Billy?

He proceeded to use my name frequently throughout our conversation, no doubt hoping to seem friendly and approachable. Instead, this approach made me conclude that he was at least slightly manipulative and perhaps not to be trusted.

Examples such as this are clearly ones which pragmatic theories should help to explain and exploring them can help us to develop our theories.[6]

12.3.6   Other data

Of course, as we said, there is no principled reason to decide in advance what kinds of data might be relevant to testing and developing a theory. There may well be relevant data which have not yet been considered. In each case, the theorist who claims that some data are relevant will need to explain how exactly the particular data are relevant. Relevance theorists, like other theorists, will continue to look for new kinds of data which will test and help to develop the theory.

12.4   Linguistic and pragmatic development, translation and evolution

One question which has been raised about Grice's approach concerns the origin of his pragmatic principles, i.e. the maxims of conversation. Are they social conventions which speakers learn? Are they innate universals which develop as individuals mature? Assumptions about the nature of the key components of relevance theory have developed over the years, but one idea present from the beginnings of the theory is the idea that it replaces the vaguer notions of a 'Cooperative Principle' and 'maxims' with generalisations about human cognition and communication. As with other aspects of cognition, we expect these proposals to lead to further investigations of how these features are acquired and develop. Even in the earliest stages of the theory, it was clear that relevance theory made more precise claims than Grice in this area since the (Communicative) Principle of Relevance was to be understood as a generalisation about communication backed by a generalisation about cognition. In more recent versions, as we have seen, both generalisations are described as 'principles'. If these assumptions are on the right lines, then we should expect to be able to investigate some of the details of how these biological systems develop as humans grow. Any theory which assumes that pragmatic principles are universal should be expected to develop an account of how the principles are acquired. In recent years, a number of studies have started to shed some light on how the story might go. This section begins by considering how pragmatic abilities might develop in general and how this might relate to language acquisition, before moving on to consider the role of pragmatics in second language acquisition and, from a much wider perspective, how pragmatic systems and abilities might have evolved.

12.4.1   Pragmatic development and language acquisition

There are a number of ways in which we might begin to investigate how pragmatic abilities develop in individuals over time and several of these have been investigated by researchers (see suggestions for further reading below). Relevant studies include ones which study general topics such as the development of 'theory of mind' abilities (a classic source on this is Baron-Cohen 1995) and ones which study specific pragmatic phenomena such as the comprehension of irony, metaphor and particular kinds of implicature. In particular, as mentioned above, there has been a considerable body of work exploring the development of scalar implicature.

In one important study, Noveck (2001) compared the way in which children and adults responded to a number of utterances when asked simply to say whether or not they agreed with them. The utterances included the following (these are English translations of French utterances used in the experiments):

(18)   Some stores are made of bubbles.

(19)   Some birds live in cages.

(20)   Some giraffes have long necks.

(18) was classified as an 'absurd' utterance, (19) as 'appropriate', (20) as 'inappropriate'. (18) is absurd so we expect subjects not to agree with it. (19) is true and 'appropriate' in that there is no pragmatic problem with it. (20) is also true but this one is 'inappropriate' for pragmatic reasons. The key difference between (19) and (20) is that some birds live in cages while others do not but most people assume that all giraffes have long necks and not only some of them. Most pragmatic theories assume that utterances containing the term *some* (*certains* in the French utterances used here) often implicate 'not all'. Given this, (20) might seem odd. If all giraffes have long necks, why state only that '*some*' do? Noveck found significant differences among children and adults in their responses to (20). 89% of children aged 7 to 8 agreed with it. 85% of children aged 10 to 11 agreed with it. Only 41% of adults agreed. This suggests, then, either that children do not draw the inference from 'some' to 'not all' as often as grownups or that they are more 'tolerant' of pragmatic infelicity.

12.4.2   Second language acquisition

Of course, we need not restrict developmental studies to what might happen when acquiring our first language or before that stage. It is also interesting to consider how pragmatics might be involved in the acquisition of second languages. A number of researchers have looked at pragmatics in second language acquisition.[7] Foster-Cohen (2000) suggests that the technical notion of 'relevance' helps to clarify ideas which have been expressed using an informal notion of relevance in the past. More specifically, of course, we assume that pragmatic principles are universal so the 'specialness' of pragmatics in second language contexts is not to do with pragmatics varying cross-linguistically but must be due to more general cultural differences, varying availability of particular contextual assumptions, and, of course, differences in linguistic competence. Jodlowiec (2010) surveys previous work in this area and makes some specific suggestions for future work, suggesting that relevance-theoretic ideas can be applied not only in developing theories of second language acquisition but also in the development of classroom practice.

12.4.3   Translation

There have been a number of studies which apply relevance-theoretic ideas to the study of translation.[8] Perhaps the most comprehensive model of translation developed within a relevance-theoretic framework is Gutt's (1991) model which considers the translator's task with reference to a model of the cognitive environments of original author, translator, original target audience and translator's target audience. Thinking of things in this way, it becomes clearer that translation is not very different from other kinds of verbal communication.

Suppose I am about to speak to you. Let's say that I want you to bring salt and pepper to the table as we are about to eat. I am just sitting down and you have just arrived in the kitchen. I could utter any of the following:

(21)   Could you bring the salt and pepper to the table please?

(22)   Go and bring the salt and pepper to the table, will you?

(23)   Damn, I forgot to bring the salt and pepper.

(24)   While you're up?

What will lead me to choose one of these over the others? Naturally, this depends on what I think you will make of each of them, which in turn depends on what range of assumptions you are likely to access when interpreting my utterance. (21) is a fairly polite request. (22) is less polite, more informal and suggests a friendly and relaxed relationship. (23) is also informal and more indirect. (24) depends on a very good understanding between speaker and hearer. It might be appropriate if the two people involved have discussed the use of this phrase before and it will depend on the hearer knowing that it is salt and pepper which the speaker wants to be brought to the table. Differences in available assumptions will affect not just whether the addressee knows that this is a request for salt and pepper but also a number of aspects of the social relationship between the speaker and the hearer.

The situation is more complicated when there is more than one addressee. When I talk in class, I try to use formulations that will make sense for everyone. Sometimes, I indicate an awareness of differences, and highlight it for the students, by saying something like (25) or (26):

(25)   Some of you will have looked at this topic before.

(26)   Have any of you looked at work on implicature before?

The situation is even more complex when audiences are particularly large, say when writing a newspaper article or a novel. Here the writer needs to represent the sets of assumptions shared by a large number of people. Of course, assumptions will vary greatly and so the writer has less control over how her utterance might be interpreted than in face-to-face speech with one other person.

What is common to all of these cases, and to all utterances, is that communicators will shape their utterances based on assumptions they make about assumptions their addressees are likely to access. Gutt's work models the more complicated situation facing translators. Translators need to model the assumptions of original communicators and their audiences and then to model the assumptions of the target audience for their translation. At each stage, they will need to make decisions about how closely the target audience's assumptions will resemble the original audience's assumptions and also about the nature of specific linguistic forms available in the two languages.

We can illustrate how this applies to specific cases by considering (21)–(24). If I am to translate one of these options into another language, I need to think about the contextual assumptions available to the original addressee and how the speaker imagined them when choosing how to formulate the utterance. Suppose, for example, that the original utterance was (22), repeated here as (27):

(27)   Go and bring the salt and pepper to the table, will you?

Let's imagine this is the first utterance in a British film appearing in 2013. The translator needs to think about how this will be understood by members of its original audience, knowing that not all members of that audience will interpret it in the same way. Simplifying greatly, assumptions the translator makes might include:

(28) a.   This is a fairly informal way of asking for the salt and pepper.
     b.   This is the kind of utterance appropriate between people who are quite close and have a friendly relationship.
     c.   Not every member of the audience will be familiar with the '*go and ...*' construction.

Part of the translator's task might be seen as to find a formulation in the new language which is similar in its informality and suggestion of a close relationship while also being one which not all members of the audience will be familiar with. Of course, translation always involves compromise. Perhaps the translator will find a form which is consistent with (28a) and (28b) but which is likely to be known to everyone in the target audience. Or perhaps she will find a form that is slightly less familiar but shares the property of not being known to everyone in the target audience. In this situation, the translator is likely to pick the former option if she prioritises implications about the relationship between the characters over the possibility of some audience members being confused by the utterance.

A pragmatic theory should also help to address more serious difficulties faced by translators. Boase-Beier (2009) discusses difficulties raised for translators by the German word *wenn* which has meanings corresponding both to English *if* and to *when*. Another example is Beckett's play *Waiting For Godot*. Beckett originally wrote the play in French with the title *En Attendant Godot*. Introducing Chekhov's play *Three Sisters*, Gilman (2003: xxx) suggests that Beckett made a mistake by not including the word *while* in his English version. Gilman suggests that this would have made more salient the idea that the play is about how the two main characters fill the time while they wait for someone who will not be arriving. Beckett had the option of including a word corresponding to *en* in his English version. However, it is not the case that *En Attendant Godot* is a straightforward equivalent to *While Waiting For Godot* nor that *Attendant Godot* is equivalent to *Waiting For Godot*. The issues raised by all of these forms are about the intentions of communicators and how particular formulations will be understood by particular audiences. Clearly, these are questions about pragmatics and we would expect a pragmatic theory such as relevance theory to help explain the processes involved in translation and to have practical implications for translators.

12.4.4   Evolution

Related to the topic of how pragmatics develops in individuals is the question of how pragmatics has evolved in humans. There has been renewed interest in questions about language evolution in recent years. This discussion is necessarily quite speculative but it is possible to develop arguments which can be scrutinised on logical and other grounds, even if it is not possible to carry out direct empirical research. Similarly, there has been increased discussion of how pragmatic abilities might have evolved, including discussion within a relevance-theoretic framework (for a general discussion, see Wharton 2006).

Sperber (1995) speculates on the development of pragmatics by imagining two human ancestors, Jack and Jill, 'a million years ago'. He imagines Jack watching Jill eating berries. As he points out, if Jack sees Jill's behaviour as intentional and attributes to her the belief that the berries are edible, then he has 'metarepresentational' ability, i.e. the ability to represent the representations of others.[9] As Sperber points out, being able to make inferences such as this means that Jack can learn things about the world which are not based on his own direct experience.

Sperber then imagines that Jill knows that Jack will make inferences based on her actions. She might, for example, not be picking the berries in order to eat them, but instead be picking them precisely in order to inform Jack that the berries are edible. She might even be trying to misinform Jack and trick him into eating berries which she actually believes are poisonous. Sperber sees this scenario as closer to verbal communication. The key difference here is that although Jill is intentionally conveying information to Jack, she is not overtly communicating. Her intention to communicate to Jack is not overt. What is needed for this to count as ostensive-inferential communication is for Jill to make mutually manifest to Jack and herself that she is intending to inform him of something. If Jill knows that Jack can understand her behaviour as ostensive, she no longer even needs to eat the berries. She can gesture towards them and mimic eating them, trusting Jack to be able to infer what she is communicating. This is not linguistic communication but it is ostensive-inferential communication of the type governed by pragmatic principles. Once language has evolved, Jill can communicate simply by saying something such as *'eat'* or *'good'*. Sperber concludes:

> The new story, then, is that human communication is a by-product of human meta-representational capacities. The ability to perform sophisticated inferences about each other's states of mind evolved in our ancestors as a means of understanding and predicting each other's behavior. This in turn gave rise to the possibility of acting openly so as to reveal one's thoughts to others. As a consequence, the conditions were created for the evolution of language. Language made inferential communication immensely more effective. It did not change its character. All human communication, linguistic or non-linguistic, is essentially inferential. Whether we give evidence of our thoughts by picking berries, by mimicry, by speaking, or by writing – as I have just done –, we rely first and foremost on our audience's ability to infer our meaning.   (Sperber 1995: 199)

This is, of course, largely speculative and merely shows that ostensive communication *might* have evolved in this way. Future work will aim to flesh out the picture, based on theoretical argument and possibly evidence from further investigation of the processes and structure of the mind, some examples of which are discussed in the next section.

12.5   Pragmatics and the mind

One of the key features of relevance theory has always been its cognitive orientation. It assumes a theory of 'mental architecture', i.e. a theory of how the mind is organised overall, which means that it can be fully explicit about how various aspects of cognitive and pragmatic processing are connected. Initially, it adopted a framework based on Fodor's modularity thesis for the mind in general and a broadly Chomskyan approach to language. (The ideas about language were only broadly Chomskyan since Chomsky explicitly rejected the idea that the linguistic system could be a module in Fodor's sense.) This section begins by discussing assumptions about modularity. It then considers non-linguistic aspects of the mind which are relevant to pragmatic processing and cases where individuals have problems with particular kinds of processing or representation. Looking at phenomena such as autistic spectrum disorder helps us to understand how the mind is organised, what is involved in pragmatic processing and how pragmatic theories might be applied in understanding and possibly developing treatments for such disorders.

12.5.1   Modularity and mental architecture

As mentioned above, relevance theory was initially developed on the assumption that it would be compatible with a broadly Chomskyan notion of language and Fodorian assumptions about the modularity of mind (Fodor 1983). The approach is Chomskyan in that it assumes a distinction between language and other aspects of cognition. Within linguistics, this distinction is often seen as one between 'formalists', who think that language can be studied independently of its function, and 'functionalists', who think that language exists in order to convey meanings and that its function may have affected its form. Chomskyan formalists assume a distinction between 'competence' and 'performance'. Functionalists such as Michael Halliday (Halliday and Matthiessen 2004; see also Thompson 2004) assume that the point of language is to convey meanings and so discussion of any linguistic form must simultaneously involve discussion of its functions. A more recent approach which rejects the separation of linguistic knowledge from cognition in general is cognitive linguistics (for an introduction, see Evans and Green 2006). On this approach, there is no autonomous language faculty and knowledge of language develops from language use. Within Chomsky's approach, connections between linguistic forms and other kinds of knowledge are dealt with at 'interfaces' such as 'Logical Form' ('LF') which is the location of the interface with meaning or 'semantic interpretation'.

In a Chomskyan approach to language, it is possible to study the linguistic system independently of how language is used. Chomsky has often suggested (e.g. in Chomsky 1986) that study of the nature of language logically precedes study of language use since we cannot study how language is used until we know what kind of thing language is. More recent Chomskyan work, in the 'minimalist' framework (for introductions, see Adger 2003; Cook and Newson 2007), has focused more closely on the nature of interfaces so that it is less far removed from accounts of actual processing than previous approaches. Fodor's approach, by contrast, sees the linguistic system as a module, or 'input system' which connects a particular kind of input (low-level phonetic representations) with a particular kind of output ('shallow' semantic representations). Relevance theory is Chomskyan in that it assumes that the linguistic system is independent of other kinds of knowledge and Fodorian in that it assumes a modular architecture.

Initially, relevance theory assumed that the output of the language module was an incomplete conceptual representation which provides input to 'unencapsulated' (non-modular) central processes. Pragmatic processing was seen as having free access to information from a wide range of sources (including perception, inference, long- and short-term memory, output from other modules, even assumptions created on the spot as part of the interpretation process). Wilson and Sperber (1986) provided strong arguments against the assumption that the linguistic input system contained a code-like 'pragmatics module' capable of assigning speaker's meanings to any utterance in context. If pragmatics is part of the central system, however, Fodor suggested we would be able to find out very little about how it works. Fodor believed that modular processes could be studied scientifically precisely because they are encapsulated and use information only from a restricted domain. He suggested that we could not expect to understand wide-ranging central processes such as scientific theorising or pragmatic processing. Sperber and Wilson's development of relevance theory was presented as an attempt to meet this challenge and show that one area of central processing, pragmatics, is indeed one which can be studied, where we can develop our understanding and where we can make testable predictions. They make this point, for example, in Chapter 2 of the book *Relevance* (Sperber and Wilson 1986) and in Wilson and Sperber (1993). They believed that this was possible because pragmatic processing is a task that we know individuals perform fast, spontaneously, and with considerable success.

More recently, relevance theorists have been rethinking the nature of the modular systems involved in pragmatics.[10] Dan Sperber (1994a, 2001) began this line of thinking by pointing out that since Fodor's work on modularity of mind, cognitive scientists had discovered many more potential modules, which were not 'input systems' in Fodor's sense, but which took conceptual representations from a particular cognitive domain as input and performed inferences over them. An early example was the so-called '"theory of mind" module', which attributed beliefs and intentions to individuals on the basis of their behaviour. This proliferation of modules had been described by Fodor (1987: 27) as 'modularity theory gone mad'.[11] Nevertheless, Sperber defends a 'massive modularity' thesis in which many inferences were performed by specialised modular mechanisms which apply only in particular domains. On this view, not all modules are 'input systems', and a rather broader definition of modules is used. Wilson describes this broader view by suggesting that modules might be understood as 'dedicated mechanisms ... which cannot be seen as special cases of more general mechanisms operating in broader domains' (Wilson 2005: 1131). Pragmatic inferences seem to be modular in this broader sense.

Recent work in relevance theory argues that pragmatic inference may be carried out by a domain-specific comprehension mechanism, which is one of a number of sub-modules or mechanisms which together account for our ability to attribute mental states to others. This ability is usually referred to as 'theory of mind'.[12] A central component of this comprehension sub-module would be the relevance-guided comprehension heuristic discussed above. Sperber and Wilson (2002) say that this approach

> defends the broadly Gricean view that pragmatic interpretation is ultimately an exercise in mind-reading, involving the inferential attribution of intentions. We argue, however, that the interpretation process does not simply consist in applying general mind-reading abilities to a particular (communicative) domain. Rather, it involves a dedicated comprehension module, with its own special principles and mechanisms.   (Sperber and Wilson 2002: 3)

They present a number of arguments for this view, partly based on considering how the processes involved in pragmatic interpretation might have evolved. They suggest that the nature of comprehension lends itself to the development of a dedicated module responsible for inferring communicators' meanings. The argument is based partly on a distinction between 'intuitive' and 'reflective' inferences. Grice's way of describing the inferences involved in deriving implicatures makes this sound like a reflective process, e.g. when he discusses inferential steps along the lines of the speaker being able to see that such-and-such an inference is required. However, Grice also describes implicature as something that is 'capable of being' worked out rather than being explicitly worked out, so he need not be seen as committing himself to a lengthy and explicit rational process. Sperber and Wilson point out that 2-year-old children who struggle with first order false belief tasks are capable of inferring communicators' meanings. This suggests that comprehension need not involve a working-out process of the complexity often assumed in Gricean and post-Gricean theories. Pragmatic processes are fast and seem to be unreflective. There are cases where individuals have specific enhanced pragmatic abilities and specific kinds of pragmatic breakdown. Wilson and Sperber claim that all of these things suggest a dedicated mechanism rather than simply the application of Fodorian central processes.

Sperber and Wilson also consider that 'mind-reading' (or the attribution of mental states to others) is so complex that there are likely to be a number of sub-modules dedicated to particular aspects of this overall task. Here they suggest a module for one of the sub-tasks involved:

> Given the complexity of mind-reading, the variety of tasks it has to perform, and the particular regularities exhibited by some of these tasks, it is quite plausible to assume that it involves a variety of sub-modules. A likely candidate for one sub-module of the mind-reading mechanism is the ability, already present in infants, to infer what people are seeing or watching from

the direction of their gaze. Presumably, the infant (or indeed the adult) who performs this sort of inference is not feeding a general-purpose inferential mechanism with, say, a conditional major premise of the form 'If the direction of gaze of a person P is towards an object O, then P is seeing O' and a minor premise of the form 'Mummy's direction of gaze is towards the cat' in order to derive the conclusion: 'Mummy is seeing the cat.' ... In other words, the inference involved is not just an application of a relatively general and internally undifferentiated mind-reading module to the specific problem of inferring perceptual state from direction of gaze. It is much more plausible that humans are equipped from infancy with a dedicated module, an Eye Direction Detector (Baron-Cohen, 1995), which exploits the de facto strong correlation between direction of gaze and visual perception, and directly attributes perceptual and attentional states on the basis of direction of gaze.   (Sperber and Wilson 2002: 12)

They take this line of reasoning also to suggest the existence of a dedicated module which carries out the tasks involved in inferring communicators' meanings on the basis of their behaviour.

The idea that there is a pragmatics module capable of inferring communicators' meanings would help to explain why pragmatic processing does have some properties of Fodorian modules, such as speed and mandatoriness. Evidence that individual performance on pragmatics can be significantly better or worse than performance in other areas also supports the idea of a pragmatics module. There is, of course, evidence for this in the developmental work and work with people with autistic spectrum disorder mentioned above which we will consider again in the next section.

12.5.2   Mind-reading, metarepresentation and theory of mind

In recent years, the term 'mind-reading' has been used to refer to the ability to infer the beliefs, desires and intentions (or more generally, mental states) of others in order to explain and predict their behaviour. The ability to 'read minds' in this way clearly involves metarepresentations, i.e. representations of representations. (29)–(31) are examples of metarepresentations:

(29)   John wants to eat some ice-cream.

(30)   John believes there is ice-cream in the fridge.

(31)   [John is walking towards the fridge because] he intends to get some ice-cream to eat.

The ability to entertain representations such as these, or to 'mind-read', has been described in the past under the slightly misleading label 'theory of mind'. Recent work has followed up on insights gained in pragmatics, in developmental studies, and in work with people with autistic spectrum disorders, to develop fuller accounts of the nature of the metarepresentational abilities involved in cognition and communication.[13]

Sperber (1994b) proposes three possible strategies which might be used in pragmatic interpretation and which vary in terms of how much metarepresentational ability they require. These are 'naïve optimism', 'cautious optimism' and 'sophisticated understanding'. An interpreter who follows the 'naïve optimist' strategy will interpret communicative acts on the assumption that the communicator is both 'competent' enough to achieve optimal relevance and 'benevolent' enough not to lead the interpreter astray. A naïve optimist will assume that the speaker of (32) knows what the hearer likes to eat and is not intending to deceive the hearer:

(32)   If you're hungry, there's something delicious in the freezer.

A naïve optimist will be satisfied as soon as they find an interpretation which seems relevant enough and will not consider other possibilities, such as that the speaker is mistaken about what is in the fridge or is trying to mislead the hearer.

A 'cautious optimist' will be able to consider the possibility that the communicator is 'benevolent' but not 'competent', and so may be able to arrive at an interpretation which, while not actually relevant, is one which a communicator aiming at optimal relevance might have intended. Suppose that the hearer of (32) does not like ice-cream but has no memory of ever mentioning this to the speaker. In this case, he might entertain the possibility that the speaker is mistakenly informing him that there is ice-cream in the freezer thinking that the hearer will consider ice-cream a delicious treat.

A 'sophisticated understander' will be aware not only that communicators sometimes make mistakes but also that they might sometimes be intentionally deceitful. This means that they may be able to arrive at interpretations which are not in fact relevant, but which a deceitful interpreter might have intended them to accept as relevant. The hearer of (32), for example, might suspect the speaker of sending them on a wild goose chase and doubt whether there really is anything interesting in the freezer. Sperber (1994b) illustrates the possibility by discussing different possible interpretations of (33) produced by someone called Carol to her partner John when they are out at a party (I've adapted the details here):

(33)   It's late.

In this context, John is likely to take Carol to be saying that it is relatively late in the evening. How late? Suppose Carol and John have a babysitter who can only stay until a certain time. Then John will assume that Carol means it's late enough for them to need to go home so that the babysitter will not be inconvenienced. Now let's suppose there is some deception here. Suppose that the babysitter has explicitly told Carol that he doesn't mind how late they come home. If John doesn't know about this, he will still think that they need to leave to relieve the babysitter. Now let's suppose that John knows that Carol knows that the babysitter can stay late. Still, he will assume that she is implicating that they should go home. He recognises Carol's intention as follows:

(34)   Carol intends John to know that Carol intends John to believe that it is time to go home.

The fact that she intends to deceive him is not inconsistent with (34) and John will still recognise Carol's intended meaning. This is possible because John has sufficient metarepresentational ability to attribute to Carol intentions which include an intention to deceive.

As Sperber points out, these strategies correspond to different levels of metarepresentational ability. A naïve optimist need not represent the communicator's thoughts at all in arriving at a hypothesis about the communicator's meaning. A cautious optimist can think about what the communicator might have thought would be an appropriate interpretation. A sophisticated understander can go even further and think about what the communicator might have intended the interpreter to think would be an appropriate interpretation. These three strategies can be linked to the more or less sophisticated expectations of relevance that hearers bring to utterances: an interpreter who is a naïve optimist will expect actual relevance, a cautious optimist will expect attempted relevance, and a sophisticated understander will expect purported relevance. These expectations may, of course, be adjusted in the course of the interpretation process. Understanding these strategies might shed light on aspects of pragmatic development and on the behaviour of people with conditions which affect pragmatic performance, such as autism or Asperger's syndrome.[14]

12.6   Words and beyond

As we have seen, the Communicative Principle of Relevance applies to both verbal and nonverbal communication. This section considers some of the different modes of verbal communication and some of the ways in which ostensive-inferential communication can take place other than with the use of words.

12.6.1   Speech, signing and writing

This section has the relatively simple aim of reminding you that verbal communication comes in different forms. It may be spoken, signed or written. Speech involves the production of sequences of sounds to be understood as realisations of linguistic forms. Signing involves bodily movements understood as realisations of linguistic forms. Writing involves the production of visual stimuli understood as realisations of linguistic forms. Writing is sometimes designed to be read silently by the reader and sometimes to be spoken or signed aloud.

Work in pragmatics tends to focus on how speech, signing and writing are understood, i.e. on the inferences made by the addressees in each case. This is what I have done in most of this book. However, it is not true that pragmatic theories in general, or relevance theory in particular, have nothing to say about the processes involved in producing acts of verbal communication. Some theorists explicitly argue that it is important to see communication as something which involves the interaction of communicators and interpreters. Jenny Thomas, for example, stresses the importance of the idea that meaning arises from interaction:

> meaning is not something that is inherent in the words alone, nor is it produced by the speaker alone, nor by the hearer alone. Making meaning is a dynamic process, involving the negotiation of meaning between speaker and hearer, the context of an utterance … and the meaning potential of an utterance.   (Thomas 1995: 22)

Even approaches which seem to be 'hearer-oriented', such as Grice and relevance theory, include statements about what speakers, signers and writers do. Here, for example, is part of Grice's 'general pattern for the working out of a conversational implicature':

> He has said that p; there is no reason to suppose that he is not observing the maxims, or at least the Cooperative Principle; he could not be doing this unless he thought that q; he knows (and knows that I know that he knows) that I can see that the supposition that he thinks that q is required; he has done nothing to stop me thinking that q; he intends me to think, or is at least willing to allow me to think, that q; and so he has implicated that q.
> (Grice 1989: 31)

While this is about an inferential process followed by the hearer, it is clear that Grice envisages the hearer making assumptions about what the speaker is thinking, including what the speaker is thinking about what the hearer is thinking. And so on.

As we have seen above, relevance theory adapts the Gricean picture about intentions using the notion of **manifestness** (where something is manifest to an individual if that individual is capable of entertaining it and representing it as true or probably true). They suggest that:

> A communicator who produces an ostensive stimulus is trying to fulfil two intentions: … the informative intention, to make manifest to her audience a set of assumptions … and the communicative intention, to make her informative intention mutually manifest.   (Sperber and Wilson 1986: 163)

So relevance theory also makes claims about what the communicator does.[15]

12.6.2   Stylistics and literary studies

Pragmatic processes are, of course, involved in understanding all kinds of ostensive acts. This section considers how ideas from relevance theory have been applied in work which aims to account for the ways in which particular linguistic formulations give rise to particular kinds of effects, i.e. stylistics, and in work which focuses on one particular kind of texts, i.e.

in literary studies. Naturally, a number of relevance theorists have suggested that accounts of how texts give rise to effects on readers must include an account of the inferential processes they give rise to, i.e. of pragmatics. There have been a number of kinds of applications of relevance theory to stylistics.[16]

Naturally, work in stylistics has implications for literary studies, since literary works illustrate the phenomena focused on by stylistic analyses. However, there are other ways in which relevance theory has been seen as relevant to literary studies. Furlong (1996, 2001, 2011) has considered the nature of literariness itself, arguing that literariness should be understood as a property of interpretations. In particular, she distinguishes 'spontaneous' from 'non-spontaneous' interpretations. Spontaneous interpretations are typical of everyday exchanges where hearers follow the relevance-guided comprehension heuristic and stop when they have found an interpretation which the communicator could have intended to be relevant. Non-spontaneous interpretations go further than this, looking for further evidence and further possible interpretations, weighing them up and considering how likely each of them are. Of course, this is a matter of degree and interpretations can be more or less spontaneous.[17]

12.6.3   Modes and media

An area of work in which there has been increased interest in recent years concerns the fact that communication comes in more than one 'mode' and often in more than one mode at the same time. A mode simply means a channel of communication. A radio broadcast is in one mode. A photograph is another. A film is in two modes: speech and image. Communication in more than one mode is referred to as 'multimodal'. Before saying something about relevance theory and different modes, there are two things which I think I should highlight. Of course, almost all discourse takes place in more than one mode. In an everyday conversation, for example, speakers will usually be visible to hearers and will accompany their speech with body movements. Even if a speaker does not do much when speaking, this can still be seen as a choice which has some effect on how the utterance is understood.

Naturally, relevance theorists have been interested in how the effects of different stimuli are combined in understanding communicative acts. Forceville (1996, 2000, 2002, 2010) has studied how images and multimodal texts are understood from a relevance-theoretic point of view. Yus (1998a, 2009) has developed a unified relevance-theoretic account of visual and verbal metaphor. A number of theorists have worked on modelling multimodal comprehension, in some cases combining this with experimental work.[18]

Work on media communication naturally involves considering how input from different modes is combined. There has been a wide range of work on this topic.[19]

12.6.4   Prosody

It is clear that prosody plays a number of important roles in utterance production and interpretation and of course linguists have been interested in this for many years. The nature of the contribution of prosody to meaning raises a number of difficult questions which any semanticist or pragmaticist will be interested in exploring. These include questions about the nature of prosody in general as well as how it contributes to specific interpretations. A number of relevance theorists have considered prosodic meaning over the years, addressing both the larger and the more specific questions. Many of these questions were the subject of sustained discussion in the work of Bolinger (see, for example, the papers collected in Bolinger 1986, 1989) and, to some extent, the relevance-theoretic work can be seen as responding to Ladd's comment:

> there has been very little real debate on [the issue of how to account for intonational meaning]. I think this is primarily because we know too little about pragmatic inference for the debate to be conclusive   (Ladd 1996: 101)

Naturally, relevance theorists and other pragmaticists are likely to think that we know more about pragmatic inference than Ladd seems to assume here. Wilson and Wharton (2006) suggest a way of addressing the larger questions within the framework of relevance theory. While other relevance-theoretic work[20] did not always presuppose the ideas discussed by Wilson and Wharton, and some of this work would not have made all of the assumptions made there, the various analyses proposed can be seen as fitting more or closely to the general approach outlined there. Fairly common assumptions include that prosody encodes procedural meaning and that intonational meaning affects the recovery of higher-level explicatures. Wilson and Wharton (2006) consider the nature of prosody in general and how it might fit into an overall account of linguistic and non-linguistic meaning. Partly based on some of Wharton's (2003a, 2003b, 2009) suggestions about how to rethink Grice's distinction between natural and non-natural meaning, they suggest that there are three types of prosodic meaning, illustrated in Figure 12.1.

This figure presupposes Wharton's discussion of natural and non-natural meaning. Wharton (2003a, 2003b, 2009) suggested some slight changes to the Gricean picture, including the suggestion of a showing–meaning$_{NN}$ continuum rather than a sharp divide between natural and non-natural meaning; this is illustrated in Figure 12.2.

12.6.5   Phatic communication and politeness

Two related areas which can be seen as going beyond considerations of what is linguistically communicated are the study of phatic communication and politeness. 'Phatic communication' is a term originating in the work of Malinowski (1923) (Malinowski's original term was 'phatic communion') to refer to communication whose main aim has to do with social relationships

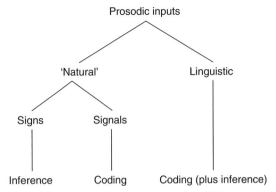

Figure 12.1 *Types of prosodic meaning (Wilson and Wharton 2006: 1563)*

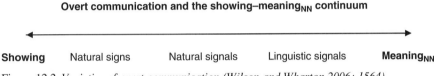

Figure 12.2 *Varieties of overt communication (Wilson and Wharton 2006: 1564)*

between interlocutors and depends relatively weakly on the encoded meanings of the words used. Politeness studies are concerned with how linguistic choices are influenced by considerations of politeness and how politeness is communicated or created by verbal and nonverbal behaviour. Within linguistics, the most influential work on politeness was carried out by Brown and Levinson (1987). Brown and Levinson's account used the notion of 'face' as developed by Goffman (1955, 1967) based, of course, on the notion of face originating in Chinese culture. They considered politeness cross-culturally and developed an account of ways in which interlocutors modify behaviour to enhance, protect or attack each other's 'face'. Both studies of phatic communication and of politeness, then, are concerned with aspects of social relationships and with something that goes beyond meanings derived directly from the linguistically encoded meanings of words. There has been considerable work within relevance theory on both of these areas (see 'further reading' below for some examples) and there is only space to mention some of the work here.

Zegarac and Clark (1999) proposed an account of phatic communication which aimed to account both for the way in which it affected social relationships, and for the intuition that phaticness did not depend closely on the meanings of the words used, without adding extra machinery to the relevance-theoretic framework. A number of other researchers have looked at phatic communication from a relevance-theoretic point of view. Manuel Padilla Cruz, for example, has explored phaticness in a series of papers (including Padilla Cruz 2007, 2008, 2009) focusing on the details of how phatic utterances are interpreted and suggesting that metarepresentation plays a key role here.

Work on politeness overlaps with work on phatic communication to some extent, since both concern the management of social relationships and researchers on both topics have seen themselves as addressing the question of how well relevance theory might be able to account for social as well as cognitive phenomena. Generally, this work has been seen as complementing or 'fleshing out' the account developed by Brown and Levinson (1987). Escandell-Vidal (1998b) argues that a cognitive account based on relevance theory can complement existing socially oriented approaches which focus on politeness strategies such as Leech's (1983) and Brown and Levinson's (1987) accounts. Christie (2007) maps out some of the implications of adopting a relevance-theoretic approach to politeness. Watts (2004) considers how relevance-theoretic ideas can be used in accounting for power relationships as well as politeness. Nowik (2005) considers general questions about politeness and social phenomena, focusing in particular on 'banter', i.e. utterances which seem on the surface to be impolite but in fact help to create a positive relationship, or a bond, between interlocutors. Nowik suggests that metarerpresentation is important here, and raises the question of where in the relevance-theoretic picture politeness and impoliteness effects might feature, i.e. whether they contribute to explicatures (higher- or lower-level) or implicatures. This last question has been considered by a number of relevance theorists.

12.7   Competitors and challenges: other views

Naturally, this book has not been able to do justice to the range of alternative approaches to relevance theory which have been developed so far. This final section mentions a number of alternative approaches which were mentioned in discussions above and one or two others which we have not explicitly discussed. There is space here only to mention alternatives briefly and not to mention all of them. I hope, though, that this will help to give the sense that relevance theory exists alongside a number of other approaches and that anyone interested in linguistic meaning and cognition can explore a number of different ways of thinking about these questions. We begin in the next section by reminding you of the terminology often used to describe pragmatic theories in terms of their relationship to Grice's foundational approach. We then remind you of the way of distinguishing approaches in terms of a contrast between 'contextualism' and 'minimalism', before mentioning a few other approaches in Section 12.7.3 and making some remarks on testing and comparing approaches in 12.7.4

12.7.1   Neo-Griceans and post-Griceans

As we saw in Chapter 2, researchers working after Grice are often divided into 'neo-Griceans', understood as theorists who maintain many of the assumptions of Grice's approach, and 'post-Griceans', who diverge more significantly from Grice's approach. We looked at Horn's (1984, 1988, 1989, 2004) and Levinson's (1987a, 1987b) neo-Gricean approaches in Chapter 2. Leech (1983) also proposed an account which is clearly neo-Gricean in that it is based on the assumption of a number of principles. Leech's approach is not reductionist, however, in that he suggested an increase in the number of maxims, including the proposal that a politeness principle exists alongside the Cooperative Principle and is realised by six further maxims. While a distinction is often made between 'neo-Gricean' and 'post-Gricean' approaches, it is not the case that 'post-Griceans' reject Grice's ideas altogether. Relevance theory falls into the 'post-Gricean' grouping but it is clear that relevance theory preserves some of the key ideas developed by Grice, including the notion of a semantics–pragmatics distinction and the assumption that pragmatic interpretation is grounded in rationality. What the 'neo-Griceans' have in common is that they maintain the notion of a set of maxim-like principles which govern interpretations while 'post-Griceans' suggest something different, such as the principles assumed within relevance theory. At the same time, it is clear that there is not an absolutely clear-cut distinction between 'neo-Griceans' and those approaches which are seen as merely 'post' Grice. Any approach which assumes pragmatic principles governing interpretation can be seen as 'neo-Gricean' to some extent.

12.7.2 Contextualism and minimalism

In Chapter 5, we considered the distinction between 'contextualist' and 'minimalist' approaches. While there is also no absolutely clear-cut distinction between contextualism and minimalism, a number of approaches have been compared in terms of the extent to which they can be labelled 'contextualist' or 'minimalist' (see discussion in Carston 2007; Jaszczolt 2006; Recanati 2007). An approach is contextualist to the extent that it assumes significant pragmatic enrichment is involved in communication, particularly with regard to the fleshing-out of semantic representations into communicated propositions. Relevance theory is, of course, radically contextualist since it assumes that semantic representations require extensive enrichment before full explicatures are derived and also that some enrichment is 'free', i.e. not motivated by the presence of linguistic material which 'triggers' the enrichment process. At the other extreme end of this continuum, theorists such as Jason Stanley (2000; Stanley and Szabó 2000) argue that any contribution to 'truth-conditional content' (here, this means contributions to the proposition expressed) must be licensed by covert or overt material in the semantic representation of the utterance which gives rise to them. In Chapter 5, we looked at the relatively contextualist approaches proposed by Bach and Recanati and at the minimalist approaches suggested by Stanley, Cappelen and Lepore, and Borg.

12.7.3   Other approaches

There is no space to discuss other approaches adequately here, but they include Burton-Roberts's representational hypothesis (Burton-Roberts 2000, 2011; Burton-Roberts and Poole 2006), Jaszczolt's default semantics (Jaszczolt 2005, 2009, 2010, 2011) and work in dynamic syntax (Cann, Kempson and Marten 2005; Cann, Kempson and Wedgwood 2012; Kempson, Meyer-Viol and Gabbay 2001; for a brief summary, see Marten and Kempson 2006). This section mentions four other approaches which we have not discussed much above.

Discourse representation theory (DRT), originally developed by Kamp (1981; see also Kamp and Reyle 1993), is a formal approach which aims explicitly to formalise mental representations of meaning and so to capture meaning at a higher than sentence level. Irene Heim's (1983) file change semantics shares many properties with this approach. What these approaches share is the aim of capturing relationships between utterances and contexts, including how contexts are changed by the interpretation of utterances. These approaches share with relevance theory a focus on contextual interpretation and they share with dynamic syntax the aim of accounting for interpretation as a 'dynamic', ongoing process rather than focusing on 'static' semantic representations. Other 'dynamic' approaches include dynamic predicate logic (Groenendijk and Stokhof 1991) and segmented discourse representation theory (Asher and Lascarides 2003; Lascarides and Asher 2007).

Optimality theory (OT) (Prince and Smollensky 2004) has been very influential in a number of areas of linguistics, including pragmatics (Blutner and Zeevat 2004). The central idea of optimality theory is that data can be accounted for in terms of a number of conflicting constraints. It is perhaps easy to see how Gricean maxims and neo-Gricean work could be understood in terms of conflicting constraints. Blutner and Zeevat (2004: 14) do, in fact, suggest that 'the idea of optimization was present in the pragmatic enterprise from the very beginning'. To some extent, optimality-theoretic pragmatics involves deciding which are the specifically pragmatic principles which are then understood to interact in the ways assumed in optimality theory more generally.

The final two approaches we will consider here are approaches to the study of language and linguistic meaning in general: cognitive linguistics (CL) and systemic-functional linguistics (SFL). These approaches are quite distinct but they do share some properties, including a focus on language and meaning and the assumption that there is no formal distinction between language and other kinds of knowledge.

Cognitive linguistics focuses on cognitive structures in the mind and their realisation in language (for an introduction, see Evans and Green 2006). With no assumed separation between language and other cognitive structures, the assumption is that linguistic structures are conceptualisations. Recent work has focused in particular on 'embodiment' in language and the notion of 'mental spaces' as focuses of conceptualisation. One area where there has been explicit discussion of possible complementarity between cognitive linguistics and relevance-theoretic approaches is in accounts of metaphor. As mentioned in Chapter 9, Gibbs and Tendahl (2006; Tendahl and Gibbs 2008) have explored the possibility that the two approaches might be seen as complementary. Wilson (2011a, 2011b) and Stöver (2011a) also explore this possibility. The fundamental underlying assumptions about language and mental architecture made by the two approaches are so different that it is not yet clear whether it might be possible to develop a fully articulated unified approach.

Systemic-functional linguistics is another very influential approach to language which makes very different foundational assumptions from those of relevance theory. This approach focuses very much on language as a functional system whose central function is 'meaning-making'. This approach developed originally in the work of Michael Halliday (for introductions, see Halliday and Matthiessen 2004; Thompson 2004) and has been particularly influential in educational contexts, including language teaching. Perceived advantages of this approach include its intuitiveness, which makes it fairly easy to explain and apply, its applicability in teaching and other contexts, and the scope for explaining how meanings from different sources are combined (see the comments above on multimodality). It is not clear whether a relevance-theoretic and a systemic-functional approach could ever interact in a meaningful way. No serious attempts in this direction have yet been made.

12.7.4   Testing and comparing approaches

Throughout the book, and in this chapter, we have considered ways of testing and comparing particular approaches. This subsection aims to make just one simple point, namely that tests and comparisons can focus on specific areas or on the whole 'story' told by a particular framework. A test which focuses on a specific sub-part might, for example, consider experimental predictions about how subjects at different ages respond to utterances containing forms such as *some X are Y* or about how ironical utterances are understood. An alternative test or comparison might consider how coherent the overall picture is. We might, for example, question the modular architecture adopted by earlier versions of the theory and how the Principles of Relevance fit into that picture. Or we might consider the 'massively modular' architecture assumed more recently. Relevance theorists have often claimed that the explicit development of an overall framework is a strength of the theory. At the same time, some relevance-theoretic research has focused on very specific areas, e.g. the meaning of the word *and* or *but*. In an important review article, discussing the book *Relevance*, Levinson (1989) adopts ideas from the philosopher Isaiah Berlin (1953) who divided thinkers into 'foxes' and 'hedgehogs' with reference to a quote from the poet Archilochus who said that 'the fox knows many things, but the hedgehog knows one big thing'. For Levinson, relevance theory aims to be a hedgehog knowing 'one big thing' while pragmatic theory raises so many questions that it might make more sense to aim only to know a number of small things. Despite Levinson's comments, it could be argued that researchers working on relevance theory can themselves be divided into foxes and hedgehogs, and that there are some individual researchers who alternate between vulpine ('foxy') and hystricine (believe it or not, this is the adjective meaning 'hedgehog-like') research activity.

12.8   What's next?

So what is the future for relevance theory? Of course, it is hard to anticipate where theorists will develop, challenge and modify particular theories or understanding of particular phenomena. Looking at past developments, there are some areas where things have moved quickly (such as the initial development of understanding of the explicature–implicature distinction), areas where things have remained relatively stable (such as the central claims expressed in the two Principles of Relevance) and areas where there seems always to be more to discover (such as the continuing development in relevance-theoretic accounts of metaphor). There are also some areas where it seems that different theorists continue to debate without clear agreement emerging about the way forward. Naturally, relevance theorists do not easily persuade theorists working with other approaches of the advantages of relevance theory and theorists working with other approaches do not easily win over relevance theorists. At the same time, there are areas where researchers working in different approaches can agree. Areas where there is considerable (but not total) agreement include the idea that pragmatic inference is quite pervasive and involved in deriving the proposition expressed (Grice's 'what is said') as much as in deriving implicatures. Areas where there seems to be ongoing agreement to disagree include discussions of exactly how to draw the semantics–pragmatics distinction. There will no doubt be considerable ongoing work in these areas. It is not clear whether major breakthroughs might emerge which will lead to an agreement to develop new accounts. It is of course also not clear what new areas of study will emerge. Current trends suggest that theorists will continue not only to look at particular phenomena but also to look for other relevant sources of data. Examples of new areas being considered in the past include the consideration of data from subjects with autistic spectrum disorders and comparison of human and primate cognition. Ultimately, of course, the aim will be to explain human cognition and communication in general. Developing fuller accounts will include developing our understanding of central notions such as communication and cognition as well as rich and detailed accounts of the interpretation of particular utterances and other communicative acts. I hope that this book has helped you to develop your understanding of the range of topics considered by work in relevance theory and has suggested some areas which you might be interested in working on yourself.

Exercise 12.1 asks you to consider questions and topics you have looked at throughout the book as a whole and to think about how far you have developed your understanding while working in it.

Exercise 12.1

- Look at the list of questions and comments on them which you have been working on throughout the book. Consider for each one how far you have come in developing answers to them. Second, consider what you might do now in order to find out more about each one.

Exercise 12.2 asks you to think about specific topics raised in the chapter and elsewhere and to consider possible projects you might develop in order to find out more.

Exercise 12.2

- Run through the list of research topics mentioned in this chapter. Make a list for each one of new questions they raise and consider how you might find out more in order to develop answers.
- Finally, consider what you have discovered about relevance theory as a whole and pragmatics from reading this book. How much do you think your understanding has developed from reading this book? How well do you think relevance theory answers the questions which any pragmatic theory aims to answer.

12.9   Summary

In this chapter, we have looked at some developments of relevance theory which were presupposed in the rest of the book and some which we had not mentioned before. We have reminded ourselves of the key things which relevance theory offers for accounts of human cognition and communication, considered the kinds of data which might be relevant, and looked at ways in which the theory has been tested and developed in a number of areas. One key point to emphasise is that we can never tell in advance what range of data might be relevant to pragmatics. We can also never know in advance all of the areas where pragmatic theories might be tested or applied. It is hard to imagine areas wider or more complex than human cognition and communication. Given the range of phenomena which seem to be relevant in explaining any act of ostensive communication or other behaviour, it might seem daunting to attempt to come up with accounts which reveal more than a very small part of the overall picture. However, we could think of this as an opportunity rather than a problem. There is a huge area to explore and room for more and more research in this area. I hope this book has given a sense of the vastness of the challenge and the excitement of developing our understanding of parts of the overall story. Even more, I hope that some readers will be inspired to work on aspects of the puzzle and to test, develop and refine (or even replace) the approach outlined here.

12.10   Finding out more

As this chapter summarises ideas discussed earlier and suggests initial reading for other topics discussed, I have not suggested any specific further reading here. I hope that you are now confident to find your own way through the existing and growing body of work on relevance theory.

The resources section at the end of the book lists some key reading on relevance theory, including useful websites, and concludes with a fuller bibliography containing all of the sources mentioned in the book. There is further help available on the book's website at: www.cambridge.org/billyclark.

Appendix: Key notions of relevance theory

This Appendix contains a brief summary of some of the key technical notions involved in understanding the central claims of relevance theory. The aim is to provide one place in the book where you can remind yourself of some of the key theoretical notions. I have focused on those which are particularly useful in relevance-theoretic accounts of how particular acts of communication or other phenomena are understood. The appendix can be used as a stand-alone presentation of key ideas as well as something to refer to while reading through the rest of the book.

Of course, all of these notions are discussed in more detail in the rest of the book and have also been much discussed in the literature. It is always hard to know whether to present complex ideas from the 'bottom up' (so that no statement presupposes anything which has not yet been introduced) or from the 'top down' (starting with the broad claims and then explaining the terms mentioned within them). The advantage of the bottom-up approach is that no part of the story at a level higher than the base level requires readers to trust that there will be an account at some stage of how the lower levels work. The advantage of the top-down approach is that the bigger picture is clearer sooner. Both directions involve trust since students or readers are asked either to trust that new terms which have not yet been explained will be defined later or to trust that there will be a valid reason for having introduced this particular series of technical terms. Here I have gone mainly with the 'bottom-up' approach starting with cognitive effects and working up to the two Principles of Relevance (although the discussion does depart from the 'bottom to top' ordering a little on the way). The order in the book is more 'top-down' than 'bottom-up'. For now, though, let's take it from the bottom.

First, we need to know what cognitive effects are:

Cognitive effects
Adjustments to the way an individual represents the world.

The definition of relevance relies on a subset of these which are positive cognitive effects:

Positive cognitive effect
A worthwhile difference to the way an individual represents the world (a cognitive effect 'that it is worth having'). Note that false assumptions

are not worth having so positive effects are ones which lead to true conclusions, even though they may not be strictly and literally true.

Three kinds of cognitive effect are usually mentioned:

(a)   Contextual implication

Where a new assumption (or set of assumptions) interacts with existing assumptions to communicate new assumptions (not derivable from either the new or the existing assumptions alone), e.g. if I see that your bicycle tyre has a puncture (new assumption) and I already know that you will fit a new inner tube if you get another puncture (existing assumption), then in this context the new assumption implies that you will fit a new inner tube. We can present this schematically and informally as follows:

> *Existing assumption:*
> You will fit a new inner tube if you have another puncture.
> *New assumption:*
> You have another puncture.
> *Contextual implication:*
> You will fit a new inner tube.

(b)   Strengthening an existing assumption

When a new assumption (or set of assumptions) provides stronger evidence for an existing assumption which is less strongly evidenced, then the new assumption strengthens the existing assumption. If I hear a hissing sound and think my tyre might be punctured and then look closely to see air escaping through a large hole in the tyre caused by a sharp piece of metal, my assumption that the tyre has a puncture is strengthened. We can present this schematically and informally as follows:

> *Existing assumption:*
> My tyre might have a puncture.
> *New assumption:*
> Air is escaping through a large hole in my tyre.
> *Strengthened assumption:*
> My tyre definitely has a puncture.

(c)   Contradicting an existing assumption

When a new assumption provides stronger evidence against an existing assumption, it may lead to the elimination of the existing assumption. If I think that it is impossible for my puncture-resistant tyres ever to be punctured, then the existence of a puncture will lead me to reject the assumption that they can never be punctured. We can represent this schematically and informally as follows:

> *Existing assumption:*
> My tyre is completely puncture-proof.

> *New assumption:*
> My tyre has a puncture.
> *New assumption:*
> My tyre is not completely puncture-proof.

Now that we know what positive cognitive effects are, and we know about some of the varieties they come in, we can understand the definition of relevance used in the theory. The key notion here is what makes a processing 'input' relevant to an individual.

> **Relevance of an input to an individual**
>
> a.   Other things being equal, the greater the positive cognitive effects achieved by processing an input, the greater the relevance of the input to the individual at that time.
>
> b.   Other things being equal, the greater the processing effort expended, the lower the relevance of the input to the individual at that time.

This notion of relevance is used to make a generalisation about all human cognition in the First, or Cognitive, Principle of Relevance:

> **First, or Cognitive, Principle of Relevance**
> Human cognition tends to be geared to the maximisation of relevance.

To understand this we need to know what is involved in maximising relevance:

> **Maximising relevance**
> To maximise relevance is to look for the greatest amount of positive cognitive effects for the least amount of processing effort.

So the claim expressed here is that human cognition is organised in such a way as to try to derive as many positive cognitive effects as possible for as little effort as possible. The claim about our expectations in communication is a more modest one, namely that we presume communicative acts are optimally relevant:

> **Second, or Communicative, Principle of Relevance**
> Every ostensive stimulus conveys a presumption of its own optimal relevance.

To understand this, we need two things. First, we need to know what it means to presume that an input is optimally relevant:

> **Presumption of optimal relevance**
>
> a.   The ostensive stimulus is relevant enough to be worth the audience's processing effort.
>
> b.   It is the most relevant one compatible with the communicator's abilities and preferences.

Second, we need to know what kinds of communication give rise to this presumption. The kind of communication which gives rise to this presumption is ostensive-inferential communication:

Ostensive-inferential communication

a.   The informative intention
       The intention to inform an audience of something.
b.   The communicative intention
       The intention to inform the audience of one's informative intention.

And from all of this follows the relevance-guided comprehension heuristic:

Relevance-guided comprehension heuristic

a.   Follow a path of least effort in computing cognitive effects: Test interpretive hypotheses (disambiguations, reference resolutions, implicatures, etc.) in order of accessibility.
b.   Stop when your expectations of relevance are satisfied (or abandoned).

Finally, relevance theory assumes that interpretation involves a process of mutual parallel adjustment:

Mutual parallel adjustment process

Tentative hypotheses about explicit and implicit content are constructed and adjusted in parallel, guided in order to satisfy the addressee's expectations of relevance.

Notes to chapters

Chapter 1

1 A 1991 film about the case was entitled *Let Him Have It* (1991, dir. Peter Medak). In 1989, Elvis Costello referred to the case in his anti-capital punishment song 'Let Him Dangle'.
2 The importance of the communicator's abilities and preferences was acknowledged in discussion around this, but these were not explicitly mentioned in the presumption itself.

Chapter 2

1 For an account of how these ideas developed, see Chapman (2005: 61–84); for discussion of these ideas and development of them within a relevance-theoretic framework, see Sperber and Wilson (1986: 21–64); for discussion with a particular focus on nonverbal communication, see Wharton (2009).
2 Wharton (2009) develops a different account, based partly on evidence such as this, where the distinction between natural and non-natural meaning is less clear-cut than suggested by Grice and involves a continuum rather than a binary contrast.
3 Notable names here include Atlas (1989), Bach (2004, 2010), Bach and Harnish (1982), Horn (1984, 1988), Huang (2007, 2010), Jaszczolt (2005, 2009), Leech (1983), Levinson (1987a, 1995, 2000) and, of course, Sperber and Wilson.

Chapter 3

1 Swinney's experiments were important not only for the specific evidence they provided but also because he developed here the cross-modal priming task which is now often used in experimental work.
2 More recent work has suggested that activation occurs whenever we encounter a sequence of sounds which could correspond to a word, even across word boundaries or as part of another word. See, for example, Gow and Gordon (1995), Tabossi (1993), Tabossi *et al.* (1995).
3 For discussion, see Barrett and Kurzban (2006), Carruthers (2006), Pinker (1997), Prinz (2006).
4 For a relevance-theoretic discussion, see Pilkington (2000).
5 For an interesting discussion of this question with regard to the material conditional, see Allott and Uchida (2009).
6 I am ignoring trivial conclusions which are not relevant here, such as disjunctions of true propositions with any other proposition and conjunctions of known propositions. If we did include them, then all propositions, or sets of propositions, would give rise to an infinite number of conclusions. Here we could conclude, for example, '$Q \vee \neg Q$', '$Q \vee T$', '$Q \& \neg R$', among others.

7 See, for example, Barsalou (1987, 1989) on how recency, frequency and context affect accessibility. The MRC Psycholinguistic database is a collection of data on many of these factors for over 150,000 words: www.psych.rl.ac.uk/

8 'Optimally processed' means processed in the most efficient way, not involving such things as mistakes, false starts, distractions or accessing non-optimal contexts.

9 As mentioned in Chapter 1, the distinction between 'personal' and 'sub-personal' processes is based on Dennett (1969).

10 The term 'phatic communion' was coined by Malinowski (1923). We will mention relevance-theoretic accounts of phatic communication in Chapter 11.

11 I have changed one word here. Where I have written 'assumption', Sperber and Wilson wrote 'fact'. I have changed it because I assume that a 'fact' is a 'true proposition' and Sperber and Wilson go on to argue that assumptions as well as facts can be manifest and that an assumption which is manifest to an individual may turn out to be false.

12 For a fuller discussion of nonverbal communication and a range of relevant examples, see Wharton (2009).

Chapter 4

1 Sperber, Cara and Girotto (1995) propose a relevance-theoretic explanation of one way in which humans notoriously get it wrong, in the 'selection task' devised by Peter Wason (Wason 1966).

2 I am ignoring here the step that takes you from 'If you are...' to 'If John is...' which is easily explained in standard logical languages.

3 This would be consistent with the findings of Swinney (1979) mentioned in Chapter 3.

4 See note 7 in Chapter 3.

5 For discussion of a range of examples of nonverbal communication from a relevance-theoretic perspective, see Wharton (2009).

Chapter 5

1 Many of the papers by Carston cited in the bibliography deal with this topic; see, in particular, Carston (1988, 2002a, 2004a, 2004b, 2007, 2008, 2009a, 2010).

2 The assumption is not, of course, that we will always represent exact times and dates in the way I have done for these examples. This is just a convenient simplification for now. Sperber and Wilson (1995: 192) suggest that a 'private logbook and an ego-centred map' might be used to represent time and space references.

3 For discussion of the notion of 'reference' in general, see Powell (2010).

4 For discussion of this phenomenon, see Haegeman and Ihsane (1999, 2001) and Haegeman (2006). For a relevance-theoretic approach, see Scott (2006, 2008, 2010).

5 Including by Bach (1994a, 1994b, 1997, 2001, 2010), Borg (2004, 2007), Cappelen and Lepore (2007), Horn (1992, 1996), Jaszczolt (2005), Levinson (2000), Recanati (2001, 2004, 2010), Stainton (1994, 2006), Stanley (2000, 2002), Stanley and Szabo (2000). For discussion, see Carston (2009a).

6 See, for example, Carston (1988, 2002a, 2004a, 2004b, 2007, 2008, 2009a, 2010).

7 For a general discussion of work in experimental pragmatics, see Sperber and Noveck (2004); for discussion of work on scalar implicatures in particular, see Noveck and Sperber (2007).

8 For a survey of different discussions of underdeterminacy, see Atlas (2005: 3–44). As well as work by herself (Carston 1988, 2002a, 2004a, 2004b) and Sperber and Wilson (1986; Wilson and Sperber 2002, 2004), Carston (2009a) mentions a wide range of approaches which can be seen as falling into this category, including work by Atlas (1989, 2005),

Bezuidenhout (1997, 2002), Elugardo and Stainton (2004), Neale (2000, 2005), Powell (2001, 2002), Recanati (1993, 2001, 2004), Soames (forthcoming), Stainton (1994, 2006) and Travis (1981, 1985).

Chapter 6

1 For further discussion, see Sperber and Wilson (1986), Wilson and Sperber (1988), Clark (1991, 1993a, 1993b), Jary (2010, 2011).
2 See, for example, Clark (2007, 2012), Clark and Lindsey (1990), Escandell-Vidal (1998a, 2002), Fretheim (1998), House (1990, 2006), Imai (1998), Vandepitte (1989), Wilson and Wharton (2006).
3 Sperber and Wilson (2008: 100) discuss another famous haiku, by Basho, focusing there on the wide range of weak implicatures which a literal utterance can give rise to.

Chapter 7

1 For discussion of phatic communication in general, see Coupland, Coupland and Robinson (1992), Laver (1974), Schneider (1988); for discussion within relevance theory, see Haicun (2005), Kisielewska-Krysiuk (2010), Nicolle and Clark (1998), Padilla Cruz (2007, 2008, 2009), Ruhi and Dogan (2001), Zegarac (1998), Zegarac and Clark (1999).
2 For discussion of, and experimental evidence about, how we decide what to say when asked the time by a stranger, see Van der Henst, Carles and Sperber (2002).
3 For discussion of the psychological processes of readers, see Gerrig (1993), Gerrig and Allbritton (1990), Allbritton and Gerrig (1991), Prentice, Gerrig and Bailis (1997), Rapp and Gerrig (in press); for the related notion of demonstrations in communication, see Clark and Gerrig (1990).
4 In discussing issues around mutual knowledge, Sperber and Wilson (1982) made the point that it is important not to treat implicated premises as having to be mutually manifest in advance of utterances.
5 For discussion of this, see Pilkington (2000).

Chapter 8

1 This concept is discussed by Sperber and Wilson (1998) in one of the key early papers developing the ideas about lexical pragmatics discussed in this chapter.
2 There is continuing discussion of this (for discussion, see Groefsema 2007, Wilson and Carston 2007); for related work on 'core' and 'non-core' features of concepts, see Rubio Fernandez (2001, 2005, 2007, 2008).
3 For discussion within relevance theory, see Carston (1997, 2002a), Sperber and Wilson (1998), Wilson (2005), Wilson and Carston (2007), Wilson and Sperber (2002). For discussion in other frameworks, see Barsalou (1987, 1993), Blutner (1998), Glucksberg, Manfredi and McGlone (1997), Lascarides and Copestake (1998), Recanati (1995).

Chapter 9

1 Sperber and Wilson (1986) made some suggestions on this, which were developed in Wilson and Sperber (1998). For more recent discussion, see Clark (1991) and Jary (2009, 2010).

2 There is, of course, a general tendency for hearers to retain a verbatim record of an utterance until they have arrived at a satisfactory interpretation. This may apply to cases of disambiguation, reference assignment, wit, theoretical works one doesn't understand, and so on. This general aspect of processing fits quite well within the framework of relevance theory, and can be explained with reference to the comprehension heuristic and the mutual adjustment process.

3 Within cognitive linguistics, the account will be based on the assumption of a mapping from surgeons to butchers focusing on properties they share (see, for example, Lakoff 1987; Lakoff and Turner 1989).

4 See, for example, Carston (2002a, 2002b), Sperber and Wilson (2008), Vega Moreno (2007), Wilson and Carston (2006, 2007, 2008).

Chapter 10

1 Including Clark and Gerrig (1984), Kumon-Nakamura, Glucksberg and Brown (1995), Walton (1990), Recanati (2000, 2004, 2007), Currie (2006).

2 See, for example, Astington, Harris and Olston (1988), Surian and Leslie (1999), Wellman, Cross and Watson (2001), Sodian (2004), Matsui, Yamamoto and McCagg (2006) and Matsui *et al.* (2009).

Chapter 11

1 Burton-Roberts (2010) raises questions about the notion of 'cancellability' which suggest, at least, that this might not be the right term. For now, though, we'll stick to this as it is how Grice thought about it.

2 See, for example, Clark (2007, 2012), Clark and Lindsey (1990), Escandell-Vidal (1998a, 2002), Fretheim (1998), House (1990, 2006), Imai (1998), Vandepitte (1989). For a more general discussion of prosodic meaning within a relevance-theoretic framework, see Wilson and Wharton (2006).

3 For work on prosody, see references in note 2; on syntactic structures, see Sperber and Wilson (1986), Wilson and Sperber (1988), Clark (1991, 1993), Jary (2010, 2011); on nonverbal communication, see Wharton (2009).

4 The most sustained discussion of these questions has been carried out by Blakemore (1987, 2002, 2007a) but they have also been explored by other authors, including Bezuidenhout (2004), Fraser (2006), Iten (2005). See Escandell-Vidal, Leonetti and Ahern (2011) for a recent collection of papers focusing on the conceptual–procedural distinction, including Wilson (2011b), who considers past, present and future research.

Chapter 12

1 For other useful summaries of more recent developments, see Blakemore (1995), Carston and Powell (2006), Clark (2011), Wilson and Sperber (2004), Sperber and Wilson (2005), Yus (2006, 2010).

2 As illustrated by this quote: '[The Principle of Relevance] warrants the selection of the first accessible interpretation consistent with the principle, if there is one, and otherwise, no interpretation at all' (Sperber and Wilson 1986: 170).

3 For a general discussion, see Hunston (2006). Introductory books include McEnery and Wilson (2001), McEnery and Hardie (2011), Teubert and Cermakova (2007).

4 See, for example, Andersen (1999), Jary (2008), de Klerk (2005), Navarro (2006), Zajac (2004), Zaki (2011).

5 See, for example, Girotto *et al.* (2001), van der Henst, Carles and Sperber (2002), van der Henst, Sperber and Politzer (2002), van der Henst and Sperber (2004), Sperber, Cara and Girotto (1995).

6 For further discussion of meaning disputes, see Durant (2010). For discussion of misunderstandings from a relevance-theoretic perspective, see Bou-Franch (2002), Jodlowiec (2009), Mirecki (2005), Yus (1998b, 1999a, 1999b).

7 See, for example, Bouton (1988, 1990, 1992a, 1992b, 1994a, 1994b, 1999), Foster-Cohen (2000, 2004a, 2004b), Jodlowiec (2010), Shively, Menke and Manzón-Omundson (2008), Sroda (2000), Yamanaka (2003).

8 See, for example, Boase-Beier (2004a, 2004b), Gutt (1991, 1998, 2004), Rosales Sequeiros (2005), Saad (2010), Setton (1999, 2005a, 2005b, 2006).

9 As Sperber points out, humans are not the only creatures who have evolved metarepresentational abilities. Chimpanzees, for example, also seem to be able to do this.

10 For discussion, see Sperber (1994a, 2001, 2005), Sperber and Wilson (2002), Wilson (2005).

11 Fodor's remark preceded the work of Sperber and others on 'massive modularity'. He referred to 'what I take to be modularity theory gone mad: the idea that modularity is the general case in cognitive architecture'. Sperber (1994b: 39) mentioned this remark when first arguing for the massive modularity thesis.

12 The term was coined by Premack and Woodruff (1978); see also Astington, Harris and Olson (1988), Baron-Cohen (1995), Carruthers and Smith (1996), Davies and Stone (1995a, 1995b), Leslie (1987), Scholl and Leslie (1999).

13 For discussion, see Sperber (1994b, 1995), Wilson (2000), Sperber and Wilson (2005).

14 Work in these areas includes Bezuidenhout and Sroda (1998), Happé (1993), Leslie and Happé (1989). Recent work on mind-reading and metarepresentational abilities includes Ifantidou (2005a, 2005b, 2005c), Mascaro and Sperber (2009), Mercier and Sperber (2009), Sperber (2000, 2001), Sperber and Wilson (2002).

15 For discussion of relevance theory and writing, see Aguilar (2008), Clark and Owtram (2012), Owtram (2010).

16 These include general discussions of how accounts of inference might be relevant (e.g. Clark 1996, 2009); accounts of particular phenomena such as metaphor (Pilkington 1991, 1992, 2000, 2001), irony (Wilson 2009; Wilson and Sperber 2012: 123–45), metarepresentations (MacMahon 1996, 2009a, 2009b), representation of speech and thought (Blakemore 1991, 1996, 2007b, 2009, 2010) and the derivation of particular kinds of aesthetic or 'poetic' effects (Fabb 1995, 1997, 2002; Pilkington 2000, 2001).

17 For discussion of relevance-theoretic work on stylistics and literary studies, see Bursey and Furlong (2006), Clark (1996, 2009), Furlong (1996, 2001), MacMahon (1996, 2001a, 2001b, 2007, 2009a, 2009b), Pilkington (1996, 2000).

18 See, for example, Landragin *et al.* (2002), Ifantidou and Tzanne (2006), Landragin (2003).

19 Examples include: Peeters (2010), Yus (1998a, 2009) on media language in general; Crook (2004), Durán Martínez (2005), Dynell (2008), Lagerwerf (2007) and Tanaka (1992, 1994) on advertising; Buckland (1992, 1995) and Desilla (2012) on meaning in film; Bekalu (2006) and Ifantidou (2009) on newspapers; Abras (2002), De Boni (2004), Pajares Tosca (2000), Yus (2008, 2011) on web-based and computer-mediated communication. Durant (2010) explores meaning 'troublespots' in media communication, i.e. cases where there is a debate about what a particular utterance meant or was intended to mean.

20 See, for example, Clark (2007, 2012), Clark and Lindsey (1990), Escandell-Vidal (1998a, 2002), Fretheim (1998), House (1990, 2006), Imai (1998), Vandepitte (1989).

Bibliography and other resources

If you're interested in reading more on relevance theory, there's no shortage of material you might look at. The bibliography below contains all of the sources referred to in the text of this book. Before that, I have mentioned some useful starting points, including other introductions to the theory (listed in full in the bibliography) and some useful web-based resources. An even fuller range of resources are mentioned on the book's website at: www.cambridge.org/billyclark.

1. Other introductions to relevance theory

A number of other sources introduce key ideas in relevance theory. Blakemore's (1992) book is a good, simple introduction to the theory. It is aimed at readers who are at an earlier stage than the target audience for this book. Two articles by Wilson and Sperber (Wilson and Sperber 2004; Sperber and Wilson 2005) are useful brief summaries of the theory. Other introductory articles include: Blakemore (1995), Carston and Powell (2006), Clark (2011), Yus (2006, 2010). Any of these would be a good starting point for beginners who would like to have a quick overview, perhaps before or alongside reading this book. For more advanced reading, possibly after having read this book, the classic source is, of course, the book *Relevance* (Sperber and Wilson 1986). Books by Diane Blakemore (2002) and Robyn Carston (2002a) are key sources which also present ideas for more advanced readers. Wilson and Sperber (2012) collects a number of important papers which have helped to develop the theory in recent years.

2. Web-based resources

There are a number of useful web-based resources. The most comprehensive is the online bibliography maintained by Francisco Yus:

Relevance Theory Online Bibliographic Service

A frequently updated and comprehensive list of sources which discuss or apply relevance-theoretic ideas is created and maintained by Francisco Yus at the Universidad de Alicante:

www.ua.es/personal/francisco.yus/rt.html

Some relevance theorists have websites with links to downloadable work. These include Dan Sperber and Deirdre Wilson. Dan Sperber's website with downloadable papers:

www.dan.sperber.fr/

Deirdre Wilson's UCL home page with downloadable papers:

www.langsci.ucl.ac.uk/home/deirdre/index.php

Finally, the International Cognition and Culture Institute website (co-hosted by the London School of Economics and the Institut Jean Nicod) has lively blog discussions which sometimes address topics relevant to relevance theory:

www.cognitionandculture.net/

3.   Bibliography

Abras, C. 2002. The principle of relevance and metamessages in online discourse: electronic exchanges in a graduate course. *Language, Literacy and Culture Review* **1**.2: 39–53.

Ackerman, B. 1983. Form and function in children's understanding of ironic utterances. *Journal of Experimental Child Psychology* **35**: 487–508.

Adger, D. 2003. *Core Syntax*. Oxford University Press.

Aguilar, M. 2008. *Metadiscourse in Academic Speech: A Relevance-theoretic Approach*. Peter Lang, Berlin.

Allbritton, D.W. and R.J. Gerrig 1991. Participatory responses in prose understanding. *Journal of Memory and Language* **30**: 603–26.

Allott, N. and H. Uchida 2009. Natural language indicative conditionals are classical. *UCL Working Papers in Linguistics* **21**: 1–17.

Andersen, G. 1999. *Pragmatic Markers and Sociolinguistic Variation: A Corpus-based Study*. PhD thesis, University of Bergen.

Asher, N. and A. Lascarides 2003. *Logics of Conversation*. Cambridge University Press.

Astington, J., P. Harris and D. Olson (eds.) 1988. *Developing Theories of Mind*. Cambridge University Press.

Atlas, J.D. 1989. *Philosophy Without Ambiguity: A Logico-linguistic Essay*. Clarendon Press, Oxford.

2005. *Logic, Meaning and Conversation: Semantical Underdeterminacy, Implicature and their Interface*. Oxford University Press.

Atlas, J.D. and S.C. Levinson. 1981. It-clefts, informativeness and logical form. In P. Cole (ed.) *Radical Pragmatics*, pp. 1–62. Academic Press, New York.

Bach, K. 1994a. Conversational impliciture. *Mind and Language* **9**: 124–62.

1994b. Semantic slack: what is said and more. In S. Tsohatzidis (ed.) *Foundations of Speech Act Theory: Philosophical and linguistic perspectives*, pp. 267–91. Routledge, London.

1997. The semantics–pragmatics distinction: what it is and why it matters. *Linguistische Berichte* **8** (Special Issue on Pragmatics): 33–50. Reprinted in K. Turner (ed.) 1999. *The Semantics–Pragmatics Interface from Different Points of View*. Elsevier Science, Oxford.

1999. The myth of conventional implicature. *Linguistics and Philosophy* **22**: 327–66.

2001. You don't say. *Synthése* **128**: 15–44.

2004. Pragmatics and the philosophy of language. In Horn and Ward (eds.), pp. 461–87.

2010. Impliciture vs. explicature: what's the difference? In B. Soria and E. Romero (eds.), pp. 126–37.

Bach, K. and R.M. Harnish 1982. *Linguistic Communication and Speech Acts*. MIT Press, Cambridge MA.

Baron-Cohen, S. 1995. *Mindblindness: An Essay on Autism and Theory of Mind*. MIT Press, Cambridge MA.

Barrett, H.C. and R. Kurzban 2006. Modularity in cognition: framing the debate. *Psychological Review* **113**.3: 628–47.

Barsalou, L. 1987. The instability of graded structure: implications for the nature of concepts. In U. Neisser (ed.) *Concepts and Conceptual Development: Ecological and Intellectual Factors in Categorization*: 101–40. Cambridge University Press.

1989. Intra-concept similarity and its implications for inter-concept similarity. In S. Vosniadou and A. Ortony (eds.) *Similarity and Analogical Reasoning*, pp. 76–121. Cambridge University Press.

1992. Frames, concepts, and conceptual fields. In E. Kittay and A. Lehrer (eds.) *Frames, Fields, and Contrasts: New Essays in Semantic and Lexical Organization*, pp. 21–74. Lawrence Erlbaum, Hillsdale NJ.

1993. Flexibility, structure, and linguistic vagary in concepts: manifestations of a compositional system of perceptual symbols. In A. Collins, S. Gathercole, A. Conway and P. Morris (eds.) *Theories of Memory*, pp. 29–101. Lawrence Erlbaum Associates, Hove.

Bekalu, M.A. 2006. Presupposition in news discourse. *Discourse & Society* **17**.2: 147–72.

Berlin, I. 1953. *The Hedgehog and the Fox: An Essay on Tolstoy's View of History*. Weidenfeld and Nicolson, New York.

Berg, J. 2002. Is semantics still possible? *Journal of Pragmatics* **34**.4: 349–59.

Bezuidenhout, A. 1997. Pragmatics, semantic underdetermination and the referential–attributive distinction. *Mind* **106**: 375–409.

2002. Truth-conditional pragmatics. *Philosophical Perspectives* **16**: 105–34.

2004. Procedural meaning and the semantics/pragmatics interface. In C. Bianchi (ed.) *The Semantics/Pragmatics Distinction*, pp. 101–31. CSLI Publications, Stanford CA.

Bezuidenhout, A. and M.S. Sroda 1998. Children's use of contextual cues to resolve referential ambiguity: an application of relevance theory. *Pragmatics and Cognition* **6**: 265–99.

Bialystok, E. 1987. Influences of bilingualism on metalinguistic development. *Second Language Research* **3**.2: 154–66.

    1991. *Language Processing in Bilingual Children*. Cambridge University Press.

    2001. *Bilingualism in Development: Language, Literacy and Cognition*. Cambridge University Press.

Birdsong, D. 1989. *Metalinguistic Performance and Interlinguistic Competence*. Springer-Verlag, New York.

Blakemore, D. 1987. *Semantic Constraints on Relevance*. Blackwell, Oxford.

    1991. Performatives and parentheticals. *Proceedings of the Aristotelian Society* **91**: 197–214.

    1992. *Understanding Utterances*. Blackwell, Oxford.

    1995. Relevance theory. In J. Verschueren, J.-O. Ostman and J. Blommaert (eds.) *Handbook of Pragmatics*, pp. 443–52. John Benjamins, Amsterdam.

    1996. Are apposition markers discourse markers? *Journal of Linguistics* **32**: 325–47.

    1997. On non-truth conditional meaning. *Linguistische Berichte* **8** (Special Issue on Pragmatics): 92–102.

    2002. *Relevance and Linguistic Meaning: The Semantics and Pragmatics of Discourse Markers*. Cambridge University Press.

    2007a. Constraints, concepts and procedural encoding. In N.C. Burton-Roberts (ed.), pp. 45–66.

    2007b. 'Or'-parentheticals, 'that is'-parentheticals and the pragmatics of reformulation. *Journal of Linguistics* **43**: 311–33.

    2009. Parentheticals and point of view in free indirect style. *Language and Literature* **18**.2: 129–53.

    2010. Communication and the representation of thought: the use of audience-directed expressions in free indirect thought representations. *Journal of Linguistics* **46**: 575–99.

Blutner, R. 1998. Lexical pragmatics. *Journal of Semantics* **15**: 115–62.

Blutner, R. and H. Zeevat 2004. *Optimality Theory and Pragmatics*. Palgrave Macmillan, Basingstoke.

Boase-Beier, J. 2004a. Knowing and not knowing: style, intention and the translation of a Holocaust poem. *Language and Literature* **13**.1: 25–35.

    2004b. Saying what someone else meant: style, relevance and translation. *International Journal of Applied Linguistics* **14**.2: 276–87.

    2009. Translation and timelessness. *Journal of Literary Semantics* **38**: 101–14.

Bolinger, D. 1986. *Intonation and its Parts: Melody in Spoken English*. Edward Arnold, London.

    1989. *Intonation and its Uses: Melody in Grammar and Discourse*. Edward Arnold, London.

De Boni, M. 2004. *Relevance in Open Domain Question Answering: Theoretical Framework and Application*. PhD thesis, University of York.

Borg, E. 2004. *Minimal Semantics*. Oxford University Press.

    2007. Minimalism versus contextualism in semantics. In G. Preyer and G. Peter (eds.) *Context-Sensitivity and Semantic Minimalism*, pp. 339–59. Oxford University Press.

Bou-Franch, P. 2002. Misunderstandings and unofficial knowledge in institutional discourse. In D. Walton and D. Scheu (eds.) *Culture and Power*, pp. 323–45. Peter Lang, Berlin.

Bouton, L.F. 1988. A cross-cultural study of ability to interpret implicatures in English. *World Englishness* **7**: 183–96.

1990. The effective use of implicature in English: why and how it should be taught in the ESL classroom. *Pragmatics and Language Learning Monograph Series*, vol.1, pp. 43–51.

1992a. The interpretation of implicature in English by NNS: does it come automatically without being explicitly taught? *Pragmatics and Language Learning* **3**: 53–65.

1992b. *Culture, Pragmatics and Implicature: Acquisition of Language – Acquisition of Culture. AFinLA Yearbook* (Publications de l'Association Finlandaise de Linguistique Appliquée) **50**, pp. 35–61.

1994a. Conversational implicature in a second language: learned slowly when not deliberately taught. *Journal of Pragmatics* **22**: 157–67.

1994b. Can NNS skill in interpreting implicature in American English be improved through explicit instruction? A pilot study. *Pragmatics and Language Learning Monograph Series*, vol. 5, pp. 88–109.

1999. Developing nonnative speaker skills in interpreting conversational implicatures in English: explicit teaching can ease the process. In E. Hinkel (ed.) *Culture in Second Language Teaching and Learning*, pp. 47–70. Cambridge University Press.

Brown, C. 2010. *The Lost Diaries*. Fourth Estate, London.

Brown, P. and S. Levinson 1978. Universals in language usage: politeness phenomena. In E. Goody (ed.) *Questions and Politeness*, pp. 56–310. Cambridge University Press.

1987. *Politeness: Some Universals in Language Usage*. Cambridge University Press.

Bryant, G. and J. Fox Tree 2002. Recognising verbal irony in spontaneous speech. *Metaphor and symbol* **17**: 99–117.

Buckland, W. 1992. *Filmic Meaning: The Semantics–Pragmatics Interface*. PhD thesis, University of East Anglia.

1995. Relevance and cognition: towards a pragmatics of unreliable filmic narration. In J.E. Müller (ed.) *Towards a Pragmatics of the Audiovisual*, vol. 2, pp. 55–66. Nodus Publikationen, Münster.

Bursey, J. and A. Furlong 2006. Cognitive gothic: relevance theory, iteration and style. In J. Tabbi and R. Shavers (eds.) *Paper Empire: William Gaddis and the World System*, pp. 118–33. University of Alabama Press, Tuscaloosa.

Burton-Roberts, N.C. 2000. Where and what is phonology? A representational perspective. In N.C. Burton-Roberts, P. Carr and G. Docherty (eds.) *Phonological Knowledge: Conceptual and empirical* issues, pp. 39–66. Oxford University Press.

(ed.) 2007. *Pragmatics*. Palgrave Macmillan, Basingstoke.

2010. Cancellation and intention. In B. Soria and E. Romero (eds.), pp. 138–55.

2011. On the grounding of syntax and the role of phonology in human cognition. *Lingua* **121**.14: 2089–102.

Burton-Roberts, N. and G. Poole 2006. 'Virtual conceptual necessity', feature-dissociation and the Saussurian legacy in generative grammar. *Journal of Linguistics* **42**.3: 575–628.

Camp, E. 2008. Showing, telling, and seeing: metaphor and 'poetic' language. *Baltic International Yearbook of Cognition, Logic and Communication*, vol. 3, pp. 1–24.

Cann, R., R. Kempson and L. Marten 2005. *The Dynamics of Language*. Elsevier, Oxford.

Cann, R., R. Kempson and D. Wedgwood 2012. Representationalism and linguistic knowledge. In R. Kempson, T. Fernando and N. Asher (eds.) *Philosophy of Linguistics*, pp. 357–401. Elsevier, Amsterdam.

Cappelen, H. and E. Lepore 2007. Relevance theory and shared content. In N.C. Burton-Roberts (ed.), pp. 115–35.

Carruthers, P. 2006. *The Architecture of the Mind: Massive Modularity and the Flexibility of Thought*. Oxford University Press.

Carruthers, P. and P. Smith (eds.) 1996. *Theories of Theories of Mind*. Cambridge University Press.

Carston, R. 1988. Implicature, explicature and truth-theoretic semantics. In R. Kempson (ed.) *Mental Representation: The Interface between language and reality*, pp. 155–81. Cambridge University Press.

1997. Enrichment and loosening: complementary processes in deriving the proposition expressed? *Linguistische Berichte* **8** (Special Issue on Pragmatics): 103–27.

1998. *Pragmatics and the Explicit–Implicit Distinction*. PhD thesis, University College London.

2002a. *Thoughts and Utterances: The Pragmatics of Explicit Communication*. Wiley-Blackwell, Oxford.

2002b. Metaphor, ad hoc concepts and word meaning: more questions than answers. *UCL Working Papers in Linguistics* **14**: 83–105.

2004a. Relevance theory and the saying–implicating distinction. In L. Horn and G. Ward (eds.), pp. 633–56.

2004b. Explicature and semantics. In S. Davis and B. Gillon (eds.) *Semantics: A Reader*, pp. 1–44. Oxford University Press.

2007. How many pragmatic systems are there? In M.J. Frapolli (ed.) *Saying, Meaning, Referring: Essays on the Philosophy of F. Recanati*, pp. 18–48. Palgrave Macmillan, Basingstoke.

2008. Linguistic communication and the semantics–pragmatics distinction. *Synthèse* **165**.3: 321–45.

2009a. The explicit/implicit distinction in pragmatics and the limits of explicit communication. *International Review of Pragmatics* **1**.1: 35–62.

2009b. Relevance theory: contextualism or pragmaticism? *UCL Working Papers in Linguistics* **21**: 19–26.

2010. Explicit communication and 'free' pragmatic enrichment. In B. Soria and E. Romero (eds.), pp. 217–85.

Carston, R. and G. Powell 2006. Relevance theory: new directions and developments. In E. Lepore and B. Smith (eds.) *Oxford Handbook of Philosophy of Language*, pp. 341–60. Oxford University Press.

Carston, R. and S. Uchida (eds). 1998. *Relevance Theory: Applications and Implications*. John Benjamins, Amsterdam.

Chalmers, A.F. 1999. *What Is This Thing Called Science?* 3rd edn. Open University Press, Buckingham.

Chapman, S. 2005. *Paul Grice: Philosopher and Linguist*. Palgrave Macmillan, Basingstoke.

Christie, C. 2007. Relevance theory and politeness. *Journal of Politeness Research* **3**: 269–94.

Chomsky, N. 1965. *Aspects of the Theory of Syntax*. MIT Press, Cambridge MA.

    1986. *Knowledge of Language*. Praeger, New York.

Clark, B. 1991. *Relevance Theory and the Semantics of Non-Declaratives'*. PhD thesis, University College London.

    1993a. Let and let's: procedural encoding and explicature. *Lingua* **90**: 173–200.

    1993b. Relevance and pseudo-imperatives. *Linguistics and Philosophy* **16**.1: 79–121.

    1996. Stylistic analysis and relevance theory. *Language and Literature* **5**.3: 163–78.

    2007. 'Blazing a trail': moving from natural to linguistic meaning in accounting for the tones of English. In R.A. Nilsen, N.A. Appiah Amfo and K. Borthen (eds.) *Interpreting Utterances: Pragmatics and its interfaces. Essays in honour of Thorstein Fretheim*, pp. 69–81. Novus, Oslo.

    2009. Salient inferences: pragmatics and *The Inheritors*. *Language and Literature* **18**.2: 173–212.

    2011. Recent developments in relevance theory. In P. Grundy and D. Archer (eds.) *The Pragmatics Reader*, pp. 129–37. Routledge, London.

    2012. The relevance of tones: prosodic meanings in utterance interpretation and in relevance theory. *The Linguistic Review*, **29**.4: 643–61.

Clark, B. and G. Lindsey 1990. Intonation, grammar and utterance interpretation: evidence from English exclamatory-inversions. *UCL Working Papers in Linguistics* **2**: 32–51.

Clark, B. and N. Owtram 2012. Imagined inference: teaching writers to think like readers. In M. Burke, S. Czabo, L. Week and J. Berkowitz (eds.) *Current Trends in Pedagogical Stylistics*, pp. 126–41. Continuum, London.

Clark, H. and R.J. Gerrig 1984. On the pretense theory of irony. *Journal of Experimental Psychology: General* **113**: 121–6.

    1990. Quotations as demonstrations. *Language* **66**: 764–805.

Cook, V.J. and M. Newson 2007. *Chomsky's Universal Grammar: An Introduction*, 3rd edn. Wiley-Blackwell, Oxford.

Coupland, J., N. Coupland and J.D. Robinson 1992. 'How are you?' Negotiating phatic communion. *Language in Society* **21**: 207–30.

Crook, J. 2004. On covert communication in advertising. *Journal of Pragmatics* **36**: 715–38.

Currie, G. 2006. Why irony is pretence. In S. Nichols (ed.) *The Architecture of the Imagination*, pp. 111–33. Oxford University Press.

Davies, M. and T. Stone (eds.) 1995a. *Mental Simulation: Philosophical and Psychological Essays*. Wiley-Blackwell, Oxford.

    (eds.) 1995b. *Folk Psychology*. Blackwell, Oxford.

Dennett, D. 1969. *Content and Consciousness*. Routledge, London.

Desilla, L. 2012. Implicatures in film: construal and functions in Bridget Jones romantic comedies. *Journal of Pragmatics* **44**: 30–53.

Dogan, G. 1992. *The Pragmatics of Indirectness of Meaning: A Relevance-Theoretic Approach to Epigrams and Graffiti in Turkish.* PhD thesis, University of Manchester.

Dowty, D.R., R.E. Wall and S. Peters. 1980. *Introduction to Montague Semantics.* Reidel, Dordrecht.

Durán-Martínez, R. 2005. Covert communication in the promotion of alcohol and tobacco in Spanish press advertisements. *Revista Electrónica de Lingüística Aplicada* **5**: 82–102.

Durant, A. 1984. *Conditions of Music.* Macmillan, London.

2010. *Meaning in the Media: Discourse, Controversy and Debate.* Cambridge University Press.

Dynell, M. 2008. Wittiness in the visual rhetoric of advertising and the quest for relevance. In E. Walaszewska, M. Kisielewska-Krysiuk, A. Korzeniowska and M. Grzegorzewska (eds.) *Relevant Worlds: Current Perspectives on Language, Translation and Relevance Theory*, pp. 48–66. Cambridge Scholars Publishing, Newcastle.

Elugardo, R. and R.J. Stainton 2004. Shorthand, syntactic ellipsis, and the pragmatic determinants of what is said. *Mind & Language* **19**.4: 442–71.

Escandell-Vidal, V. 1998a. Intonation and procedural encoding: the case of Spanish interrogatives. In V. Rouchota and A. Jucker (eds.), pp. 169–204.

1998b. Politeness: a relevant issue for relevance theory. *Revista Alicantina de Estudios Ingleses* **11**: 45–57.

2002. Echo-syntax and metarepresentations. *Lingua* **112**: 871–900.

Escandell-Vidal, V., M. Leonetti and A. Ahern (eds.) 2011. *Procedural Meaning: Problems and Perspectives.* Emerald Group Publishing, Bingley.

Evans, V. and M. Green 2006. *Cognitive Linguistics: An Introduction.* Edinburgh University Press.

Fabb, N. 1995. The density of response: a problem for literary criticism and cognitive science. In J. Payne (ed.) *Linguistic Approaches to Literature: Papers in Literary Stylistics*, pp. 143–57. English Language Research, University of Birmingham.

1997. *Linguistics and Literature.* Wiley-Blackwell, Oxford.

2002. *Language and Literary Structure.* Cambridge University Press.

Fauconnier, G. and M. Turner 2002. *The Way We Think.* Basic Books, New York.

Fiddick, L., L. Cosmides and J. Tooby 2000. No interpretation without representation: the role of domain-specific representations in the Wason selection task. *Cognition* **77**: 1–79.

Fodor, J.A. 1975. *The Language of Thought.* Harvard University Press, Cambridge MA.

1983. *The Modularity of Mind.* MIT Press, Cambridge MA.

1987. *Psychosemantics: The Problem of Meaning in the Philosophy of Mind.* MIT Press, Cambridge MA.

1990. *A Theory of Content and Other Essays.* MIT Press, Cambridge MA.

1994. *The Elm and the Expert.* MIT Press, Cambridge MA.

2008. *LOT 2: The Language of Thought Revisited.* Oxford University Press.

Forceville, C. 1996. *Pictorial Metaphor in Advertising.* Routledge, London.

2000. Compasses, beauty queens and other PCs: pictorial metaphors in computer advertisements. *Hermes* **24**: 31–55.

2002. The identification of target and source in pictorial metaphors. *Journal of Pragmatics* **34**: 1–14.

2010. Why and how study metaphor, metonymy and other tropes in multimodal discourse? In R. Caballero and M.J. Pinar Sanz (eds.) *Ways and Modes of Human Communication*, pp. 57–76. Universidad de Castilla-La Mancha, Servicio de Publicaciones y AESLA, Ciudad Real.

Foster-Cohen, S.H. 2000. Review article on *Relevance: Communication and Cognition*. *Second Language Research* **16**.1: 77–92.

2004a. Relevance theory and second language learning/ behaviour. *Second Language Research* **20**.3: 189–92.

2004b. Relevance theory, action theory and second language communication strategies. *Second Language Research* **20**.3: 289–302.

Fraser, B. 2006. On the conceptual–procedural distinction. *Style* 40.1–2. Available at: http://findarticles.com/p/articles/mi_m2342/is_1–2_40/ai_n17113874/

Fretheim, T. 1998. Intonation and the procedural encoding of attributed thoughts: the case of Norwegian negative interrogatives. In V. Rouchota and A. Jucker (eds.), pp. 205–36.

Furlong, A. 1996. *Relevance Theory and Literary Interpretation*. PhD. thesis, University College London.

2001. Is it a classic if no one reads it? In *Proceedings of the 24th Annual Meeting of the Atlantic Provinces Linguistics Association (APLA)*, pp. 54–60. Université de Moncton, Moncton NB.

2011. The soul of wit: a relevance-theoretic discussion. *Language and Literature* **20**.2: 136–50.

Gerrig, R.J. 1993. *Experiencing Narrative Worlds: On the Psychological Activities of Reading*. Yale University Press, New Haven CT.

Gerrig, R.J. and D.W. Allbritton 1990. The construction of literary character: a view from cognitive psychology. *Style* **24**: 380–91.

Gibbs, R. 1994. *The Poetics of Mind: Figurative Thought, Language and Understanding*. Cambridge University Press.

2001. Evaluating contemporary models of figurative language understanding. *Metaphor and Symbol* **16**: 317–33.

Gibbs, R. and J. Moise 1997. Pragmatics in understanding what is said. *Cognition* **62**: 51–74.

Gibbs, R. and M. Tendahl 2006. Cognitive effort and effects in metaphor comprehension: relevance theory and psycholinguistics. *Mind and Language* **21**.3: 379–403.

Gigerenzer, G., P. Todd and the ABC Research Group 1999. *Simple Heuristics That Make Us Smart*. Oxford University Press.

Gilman, R. 2003. Introduction. In R. Gilman (ed.) *Anton Chekhov: Plays*, pp. vii-xxxii. Penguin, London.

Girotto, V., M. Kemmelmeier, D. Sperber and J.-B. van der Henst, 2001. Inept reasoners or pragmatic virtuosos? Relevance and the deontic selection task. *Cognition*, **81**: 69–76.

Glucksberg, S. 2001. *Understanding Figurative Language*. Oxford University Press.

2004. On the automaticity of pragmatic processes: a modular proposal. In I. Noveck and D. Sperber (eds.), pp. 72–93.

Glucksberg, S., D. Manfredi and M.S. McGlone 1997. Metaphor comprehension: How metaphors create new categories. In T. Ward, S. Smith and J. Vaid (eds.), pp. 327–50.

Goffman, E. 1959. *The Presentation of Self In Everyday Life*. Anchor Doubleday, Garden City NY.

1967. *Interaction Ritual: Essays on face-to-face behavior*. Anchor Doubleday, Garden City NY.

van Gompel, R.P.G. 2006. Sentence processing. In K. Brown (ed.) *Encyclopedia of Language and Linguistics*, 2nd edn, vol. 11, pp. 251–5. Elsevier, Oxford.

Gow, D.W. and P.C. Gordon 1995. Lexical and prelexical influences on word segmentation: evidence from priming. *Journal of Experimental Psychology: Human Perception and Performance* **21**: 344–59.

Grice, H.P. 1957. Meaning. *The Philosophical Review* **66**: 377–88. Reprinted in H. P. Grice (1989), pp. 213–23.

1967. *Logic and Conversation. The William James Lectures*. Harvard University. Published as Grice (1975) and reprinted in Grice (1989).

1975. Logic and conversation. In P. Cole and J. Morgan (eds.) *Syntax and Semantics 3: Speech Acts*, pp. 41–58. Academic Press, New York. Reprinted in Grice (1989), pp. 86–116.

1989. *Studies in the Way of Words*. Harvard University Press, Cambridge MA.

Groefsema, Marjolein. 2007. Concepts and word meaning in relevance theory. In N.C. Burton-Roberts (ed.), pp. 136–57.

Groenendijk, J. and M. Stokhof 1991. Dynamic predicate logic. *Linguistics and Philosophy* **14**: 39–100.

Gutt, E.-A. 1991. *Translation and Relevance: Cognition and Context*. Blackwell, Oxford. (2nd edn 2000. St Jerome Publishing, Manchester.)

1998. Pragmatic aspects of translation: some relevance-theoretic observations. In L. Hickey (ed.) *The Pragmatics of Translation*, pp. 41–53. Multilingual Matters, Clevedon.

2004. Translation, metarepresentation and claims of interpretive resemblance. In S. Arduini and R. Hodgson (eds.) *Proceedings of the International Conference on Similarity and Translation*, pp. 93–101. Guaraldi, Rimini.

Haegeman, L. 2006. Register variation: Core grammar and periphery. In K. Brown (ed.) *Encyclopedia of Language and Linguistics*, 2nd edn, pp. 468–74. Elsevier, Oxford.

Haegeman, L. and T. Ihsane. 1999. Subject ellipsis in embedded sentences in English. *English Language and Linguistics* **3**: 117–45.

2001. Adult null subjects in the non-pro drop languages: two diary dialects. *Language Acquisition* **9**.4: 329–46.

Haicun, L. 2005. Explaining phatic utterance within the theory of relevance. In A. Korzeniowska and M. Grzegorzewska (eds.) *Relevance Studies in Poland*, vol. 2, pp. 81–7. The Institute of English Studies, University of Warsaw.

Hall, A. 2009. 'Free' enrichment and the nature of pragmatic constraints. *UCL Working Papers in Linguistics* **21**: 93–123.

Halliday, M.A.K. and C.M.I.M. Matthiessen. 2004. *An Introduction to Functional Grammar*, 3rd edn. Hodder Arnold, London.

Hampton, J. 1997. Emergent attributes in combined concepts. In T. Ward, S. Smith and J. Vaid (eds.), pp. 83–110.

Hann, M. 2007. Meh – the word that's sweeping the internet. *The Guardian*, 5th March 2007. Available at: www.guardian.co.uk/media/2007/mar/05/newmedia. broadcasting

Happé, F. 1993. Communicative competence and theory of mind in autism: a test of relevance theory. *Cognition* **48**: 101–19.

Hawkins, J.A. 1991. On (in)definite articles: implicatures and (un)grammaticality prediction. *Journal of Linguistics* **27**: 405–42.

Heim, I. 1983. File change semantics and the familiarity theory of definiteness. In R. Bäuerle, C. Schwarze and A. von Stechow (eds.) *Meaning, Use and Interpretation of Language*, pp. 164–89. De Gruyter, Berlin.

Horn, L.R. 1972. *On the Semantic Properties of Logical Operators in English*. PhD thesis, UCLA.

   1984. Towards a new taxonomy for pragmatic inference: Q- and R-based implicature. In D. Schiffrin (ed.) *Meaning, Form, and Use in Context*, pp. 11–42. Georgetown University Round Table on Languages and Linguistics. Georgetown University Press, Washington DC.

   1988. Pragmatic theory. In F. Newmeyer (ed.) *Linguistics: The Cambridge Survey*, vol. 1: *Linguistic Theory: Foundations*, pp. 113–45. Cambridge University Press.

   1989. *A Natural History of Negation*. University of Chicago Press.

   1992. The said and the unsaid. *Ohio State Working Papers in Linguistics (Proceedings of SALT II: The Second Conference on Semantics and Linguistic Theory)* **40**: 163–202.

   1996. Presupposition and implicature. In S. Lappin (ed.) *The Handbook of Contemporary Semantic Theory*, pp. 299–320. Blackwell, Oxford.

   2004. Implicature. In L.R. Horn and G. Ward (eds.), pp. 3–28.

Horn, L.R. and G. Ward (eds.) 2004. *The Handbook of Pragmatics*. Wiley-Blackwell, Oxford.

House, J. 1990. Intonation structures and pragmatic interpretation. In S. Ramsaran (ed.) *Studies in the Pronunciation of English*, pp. 38–57. Routledge, London.

   2006. Constructing a context with intonation. *Journal of Pragmatics* **38**.10: 1542–58.

Huang, Y. 1991. A neo-Gricean pragmatic theory of anaphora. *Journal of Linguistics* **27**: 301–35.

   2007. *The Syntax and Pragmatics of Anaphora: A Study with Special Reference to Chinese*. Cambridge University Press.

   2010. Neo-Gricean pragmatic theory of conversational implicature. In B. Heine and H. Narrog (eds.) *The Oxford Handbook of Linguistic Analysis*, pp. 607–31. Oxford University Press.

Hunston, S. 2006. Corpus linguistics. In K. Brown (ed.) *Encyclopedia of Language and Linguistics*, 2nd edn, pp. 234–48. Elsevier, Oxford.

Ifantidou, E. 2001. *Evidentials and Relevance*. John Benjamins, Amsterdam.

   2005a. Evidential particles and mind-reading. *Pragmatics & Cognition* **13**.2: 253–95.

2005b. Hearsay devices and metarepresentation. In S. Marmaridou, E. Antonopoulou and V. Nikiforidou (eds.) *Reviewing Linguistic Thought: Converging trends in the 21st Century*, pp. 401–20. Mouton de Gruyter, Berlin.

2005c. The semantics and pragmatics of metadiscourse. *Journal of Pragmatics* **37**: 1325–53.

2009. Newspaper headlines and relevance: ad hoc concepts in ad hoc contexts. *Journal of Pragmatics* **41**.4: 699–720.

Ifantidou, E. and A. Tzanne 2006. Multimodality and relevance in the Athens 2004 Olympic Games televised promotion. *Revista Alicantina de Estudios Ingleses* **19**: 191–210.

Imai, K. 1998. Intonation and relevance. In R. Carston and S. Uchida (eds.) *Relevance Theory: Applications and implications*, pp. 69–86. John Benjamins, Amsterdam.

Iten, C. 2005. *Linguistic Meaning, Truth Conditions and Relevance*. Palgrave Macmillan, Basingstoke.

Jackendoff, R. 2002. *Foundations of Language: Brain, Meaning, Grammar, Evolution*. Oxford University Press.

Jary, M. 2008. The relevance of complement choice: a corpus study of 'believe'. *Lingua* **118**: 1–18.

2009. Relevance, assertion and possible worlds: a cognitive approach to the Spanish subjunctive. In P. de Brabanter and M. Kissine (eds.) *Utterance Interpretation and Cognitive Models*, pp. 235–77. Emerald Group Publishing, Bingley.

2010. *Assertion*. Palgrave Macmillan, Basingstoke.

2011. Assertion, relevance and the declarative mood. In V. Escandell-Vidal, M. Leonetti and A. Ahern (eds), pp. 267–89.

Jaszczolt, K.M. 2005. *Default Semantics: Foundations of a Compositional Theory of Acts of Communication*. Oxford University Press.

2006. Default semantics. In K. Brown (ed.) *Encyclopedia of Language and Linguistics*, vol. 3, 2nd edn, pp. 388–92. Elsevier, Oxford.

2009. *Representing Time: An Essay on Temporality as Modality*. Oxford University Press.

2010. Default semantics. In B. Heine and H. Narrog (eds.) *The Oxford Handbook of Linguistic Analysis*, pp. 193–221. Oxford University Press.

2011. Default meanings, salient meanings and automatic processing. In K.M. Jaszczolt and K. Allan (eds.) *Salience and Defaults in Utterance Processing*, pp. 11–33. Mouton de Gruytes, Berlin.

Jodlowiec, M. 2009. Relevance and misunderstanding. In E. Tarasti, P. Forsell and R. Littlefield (eds.) *Communication: Understanding/Misunderstanding. Proceedings of the 9th Congress of the IASS-AIS, Helsinki-Imatra*. Vol. 1: *Acta Semiotica Fennica* XXXIV, pp. 651–61. International Semiotics Institute/Helsinki: Semiotic Society of Finland, Imatra.

2010. The role of relevance theory in SLA studies. In M. Pütz and L. Sicola (eds.) *Cognitive Processing in Second Language Acquisition*, pp. 49–66. John Benjamins, Amsterdam.

Johnson-Laird, P.N. 1983. *Mental Models: Towards a Cognitive Science of Language, Inference and Consciousness*. Cambridge University Press.

2004. The history of mental models. In K. Manktelow and M.C. Chung (eds.) *Psychology of Reasoning: Theoretical and Historical Perspectives*, pp. 179–212. Psychology Press, New York.

2006. *How We Reason*. Oxford University Press.

Johnson-Laird, P.N. and R.M.J. Byrne 1991. *Deduction*. Psychology Press, New York.

Jorgensen, J., G. Miller and D. Sperber 1984. Test of the mention theory of irony. *Journal of Experimental Psychology: General* **113**: 112–20.

Kamp, H. 1981. A theory of truth and semantic representation. In J.A.G. Groenendijk, T.M.V. Janssen and M.J.B. Stokhof (eds.) *Truth, Interpretation and Information*, pp. 1–41. Foris, Dordrecht.

Kamp, H. and U. Reyle 1993. *From Discourse to Logic*. Reidel, Dordrecht.

Katz, J.J. and J.A. Fodor 1963. The structure of a semantic theory. *Language* **39**.2: 170–210.

Katz, J.J. and P.M. Postal 1964. *An Integrated Theory of Linguistic Descriptions*. MIT Press, Cambridge MA.

Keenan, E.I. 1976. The universality of conversational postulates. *Language in Society* **5**: 67–80.

Kempson, R., W. Meyer-Viol and D. Gabbay 2001. *Dynamic Syntax*. Wiley-Blackwell, Oxford.

King, J. and J. Stanley 2005. Semantics, pragmatics, and the role of semantic content. In Z.G. Szabo (ed.) *Semantics vs. Pragmatics*, pp. 111–64. Oxford University Press.

Kisielewska-Krysiuk, M. 2010. Banter – a case of phatic communication? In E. Walaszewska, M. Kisielewska-Krysiuk and A. Piskorska (eds.) *In the Mind and across Minds: A relevance-theoretic perspective on communication and translation*, pp. 188–207. Cambridge Scholars Publishing, Newcastle.

de Klerk, V. 2005. Procedural meanings of 'well' in a corpus of Xhosa English. *Journal of Pragmatics* **37**: 1183–1205.

Kripke, S. 1977. Speaker's reference and semantic reference. *Midwest Studies in Philosophy* **2**: 255–76.

Kumon-Nakamura, S., S. Glucksberg and M. Brown 1995. How about another piece of pie: the allusional pretense theory of discourse irony. *Journal of Experimental Psychology: General* **124**: 3–21.

Ladd, R. 1996. *Intonational Phonology*. Cambridge University Press.

Lagerwerf, L. 2007. Irony and sarcasm in advertisements: effects of relevant inappropriateness. *Journal of Pragmatics* **39**: 1702–21.

Lakoff, G. 1987. *Women, Fire and Dangerous Things*. University of Chicago Press.

Lakoff, G. and M. Johnson 1980. *Metaphors We Live By*. University of Chicago Press. 1999. *Philosophy In The Flesh: The Embodied Mind and its Challenge to Western Thought*. Basic Books, New York.

Lakoff, G. and M. Turner 1989. *More Than Cool Reason: A Field Guide to Poetic Metaphor*. University of Chicago Press.

Landragin, F. 2003. Clues for the identification of implicit information in multimodal referring actions. In C. Stephanidis and J. Jacko (eds.) *Human-Computer Interaction*, vol. 2, pp. 711–15. Lawrence Erlbaum Associates, Mahwah NJ.

Landragin, F., A. De Aangeli, F. Wolff, P. Lopez and L. Romary 2002. Relevance and perceptual constraints in multimodal referring actions. In K. Van Deemter and R. Kibble (eds.) *Information Sharing: Reference and Presupposition in Language Generation and Interpretation*, pp. 391–410. CSLI Publications, Chicago.

Lascarides, A. and N. Asher 2007. Segmented discourse representation theory: dynamic semantics with discourse structure. In H. Bunt and R. Muskens (eds.) *Computing Meaning*, vol. 3, pp. 87–124. Springer-Verlag, New York.

Lascarides, A. and A. Copestake 1998. Pragmatics and word meaning. *Journal of Linguistics* **34**: 387–414.

Laver, J. 1974. *Semiotic Aspects of Spoken Communication*. Edward Arnold, London.

Leech, G. 1983. *Principles of Pragmatics*. Longman, London.

Leslie, A. 1987. Pretense and representation: the origins of 'theory of mind'. *Psychological Review* **94**: 412–26.

Leslie, A. and F. Happé. 1989. Autism and ostensive communication: the relevance of metarepresentation. *Development and Psychopathology* **1**: 205–12.

Levinson, S.C. 1983. *Pragmatics*. Cambridge University Press.

    1987a. Minimization and conversational inference. In J. Verschueren and M. Bertuccelli-Papi (eds.) *The Pragmatic Perspective*, pp. 61–129. John Benjamins, Amsterdam.

    1987b. Pragmatics and the grammar of anaphora: a partial pragmatic reduction of binding and control phenomena. *Journal of Linguistics* **23**: 379–434.

    1987c. Implicature explicated? *Behavioral and Brain Sciences*, **10**.4: 722–3.

    1989. A review of 'Relevance'. *Journal of Linguistics* **25**: 455–72.

    1995. Three levels of meaning. In F. Palmer (ed.) *Grammar and Meaning: Essays in honour of Sir John Lyons*, pp. 90–119. Cambridge University Press.

    2000. *Presumptive Meanings: The Theory of Generalized Conversational Implicature*. MIT Press, Cambridge MA.

Lewis, D. 1970. General semantics. *Synthèse* **22**: 18–67.

MacMahon, B. 1996. Indirectness, rhetoric and interpretive use: communicative strategies in Browning's 'My Last Duchess'. *Language and Literature* **5**: 209–23.

    2001a. The effects of word substitution in slips of the tongue, *Finnegans Wake* and *The Third Policeman*. *English Studies* **3**: 231–46.

    2001b. Relevance theory and the use of voice in poetry. *Belgian Journal of Linguistics* **15**: 11–34.

    2007. The effects of sound patterning in poetry: a cognitive pragmatic approach. *Journal of Literary Semantics* **36**.2: 103–20.

    2009a. Metarepresentation and decoupling in *Northanger Abbey*: Part I. *English Studies* **90**.5: 518–44.

    2009b. Metarepresentation and decoupling in *Northanger Abbey*: Part II. *English Studies* **90**.6: 673–94.

Malinowski, B. 1923. The problem of meaning in primitive languages. In C.K. Ogden and I.A. Richards (eds.) *The Meaning of Meaning*, pp. 146–52. Routledge, London.

Margolis, E. and S. Laurence (eds.) 1999. *Concepts: Core Readings*. MIT Press, Cambridge MA.

Marten, L. and R. Kempson 2006. Dynamic syntax. In K. Brown (ed.) *Encyclopedia of Language and Linguistics*, vol. 4, 2nd edn, pp. 33–37. Elsevier, Oxford.

Martí, L. 2006. Unarticulated constituents revisited. *Linguistics and Philosophy* **29**: 135–66.

Mascaro, O. and D. Sperber 2009. The moral, epistemic, and mindreading components of children's vigilance towards deception. *Cognition* **112**: 367–80.

Matsui, T., T. Yamamoto and P. McCagg. 2006. On the role of language in children's early understanding of others as epistemic beings. *Cognitive Development* **21**: 158–73.

Matsui, T., H. Rakoczy, Y. Miura and M. Tomasello 2009. Understanding of speaker certainty and false-belief reasoning: a comparison of Japanese and German preschoolers. *Developmental Science* **12**.4: 602–13.

McEnery, A.M. and A. Hardie 2011. *Corpus Linguistics: Method, Theory and Practice.* Cambridge University Press.

McEnery, A.M. and A. Wilson 2001. *Corpus Linguistics*, 2nd edn. Edinburgh University Press.

Mercier, H. and D. Sperber 2009. Intuitive and reflective inferences. In J. Evans and K. Frankish (eds.) *In Two Minds: Dual processes and beyond*, pp. 149–70. Oxford University Press.

Mirecki, P. 2005. Misunderstanding: a starting point for successful communication. A view from the relevance-theoretic perspective. In A. Korzeniowska and M. Grzegorzewska (eds.) *Relevance Studies in Poland*, vol. 2, pp. 45–51. The Institute of English Studies, University of Warsaw.

Montague, R. 1974. *Formal Philosophy: Selected Papers of Richard Montague* (ed. R.H. Thomason). Yale University Press, New Haven CT.

Morgan, J. and G. Green 1987. On the search for relevance. *Behavioral and Brain Sciences* **10**: 726–7.

Müller-Lyer, F.C. 1889. Optische Urteilstauschungen. Archiv fur Anatomie und Physiologie. *Physiologische Abteilung*, **2**: 263–70.

Navarro, M.P. 2006. Enrichment and loosening: an on-going process in the practice of translation. A study based on some translations of *Gulliver's Travels*. In A.M. Hornero, M.J. Luzón and S. Murillo (eds.) *Corpus Linguistics: Applications for the Study of English*, pp. 269–86. Peter Lang, Berlin.

Neale, S. 2000. On being explicit. *Mind and Language* **15**: 284–94.

2005. Pragmatism and binding. In Z. Szabó (ed.) *Semantics vs. Pragmatics*, pp. 165–285. Clarendon Press, Oxford.

Nicolle, S. and B. Clark 1998. Phatic interpretations: standardisation and conventionalisation. *Revista Alicantina de Estudios Ingleses* **11**: 183–91.

1999. Experimental pragmatics and what is said: a response to Gibbs and Moise. *Cognition* **66**: 337–54.

Noveck, I. 2001. When children are more logical than adults: investigations of scalar implicature. *Cognition* **78**.2: 165–88.

Noveck, I., M. Bianco and A. Castry 2001. The costs and benefits of metaphor. *Metaphor and Symbol* **16**: 109–21.

Noveck, I. and D. Sperber 2004. *Experimental Pragmatics*. Palgrave Macmillan, Basingstoke.

2007. The why and how of experimental pragmatics: the case of 'scalar inferences'. In N.C. Burton-Roberts (ed.), pp. 184–212.

Nowik, E.K. 2005. Politeness of the impolite: relevance theory, politeness and banter. In A. Korzeniowska and M. Grzegorzewska (eds.) *Relevance Studies in Poland*, vol. 2, pp. 157–66. The Institute of English Studies, University of Warsaw.

Ogden, C.K. and I.A. Richards 1923. *The Meaning of Meaning: A Study of the Influence of Language upon Thought and of the Science of Symbolism*. Kegan Paul, Trench, Trubner, London. Also available in a version edited by W.T. Gordon (1994). Continuum, London.

Owtram, N. 2010. *The Pragmatics of Academic Writing*. Peter Lang, Berlin.

Padilla Cruz, M. 2007. Metarepresentations and phatic utterances: a pragmatic proposal about the generation of solidarity between interlocutors. In P. Cap and J. Nikakowska (eds.) *Current Trends in Pragmatics*, pp. 110–28. Cambridge Scholars Publishing, Newcastle.

    2008. Three different pragmatic approaches to the teaching of the (im)politeness of phatic utterances in English. In C. Estébanez and L. Pérez Ruiz Valladolid (eds.) *Language Awareness in English and Spanish*, pp. 131–52. University of Valladolid.

    2009. Understanding and overcoming pragmatic failure when interpreting phatic utterances. In R. Gómez Morón, M. Padilla Cruz, L. Fernández Amaya and M.O. Hernández López (eds.) *Pragmatics Applied to Language Teaching and Learning*, pp. 87–108. Cambridge Scholars Publishing, Newcastle.

Pajares Tosca, S. 2000. A pragmatics of links. In *Proceedings of Hypertext 2000*, San Antonio, TX, pp. 77–84. Also in *Journal of Digital Information* **1**.6. Available at: http://journals.tdl.org/jodi/article/viewArticle/23/24

Peeters, S. 2010. Metaphors in media discourse: from a conceptual metaphor approach to the relevance-theoretic 'continuity view' (and back again). In I. Witczak-Plisiecka (ed.) *Pragmatic Perspectives on Language and Linguistics*. Vol. I: *Speech Actions in Theory and Applied Studies*, pp. 327–59. Cambridge Scholars Publishing, Newcastle.

Pilkington, A. 1991. Poetic effects: a relevance theory perspective. In R. Sell (ed.) *Literary Pragmatics*, pp. 44–61. Routledge, London.

    1992. Poetic effects. *Lingua* **87**: 29–51.

    1996. Introduction: relevance theory and literary style. *Language and Literature* **5**.3: 157–62.

    2000. *Poetic Effects*. John Benjamins, Amsterdam.

    2001. Non-lexicalised concepts and degrees of effability: poetic thoughts and the attraction of what is not in the dictionary. *Belgian Journal of Linguistics* **15**: 1–10.

Pinker, S. 1997. *How The Mind Works*. Penguin, London.

Powell, G. 2001. The referential–attributive distinction. *Pragmatics and Cognition* **9**.1: 69–98.

    2002. Underdetermination and the principles of semantic theory. *Proceedings of the Aristotelian Society* **102**.3: 271–78.

    2010. *Language, Thought and Reference*. Palgrave Macmillan, Basingstoke.

Premack, D. and G. Woodruff. 1978. Does the chimpanzee have a theory of mind? *Behavioral and Brain Sciences* **4**: 515–26.

Prentice, D.A., R.J. Gerrig and D.S. Bailis 1997. What readers bring to the processing of fictional texts. *Psychonomic Bulletin & Review* **4**: 416–20.

Prince, A. and P. Smollensky 2004. *Optimality Theory: Constraint Interaction in Generative Grammar*. Wiley-Blackwell, Oxford.

Prinz, J.J. 2009. Is the mind really modular? In R. Stainton (ed.) *Contemporary Debates in Cognitive Science*, pp. 22–36. Wiley-Blackwell, Oxford.

Rapp, D.N. and R.J. Gerrig. In press. Predilections for narrative outcomes: the impact of story contexts and reader preferences. To appear in *Journal of Memory and Language*.

Recanati, F. 1989. The pragmatics of what is said. *Mind & Language* **4**: 295–329.

———. 1993. *Direct Reference: From Language to Thought*. Wiley-Blackwell, Oxford.

———. 1995. The alleged priority of literal interpretation. *Cognitive Science* **19**: 207–32.

———. 2000. *Oratio Obliqua, Oratio Recta: The Semantics of Metarepresentations*. MIT Press, Cambridge, MA.

———. 2001. What is said. *Synthèse* **128**: 75–91.

———. 2002a. Unarticulated constituents. *Linguistics and Philosophy* **25**: 299–345.

———. 2002b. Does linguistic communication rest on inference? *Mind & Language* **17**: 105–26. (Special Issue on Pragmatics and Cognitive Science.)

———. 2004. *Literal Meaning*. Cambridge University Press.

———. 2007. Indexicality, context and pretence. In N.C. Burton-Roberts (ed.), pp. 213–29.

———. 2010. Pragmatics and logical form. In B. Soria and E. Romero (eds.), pp. 25–41.

Rockwell, P. 2000. Lower, slower, louder: vocal cues of sarcasm. *Journal of Psycholinguistics Research* **29**: 483–95.

Romero, E. and B. Soria 2007. A view of novel metaphor in the light of Recanati's proposals. In M.J. Frápolli (ed.) *Saying, Meaning and Referring: Essays on François Recanati's Philosophy of Language*, pp. 145–59. Palgrave Macmillan, Basingstoke.

Rosales Sequeiros, X. 2005. *Effects of Pragmatic Interpretation on Translation: Communicative Gaps and Textual Discrepancies*. Lincom Studies in Pragmatics 13. Lincom, München.

Rouchota, V. 1988. Procedural meaning and parenthetical discourse markers. In A. Jucker and Y. Ziv (eds.) *Discourse Markers: Descriptions and Theory*, pp. 96–126. Amsterdam: John Benjamins.

Rouchota, V. and Jucker, A. (eds) 1998. *Current Issues in Relevance Theory*. John Benjamins, Amsterdam.

Rubio Fernandez, P. 2001. The inhibition of core features in metaphor interpretation. *Cambridge Working Papers in English and Applied Linguistics* **8**: 73–100.

———. 2005. *Pragmatic Processes and Cognitive Mechanisms in Lexical Interpretation: The On-line Construction of Concepts*. PhD thesis, Cambridge University.

———. 2007. Suppression in metaphor interpretation: differences between meaning selection and meaning construction. *Journal of Semantics* **24**: 345–71.

———. 2008. Concept narrowing: the role of context-independent information. *Journal of Semantics* **25**.4: 381–409.

Ruhi S. and G. Dogan 2001. Relevance theory and compliments as phatic communication: the case of Turkish. In A. Bayraktaroglu and M. Sifianou (eds.) *Linguistic Politeness Across Boundaries*, pp. 341–90. John Benjamins, Amsterdam.

Saad, J. 2010. *Explicating the Implicit: An Exploration into the Pragmatic Competence of Arabic-speaking Trainee Translators*. PhD thesis, Heriot-Watt University, Edinburgh.

Schegloff, E.A. and H. Sacks 1973. Opening up closings. *Semiotica* **7**.4: 289–327.

Schneider, K.P. 1988. *Small Talk: Analysing Phatic Discourse*. Hitzeroth, Marburg.

Scholl, B. and A. Leslie 1999. Modularity, development and 'theory of mind'. *Mind and Language* **14**: 131–53.

Schütze, C.T. 1996. *The Empirical Base of Linguistics: Grammaticality Judgments and Linguistic Methodology*. University of Chicago Press.

Scott, K. 2006. When less is more: implicit arguments and relevance theory. *UCL Working Papers in Linguistics* **18**: 139–70.

2008. Reference, procedures and implicitly communicated meaning. *UCL Working Papers in Linguistics* **20**: 275–301.

2010. *The Relevance of Referring Expressions: The Case of Diary Drop in English*. PhD thesis, University College London.

2011. Beyond reference: concepts, procedures and referring expressions. In V. Escandell-Vidal, M. Leonetti and A. Ahern (eds.), pp. 183–203.

Searle, J. 1979. Literal meaning. In J. Searle, *Expression and Meaning*, pp. 117–36. Cambridge University Press.

Setton, R. 1999. *Simultaneous Interpretation: A Cognitive-Pragmatic Analysis*. John Benjamins, Amsterdam.

2005a. Pointing to contexts: a relevance-theoretic approach to assessing quality and difficulty in interpreting. In H.V. Dam, J. Engberg and H. Gerzymisch-Arbogast (eds.) *Knowledge Systems and Translation*, pp. 275–312. Walter de Gruyter, Berlin and New York.

2005b. So what is so interesting about simultaneous interpreting? *Skase Journal of Translation and Interpretation* **1**.1: 70–84.

2006. Context in simultaneous interpretation. *Journal of Pragmatics* **38**.3: 374–89.

Shively, R.L., R.M. Menke and S.M. Manzón-Omundson 2008. Perception of irony by L2 learners of Spanish. *Issues in Applied Linguistics* **16**.2: 101–32

Smith, N.V. 2004. *Chomsky: Ideas and Ideals*, 2nd edn. Cambridge University Press.

Soames, S. Forthcoming. The gap between meaning and assertion: why what we literally say often differs from what our words literally mean. In M. Hackl and R. Thornton (eds.) *Asserting, Meaning, and Implying*. Oxford University Press.

Sodian, B. 2004. Theory of mind: the case for conceptual development. In W. Schneider, R. Schumann-Hengsteler and B. Sodian (eds.) *Young Children's Cognitive Development*, pp. 95–131. Routledge, London.

Soria, B. and E. Romero (eds.) 2010. *Explicit Communication: Robyn Carston's Pragmatics*. Palgrave Macmillan, Basingstoke.

Sperber, D. 1984. Verbal irony: pretense or echoic mention? *Journal of Experimental Psychology: General* **113**: 130–6.

1994a. The modularity of thought and the epidemiology of representations. In L.A. Hirschfeld and S.A. Gelman (eds.) *Mapping The Mind: Domain Specificity in Cognition and Culture*, pp. 39–67. Cambridge University Press.

1994b. Understanding verbal understanding. In J. Khalfa (ed.) *What is Intelligence?*, pp. 179–98. Cambridge University Press.

1995. How do we communicate? In J. Brockman and K. Matson (eds.) *How Things Are: A Science Toolkit for the Mind*, pp. 191–9. Morrow, New York.

2000. Metarepresentations in an evolutionary perspective. In D. Sperber (ed.) *Metarepresentations: An Interdisciplinary Perspective*, pp. 117–37. Oxford University Press.

2001. In defense of massive modularity. In E. Dupoux (ed.) *Language, Brain and Cognitive Development: Essays in Honor of Jacques Mehler*, pp. 47–57. MIT Press, Cambridge MA.

2005. Modularity and relevance: How can a massively modular mind be flexible and context-sensitive? In P. Carruthers, S. Laurence and S. Stich (eds.) *The Innate Mind: Structure and contents*, pp. 53–68. Oxford University Press.

Sperber, D., F. Cara and V. Girotto. 1995. Relevance theory explains the selection task. *Cognition* **57**: 31–95.

Sperber, D. and V. Girotto 2002. Use or misuse of the selection task? Rejoinder to Fiddick, Cosmides and Tooby. *Cognition* **85**: 277–90.

2003. Does the selection task detect cheater detection? In K. Sterleny and J. Fitness (eds.) *From Mating to Mentality: Evaluating Evolutionary Psychology*, pp. 197–226. Macquarie Monographs in Cognitive Science. Psychology Press, New York and Hove.

Sperber, D. and I. Noveck. 2004. Introduction. In I. Noveck and D. Sperber (eds.), pp. 1–22.

Sperber, D. and D. Wilson. 1982. Mutual knowledge and relevance in theories of comprehension. In N.V. Smith (ed.) *Mutual Knowledge*, pp. 61–85. Academic Press, London.

1985. Loose talk. *Proceedings of the Aristotelian Society* **LXXXVI**: 153–71.

1986. *Relevance: Communication and Cognition*. Wiley-Blackwell, Oxford and Harvard University Press, Cambridge MA (2nd edn 1995).

1987a. Précis of relevance. *Behavioral and Brain Sciences* **10**.4: 697–710.

1987b. Presumptions of relevance. *Behavioral and Brain Sciences* **10**.4: 736–53.

1990a. Spontaneous deduction and mutual knowledge. *Behavioral and Brain Sciences* **13**.1: 179–84.

1990. Rhetoric and relevance. In J. Bender and D. Wellbery (eds.) *The Ends of Rhetoric: History, Theory, Practice*, pp. 140–56. Stanford University Press.

1995. Postface to the second edition of *Relevance: Communication and Cognition*. Wiley-Blackwell, Oxford.

1998. The mapping between the mental and the public lexicon. In. P. Carruthers and J. Boucher (eds.) *Language and Thought: Interdisciplinary Themes*, pp. 184–200. Cambridge University Press.

2002. Pragmatics, modularity and mindreading. *Mind & Language* **17**: 3–23.

2005. Pragmatics. In F. Jackson and M. Smith (eds.) *Oxford Handbook of Contemporary Philosophy*, pp. 468–501. Oxford University Press.

2008. A deflationary account of metaphor. In R. Gibbs (ed.) *Handbook of Metaphor and Thought*, pp. 84–108. Cambridge University Press.

Sroda, M.S. 2000. *Relevance Theory and the Markedness Model in SLA: Cognitive Approaches to Pragmatics and Second Language Acquisition*. PhD thesis, University of South Carolina.

Stainton, R. 1994. Using non-sentences: an application of relevance theory. *Pragmatics and Cognition* **2**: 269–84.

2006. *Words and Thoughts: Subsentences, Ellipsis, and the Philosophy of Language*. Oxford University Press.

Stanley, J. 2000. Context and logical form. *Linguistics and Philosophy* **23**: 391–434.

2002. Making it articulated. *Mind & Language* **17** 1&2: 149–68.

Stanley, J. and Z.G. Szabó 2000. On quantifier domain restriction. *Mind & Language* **15**: 219–61.

Stöver, H. 2011a. Awareness in metaphor understanding: the lingering of the literal. *Review of Cognitive Linguistics* **9**.1: 65–82.

2011b. *Metaphor and Relevance Theory: A New Hybrid Model*. PhD thesis, University of Bedfordshire.

Strawson, P.F. 1964[1971]. Intention and convention in speech acts. *Philosophical Review* **73**: 439–60. Reprinted in P. F. Strawson (1971) *Logico-Linguistic Papers*, pp. 170–89. Methuen, London.

Surian, L. and A. Leslie 1999. Competence and performance in false belief understanding: a comparison of autistic and normal 3-year-old children. *British Journal of Developmental Psychology* **17**: 141–55.

Swinney, D. 1979. Lexical access during sentence comprehension: (Re)consideration of context effects. *Journal of Verbal Learning and Verbal Behavior* **18**: 645–59.

Tabossi, P. 1993. Connections, competitions and cohorts. In G.T.M. Altmann and R.C. Shillcock (eds.) *Cognitive Models of Speech Processing: The second Sperlonga Meeting*, pp. 277–94. Lawrence Erlbaum Associates, Hove.

Tabossi, P., C. Burani and D. Scott. 1995. Word identification in fluent speech. *Journal of Memory and Language* **34**: 440–67.

Tanaka, K. 1992. The pun in advertising: a pragmatic approach. *Lingua* **87**: 91–102.

1994. *Advertising Language: A Pragmatic Approach to Advertisements in Britain and Japan*. Routledge, London.

Tendahl, M. and R. Gibbs 2008. Complementary perspectives on metaphor: cognitive linguistics and relevance theory. *Journal of Pragmatics* **40**.11: 1823–64.

Teubert, W. and A. Cermakova 2007. *Corpus Linguistics: A Short Introduction*. Continuum, London.

Thomas, J. 1995. *Meaning in Interaction: An Introduction to Pragmatics*. Longman, London.

Thompson, G. 2004. *Introducing Functional Grammar*, 2nd edn. Hodder Arnold, London.

Tomasello, M. 2005. *Constructing a Language: A Usage-based Theory of Language Acquisition*. Harvard University Press, Cambridge MA.

Tomlinson, C. (ed.) 2000. *William Carlos Williams: Selected poems*. Penguin, London.

Travis, C. 1981. *The True and the False: The Domain of the Pragmatic*. John Benjamins, Amsterdam.

1985. On what is strictly speaking true. *Canadian Journal of Philosophy* **15**: 187–229.

1991. Annals of analysis: *Studies in the Way of Words* by H. P. Grice. *Mind* **100**: 237–64.

Van der Henst, J.-B., L. Carles and D. Sperber 2002. Truthfulness and relevance in telling the time. *Mind & Language* **17**.5: 457–66.

Van der Henst, J.-B. and D. Sperber 2004. Testing the cognitive and the communicative principles of relevance. In I. Noveck and D. Sperber (eds.), 141–69.

Van der Henst, J.-B., D. Sperber and G. Politzer 2002. When is a conclusion worth deriving? A relevance-based analysis of indeterminate relational problems. *Thinking & Reasoning* **8**: 1–20.

Vandepitte, S. 1989. A pragmatic function of intonation. *Lingua* **79**: 265–97.

Vega Moreno, R. 2004. Metaphor interpretation and emergence. *UCL Working Papers in Linguistics* **16**: 297–322.

2005. *Creativity and Convention: The Pragmatics of Everyday Figurative Speech.* PhD thesis, University College London.

2007. *Creativity and Convention: The Pragmatics of Everyday Figurative Speech.* John Benjamins, Amsterdam.

Walton, K. 1990. *Mimesis as Make-believe: On the Foundations of the Representational Arts.* Harvard University Press, Cambridge, MA.

Ward, T., S. Smith and J. Vaid (eds.) 1997. *Creative Thought: An Investigation of Conceptual Structures and Processes.* American Psychological Association, Washington DC.

Wason, P. 1966. Reasoning. In B.M. Foss (ed.) *New Horizons in Psychology.* Penguin, Harmondsworth.

Watts, R.J. 2004. *Politeness.* Cambridge University Press.

Wellman, H.M., D. Cross and J. Watson 2001. Meta-analysis of theory-of-mind development: the truth about false belief. *Child Development* **72**: 655–84.

Wharton, T. 2003a. Natural pragmatics and natural codes. *Mind and Language* **18**.5: 447–77.

2003b. Interjections, language and the 'showing-waying' continuum. *Pragmatics and Cognition* **11**.1: 39–91.

2006. Evolution of pragmatics. In K. Brown (ed.) *Encyclopedia of Language and Linguistics*, 2nd edn, pp. 338–45. Elsevier, Oxford.

2009. *Pragmatics and Non-Verbal Communication.* Cambridge University Press.

Wilson, D. 1995. Is there a maxim of truthfulness? *UCL Working Papers in Linguistics* **7**: 197–212.

2000. Metarepresentation in linguistic communication. In D. Sperber (ed.) *Metarepresentations: An Interdisciplinary Perspective*, pp. 411–48. Oxford University Press.

2005. New directions for research on pragmatics and modularity. *Lingua* **115**: 1129–46.

2006. The pragmatics of verbal irony: echo or pretence? *Lingua* **116**: 1722–43.

2009. Irony and metarepresentation. *UCL Working Papers in Linguistics* **21**: 183–226.

2011a. Parallels and differences in the treatment of metaphor in relevance theory and cognitive linguistics. *Intercultural Pragmatics* **8**.2: 177–96.

2011b. Conceptual-procedural distinction: past, present and future. In V. Escandell-Vidal, M. Leonetti and A. Ahern (eds.), pp. 3–31.

Wilson, D. and R. Carston 2006. Metaphor, relevance and the emergent property issue. *Mind and Language* **21**.3: 404–33.

2007. A unitary approach to lexical pragmatics: relevance, inference and ad hoc concepts. In N.C. Burton-Roberts (ed.), pp. 230–59.

2008. Metaphor, relevance and the 'emergent property' problem. *The Baltic International Yearbook of Cognition, Logic and Communication* **3**: 1–40.

Wilson, D and D. Sperber 1981. On Grice's theory of conversation. In P. Werth (ed.) *Conversation and Discourse*, pp. 155–78. Croom Helm, London.

1986. Pragmatics and modularity. *Chicago Linguistic Society 22, Parasession on Pragmatics and Grammatical Theory*, pp. 68–74.

1988. Mood and the analysis of non-declarative sentences. In J. Dancy, J. Moravcsik and C. Taylor (eds.) *Human Agency: Language, Duty and Value*, pp. 77–101. Stanford University Press. Reprinted in A. Kasher (ed.) 1998, vol. II, pp. 262–89.

1993. Linguistic form and relevance. *Lingua* **90**: 1–25.

1998. Pragmatics and time. In R. Carston and S. Uchida (eds.), pp. 1–22.

2002. Truthfulness and relevance. *Mind* **111**: 583–632.

2004. Relevance theory. In L.R. Horn and G. Ward (eds.), pp. 607–32.

2012. *Meaning and Relevance*. Cambridge University Press.

Wilson, D. and T. Wharton 2006. Relevance and prosody. *Journal of Pragmatics* **38**.10: 1559–79.

Wimmer, H. and J. Perner 1983. Beliefs about beliefs: representation and constraining function of wrong beliefs in young children's understanding of deception. *Cognition* **13**.1: 103–28.

Yamanaka, E.J. 2003. Effect of proficiency and length of residence on the pragmatic comprehension of Japanese ESL. *Second Language Studies* **22**.1: 107–75.

Yus, F. 1998a. Relevance theory and media discourse: a verbal-visual model of communication. *Poetics* **25**: 293–309.

1998b. The 'what-do-you-mean syndrome': a taxonomy of misunderstandings in Harold Pinter's plays. *Estudios Ingleses de la Universidad Complutense* **6**: 81–100.

1999a. Towards a pragmatic taxonomy of misunderstandings. *Revista Canaria de Estudios Ingleses* **38**: 218–39.

1999b. Misunderstandings and explicit/implicit communication. *Pragmatics* **9**.4: 487–517.

2006. Relevance theory. In K. Brown (ed.) *Encyclopedia of Language and Linguistics*, vol. 10, 2nd edn, pp. 512–19. Elsevier, Oxford.

2008. Alterations of relevance in cyber-media. *Universitas Psychologica* **7**.3: 623–36.

2009. Visual metaphor versus verbal metaphor: a unified account. In C. Forceville and E. Uriós-Aparisi (eds.) *Multimodal Metaphor*, pp. 145–72. Mouton de Gruyter, Berlin.

2010. Relevance theory. In B. Heine and H. Narrog (eds.) *Oxford Handbook of Linguistic Analysis*, pp. 679–701. Oxford University Press.

2011. *Cyberpragmatics: Internet-Mediated Communication in Context.* John Benjamins, Amsterdam.

Zajac, M. 2004. Polish quantified sentences. From logical form to explicature: an analysis of selected examples from a corpus of young Poles' everyday conversation. In E. Mioduszewska (ed.) *Relevance Studies in Poland*, pp. 143–53. The Institute of English Studies, University of Warsaw.

Zaki, M. 2011. *The Semantics and Pragmatics of Demonstratives in English and Arabic*. PhD thesis, Middlesex University.

Zegarac, V. 1998. What is 'phatic communication'? In V. Rouchota and A. Jucker (eds.), pp. 327–62.

Zegarac, V. and B. Clark 1999. Phatic interpretations and phatic communication. *Journal of Linguistics* **35**.2: 321–46.

Index

Note: Since the work of Dan Sperber and Deirdre Wilson is a central focus throughout the book, their names have not been indexed here.